Management of Alcohol, Tobacco and Other Drug Problems

A PHYSICIAN'S MANUAL

EDITED BY
Bruna Brands, PhD

ASSOCIATE EDITORS:
Meldon Kahan, MD, CCFP, FRCPC
Peter Selby, MBBS, CCFP
Lynn Wilson, MD, CCFP

Centre for Addiction and Mental Health
Centre de toxicomanie et de santé mentale

Addiction Research Foundation

Clarke Institute of Psychiatry

Donwood Institute

Queen Street Mental Health Centre

A World Health Organization Centre of Excellence

Canadian Cataloguing in Publication Data
Main entry under title:

Management of alcohol, tobacco and other drug problems: a physician's manual

Includes bibliographical references and index.
ISBN 0-88868-306-5

1. Drug abuse – Treatment – Handbooks, manuals, etc. 2. Substance abuse – Treatment – Handbooks, manuals, etc. I. Brands, Bruna. II. Centre for Addiction and Mental Health.

RC564.15.M36 2000   616.86   C00-930714-1

Printed in Canada

For information on this and other Centre for Addiction and Mental Health resource materials, or to place an order, please contact:
Marketing and Sales Services
Centre for Addiction and Mental Health
33 Russell Street
Toronto, Ontario M5S 2S1
Tel.: 1-800-661-1111 or (416) 595-6059 in Toronto.
E-mail: marketing@camh.net

www.camh.net

SECTION 9: OTHER FREQUENTLY ABUSED SUBSTANCES . . 283

SECTION 10: POLYSUBSTANCE ABUSE 301

SECTION 11: EMERGENCY MANAGEMENT OF
INTOXICATIONS AND OVERDOSES 307

SECTION 12: COMPLICATIONS OF INJECTION
DRUG USE 323

SECTION 13: OLDER ADULTS AND SUBSTANCE USE 347

SECTION 14: WOMEN AND SUBSTANCE USE 359

SECTION 15: ADOLESCENT SUBSTANCE USE
AND THE FAMILY 371

Contents

FOREWORD

In helping patients with alcohol, tobacco and other drug problems, physicians confront a wide range of complex clinical issues. Whether in a hospital emergency room, a family practice, or some other clinical setting, primary care physicians regularly encounter patients with substance use problems — occurring either on their own or concurrently with other medical or psychiatric conditions. As a result, physicians are often required to manage a spectrum of clinical situations, from screening, brief interventions and case management to complex drug interactions, overdose and withdrawal. Yet while substance use and related problems represent a major clinical challenge, through early identification, prompt intervention and ongoing management, physicians can have a significant impact on their patient's health and on the social and economic costs of substance abuse.

To identify and treat substance-related problems effectively, physicians and other health professionals need access to the latest clinically relevant findings in an easily usable form. Providing practical, research-based resources is a key part of the mandate of the Centre for Addiction and Mental Health. By marshalling the expertise of its four founding organizations — the Addiction Research Foundation, the Clarke Institute of Psychiatry, the Donwood Institute and the Queen Street Mental Health Centre — the Centre is working to develop innovative curricula, training and continuing education for health professionals, as well as research-based clinical tools and programs.

Management of Alcohol, Tobacco and Other Drug Problems: A Physician's Manual is another important product of that effort. Written and edited by physicians, scientists and clinicians at the Centre and their colleagues, the manual provides both practical guidelines for quick reference and more detailed discussion of significant clinical issues. Building on the earlier *Physician's Handbook,* published in 1986 by the Addiction Research Foundation and the Ontario Medical Association, the revised and expanded manual continues an important tradition of putting knowledge into the hands of professionals who are best placed to make a difference. It is our hope that the *Physician's Manual* will prove an invaluable resource to any physician whose patients experience problems related to alcohol, tobacco or other drugs.

Paul Garfinkel, MD, FRCPC
President and CEO
Centre for Addiction and Mental Health

PREFACE

This manual reflects changes in knowledge and practice, and increased awareness of the potential roles for physicians who care for patients with substance use disorders. The *Management of Alcohol, Tobacco and Other Drug Problems: A Physician's Manual* includes information about screening for alcohol, tobacco and other drug problems, providing brief interventions to smokers and "problem drinkers," and treating medical complications. It also covers effective withdrawal treatment, implementing harm reduction strategies such as hepatitis B immunization, referring patients for specialized treatment, and addressing particular issues faced by women, adolescents and families, and people with problems relating to both substance use and mental health.

The manual also addresses an issue that physicians in practice frequently ask about — the management of drug-seeking behavior. In addition, because it is important to look after ourselves and our colleagues as well as our patients, a section on the impaired physician has been included.

We have endeavored to maintain the easy-to-use qualities of the original publication, the *Physician's Handbook,* by providing an expanded table of contents at the beginning of each section followed by more detailed information. Another new feature of this edition is the inclusion of patient information sheets on most major substances. These are provided as an appendix, in a format that can be easily photocopied and given to patients.

The *Physician's Handbook* was first published in 1986 by the Addiction Research Foundation and the Ontario Medical Association. Distributed to all members of the Ontario Medical Association, the handbook was lauded for its practical guidelines and management recommendations. We are gratified by the response of physicians to the original manual, and grateful to its editors, Drs. Paul Devenyi and Sarah J. Saunders. We hope this edition continues to serve as a resource that resides on the desktops of many clinicians.

We are indebted to our colleagues for their work in authoring and collaborating on sections for the manual:

Michael Anderson, MLT, B.Sc. (Chem), and Bruna Brands, PhD

Laurence Blendis, MD, FRCPC

Gloria Chaim, MSW

Graeme Cunningham, MD, FRCPC

Douglas L. Gourlay, M.Sc., MD, FRCPC

Richard Frecker, MD, PhD, FRCPC

Louis Fornazzari, MD, FRCPC

Yasemin Ikizler, MD, CCFP

David C. Marsh, MD

Blenos A.T. Pedersen, MD, FRCPC

Nicholas Pimlott, MD, PhD, FRCPC

Margaret Thompson, MD, FRCPC

Morris Sherman, MB B.Ch., PhD, FRCPC

Patrick D. Smith, PhD

Thea Weisdorf, MD, CCFP

Florence Wong, MD, FRCPC

We would also like to thank and acknowledge the important roles played by the reference librarians and the staff of the Centre for Addiction and Mental Health's Addiction Research Foundation Division library, Eleanor Liu of the ARF Division Clinical Training and Research Institute, Pearl Isaac, B.Sc. Phm and the ARF Division pharmacy, Dr. Helen Ross, Marilyn Pope, Dr. Juan Carlos Negrete, Dr. Paul Casola and Dr. Shelly McMain. We would also like to thank Dr. Trevor Hall, Dr. Raju Hajela and Dr. Shelley Doumani.

Production of this book was completed by the staff of the Centre for Addiction and Mental Health's Communications and Marketing Department, including product design by Mary Quartarone, copy-editing by Andrew Johnson, editorial co-ordination by Myles Magner and graphic design by Nancy Leung.

Bruna Brands, PhD, Editor; Meldon Kahan, MD, CCFP, FRCPC, Peter Selby, MBBS, CCFP, Lynn Wilson, MD, CCFP, Associate Editors.

AN IMPORTANT NOTE

Medicine is an evolving science. As new research and clinical experience broaden our knowledge, changes in treatment and drug therapy are required. In revising this manual, the editors and publishers have referred to sources that are believed to be reliable. The contents of this manual are based upon information available as of 1999. However, in view of the possibility of human error or changes in medical science, neither the authors, editors, publishers nor any other party who has been involved in the preparation or publication of this manual warrant that the information herein is in every respect accurate or complete, and they are not responsible for any errors or omissions or for the results obtained from the use of such information. Readers are encouraged to confirm the information contained herein with other sources.

Readers are particularly advised to check the product information sheet included in the package of each drug they plan to administer to be certain that the information in this manual is accurate and that changes have not been made in the recommended dose or in the contraindications for administration. This is of particular importance in connection with new or infrequently used drugs.

Introduction

The adverse effects of alcohol, tobacco and other drug use constitute a serious public health problem in most countries. Some studies have estimated that 20 to 40 per cent of all inpatients admitted to hospitals have substance use disorders. Studies also show that physicians often underdiagnose and inadequately treat patients with alcohol, tobacco and other drug problems. This manual is designed to help medical practitioners address these problems by providing them with accurate, practical information in an easy-to-use format.

USING THIS MANUAL

The contents of this manual have been organized to promote quick access to topics of interest to physicians. The 18 sections cover screening and assessment, treatment options, specific drugs and drug groups, emergency management of intoxications and overdoses, complications of drug use, issues relating to older adults, women, youth and the family, identifying and treating concurrent disorders, drug-seeking behavior in patients and impaired physicians.

The manual can be used by physicians to:

❑ screen patients for alcohol, tobacco and other drug problems with specific information for screening women, youth and older adults

❑ assess patients' need for treatment

❑ understand the range of treatment options available, including details of settings, indications and requirements, type and duration of treatments

❑ understand and use counselling strategies that focus on brief interventions (drawing on theories of motivational interviewing and the stages of change)

1

❑ treat patients with acute problems (intoxications and overdoses) through emergency medical measures

❑ understand and manage withdrawal from, and treatment for, alcohol and other drug dependence using withdrawal assessment tools

❑ manage withdrawal procedures for patients

❑ provide smoking cessation treatment for patients

❑ gain familiarity with relevant medical issues for a range of prescription and illicit drugs including: cocaine, benzodiazepines, opioids (including methadone), barbiturates, cannabis, methylphenidate (Ritalin®), dimenhydrinate (Gravol®, Dramamine®), MDMA ("ecstasy")

❑ understand and treat the complications of drug use in specific high-risk cases (e.g., HIV, hepatitis C)

❑ understand and manage concurrent disorders (mental disorders and substance use)

❑ recognize and manage drug-seeking behaviors in patients

❑ obtain assistance for the impaired physician

❑ become familiar with the epidemiology of substance abuse in Canada and the U.S.

ACCESSING INFORMATION

This manual has been designed to be easy to use. As well as using the manual's main table of contents to find information, physicians should refer to the expanded, more detailed directories at the start of each section. These directories list the diagnostic assessment tools, withdrawal and treatment protocols, medical complications and clinical guidelines discussed in each section. A detailed index has also been provided.

DRUG INFORMATION SHEETS FOR PATIENTS

An added feature of the manual is the inclusion of drug information sheets for patients called "Facts for Patients." The sheets highlight information about specific drugs of abuse, including alcohol, cocaine, nicotine, ecstasy and benzodiazepines. Provided in Appendix 3, they have been designed to be photocopied and distributed directly to patients.

RESOURCES FOR PROFESSIONALS

Included in Appendix 4 is information about alternative resources that support physicians when substance use issues are encountered in their practices. In addition to telephone hotlines that provide support and/or professional advice to physicians in specific jurisdictions, there is a short listing of Internet resources that physicians, regardless of their locale, can access for reliable, up-to-date information.

DEFINITIONS AND CLASSIFICATIONS OF SUBSTANCE ABUSE

This manual refers to a number of terms that relate to alcohol, tobacco and other drug problems. Definitions for the terms are taken from current sources, including the American Psychiatric Association's *Diagnostic and Statistical Manual of Mental Disorders,* Fourth Edition (DSM-IV), and the World Health Organization's *International Classification of Diseases - 10* (ICD-10), as well as various publications of the American Society of Addiction Medicine and the Addiction Research Foundation Division of the Centre for Addiction and Mental Health. Defined below are some terms used in the manual.

Addiction
The American Society of Addiction Medicine defines an addiction as "a disease process characterized by the continued use of a specific psychoactive substance despite physical, psychological or social harm" (Steindler, 1994).

Alcohol, tobacco and other drug problems
The full range of medical, psychiatric and social problems caused by substance use.

Chemical dependency
A generic term relating to psychological or physical dependency, or both, on one or more psychoactive substances.

Dependence
Dependence is a term that is used in three ways:
i)   Physical dependence. "Physiologic state of adaptation to a specific psychoactive substance, characterized by the emergence of a withdrawal syndrome during abstinence, which may be relieved in total or part by re-administration of the substance" (Fleming & Barry, 1992).
ii) Psychological dependence. "Subjective sense of need for a specific psychoactive substance, either for its positive effects or to avoid negative effects associated with its absence" (Fleming & Barry, 1992).

iii) Substance dependence. A category of substance use disorder described in DSM-IV (see Table 3).

Low-risk drinking

A pattern of alcohol consumption associated with the lowest risk of adverse effects while securing the benefits derived from alcohol's protective effect against heart disease. Physicians must have a clear understanding of what constitutes low-risk drinking in order to identify and manage alcohol problems appropriately. New guidelines for low-risk drinking include:

• Drink no more than two standard drinks on any day.

• Limit your weekly intake to 14 or fewer standard drinks for men and nine or fewer standard drinks for women.

• These guidelines were developed and endorsed by the Addiction Research Foundation (now part of the Centre for Addiction and Mental Health) and other Canadian health care organizations including the College of Family Physicians of Canada. The guidelines are based on scientific evidence and may not apply to special populations. In particular they may not apply for certain individuals with alcohol dependence or multiple physical complications arising from alcohol use. (See Section 3.5 for a full description.)

Problem drinking

A term commonly used in the literature on brief counselling interventions to describe alcohol use in excess of the recommended limits for low-risk drinking that may have contributed to one or more alcohol-related physical or social problems. Problem drinkers may not meet the DSM-IV criteria for alcohol abuse.

Standard drink

A standard drink is defined as one 341 mL (12 oz.) bottle of beer (5% alcohol); one 142 mL (5 oz.) glass of table wine (12% alcohol); one 43 mL ($1^1/_2$ oz.) shot of liquor (40% alcohol); or one 85 mL (3 oz.) serving of fortified wine, such as sherry or port (18% alcohol).

Substance/Substance of abuse

The term "substance" or "substance of abuse" refers to a psychoactive substance that has the potential to create dependence or abuse. Substances of abuse are frequently classified according to their CNS effects, i.e., depressants, stimulants or hallucinogens (see Table 1). However in the DSM-IV substances of abuse are grouped into 11 classes: alcohol, amphetamines and other stimulants, caffeine, cannabis, cocaine, hallucinogens, inhalants, nicotine, opioids, phencyclidine (PCP) and sedatives, hyponotics and anxiolytics.* The diagnoses associated with each of these groups are shown in Table 2.

Substance-Related Disorders
As defined in the DSM-IV, these are divided into two groups: Substance Use Disorders and Substance-Induced Disorders.

Substance Use Disorders
These include Substance Dependence and Substance Abuse.

Substance Dependence
See Table 3 for DSM-IV criteria for Substance Dependence.

Substance Abuse
See Table 4 for DSM-IV criteria for Substance Abuse.

Substance-Induced Disorders
As defined in the DSM-IV, these are:
Substance Intoxication, Substance Withdrawal, Substance-Induced Delirium, Substance-Induced Persisting Dementia, Substance-Induced Psychotic Disorder, Substance-Induced Mood Disorder, Substance-Induced Anxiety Disorder, Substance-Induced Sexual Dysfunction and Substance-Induced Sleep Disorder.

TABLE 1: Classification of Substances of Abuse

1. CNS Depressants	
Alcohol	Mixed Agonists-Antagonists: pentazocine, butorphanol, nalbuphine (not available in Canada)
Sedative/Hypnotics and Anxiolytics: barbiturates benzodiazepines	Inhalants Aliphatic hydrocarbons: propane
Opioid Analgesics Pure Opioid Agonists: naturally occurring alkaloids (opium) morphine, codeine Semi-synthetic: heroin Synthetic: oxycodone, methadone, fentanyl, meperidine, hydrocodone, propoxyphene	Aromatic hydrocarbons: toluene, xylene Chlorinated hydrocarbons: carbon tetrachloride Mixed hydrocarbons: gasoline Ketones: acetone Halogenated compounds: halothane Other: nitrous oxide

*Sedatives, hypnotics and anxiolytics are grouped together in this text, and are referred to as sedative/hypnotics.

Table 1 continued

2. Stimulants	Caffeine
Amphetamines: dexamphetamine, dextroamphetamine amphetamine methamphetamine methylphenidate ephedrine MDA, MDMA	Cocaine Nicotine
	3. Hallucinogens
	LSD Mescaline Cannabis PCP

TABLE 2: Diagnoses Associated with Class of Substances†,††

	Dependence	Abuse	Intoxication	Withdrawal	Intoxication Delirium	Withdrawal Delirium	Dementia	Amnestic Disorder	Psychotic Disorders	Mood Disorders	Anxiety Disorders	Sexual Dysfunctions	Sleep Disorders
ALCOHOL	x	x	x	x	I	W	P	P	I/W	I/W	I/W	I	I/W
AMPHETAMINES	x	x	x	x	I				I	I/W	I	I	I/W
CAFFEINE			x								I		I
CANNABIS	x	x	x		I				I		I		
COCAINE	x	x	x	x	I				I	I/W	I/W	I	I/W
HALLUCINOGENS	x	x	x		I				I†††	I	I		
INHALANTS	x	x	x		I		P		I	I	I		
NICOTINE	x			x									
OPIOIDS	x	x	x	x	I				I	I		I	I/W
PHENCYCLIDINE	x	x	x		I				I	I	I		
SEDATIVES, HYPNOTICS, OR ANXIOLYTICS	x	x	x	x	I	W	P	P	I/W	I/W	W	I	I/W
POLYSUBSTANCE	x												
OTHER	x	x	x	x	I	W	P	P	I/W	I/W	I/W	I	I/W

† Reprinted with permission from *Diagnostic and Statistical Manual of Mental Disorders* (4th edition). Copyright 1994, American Psychiatric Association.

†† X, I, W, I/W, or P indicates that the category is recognized in DSM-IV. In addition, *I* indicates that the specifier With Onset During Intoxication may be noted for the category (except for Intoxication Delirium); *W* indicates that the specifier With Onset During Withdrawal may be noted for the category (except for Withdrawal Delirium); and *I/W* indicates that either With Onset During Intoxication or With Onset During Withdrawal may be noted for the category. *P* indicates that the disorder is Persisting.

††† Also Hallucinogen Persisting Perception Disorder (Flashbacks)

TABLE 3: DSM-IV Criteria for Substance Dependence†

A maladaptive pattern of substance use, leading to clinically significant impairment or distress, as manifested by three (or more) of the following, occurring at any time in the same 12-month period:

1. Tolerance, as defined by either of the following:

   (a) a need for markedly increased amounts of the substance to achieve intoxication or desired effect

   (b) markedly diminished effect with continued use of the same amount of the substance.

2. Withdrawal, as manifested by either of the following:

   (a) the characteristic withdrawal syndrome for the substance (refer to Criteria A and B of the criteria sets for withdrawal from the specific substances)

   (b) the same (or a closely related) substance is taken to relieve or avoid withdrawal symptoms.

3. The substance is often taken in larger amounts or over a longer period than was intended.

4. There is a persistent desire or unsuccessful efforts to cut down or control substance use.

5. A great deal of time is spent in activities necessary to obtain the substance (e.g., visiting multiple doctors or driving long distances), use the substance (e.g., chain-smoking), or recover from its effects.

6. Important social, occupational, or recreational activities are given up or reduced because of substance use.

7. The substance use is continued despite knowledge of having a persistent or recurrent physical or psychological problem that is likely to have been caused or exacerbated by the substance (e.g., current cocaine use despite recognition of cocaine-induced depression, or continued drinking despite recognition that an ulcer was made worse by alcohol consumption).

Table 3 continued

Specify if:

With Physiological Dependence: evidence of tolerance or withdrawal (i.e., either Item 1 or 2 is present).

Without Physiological Dependence: no evidence of tolerance or withdrawal (i.e., neither Item 1 or 2 is present).

---

† Reprinted with permission from *Diagnostic and Statistical Manual of Mental Disorders* (4th edition). Copyright 1994, American Psychiatric Association.

TABLE 4: DSM-IV Criteria for Substance Abuse†

A. A maladaptive pattern of substance use leading to clinically significant impairment or distress, as manifested by one (or more) of the following, occurring within a 12-month period:

1. Recurrent substance use resulting in a failure to fulfil major role obligations at work, school, or home (e.g., repeated absences or poor work performance related to substance use; substance-related absences, suspensions, or expulsions from school; neglect of children or household)

2. Recurrent substance use in situations in which it is physically hazardous (e.g., driving an automobile or operating a machine when impaired by substance use)

3. Recurrent substance-related legal problems (e.g., arrests for substance-related disorderly conduct)

4. Continued substance use despite having persistent or recurrent social or interpersonal problems caused or exacerbated by the effects of the substance (e.g., arguments with spouse about consequences of intoxication, physical fights)

B. The symptoms have never met the criteria for Substance Dependence for this class of substance.

---

† Reprinted with permission from *Diagnostic and Statistical Manual of Mental Disorders* (4th edition). Copyright 1994, American Psychiatric Association.

R E F E R E N C E S

American Psychiatric Association. (1994). *Diagnostic and Statistical Manual of Mental Disorders* (4th ed.). Washington, DC: American Psychiatric Association.

Fleming, M.F. & Barry, K.L. (Eds.). (1992). *Addictive Disorders*. St. Louis, MO: Mosby Year Book.

Steindler, E.M. (1994). Addiction terminology. In N.S. Miller (Ed.), *Principles of Addiction Medicine*. Chevy Chase, MD: American Society of Addiction Medicine.

World Health Organization. (1992). *ICD-10 Classification of Mental and Behavioural Disorders: Clinical Descriptions and Diagnostic Guidelines*. Geneva: World Health Organization.

Screening and Assessment

1.1 SCREENING OF ALCOHOL, TOBACCO AND OTHER DRUG PROBLEMS

1.2 ASSESSMENT OF ALCOHOL, TOBACCO AND OTHER DRUG PROBLEMS

1.3 TOXICOLOGY TESTING

REFERENCES

TABLES AND FIGURES

1.1

SCREENING OF ALCOHOL, TOBACCO AND OTHER DRUG PROBLEMS

Meldon Kahan, MD

Routine screening for alcohol and drug problems should be standard in all physicians' practices. Available screening techniques are sensitive, practical and acceptable to the general population. Routine screening is justified because controlled trials have shown that treatment interventions for alcohol and other drug problems are highly cost-effective.

SCREENING AND EARLY DETECTION OF ALCOHOL PROBLEMS

Physicians from all medical disciplines have a low rate of detection of alcohol-related problems among inpatients and outpatients. Depending on the methodology and the patient population, detection rates vary from 60 per cent to under 10 per cent (Moore, Bone et al., 1989). Lack of detection leads to treatment delays and unnecessary morbidity and mortality.

Physicians are most likely to miss problems in women and the elderly. In part this reflects the reluctance of women and elderly patients to disclose their drinking due to shame or social stigma. Physicians, in turn, may maintain stereotypes that make them less likely to ask about or suspect alcohol problems in these groups.

Detection rates can be increased by taking a careful alcohol history of all patients, being alert to clinical presentations of heavy drinking and using screening questionnaires and laboratory markers. Physicians should incorporate questions about alcohol consumption into their routine baseline questions about smoking, exercise, diet, past health, family history and medication use. Patients are rarely upset by routine, matter-of-fact questioning about alcohol use.

Physicians should routinely ask all patients about alcohol use in the following circumstances:

- at initial presentation
- during complete physical examinations (e.g., annual health exams, admission histories)
- during prenatal visits
- when prescribing medications that may interact with alcohol
- with any presentation that may be related to alcohol.

Physicians should screen for alcohol use on repeated occasions. Patients become more open with their physicians as they get to know them, and drinking patterns can change dramatically over time.

Alcohol consumption history

The sensitivity of the alcohol history can be enhanced by observing the points listed in the table below.

TABLE 1: Taking an Alcohol Consumption History

1. Take a history of everyone, regardless of age, gender or socioeconomic status.

2. Elicit a specific weekly consumption ("I just drink socially" means little because patients' social groups may consist of heavy drinkers).

3. Convert the patient's response into standard drinks containing equivalent amounts of ethanol.

A "standard drink" =

43 mL (1.5 oz.)		142 mL (5 oz.)		341 mL (12 oz.)		85 mL (3 oz.)
spirit	or	table wine	or	regular beer	or	fortified wine
(40% alcohol)		(12% alcohol)		(5% alcohol)		(18% alcohol)

4. Patients who drink wine or spirits at home usually pour more than a standard drink into their glass. Ask these patients how many bottles of wine or spirits they consume per week, and the size of the bottles.

Table 1 continued

---

5. Ask about maximum consumption at one sitting in the previous month. (When patients are asked only about their average or typical weekly consumption, they often exclude sporadic heavy drinking days.)

6. For patients who give vague responses:
   - ask about their previous week's drinking (this is the week that is most precisely remembered)
   - present them with a wide range of consumption: "Would you say your drinking is more on the order of 14 drinks per week or 30 drinks per week?"

ALCOHOL SCREENING QUESTIONNAIRES

Screening questionnaires can markedly enhance detection rates with demonstrated sensitivities of 75 to 85 per cent in a general practice setting (King, 1986; Cyr & Wartman, 1988). Short questionnaires such as CAGE can be used in a clinical interview, whereas longer questionnaires such as AUDIT can be incorporated into waiting room questionnaires. The most commonly used screening questionnaires are as follows:

CAGE questionnaire

The CAGE questionnaire (Table 2) has been validated in a number of clinical settings (King, 1986). Two out of four positive responses suggests a current or past alcohol problem, although even one positive response warrants further assessment. A recent meta-analysis found that a single positive response was clinically significant for women (Bradley, Boyd-Wickizer et al., 1998). Since the CAGE questions are retrospective, a positive response may indicate a past rather than a current problem. The physician needs to interpret the CAGE in light of information on the amount and frequency of alcohol consumption, since the CAGE does not inquire about this.

TABLE 2: CAGE Questionnaire[†]

- Have you ever felt you should **C**UT DOWN on your drinking?
- Have people **A**NNOYED you by criticizing your drinking?
- Have you ever felt bad or **G**UILTY about your drinking?
- Have you ever had a drink first thing in the morning to steady your nerves or to get rid of a hangover (**E**YE-OPENER)?

Item responses on the CAGE are scored 0 or 1, with a higher score indicative of alcohol problems. A total score of 2 or greater is considered clinically significant.[††]

---

† Reprinted with permission from Mayfield, D., McLeod, G. & Hall, P. (1974). The CAGE questionnaire: Validation of a new alcoholism screening instrument. *American Journal of Psychiatry, 131(10),* 1121–1123.
†† A score of 1 may be clinically significant for women.

"Problem" questionnaire

The "Problem" questionnaire (Cyr & Wartman, 1988) is even simpler than the CAGE questionnaire, although studies have had conflicting results on its validity. The second question ("When was your last drink?") is considered positive if the response indicates consumption within the past 24 hours.

TABLE 3: "Problem" Questionnaire

- Have you ever felt you had a problem with alcohol?
- When was your last drink?

A positive response to both questions indicates a potential alcohol problem.

Alcohol Use Disorders Identification Test (AUDIT)

AUDIT, a 10-item multiple-choice questionnaire (Table 4), can be used as a waiting-room survey (Babor, de la Fuente et al., 1989). Developed by the World Health Organization, the AUDIT has been shown to be valid and reliable in a number of different languages. It includes questions on the quantity and frequency of alcohol consumption, blackouts, injuries, failure to fulfil obligations, as well as questions from the CAGE questionnaire.

TABLE 4: Alcohol Use Disorders Identification Test (AUDIT)†

Circle the number that comes closest to your actions during the past year.

1. How often do you have a drink containing alcohol?

   Never (0)
   Monthly or less (1)
   2 to 4 times a month (2)
   2 to 3 times a week (3)
   4 or more times a week (4)

2. How many drinks containing alcohol do you have on a typical day when you are drinking?

   1 or 2 (0)
   3 or 4 (1)
   5 or 6 (2)
   7 to 9 (3)
   10 or more (4)

16

Table 4 continued

3. How often do you have six or more drinks on one occasion?
    Never   (0)
    Less than monthly   (1)
    Monthly   (2)
    Weekly   (3)
    Daily or almost daily   (4)

4. How often during the past year have you found that you were not able to stop drinking once you had started?
    Never   (0)
    Less than monthly   (1)
    Monthly   (2)
    Weekly   (3)
    Daily or almost daily   (4)

5. How often during the last year have you failed to do what was normally expected from you because of drinking?
    Never   (0)
    Less than monthly   (1)
    Monthly   (2)
    Weekly   (3)
    Daily or almost daily   (4)

6. How often during the last year have you needed a first drink in the morning to get yourself going after a heavy drinking session?
    Never   (0)
    Less than monthly   (1)
    Monthly   (2)
    Weekly   (3)
    Daily or almost daily   (4)

7. How often during the last year have you had a feeling of guilt or remorse after drinking?
    Never   (0)
    Less than monthly   (1)
    Monthly   (2)
    Weekly   (3)
    Daily or almost daily   (4)

Table 4 continued

---

8. How often during the last year have you been unable to remember what happened the night before because you had been drinking?

Never	(0)
Less than monthly	(1)
Monthly	(2)
Weekly	(3)
Daily or almost daily	(4)

9. Have you or someone else been injured as a result of your drinking?

No	(0)
Yes, but not in the last year	(2)
Yes, during the last year	(4)

10. Has a relative or friend or a doctor or other health worker been concerned about your drinking or suggested you cut down?

No	(0)
Yes, but not in the last year	(2)
Yes, during the last year	(4)

Record sum of item scores: _____

Scoring: Each answer is weighted from 0 to 4 as indicated in the brackets. Please note that questions 9 and 10 are scored 0, 2 or 4. A score of 8 or more indicates that a harmful level of alcohol consumption is likely.

---

† Reprinted with permission from *AUDIT: The Alcohol Use Disorders Identification Test: Guidelines for Use in Primary Care.* Copyright 1989, World Health Organization.

ALCOHOL SCREENING QUESTIONNAIRES FOR WOMEN

T-ACE

The T-ACE screening test (Table 5) was developed and validated for use by pregnant women (Sokol, Martier & Ager, 1989). It is similar to the CAGE except that the question about guilt is replaced by a question about tolerance. The question was changed because it was felt that pregnant women tend to feel guilty about any amount of alcohol use. The T-ACE has been validated in non-pregnant populations as well.

TABLE 5: T-ACE Test †

T	How many drinks does it take to make you feel high? (**T**OLERANCE).	Record # of drinks	
A	Have people **A**NNOYED you by criticizing your drinking?	Y	N
C	Have you felt you ought to **C**UT DOWN on your drinking?	Y	N
E	Have you ever had a drink first thing in the morning to steady your nerves or get rid of a hangover? (**E**YE-OPENER).	Y	N

Scoring the T-ACE:
T: 2 points if it takes 2 or more drinks to make her feel high
A,C,E: 1 point for each yes
A total of 2 or more points indicates that the patient is likely to have an alcohol problem.

† Reprinted with permission from R.J. Sokol, S.S. Martier & J.W. Ager. (1989). The T-ACE questions: Practical prenatal detection of risk-drinking. *American Journal of Obstetrics & Gynecology 160*, 863–870. Copyright 1989.

TWEAK

The TWEAK test is another validated screening tool designed to be used with women (Table 6), but it has also been shown to be valid for men.

TABLE 6: TWEAK Test †

T	**T**OLERANCE: How many drinks does it take to feel the first effects of alcohol? (record number of drinks)	Record # of drinks	
W	**W**ORRY: Have close friends or relatives worried or complained about your drinking in the past year?	Y	N
E*	**E**YE OPENER: Do you sometimes have a drink in the morning when you first get up?	Y	N
A	**A**MNESIA (Blackouts): Has a friend or family member ever told you about things you said or did while you were drinking that you could not remember?	Y	N
K(C)	**C**UT DOWN: Do you sometimes feel the need to cut down on your drinking?	Y	N

Table 6 continued

Scoring the TWEAK:	
T	2 points if it takes 3 or more drinks to feel the effects of alcohol
W	2 points if "Yes"
E, A, K	1 point for each "Yes"
	A total score of three or more points indicates that the woman is likely to have a drinking problem.

† When using the TWEAK test with women, the "E" or "Eye-opener" question might provide more useful information if phrased as follows: "Have you ever needed a drink or medication of some kind first thing in the morning to steady your nerves or get over a hangover?" (Blume, 1994).

CLINICAL DETECTION OF ALCOHOL PROBLEMS

Laboratory markers — alcohol screening

The best laboratory markers currently available are the gamma glutamyl transferase (GGT) and mean cell volume (MCV). However, in a general practice setting their sensitivity is only 30 to 50 per cent for detecting consumption of four to six drinks per day or more. The half-life of GGT is four to six weeks; the half-life of MCV is three months. GGT can be elevated by obesity, diabetes, biliary tract disease, non-alcoholic liver disease and microsomal enzyme inducers such as phenytoin or barbiturates. MCV can be elevated by hypothyroidism, folate or B_{12} deficiency, smoking, liver disease and drugs such as valproic acid. Thrombocytopenia due to bone marrow suppression or hypersplenism is also commonly seen in heavy drinkers.

Clinical presentations of alcohol use

Physicians need to be alert to clinical presentations associated with heavy drinking (Table 7). The most common presentations in a family practice setting are trauma, gastrointestinal symptoms, hypertension, depression, anxiety, insomnia, sexual problems and social and family dysfunction.

TABLE 7: Common Presentations of Heavy Drinking

PHYSICAL EXAMINATION	smell of alcohol on breath
	hepatomegaly and other signs of chronic liver disease
NEUROLOGICAL	tremors
	ataxia

20

Table 7 continued

CARDIOVASCULAR	hypertension hemorrhagic stroke tachyarrhythmias
GASTROINTESTINAL	gastritis non-specific dyspepsia recurrent diarrhea pancreatitis fatty liver
REPRODUCTIVE	impotence menstrual irregularities infertility
MUSCULOSKELETAL	trauma
PSYCHOLOGICAL	insomnia fatigue depression anxiety prescription, illicit drug use
BEHAVIORAL	missed appointments non-compliance
SOCIAL	marital discord family violence work, school absenteeism and poor performance impaired driving charges

SCREENING AND EARLY DETECTION OF NICOTINE DEPENDENCE

Despite overwhelming evidence of the health risks of tobacco and the cost-effectiveness of smoking cessation strategies, a large proportion of smokers report that they did not receive any advice from their physician about smoking. Patients who have serious tobacco-related health problems are far more likely to report receiving advice than healthy smokers.

All patients from age nine onwards should be asked about smoking on initial presentation and during physical examinations and prenatal visits. Screening for nicotine dependence should also be undertaken in patients with chronic cardiac or respiratory disease or with risk factors for cardiovascular disease such as hypertension. Screening should also be undertaken in patients presenting with acute respiratory illness such as bronchitis, asthma or sinusitis, and among the parents of children presenting with otitis media, asthma or respiratory infections.

Patients who smoke should be asked at frequent intervals whether they are still smoking. This conveys the message that the physician considers their smoking a serious health problem. Patients should then be asked if they are interested in quitting, and if so, when. Patients who report that they would like to quit within the next six months should be offered a follow-up visit to discuss smoking cessation (see Section 4.4).

SCREENING AND EARLY DETECTION OF DRUG PROBLEMS

Screening for and identifying drug problems is even more challenging than for alcohol problems because of the greater stigma attached to drug use. The following strategies will increase detection rates. (Patients in whom a drug problem is suspected should have a more comprehensive assessment.)

TABLE 8: Taking an Initial Drug History

All patients under the age of 45 should be asked about use of street drugs.

All patients, regardless of age, should be asked about prescription benzo-diazepines, prescription opioids, over-the-counter and non-prescribed medications.

For patients who report use of street or non-prescribed psychoactive medications

☐ Ask about use of drugs/major drug classes: cannabis, cocaine, heroin and prescription opioids, benzodiazepines, hallucinogens.
☐ Ask about frequency, amount and route (injection, smoking, sniffing, oral). Have patients quantify their use in grams or dollars rather than "lines" or "hits."
☐ Ask about *maximum* use on any one day in the past three months.
☐ Ask patients whether they have any concerns about the drug use, or whether it has created any problems.

Laboratory markers — drug screening

Urine drug screens can be used to detect drug use. Cocaine and most opioids are detectable for one to three days after the last use; cannabis and benzodiazepines may be detected for up to a month. Physicians should inform patients before ordering a urine drug screen (see Section 1.3).

Clinical presentations of drug use

The following table outlines some of the common presentations of drug use encountered in a general medical setting. The drugs most likely to be associated with the presentation are in brackets.

TABLE 9: Common Presentations of Drug Use

MUSCULOSKELETAL	trauma *(all)*
GASTROINTESTINAL	viral hepatitis *(injection drugs)* unexplained elevations in ALT *(injection drugs)*
PHYSICAL EXAMINATION	weight loss *(especially cocaine, heroin)* injected conjunctiva *(cannabis)* pinpoint pupils *(opioids)* track marks *(injection drugs)*
BEHAVIORAL	missed appointments *(all)* non-compliance *(all)* drug-seeking *(especially benzodiazepines, opioids)*
PSYCHOLOGICAL	insomnia *(all)* fatigue *(all)* depression *(all)* anxiety *(all)* flat affect *(benzodiazepines, barbiturates)* paranoia *(cocaine)* psychosis *(cocaine, cannabis, hallucinogens)*
SOCIAL (ALL)	marital discord family violence work/school absenteeism and poor performance

1.2

ASSESSMENT OF ALCOHOL, TOBACCO AND OTHER DRUG PROBLEMS

Meldon Kahan, MD, and Lynn Wilson, MD

ASSESSMENT PROTOCOL

Once an alcohol or drug problem is suspected, a more detailed assessment should be undertaken to identify treatable medical, psychiatric and social problems and formulate a treatment plan. The assessment should include the following components:

- alcohol and drug consumption history
- withdrawal symptoms
- psychiatric history (depression/anxiety, suicidal ideation)
- consequences of alcohol and other drug use, including physical and social consequences
- driving while impaired
- sexual practices (birth control, safe sex)
- injection drug use (needle sharing, HIV, hepatitis B and C)
- physical and laboratory examination (CBC, liver function tests)

TAKE A COMPLETE ALCOHOL AND DRUG CONSUMPTION HISTORY
Polydrug abuse is common, especially among younger substance users. Physicians should inquire about the use of sedative/hypnotics and both prescription and over-the-counter opioid analgesics, as well as cannabis, cocaine and heroin.

DETERMINE IF THE PATIENT HAS SYMPTOMS OF WITHDRAWAL
For alcohol and sedative/hypnotics, withdrawal symptoms consist of tremor, sweating, anxiety and seizures (see Table 10). For opioids such as heroin, withdrawal symptoms include insomnia, myalgias, nausea and diarrhea.

Cocaine withdrawal symptoms include depression, hypersomnia followed by insomnia, and drug cravings.

TABLE 10: Withdrawal Symptoms of Different Drug Classes

ALCOHOL	morning relief drinking, tremor, sweating, anxiety, seizures, delirium tremens
SEDATIVES	tremor, sweating, anxiety, insomnia, seizures
OPIOIDS	insomnia, drug craving, diarrhea, nausea, myalgias, lacrimation, rhinorrhea
COCAINE	depression, hypersomnia or insomnia, nightmares, drug craving

TAKE A BRIEF PSYCHIATRIC HISTORY

Inquire about symptoms of depression, anxiety, panic disorder and psychosis. Ask specifically about suicidal ideation. Substance users have a high prevalence of affective and anxiety disorders. Suicidal ideation commonly accompanies dependence on opioids, cocaine, alcohol and sedative/hypnotics.

DETERMINE THE CONSEQUENCES OF ALCOHOL AND DRUG USE

Inquire about the effects of substance use on the major domains of patients' lives: social, occupational, financial, legal and physical. Patients should be encouraged to discuss the subtle effects of substance use (feeling tired in the morning, spending less time with the family).

TAKE A SOCIAL HISTORY

Ask about:
- Substance abuse among family members. (Substance use or abuse among spouses or family members may have a major impact on patients' treatment and prognosis.)
- Social situation. (Determine current living arrangements, partners and vocational status. The social situation can have a bearing on treatment plans.)
- Physical abuse. (Partners of male substance abusers experience an increased incidence of assault. Female substance users also experience an increased incidence of assault in both past and current relationships.)
- Parenting arrangements. (The safety of children living at home should be determined.)

25

ASK ABOUT ALCOHOL OR DRUG USE AND DRIVING

The answer should be documented. Physicians should follow the requirements in their jurisdiction regarding reporting of impaired driving.

SCREEN FOR PREGNANCY AND SEXUALLY TRANSMITTED DISEASES

Ask about sexual practices. Alcohol and drug users tend to use birth control sporadically and engage in unsafe sexual practices. Because their menstrual periods are often irregular, female drug users may not realize they are pregnant.

SCREEN FOR HIV AND HEPATITIS B AND C

Ask about injection drug use and sharing paraphernalia (spoons, filters, syringes; see Section 12).

CONDUCT A PHYSICAL EXAMINATION

Physical assessment for patients with suspected alcohol problems should include the measurement of blood pressure and an examination of the liver. Even young patients may have alcohol-induced hypertension or signs of liver disease such as fatty liver. Older patients with a long drinking history should also have a neurological exam to rule out peripheral neuropathy, cerebellar disease and dementia.

Injection drug users should be examined for track marks in the antecubital fossae or wrists. Other injection sites include the external jugular veins, the superficial thoracic or abdominal veins, the femoral veins, and other veins of the lower extremity. They should also be examined for signs of infectious complications of injection drug use, such as viral hepatitis, bacterial endocarditis and cellulitis (see also Section 12).

Because a large proportion of alcohol and drug users also smoke, a respiratory and cardiovascular exam is indicated, particularly for older patients. Women should have Pap smears and cervical cultures for gonorrhea and chlamydia.

Diagnosis

The physician is in a position to make a tentative diagnosis of substance abuse or dependence once the assessment is completed. Table 11 lists useful questions for the clinician when determining if patients meet the DSM-IV criteria for alcohol dependence. (The DSM-IV criteria for Substance Dependence are provided in the Introduction.) The diagnosis is established if three or more criteria occur at any time in the same 12-month period.

TABLE 11: Questions to Elicit DSM-IV Criteria for Alcohol Dependence†

Tolerance

Does it take more drinks than before to get "high" or get the same effect?

Withdrawal

Do you have a drink in the morning to calm your nerves?

Do you ever experience trembling or sweating the morning after drinking?

Have you ever had seizures or hallucinations after you stopped or cut down your drinking?

Taking larger amounts than intended

Do you often drink more than you had planned?

Unsuccessful efforts to reduce alcohol use

Have you ever tried to cut down or stop drinking altogether? Were you successful?

Preoccupation with drinking

Do you spend a lot of time doing things and planning ways to get alcohol?

Reduction of important activities because of alcohol

Does your drinking cause you to miss a lot of time from work or spend less time with family or friends?

Continued drinking despite knowledge of alcohol-related physical or psychological problem

Does drinking cause you any physical problems? Do you ever feel anxious or depressed? Have you had any other type of psychological problem?

---

† Reprinted with permission from M. Zimmerman. (1994). *Diagnosing DSM-IV Psychiatric Disorders in Primary Care Settings: An Interview Guide for the Non-Psychiatric Physician.* Copyright 1994 Psych Products Press.

Treatment Planning

Once the assessment is completed, the physician needs to work with the patient to develop a treatment plan, the components of which will include management of withdrawal, referral to a treatment program, treatment of medical complications, and ongoing education and support (see Section 2).

1.3

TOXICOLOGY TESTING

Michael Anderson, MLT, B.Sc.(Chem), and Bruna Brands, PhD

Urine drug screens can be used to detect and monitor drug use. The physician should inform patients before ordering urine drug screens. Immunoassay and chromatographic techniques dominate current methods for the detection of drugs in modern laboratories.

Immunoassay techniques include:
- enzyme immunoassay (EIA)
- enzyme-multiplied immunoassay technique (EMIT®)
- fluorescence polarization immunoassay (TDx®, AxSym®).

Chromatographic techniques include:
- high performance liquid chromatography (HPLC; e.g., Bio-Rad's Remedi® drug profiling system)
- gas chromatography (GC; not typically used for routine screening; more suited to emergency toxicology)
- gas chromatography-mass spectroscopy (GC-MS; used for confirmation in some laboratories; expensive and requires a great deal of expertise).

IMMUNOASSAY TECHNIQUES

Immunoassay techniques tend to be used for screening classes of drugs (opioids, benzodiazepines, barbiturates, amphetamines), although some assays are available to detect specific compounds (cocaine metabolite, methadone, cannabis [THC], phencyclidine [PCP]). Immunoassay techniques are generally more sensitive and therefore tend to detect drugs for longer periods of time than standard chromatographic techniques, though important exceptions exist (see Table 14). In addition, each assay is "tuned" to a specific drug in the class the assay is designed to detect. This accounts for variable cross-reactivity to specific drugs within a class and to problems with interpretation in inexperienced hands.

These techniques tend to be more prone to invalidation by adulteration/tampering than chromatographic techniques.

Summarized in Table 12 are some general comments about specific immunoassay tests. These comments may not be valid for every immunoassay kit available since formulations differ between manufacturers and sometimes within a manufacturer's kit selection. The laboratory using the assay should be able to provide information on or assistance in interpreting results for the kits they use.

The cut-offs listed in Table 12 are not applicable to all immunoassay products on the market. As well, the laboratory may have established its own in-house cut-off. Consult your service laboratory for their specific cut-offs, the drugs detected by their immunoassay screens and any limitations inherent in their assays.

TABLE 12: Immunoassay Testing for Drugs of Abuse

Immunoassay	Use	Comments
BENZODIAZEPINES Cut-off: 300 ng/mL or 200 ng/mL	detects various benzodiazepines and their metabolites	• does not cross-react equally to all benzodiazepines • certain benzodiazepines therefore may not always be detected (e.g., lorazepam, bromazepam)
AMPHETAMINES Cut-off: 300 ng/mL or 1000 ng/mL	intended to detect amphetamine and methamphetamine	• historically has been the most prone to cross-reactivity • phenylpropanolamine, pseudoephedrine, chlorpromazine, promethazine have been implicated in producing false positives by this assay • an alternate confirmation method is a must if this assay is used
OPIOIDS Cut-off: 300 ng/mL	detects various opioids	• assay may be more sensitive to some opioids (especially morphine) than others • some assays may not detect oxycodone or meperidine at "normal" levels, making this assay inappropriate for monitoring use of these drugs

29

Table 12 continued

Immunoassay	Use	Comments
		• the result is a total opioid (one or more opioids may be present in the urine)
COCAINE METABOLITE Cut-off: 300 ng/mL	detects the cocaine metabolite, benzoylecgonine	• tends to be very sensitive and specific to benzoylecgonine • little cross-reactivity to cocaine • lidocaine does not cross-react
BARBITURATES Cut-off: 300 ng/mL or 200 ng/mL	detects various barbiturates	• does not detect every barbiturate equally • may not be as sensitive as some chromatographic techniques for certain barbiturates (e.g., phenobarbital)
CANNABINOID METABOLITE Cut-off: Variable — 20, 50 or 100 ng/mL	detects cannabinoids	• tends to be specific, although some reports of cross-reactivity persist

CHROMATOGRAPHIC TECHNIQUES

Common chromatographic techniques are generally less sensitive than immunoassay techniques but are more specific. For example, opioid use would appear as an opioid-positive result using an immunoassay technique whereas a chromatographic technique would differentiate between morphine, codeine, hydromorphone, oxycodone and other opioids.

Chromatographic techniques are invaluable in determining methadone compliance. Methadone and its primary metabolite, 2-ethylidene-1,5-dimethyl-3, 3-diphenylpyrrolidine (EDDP), are distinguishable and reportable by many chromatographic techniques. Immunoassay techniques for methadone detect the parent compound only and are therefore not recommended as the best method for methadone compliance testing.

The ability of chromatographic techniques to detect metabolites allows for a more meaningful interpretation of some results. The detection of 6-monoacetyl-morphine (MAM) is a clear indicator of heroin use. This metabolite is not produced or available from any other source. The opioid immunoassay would simply be positive.

These techniques can provide a more complete picture of overall drug intake including antidepressants, antipsychotics, cardiac drugs, antihistamines, etc., and can therefore assist in monitoring compliance to prescribed drugs. They can also alert the physician to the possibility of double-doctoring or self-medication.

When available, gas chromatography-mass spectrometry techniques provide a level of accuracy unmatched by the other techniques. This is currently the best technology available for the identification of drugs. It is used primarily in employee drug testing and in legal cases that may be challenged in a court.

Interpretation of results

The laboratory performing the analysis should be able to assist in the interpretation of lab results. Drug screening results may be difficult to interpret because of the various methodologies available.

Confirmation testing

The laboratory should be able to provide confirmation testing by analysing a sample using a different technique than that used for the initial analysis. Confirmation testing relies on a different chemical or physical property of the drug for detection compared with the initial testing method. This increases the confidence level in the result. GC-MS, although expensive, is the ideal method for confirmation testing. Confirmation testing does not mean running the same assay a second time. Unless there was an initial error, repeating a test would not change the confidence in the result.

Properly performed and interpreted drug screens are essential for a comprehensive understanding of drug-screening results. Properly interpreted results can strengthen the treatment relationship with patients and reduce the risk of unnecessary confrontation.

INTERPRETATION OF OPIOID RESULTS

The table below lists some possible opioid results and some possible drug uses that would account for them.

TABLE 13: Opioid Test Results and Possible Interpretations

If lab reports:	Possibilities for drug use:
MONOACETYLMORPHINE (MAM) + AND MORPHINE + AND CODEINE +/-	heroin (recent, probably within the last 24 hrs)
CODEINE +	codeine
CODEINE + AND MORPHINE +	i) codeine alone ii) codeine and morphine iii) heroin (more than 24 hrs ago, with or without morphine and/or codeine) iv) poppy seeds
MORPHINE +	i) heroin (more than 24 hrs ago) ii) codeine (crossover)[†] iii) poppy seeds iv) morphine
OPIOIDS +	any of the above plus hydromorphone, meperidine (high), oxycodone, etc.

† A specific stage in codeine metabolism in which the concentration of morphine exceeds the concentration of codeine. At this time the codeine may not be detectable by the assay.

DURATION OF DETECTABILITY OF COMMONLY ABUSED DRUGS IN URINE

Detection depends on a number of factors, including:
- method of detection (laboratory methods vary in sensitivity to the drug[s] being detected, in specificity to the drug including variable specificity within the drug class and in ability to differentiate between drugs)
- metabolism of the drug, half-life ($t_{1/2}$), excretion characteristics, method and frequency of drug intake
- characteristics of the individual (e.g., body composition, disease state)
- concentration of the urine (influenced by fluid intake, time of day).

The detection times provided below are generalized observations meant as a guide only. Individuals may fall out of these ranges (see variables above). Consult the laboratory to assist in the interpretation of results of concern.

Chromatographic techniques tend to offer differentiation while EIA techniques tend to offer sensitivity. Table 14 illustrates these facts and highlights important exceptions.

TABLE 14: Duration of Detectability of Commonly Abused Drugs in Urine

Drug/Drug Class	Common Chromatographic Technique	Common EIA Technique
AMPHETAMINE(S)	1–3 days	not recommended without confirmation susceptible to cross-reactivity (phenylpropanolamine, promethazine, chlorpromazine, etc.)
BARBITURATES	differentiates barbiturates short-acting (secobarbital): 1–2 days long-acting (phenobarbital): 3+ weeks	does not differentiate barbiturates 1 day–3+ weeks depending on barbiturate present
BENZODIAZEPINES[†]	not commonly available	does not differentiate benzodiazepines after single dose (diazepam): approximately 7 days after chronic use (diazepam): up to 3+ weeks depending on extent of diazepam use

Table 14 continued

Drug/Drug Class	Common Chromatographic Technique	Common EIA Technique
CANNABINOIDS	not commonly available	after cessation of short-term use: up to 10 days after cessation of chronic use: 3+ weeks
COCAINE	1–2 days (parent drug) various metabolites may be detected and reported	parent not normally detected assay sensitive to benzoylecgonine (cocaine metabolite)
Benzoylecgonine (cocaine metabolite)	not commonly available	3–7 days
OPIOIDS		3–7 days does not differentiate between various opioids
Codeine	1–2 days	
Morphine	1–3 days	
Meperidine	1 day also detects normeperidine (1–2 days)	insensitive to therapeutic levels meperidine method not recommended for monitoring meperidine use
Hydromorphone	1–2 days (insensitive to therapeutic levels)	
Oxycodone	1–2 days	limited value for oxycodone detection

Table 14 continued

Drug/Drug Class	Common Chromatographic Technique	Common EIA Technique
METHADONE AND METHADONE METABOLITE (EDDP)[††]	method distinguishes between methadone and EDDP 1–4 days (laboratory could provide estimate of progress of elimination)	common EIAs detect parent only

[†] Detection of other benzodiazepines varies greatly with specific drug. Lorazepam and bromazepam exhibit greatly reduced cross-reactivity in common EIA. This may be seen as fluctuating results (+, -, then +). These results may imply use, abstinence and reuse. They may also be a result of being just over, then under and then over the cut-off set for the assay. Consequently, patients on therapeutic doses of these drugs may seem not to be in compliance when they actually are.

[††] For compliance testing, it is important to be able to distinguish between methadone and its major metabolite (EDDP). Absence of the metabolite may indicate non-compliance. Methods that do not distinguish between methadone and EDDP are susceptible to fraudulent abuses. Common methods do not allow for the distinction of patients taking legitimate methadone doses from those that supplement with illicit methadone.

ETHANOL

Blood alcohol concentration

Blood alcohol concentration (BAC) levels peak 30–90 minutes after ingestion (Kalant and Rosclou, 1989), followed by an approximate rate of decline of 15 mg% per hour (3.26 mmol/L per hour). Unlike many drugs, ethanol is completely eliminated in hours rather than days.

Testing

Ethanol can be tested for in blood, urine or breath. The availability of an alcohol breath analyser in the physician's office is highly recommended if there is a high prevalence of alcohol problems in the practice. This allows immediate testing and intervention as required. Breath analysers must be maintained (i.e., calibrated) on a regular basis. Urines with a glucose content can produce in vitro ethanol and may give a false positive urine ethanol result. The storage temperature and length of time between collection and testing will influence the test results.

Useful concentrations and conversions

Although in Canada the "legal limit" of blood alcohol concentration is 80 mg%, driving ability may be impaired at considerably lower levels, particularly in non-tolerant individuals. Ethanol levels are expressed in numerous concentration units. Laboratories use the S.I. units of mmol/L, while breath analysers may report levels in mg%.

80 mg% = 80 mg/100 mL = 80 mg/dL = 0.08% (wt) = 17.4 mmol/L

A useful conversion factor is: mmol/L x 4.6 = mg%.

R E F E R E N C E S

Babor, T.F., de la Fuente, J.R., Saunders, J. & Grant, M. (1989). *AUDIT: The Alcohol Use Disorders Identification Test: Guidelines for Use in Primary Care.* Geneva: World Health Organization.

Blume, S.B. (1994). Women and addictive disorders. In N.S. Miller (Ed.), *Principles of Addiction Medicine.* (Sec.XVI, Chap.1). Chevy Chase, MD: American Society of Addiction Medicine.

Bradley, K.A., Boyd-Wickizer, J., Powell, S.H. & Burman, M.L. (1998). Alcohol screening questionnaires in women: A critical review. *Journal of the American Medical Association, 280* (2), 166-171.

Cyr, M.G. & Wartman, S.A. (1988). The effectiveness of routine screening questions in the detection of alcoholism. *Journal of the American Medical Association, 259,* 51-54.

Kalant, H. and Rosclou, W.H.E. (1989). *Principles of Medical Pharmacology* (5th ed.). Toronto: B.C. Decker.

King, M. (1986). At risk drinking among general practice attenders: Validation of the CAGE questionnaire. *Psychological Medicine, 16,* 213-217.

Moore, R.D., Bone, L.R., Geller, G., Mamon, J.A., Stokes, E.J. & Levin, D.M. (1989). Prevalence, detection and treatment of alcoholism in hospitalized patients. *Journal of the American Medical Association, 261(3),* 403-407.

Sokol, R.J., Martier, S.S. & Ager, J.W. (1989). The T-ACE questions: Practical prenatal detection of risk-drinking. *American Journal of Obstetrics & Gynecology, 160,* 863-870.

Zimmerman, M. (1994). *Diagnosing DSM-IV Psychiatric Disorders in Primary Care Settings: An Interview Guide for the Non-Psychiatric Physician.* Philadelphia: Psych Products Press.

Overview of Treatment Options

2.4 PHARMACOTHERAPY IN TREATMENT

2.5 COUNSELLING PATIENTS IN A PRIMARY CARE SETTING

REFERENCES

TABLES AND FIGURES

2.1

TREATMENT CONSIDERATIONS

Meldon Kahan, MD, Peter Selby, MBBS, and Lynn Wilson, MD

TREATMENT EFFECTIVENESS

While physicians commonly hold pessimistic attitudes towards substance-dependent patients, there is strong and consistent evidence that treatment for substance abuse leads to substantial reductions in mortality, morbidity and health care costs. The cost-effectiveness of substance abuse treatment compares favorably with that of other chronic medical conditions.

PROGNOSIS

The effectiveness of addiction treatment has been extensively studied in the U.S. One-year abstinence rates after intensive treatment for an alcohol or drug problem range from 45 to 60 per cent. However, 90 per cent of patients will maintain abstinence if they continue in aftercare programs and/or mutual aid groups (Hoffman, 1994). Young, socially stable patients have a better prognosis than patients with longer drinking histories, fewer social supports or polydrug addiction.

RECOVERY, LAPSE AND RELAPSE

Recovery is defined as "the process of initiating and maintaining abstinence from alcohol or other drug use as well as making intrapersonal and interpersonal changes." A lapse is defined as "the initial episode of drug or alcohol use after a period of recovery." A lapse may end quickly or lead to a relapse. A relapse is a "failure to maintain abstinence over a period of time" (Daley & Marlatt, 1997). Many patients require several treatment attempts before achieving long-term abstinence, and relapses are common. This can be discouraging for both patient and physician. However, if addiction is viewed as a chronic condition similar to diabetes or heart disease, then relapses can be viewed not as a treatment failure but as a learning experience that also calls for a review of the treatment plan. The physician should approach a relapse in a manner similar to that of a patient with a sudden worsening of diabetes: analyse potential causes, address patient compliance, change or intensify treatment and consult with colleagues.

TREATMENT APPROACHES

No one treatment approach is appropriate for all patients. Rather, the treatment plan should be matched to the needs of the individual. A team approach to treatment should be employed wherever possible, involving the physician, addiction counsellors, psychiatrists and other services as needed, as well as family members.

FIGURE A: Overview of Treatment Options

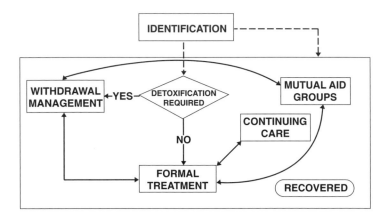

2.2

ROLES OF THE PHYSICIAN IN TREATMENT

Meldon Kahan, MD, Peter Selby, MBBS, and Lynn Wilson, MD

The physician has a number of important roles to play in the treatment of a substance user. These include initial assessment and diagnosis, followed by the presentation of the diagnosis and the initiation of treatment (including recommendation of mutual aid groups and referral to formal treatment programs). The physician is also responsible for the management of withdrawal, pharmacotherapy, medical complications and concurrent disorders. Another central role is providing educational and supportive counselling to family members.

COMMUNICATING WITH SUBSTANCE USERS

When communicating with substance-dependent patients, the following tips are helpful:

- Work on establishing a trusting physician-patient relationship.
- Do not attempt to counsel an intoxicated patient.
- If you think your patient has a diagnosis of substance dependence, tell him or her and present the evidence for this diagnosis.
- Do not use negative labels (e.g., "alcoholic," "drug addict"), unless the patient uses the label — use terms such as alcohol dependence, heroin dependence, etc.
- Tell the patient he or she is suffering from an illness, not a moral weakness.
- Tell the patient his or her illness is treatable and that you can help.
- Try to get the patient to acknowledge that his or her troubles are caused or worsened by substance use, and not the other way around (but do not argue).
- Offer to refer him or her to a substance abuse treatment program.
- Tell the patient about mutual aid groups and provide him or her with local meeting lists.
- Get to know some mutual aid groups for referral purposes.

For further information see Section 2.5.

HELPING PATIENTS IN RECOVERY*

Patients in recovery will benefit from the ongoing support of their primary care physician. Positive steps to support the patient include:

- emphasizing the need to attend a continuing care program
- encouraging frequent contact with a sponsor
- encouraging frequent attendance at mutual aid meetings
- monitoring response to pharmacotherapy
- avoiding the prescription of sedative/hypnotics
- prescribing opioids with caution, particularly for chronic non-malignant pain
- acknowledging "dry-dates" and recovery anniversaries
- looking for clues of potential relapse (e.g., missed appointments, requests for mood-altering medications, labile affect)
- when lapse or relapse occurs, helping the patient to see it as a learning experience and to develop new strategies for dealing with triggers to substance use. (Do not worsen the patient's guilt and self-blame.)

WHEN PATIENTS DO NOT ACCEPT A DIAGNOSIS OF SUBSTANCE ABUSE

Some substance abusers will not accept the diagnosis presented to them, or will insist that they have their substance use under control. This is often referred to as "denial" and may be due to conscious and/or unconscious motives for hiding their condition. Denial may be intensified by negative attitudes and behaviors on the part of the physician. It may also be intensified by cognitive deficits secondary to heavy use.

In this situation it is important to remember that the patient is suffering from a chronic condition that may not respond to initial interventions. Do not give up. Readdress the issue in a non-judgmental manner whenever possible. It is particularly helpful to link presenting complaints to the patient's substance use. Provide support to family members, and encourage them to attend a mutual support group such as Al-Anon.

* Adapted from Fleming & Barry, 1992.

2.3

TREATMENT OPTIONS AND SETTINGS

Meldon Kahan, MD, Peter Selby, MBBS, and Lynn Wilson, MD

Treatment can be divided into four phases: assessment and referral, detoxification or withdrawal management, active treatment and continuing care (see Table 1: Treatment Options and Settings).

Assessment and Referral

A comprehensive assessment is an essential component of treatment planning (see Section 1). Many jurisdictions have specialized addictions assessment and referral centres.

Detoxification or Withdrawal Management

Detoxification, which is increasingly referred to by health professionals as withdrawal management, is often a necessary first step towards recovery. As long as patients need to drink or use drugs throughout the day in order to avoid withdrawal symptoms, they will have difficulty following through with treatment recommendations. Detoxification in itself, however, rarely leads to long-term recovery unless it is expeditiously followed by intensive treatment. Detoxification can occur in the following settings:

Home detoxification

Home detoxification is appropriate for patients in mild withdrawal who have a stable, supportive home environment. Family members should be counselled about the nature and treatment of withdrawal, and the importance of not providing the patient with alcohol or other unauthorized substances.

Withdrawal management or detoxification centres

Detoxification can usually be managed safely in non-medical settings such as detoxification centres. The staff, although non-medical, are generally experienced in assessing withdrawal and other complications and will promptly refer patients who require urgent medical attention. They also provide supportive care and counselling and assist patients in enrolling in treatment programs. Detoxification centres are usually not equipped to dispense psychoactive medications such as benzodiazepines or opioids.

Medically supervised detoxification

Medical supervision is necessary when there is a risk of complications of withdrawal such as seizures (e.g., an alcohol-dependent individual with past withdrawal seizures), miscarriage (e.g., a pregnant woman withdrawing from opioids) or suicide. Criteria for medical supervision and inpatient admission are given in individual sections of this manual.

Formal treatment programs

Many treatment programs provide supervised and medically assisted detoxification, ensuring a smooth transition to the active treatment phase.

ACTIVE TREATMENT

Formal treatment approaches

Formal outpatient, day or inpatient rehabilitation programs use a combination of group therapy, individual counselling and health education. Specific programs are often available for women, adolescents, the elderly and patients with concurrent psychiatric disorders. Programs are also organized by substance (cocaine, heroin, alcohol, nicotine). Most treatment programs have continuing care sessions in which patients meet weekly to monthly for up to two years.

Outpatient treatment programs are the preferred initial treatment for most patients because they are generally as effective as, and less costly than, inpatient programs (Hoffman, 1994). Inpatient programs are indicated for homeless patients, those with an abusive or addicted spouse at home, patients with serious medical or psychiatric problems, and those who have failed at outpatient treatment. Outpatient or day programs are preferred for patients who are working outside the home, are caring for children, or who have a supportive family. Physicians should be familiar with treatment resources and registries in their community (see Appendix 4).

Mutual aid groups

Patients should be encouraged to try mutual aid groups such as Alcoholics Anonymous (AA), Narcotics Anonymous (NA) or Women for Sobriety. Physicians should have an AA contact, perhaps a patient in their practice, who will (with mutual consent) meet with patients new to AA and take them to one or two meetings. Patients should be encouraged to try several AA groups until they find one they feel comfortable attending on an ongoing basis.

The 12-step program (see Table 2) offers many patients a deeply meaningful approach to recovery. Mutual aid groups also provide wisdom, experience and practical advice to help their members avoid relapse and maintain a balanced, healthy lifestyle. For example, AA members are advised to avoid "HALT" states (Hungry, Angry, Lonely, Tired) as these are common triggers for relapse. Mutual aid groups have several additional strengths:

- **Acceptance.** By admitting that they have an alcohol problem to others in the group, and being met with acceptance and empathy rather than reproach, the burden of shame and guilt is lifted and patients can develop a more positive approach to recovery.
- **Social Support.** For many patients, becoming abstinent means giving up friends, relatives and even family members. The result is loneliness and social isolation in the initial period of abstinence, leaving them at risk for relapse. Mutual aid groups provide a social circle of supportive, abstinent people to fill the gap. A close bond can develop between group members.
- **Mentoring.** A group member can choose a more senior group member as a sponsor or mentor. The sponsor often plays a crucial role in the patient's recovery, providing support, advice and empathy.

Mutual aid groups conduct both open meetings (open to the general public) and closed meetings (attended only by group members). Closed meetings enable members to discuss difficult personal issues in confidence.

CONTINUING CARE

Due to the chronic, relapsing and remitting nature of substance use disorders, ongoing counselling or "continuing care" is recommended following successful completion of the intensive phase of treatment. The primary aim is to consolidate the gains made by patients during the intensive phase while they develop a drug-free lifestyle. Continuing care emphasizes relapse-prevention techniques and lifestyle modification. The format may include group or individual outpatient therapy. The intensity of treatment may be individualized, but it is usually for one or two hours once or twice weekly for several months. During vulnerable times for relapse, the frequency of contact with treatment providers may need to be increased.

Halfway houses
In some jurisdictions, halfway houses provide supportive housing for patients who have completed a treatment program. They can live in a halfway house, typically for six months or longer, enabling them to find work and permanent accommodation. Abstinence is required.

TABLE 1: Treatment Options and Settings†

	Intervention	Indication and Requirements	Description	Usual Duration
Assessment and Referral		• patient suspected of having a substance use disorder • patient should not be intoxicated at the time of interview	• assessment can be done by MD, RN, psychologist, social worker or addictions counsellor • exploration of the pattern and consequences of substance use in the patient's life • development of a treatment plan to meet patient's need for local program or specialized treatment	• 45 minutes to two-hour interview: patient may need to be seen at more than one office visit
Detoxification (withdrawal management)	**INPATIENT** Non-medical	• young, otherwise healthy adults who want to withdraw from drugs in a supportive and supervised environment	• staffed by addictions counsellors • meals and supportive care provided • access to medical services, both emergency and non-emergency, though not always on-site • facilitation of referral to treatment programs and mutual aid groups	• three to five days

Table 1 continued

	Intervention	Indication and Requirements	Description	Usual Duration
Detoxification (withdrawal management) – cont'd	Medical	• concurrent medical or psychiatric disorder requiring medical monitoring • unsafe to try non-medical detoxification due to risks of complications	• in a general hospital in a unit experienced in the management of withdrawal, or under supervision of knowledgeable physician	• one to seven days
	OUTPATIENT Non-medical	• usually when there are access issues (e.g., rural communities or the elderly)	• usually done with trained staff visiting the patient at home	• three to five days
	Medical	• in cases of alcohol dependence, opioid dependence, and slow benzodiazepine tapers	• outpatient clinic for patients unwilling/unable to access detoxification facilities and wanting medical assistance for withdrawal	• alcohol and opioids: three to 10 hours in an office setting with frequent follow-up visits • benzodiazepines: weeks to months for tapering
Intensive Treatment	**RESIDENTIAL** Short-term	• long-standing history of substance use • unsuccessful outpatient treatment • multiple psychosocial issues	• usually multidisciplinary model, depending upon philosophy • includes group therapy, psychoeducation, lifestyle modification, coping	• 21–30 days

Table 1 continued

	Intervention	Indication and Requirements	Description	Usual Duration
Intensive Treatment - cont'd		• must be abstinent for at least a week prior to admission	skills, and linkage to mutual aid groups	
	Long-term	• long-standing history of substance dependence with associated social, employment and housing problems • unsuccessful in less intensive programs • must be abstinent for at least seven days prior to admission	• enhanced services as compared with short-term residential, but includes the provision of services to facilitate rehabilitation into the community upon discharge	• six weeks to six months
	Therapeutic Community	• for heroin and cocaine users interested in rebuilding their lives who are unable to achieve abstinence • must be drug-free prior to admission and have a medical and psychiatric examination prior to admission	• regimented living in a closed community • radical lifestyle adjustments including the interventions offered in short-term residential settings • must be willing to participate in chores and care of the treatment setting	• six to 15 months

Table 1 continued

	Intervention	Indication and Requirements	Description	Usual Duration
Intensive Treatment - cont'd	**OUTPATIENT**			
	Brief Interventions	• early problems with substance use • smoking cessation programs • must be socially stable	• time-limited, structured sessions including education, readings and assignments, goal-setting, skills training and relapse prevention techniques	• one or two sessions per week for one to three months
	Day/evening Programs	• alcohol and/or other drug dependence with moderate to severe impairment	• similar components as above including group counselling	• two to five hours per weekday for two to five weeks
	Mutual Aid Groups	• alcohol and/or other drug dependence • must have the desire to stop drug/alcohol use, respect the principles of the group • detoxification is not a prerequisite	• social group: no payment necessary • members support each other by sharing experiences, strengths and hope • structured program of recovery (e.g., AA's 12-Step program; see Table 2), where senior members act as mentors or sponsors for new members	• one- to two-hour meetings held in most cities and countries daily
	Individual	• problem drinkers • smokers who do not have poly-substance use disorders	• private and anonymous • use printed material outlining methods others have used to quit	• variable

Table 1 continued

	Intervention	Indication and Requirements	Description	Usual Duration
Continuing Care	Weekly Counselling	• completed a substance use treatment program	• relapse prevention • lifestyle modification counselling: individual or group	• months to years
	Halfway (Supportive) Houses	• completed an inpatient treatment program and requires bridging arrangements before re-integration into the community	• home like environment • empowerment to live independently • practise life-skills • counselling and case-management offered • must be drug-free and involved in other activities outside the house • payment of board and lodging if possible	• six months to one year

† Adapted from Addiction Research Foundation, 1994. *Alcohol and Drug Treatment in Ontario: A Guide for Helping Professionals.* Toronto: Addiction Research Foundation.

TABLE 2: The Twelve Steps of Alcoholics Anonymous†

1. We admitted we were powerless over alcohol — that our lives had become unmanageable.
2. Came to believe that a Power greater than ourselves could restore us to sanity.
3. Made a decision to turn our will and our lives over to the care of God *as we understood Him.*
4. Made a searching and fearless moral inventory of ourselves.
5. Admitted to God, to ourselves and to another human being the exact nature of our wrongs.
6. Were entirely ready to have God remove all these defects of character.
7. Humbly asked Him to remove our shortcomings.
8. Made a list of all persons we had harmed, and became willing to make amends to them all.
9. Made direct amends to such people wherever possible, except when to do so would injure them or others.
10. Continued to take personal inventory and when we were wrong promptly admitted it.
11. Sought through prayer and meditation to improve our conscious contact with God *as we understood Him,* praying only for knowledge of His will for us and the power to carry that out.
12. Having had a spiritual awakening as the result of these Steps, we tried to carry this message to alcoholics, and to practice these principles in all our affairs.

† Twelve Steps are reprinted with permission of Alcoholics Anonymous World Services, Inc. Permission to reprint Twelve Steps does not mean that AA has reviewed or approved the contents of this publication, or that AA agrees with the views expressed herein. AA is a program of recovery from alcoholism only — use of Twelve Steps in connection with programs and activities which are patterned after AA but which address other problems, or in any other non-AA context, does not imply otherwise.

2.4

PHARMACOTHERAPY IN TREATMENT

Meldon Kahan, MD, Peter Selby, MBBS, and Lynn Wilson, MD

Pharmacotherapy can play a critical role in recovery. Medications such as diazepam or clonidine are useful in the treatment of withdrawal. Replacement or substitution treatment (e.g., the nicotine patch and methadone) relieve withdrawal symptoms, reduce drug cravings and promote long-term abstinence. Aversive therapy (disulfiram) prevents patients from drinking alcohol impulsively. Anti-craving medications such as naltrexone reduce the intensity and frequency of alcohol binges. Medications such as buspirone and selective serotonin reuptake inhibitors (SSRIs) treat psychiatric conditions that predispose individuals to substance use. Medications are also used in the treatment of the medical complications of substance use (e.g., propylthiouracil for alcoholic cirrhosis). These and other medications are reviewed in detail in later chapters.

Pharmacotherapy is of limited effectiveness as a sole treatment and should always be accompanied by a comprehensive program consisting of supportive counselling, formal inpatient or outpatient programs, mutual aid groups and long-term medical care.

NEUROBIOLOGY OF ADDICTION

The human brain has a highly evolved neural network with several neurotransmitter systems regulating different functions. Drugs tend to have abuse liability if they are reinforcing or prevent withdrawal symptoms (Gold, 1994). Neurotransmitters implicated in addictive disorders are primarily associated with the brain's reward system. They include dopamine, serotonin, endorphins, norepinephrine, gamma-amino butyric acid (GABA), and glutamate. All drugs of abuse, including opioids, enhance the firing rate of dopaminergic neurons projecting from the ventral tegmental area (VTA) to the nucleus accumbens, what is referred to as the mesolimbic dopamine system. Drugs of abuse tend to either increase the release of dopamine (amphetamines), or inhibit the reuptake of dopamine (cocaine). Even opioids elevate dopamine levels due to the extensive interaction between the opioid and dopaminergic systems in the mesotelencephalic regions of the brain. This is thought to lead to the experience of pleasure and hence make the drug reinforcing and addictive. Figure B is a schematic overview of the brain reward pathway and putative site(s) of action for drugs of abuse. By increasing our understanding of the biological basis of addiction more effective biological interventions can be developed.

FIGURE B: Brain Reward Circuit

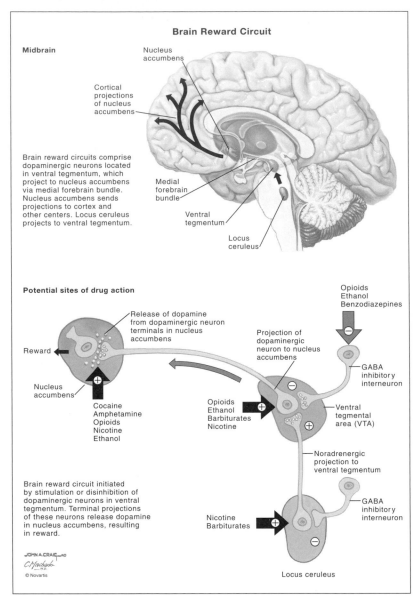

† Reproduced by permission. Copyright 1996 CIBA.

2.5

COUNSELLING PATIENTS IN A PRIMARY CARE SETTING

David C. Marsh, MD

COUNSELLING CONSIDERATIONS

Counselling and psychotherapy are integral and necessary components of primary care medicine. The interaction between patient and doctor builds the therapeutic relationship, and the nature of psychosocial interventions provided to patients can set the tone for all interactions between patients and staff. This will be particularly important to family physicians who integrate the treatment of substance use disorders into their regular practice. Non-medical staff and other patients will take their attitude towards patients from the physician. Building an atmosphere of mutual trust, honesty and co-operation can mean the difference between success and failure.

Individualized treatment
The needs of an individual with a substance use disorder will vary from person to person and within the same person over time. From the time the patient is first seen, the physician has an ongoing opportunity to assess his or her readiness for change. By matching interventions to the patient's readiness to address a problem, the clinician can be more effective in working with the patient. For those with substance dependence, which can be seen as a chronic relapsing illness, other issues may arise after substance use is no longer the primary focus. In some cases patients may be estranged from their families and friends because all of their social networks revolve around acquiring and using alcohol or other drugs.

Developing a strong therapeutic relationship requires a little time, but is well worth the effort. Such a relationship allows the primary care physician to deepen his or her understanding of the patient and to identify areas they can work on together or that require referral to other health care or social service resources. It creates the conditions necessary to support the client towards therapeutic change.

Concurrent disorders

In some groups of substance users, psychopathology is more common than among the general population (Rounsaville, Glazer et al., 1983), though the presence or nature of psychopathology may not become apparent until the chronic cycle of intoxication and withdrawal is interrupted. Whatever psychosocial difficulties arise for the patient as she or he moves from chronic substance use, the physician must be attuned to the patient's needs. (See also Section 16.)

THERAPEUTIC ALLIANCE

Clinicians and researchers have described factors common to all psychotherapies that are strong determinants of success (Frank, 1961; Strupp, 1986). The patient should view the physician as open, honest, empathic and reliable. The intent is to build an air of mutual respect in which the patient co-operates with the caregiving team. Useful strategies include:

- Trying to build self-reliance in patients as they take responsibility for their present actions and the consequences of their past actions.
- Creating a non-judgmental, understanding environment where patients feel safe discussing and expressing their innermost emotions. This will mean they will be less likely to act out their feelings in drug use or disruptive, violent behavior.
- Approaching patients with hope and optimism even as they work through their problems, often making the same mistakes over and over before incorporating new learning into their behavior.

Starting points — physician's attributes

Integral to the building of a strong therapeutic alliance is the physician's awareness of her or his own beliefs, attitudes, prejudices and emotions. Such awareness is important because substance-dependent individuals are sensitive to dismissive, judgmental or condescending attitudes. Usually they will have been repeatedly treated as "drunks" and "losers" by family, friends, teachers, health care professionals, the police and even individuals working within addictions treatment services. They may have come to accept or internalize these critical messages, with a resulting chronic erosion of self-esteem. By approaching each patient as a unique person with positive and negative attributes, the physician can help him or her recognize and build on his or her strengths. Over time, patients will develop a healthy awareness of the ambivalence inherent in all relationships including the relationship to one's self. This approach is an essential starting point to building a strong therapeutic alliance.

All members of the caregiving team should display attitudes of openness, honesty and respect towards patients. At the same time it is essential to maintain clear, consistent boundaries with patients. They should know exactly what can and cannot be expected from the physician and the caregiving team. Patients will be very sensitive to being treated differently by different team members or to rules applied differently to other patients. The physician must communicate openly and frequently with the team of caregivers to encourage consistency of treatment for the patients. When conflicts arise, the physician should focus the patient on what is in that patient's best interest. Such boundary issues are particularly important when treating patients with borderline or antisocial personality disorders, though they apply to all patients.

PROCESS OF CHANGE

Prochaska and DiClemente (1982) outline a model of personal change that attempts to describe how individuals alter behavior of all types. They view change as a process of six stages through which individuals may cycle several times before maintaining a permanent change in behavior. The stages are:

- precontemplation
- contemplation
- preparation
- action
- maintenance
- relapse.

Motivational interviewing and stages of change

Miller and Rollnick (1991) have used this model of change to develop techniques of motivational interviewing. The physician attempts to identify the stage a patient is at and then apply interventions that are specifically designed to help the patient move to the next stage. Interventions that do not fit the individual's readiness to change are likely to raise defensiveness, frustrate the physician and lead to the patient resisting change.

Precontemplation means the patient does not consider the substance use to be a problem. At this stage the physician should reflect back to the patient the results of a complete biopsychosocial assessment, emphasizing the consequences of substance use in a non-judgmental way. The physician can then listen empathically as the patient assimilates this knowledge.

As the patient considers the meaning of the assessment results he or she may move from *precontemplation* to *contemplation.* At this point the patient and physician can work together to construct a comparison of the advantages and disadvantages of continued substance use and of stopping substance use. By listening attentively and asking open-ended questions, the physician can discover what may motivate the patient to change and what beliefs support the present behavior. By challenging false beliefs and emphasizing the benefits of stopping substance use, the patient can be helped towards a decision.

Only in the *preparation* and *action* phases is it worthwhile for the physician to work with the patient to formulate a plan for change. However, the physician should keep a careful record of the motivating factors identified. The physician can return to this record to support the change (maintenance) or to facilitate another attempt at change following *relapse*. (See Table 3 for recommended strategies and sample questions for the patient in the precontemplation, contemplation, preparation and action stages.)

The stages-of-change approach emphasizes the collaborative nature of the clinical endeavor. By accepting that relapse will frequently occur the clinician is able to maintain hopefulness and empathy, two important elements of the therapeutic alliance. The collaborative nature of the motivational model helps build the patient's sense of self-efficacy or confidence in his or her ability to change. Ultimately this empowers patients to maintain the change without reliance on the physician.

TABLE 3: Strategies for Patients at the Precontemplation, Contemplation, Preparation and Action Stages†

	Precontemplation	Contemplation	Preparation and Action
DESCRIPTION OF STAGE	• doesn't see substance use as a problem	• ambivalent: substance use causes problems but has benefits • weighing pros and cons of changing vs. staying the same	• committed to doing something about substance use
PHYSICIAN STRATEGY	• discuss the role substance use plays in patient's life • provide information based on bio-psychosocial assessment	• explore patient's reasons for concern about patient's using and patient's arguments for change	• give treatment options

Table 3 continued

	Precontemplation	Contemplation	Preparation and Action
SAMPLE QUESTIONS	• "Tell me about a typical day. Where does your use of substances fit in?" • "How does your substance use affect your health?" • "Would you be interested in knowing more about the effects of substance use on...?"	• "What are some of the good things about your use of... ?" • "What are some of the not-so-good things about your use of...?" • "How does your substance use affect you at the moment?" • "How would you like things to be different in the future?" • "What concerns do you have about your substance use?" • "What concerns do you have about changing your substance use?"	• "Where does this leave you now?" • Emphasize "You are the best judge of what will be best for you."

† Adapted from Miller & Rollnick, 1991.

THERAPEUTIC ROLES OF PRIMARY CARE PHYSICIANS

The primary care physician is ideally positioned to recognize and begin treatment for most substance use disorders and to offer supportive counselling. Frequent contact with affected individuals and their families over the course of many years allows the physician to establish a strong, trusting relationship that can overcome patients' sense of guilt, denial and self-criticism at times of relapse.

Some family physicians may also choose to obtain further training and devote time to more intensive psychotherapeutic techniques. Behavioral, cognitive, psychodynamic, group and family therapy approaches have all been shown to be beneficial for substance use disorders when applied appropriately. It is essential, however, for physicians to recognize the limits of their training and experience, to be familiar with other resources available in their community and to refer appropriately. In many communities the most widely available form of therapy for substance dependence is social support or mutual aid groups.

Fostering social support

Problematic substance use, especially illicit drug use, is a behavior that tends to isolate users, making them secretive and marginalized. It introduces them to a set of social contacts that can reinforce continued drug use, often depriving them of contact with others who might encourage them away from harmful behaviors.

The physician can work to identify and promote social support for substance users at a number of levels. The most obvious is the family. The patient may also have peers who are concerned and willing to play a supportive role. The key consideration is to identify someone the patient sees as a positive force in their lives. For many individuals Alcoholics Anonymous or other mutual aid groups fulfil this role. The support provided by meeting and sharing with others with substance use concerns in an environment of mutual aid and self-help can have immediate and ongoing impact for the recovering substance user. The support groups that are available for families and friends of people who are substance-dependent are often highly valued by those who make use of these resources. Again, the physician can play a facilitative role by encouraging and supporting patients, and those close to them, to access these services, either as an adjunct to the formal treatment or as the primary therapeutic intervention.

Counselling goals

There are very practical steps that the primary care physician can take in counselling patients with substance use disorders. Within the basic framework of a working therapeutic relationship, it is important for the physician to:

- orient patients to treatment expectations
- explore and understand patients' needs and goals
- develop a clear treatment contract
- assess progress on a continuing basis to identify positive and negative change and to provide supportive counselling
- identify issues that require referral
- provide support to family members.

The physician's counselling relationship needs to be seen within the broader context of community services and supports. These can include the patient's partner, family and peers, and can extend to mutual support groups and beyond to formal social services and health care resources. Particularly where there are complex problems, the primary care physician will need to draw on the support of these formal and informal resources and to recognize the limits of what he or she can provide personally. However, in situations where the physician has developed an empathic and effective working relationship with the patient, it is just as likely that the patient will extend trust to the doctor and turn to him or her for counsel, advice, support and healing.

R E F E R E N C E S

Addiction Research Foundation (1994). *Alcohol and Drug Treatment in Ontario: A Guide for Helping Professionals.* Toronto: Addiction Research Foundation.

Daley, D.C. & Marlatt, G.A. (1997). Relapse prevention. In J.H. Lowinson, P. Ruiz & J.G. Langrod (Eds.), *Substance Abuse: A Comprehensive Textbook.* (3rd. ed.). Baltimore: Williams and Wilkins.

Fleming, M.F. & Barry, K.L. (Eds.). (1992). *Addictive Disorders.* St Louis, MO: Mosby Year Book.

Frank, J.D. (1961). *Persuasion and Healing: A Comparative Study of Psychotherapy.* Baltimore: Johns Hopkins Press.

Gold, M.S. (1994). Clinical implications of the neurobiology of addiction. In N.S. Miller (Ed.), *Principles of Addiction Medicine.* Chevy Chase, MD: American Society of Addiction Medicine.

Hoffman, N.G. (1994). Assessing treatment effectiveness. In N.S. Miller (Ed.), *Principles of Addiction Medicine.* Chevy Chase, MD: American Society of Addiction Medicine.

Miller, W.R. & Rollnick, S. (1991). *Motivational Interviewing: Preparing People to Change Addictive Behavior.* New York: Guilford Press.

Prochaska, J.O. & DiClemente, C.C. (1982). Transtheoretical therapy: Toward a more integrative model of change. *Psychotherapy: Theory, Research, and Practice, 19(3),* 276-288.

Rounsaville, B.J., Glazer, W., Wilber, C.H., Weissman, M.M. & Kleber, H.D. (1983). Short-term interpersonal psychotherapy in methadone-maintained opiate addicts. *Archives of General Psychiatry, 40,* 629-636.

Strupp, H.H. (1986). The nonspecific hypothesis of therapeutic effectiveness: A current assessment. *American Journal of Orthopsychiatry, 56(4),* 513-520.

Alcohol

3.1 METABOLISM AND ACUTE EFFECTS

3.2 ALCOHOL WITHDRAWAL

3.3 ALCOHOLIC LIVER DISEASE

3.4 OTHER MEDICAL COMPLICATIONS OF ALCOHOL USE

3.5 GUIDELINES ON LOW-RISK DRINKING

3.6 IDENTIFYING PROBLEM DRINKERS

3.7 BRIEF ADVICE PROTOCOL FOR PROBLEM DRINKERS

3.8 PHARMACOTHERAPY FOR ALCOHOL DEPENDENCE

REFERENCES

TABLES AND FIGURES

3.1

METABOLISM AND ACUTE EFFECTS*

Meldon Kahan, MD

Alcohol is second only to tobacco in its contribution to morbidity, mortality and health care costs. The adverse health and social consequences of alcohol abuse outweigh those of all other drugs of abuse combined. It is estimated that in Canada in 1992, the total cost of alcohol use (including direct health care costs, lost productivity and legal costs) was $7.5 billion (Single, Robson et al., 1996). Approximately one in 10 drinkers has had at least one alcohol-related problem in the past year — including problems in social life, health, happiness, home life, work and/or finances (Canadian Centre on Substance Abuse and Addiction Research Foundation, 1997).

Physicians can play a critical role in reducing alcohol-related morbidity and mortality. In order to effectively manage alcohol problems, physicians need to be familiar with the pharmacology of alcohol, the treatment of withdrawal and other medical complications, and the treatment of problem drinking and alcohol dependence.

DOSAGE

Dosage levels of alcohol are typically described in terms of a given number of standard drinks, each containing 13.6 grams of pure alcohol.

* Adapted from Brands, Sproule & Marshman, 1998, and Devenyi & Saunders, 1986.

TABLE 1: Definition of a Standard Drink

Type of drink	oz.	mL	g alcohol	% absolute alcohol
ABSOLUTE ALCOHOL	0.6	17	13.6	100
SPIRITS	1.5	43	13.6	40
WINE	5	142	13.6	12
FORTIFIED WINE (SHERRY)	3	85	13.6	18
BEER	12	341	13.6	5

METABOLISM

Alcohol is rapidly absorbed and widely distributed to body organs. While a small amount is excreted unchanged in the urine and breath, most of it is metabolized by alcohol dehydrogenase (a cytosolic enzyme) to water and carbon dioxide in the liver. Heavy consumption causes induction of the microsomal enzyme system.

FIGURE A: Metabolism of Alcohol

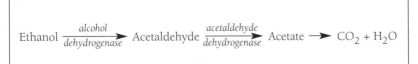

$$\text{Ethanol} \xrightarrow[\text{dehydrogenase}]{\text{alcohol}} \text{Acetaldehyde} \xrightarrow[\text{dehydrogenase}]{\text{acetaldehyde}} \text{Acetate} \longrightarrow CO_2 + H_2O$$

Alcohol is metabolized at a constant rate of approximately 10 grams of alcohol per hour (somewhat less than a standard drink). Heavy drinkers may have almost double this rate of metabolism. Depending on body size and tolerance, many men will attain blood alcohol concentrations (BAC) of 30, 50 and 80 mg% (mg/100 mL) after consuming 1.5, 2.5 and four drinks in an hour respectively.* Because women have a smaller volume of distribution, they will attain similar BACs with two-thirds of that consumption (Lowenstein and Hunt, 1990).

*100 mL = 1 dL = 0.1 litres. Therefore, a blood alcohol concentration of 80 mg/100 mL may also be expressed as 0.08 g/dL or 0.08 per cent. Driving in Canada with a blood alcohol concentration in excess of 80 mg% is an offence under the Criminal Code.

The table below can be used to estimate blood alcohol concentrations for a given rate of alcohol consumption. Weights are based on ideal body weight; 15 mg% is subtracted per hour from the time of the first drink (this assumes a constant rate of consumption over the drinking episode). For example, a 68-kg woman who consumes three drinks in one hour will have a BAC of 86 mg%.

TABLE 2: BAC (mg%) for Different Rates of Alcohol Consumption†

FEMALES

Body Weight Number of drinks

Kg	Lbs.	1	2	3	4	5	6	7	8	9	10
45	100	50	101	152	203	253	304	355	406	456	507
57	125	40	80	120	162	202	244	282	324	364	404
68	150	34	68	101	135	169	203	237	271	304	338
79	175	29	58	87	117	146	175	204	233	262	292
91	200	26	50	76	101	126	152	177	203	227	253
102	225	22	45	68	91	113	136	159	182	204	227
114	250	20	41	61	82	101	122	142	162	182	202

MALES

Body Weight Number of drinks

Kg	Lbs.	1	2	3	4	5	6	7	8	9	10
45	100	43	87	130	174	217	261	304	348	391	435
57	125	34	69	103	139	173	209	242	278	312	346
68	150	29	58	87	116	145	174	203	232	261	290
79	175	25	50	75	100	125	150	175	200	225	250
91	200	22	43	65	87	108	130	152	174	195	217
102	225	19	39	58	78	97	117	136	156	175	195
114	250	17	35	52	70	87	105	122	139	156	173

Hours since first drink	1	2	3	4	5
Subtract from BAC	15	30	45	60	75

Note: 80 mg% is the equivalent of 17 mmol/L.

† Reprinted with permission from *Smashed*. Copyright 1987, Transport Canada.

Clinical interpretation of blood alcohol concentration

In most "naive," that is, non-tolerant individuals, a BAC of approximately 160 mg% (34 mmol/L) will be associated with clinically obvious alcohol intoxication, with its well-known signs and symptoms. In alcohol-dependent persons, considerable metabolic and CNS tolerance to the behavioral effects of alcohol may develop. It is not unusual to see some patients appear to be relatively unimpaired with a BAC of 280–320 mg% (60 or 70 mmol/L). Coma develops in most individuals at a BAC between 400–560 mg% (90 and 120 mmol/L).

Alcohol intoxication

Low doses of alcohol depress the inhibitory and behavioral control centres of the brain, causing relaxation and decreased social inhibition. Higher doses produce emotional lability and impaired cognition and motor function. Intoxication can also result in aspiration, pneumonia and cardiac arrhythmias.

Drug interactions

Acute intoxication inhibits the metabolism of long-acting benzodiazepines, phenothiazines, tricyclic antidepressants and barbiturates. Long-term alcohol use increases the rate of metabolism of warfarin, diazepam and propanolol. Cimetidine and ranitidine inhibit gastric alcohol dehydrogenase, elevating blood alcohol concentrations. Patients who drink alcohol while on metronidazole, sulfonylureas or certain cephalosporins will experience disulfiram-like reactions.

ADVERSE EFFECTS OF INTOXICATION

Blackouts

People who cannot remember some or all of the events that occurred during a bout of heavy drinking are said to have experienced a blackout. They are conscious during a blackout but sometimes act in an uncharacteristic or even a dangerous manner. Patients being assessed for an alcohol problem should be asked about blackouts, which are often an early warning sign of a worsening alcohol problem.

Psychiatric effects

Alcohol intoxication can cause depression, impaired judgment, impulsivity and disinhibition, putting patients at risk for suicide.

Trauma

Alcohol is a major cause of traumatic injury and death, including motor vehicle and other accidents, pedestrian fatalities and violence.

Tolerance

Tolerance is a function of the dose and duration of alcohol consumed and genetic factors. It can develop within a few days of heavy drinking and it decreases with abstinence. Heavy drinkers are often relatively tolerant to the effects of benzo-diazepines and barbiturates even if they have not taken these drugs previously, a phenomenon known as cross-tolerance.

3.2

ALCOHOL WITHDRAWAL*

Meldon Kahan, MD, and Lynn Wilson, MD

Treatment of alcohol withdrawal is a crucial first step in the recovery process. Untreated withdrawal makes it difficult for patients to reduce their drinking because they need to maintain a constant blood alcohol concentration (BAC) in order to avoid withdrawal symptoms. Treatment of withdrawal symptoms, however, rarely leads to prolonged abstinence in the absence of other interventions.

ASSESSMENT

Alcohol withdrawal is common among patients consuming more than 40 drinks per week. An inquiry should be made about previous withdrawal episodes and current drinking patterns because these are the best predictors of future withdrawal. Patients who have had withdrawal seizures or delirium tremens are at high risk for recurrence if their drinking pattern remains unchanged. Repeated episodes of withdrawal over time may predispose the patient to more severe withdrawal, a phenomenon known as "kindling."

Because diazepam loading is insufficient for treating patients also dependent on benzodiazepines or barbiturates, a careful drug history is required.

Patients should be examined for hypertension, fever, tachycardia, tremor or sweating, and dehydration. The heart, lungs and abdomen should be examined, looking in particular for signs of dysrhythmias and signs of alcoholic liver disease. A mental status exam should be conducted to assess level of consciousness, orientation, perceptual disturbances (hallucinations or illusions), mood and thought processes including suicidal ideation and cognitive deficits.

*Adapted from Devenyi & Saunders, 1986.

Patients who are in severe withdrawal, are febrile or appear ill require a more detailed assessment. The assessment should examine for infection, trauma, pancreatitis, dehydration, subdural hematoma, electrolyte abnormalities and hypoglycemia.

The Clinical Institute Withdrawal Assessment for Alcohol (CIWA-A) is a scoring system that nurses and physicians can use to assess the severity of withdrawal and monitor response to treatment.

TABLE 3: Clinical Institute Withdrawal Assessment for Alcohol

---

Date (mm/dd/yy): _____ Time: _____

Pulse or heart rate taken for 1 minute: _____ Blood Pressure: _____

NAUSEA AND VOMITING – Ask "Do you feel sick to your stomach? Have you vomited?" Observation.

    0 no nausea and no vomiting
    1
    2
    3
    4 intermittent nausea with dry heaves
    5
    6
    7 constant nausea, frequent dry heaves and vomiting

TACTILE DISTURBANCES – Ask "Have you any itching, pins and needles sensations, any burning, any numbness or do you feel bugs crawling on or under your skin?" Observation.

    0 none
    1 very mild itching, pins and needles, burning or numbness
    2 mild itching, pins and needles, burning or numbness
    3 moderate itching, pins and needles, burning or numbness
    4 moderately severe hallucinations
    5 severe hallucinations
    6 extremely severe hallucinations
    7 continuous hallucinations

Table 3 continued

TREMOR – Arms extended and fingers spread apart. Observation.

0 no tremor

1 not visible, but can be felt fingertip to fingertip

2

3

4 moderate, with patient's arms extended

5

6

7 severe, even with arms not extended

AUDITORY DISTURBANCES – Ask "Are you more aware of sounds around you? Are they harsh? Do they frighten you? Are you hearing anything that is disturbing you? Are you hearing things you know are not there?"
Observation.

0 not present

1 very mild harshness or ability to frighten

2 mild harshness or ability to frighten

3 moderate harshness or ability to frighten

4 moderately severe hallucinations

5 severe hallucinations

6 extremely severe hallucinations

7 continuous hallucinations

PAROXYSMAL SWEATS – Observation.

0 no sweat visible

1 barely perceptible sweating, palms moist

2

3

4 beads of sweat obvious on forehead

5

6

7 drenching sweats

VISUAL DISTURBANCES – Ask "Does the light appear to be too bright? Is its color different? Does it hurt your eyes? Are you seeing anything that is disturbing to you? Are you seeing things you know are not there?" Observation.

0 not present

1 very mild sensitivity

2 mild sensitivity

3 moderate sensitivity

4 moderately severe hallucinations

Table 3 continued

> 5 severe hallucinations
> 6 extremely severe hallucinations
> 7 continuous hallucinations

ANXIETY – Ask "Do you feel nervous?" Observation.

> 0 no anxiety, at ease
> 1 mildly anxious
> 2
> 3
> 4 moderately anxious, or guarded, so anxiety is inferred
> 5
> 6
> 7 acute panic as seen in severe delirium or acute schizophrenic reactions

---

HEADACHE, FULLNESS IN HEAD – Ask "Does your head feel different? Does it feel like there is a band around your head?" Do not rate for dizziness or light-headedness. Otherwise, rate severity.

> 0 not present
> 1 very mild
> 2 mild
> 3 moderate
> 4 moderately severe
> 5 severe
> 6 very severe
> 7 extremely severe

AGITATION – Observation.

> 0 normal activity
> 1 somewhat more than normal activity
> 2
> 3
> 4 moderately fidgety and restless
> 5
> 6
> 7 paces back and forth during most of the interview, or constantly thrashes about

---

ORIENTATION AND CLOUDING OF SENSORIUM – Ask "What day is this? Where are you? Who am I?"

> 0 oriented and can do serial additions
> 1 cannot do serial additions or is uncertain about date

Table 3 continued

2	disoriented for date by no more than 2 calendar days
3	disoriented for date by more than 2 calendar days
4	disoriented for place and/or person

Total Score: ❏ ❏ (maximum possible score = 67)

Signature: _____

CIWA-Ar Severity[†]	Score
Mild	< 10
Moderate	10–20
Severe	> 20

† CIWA scoring should not be confused with the classification of alcohol withdrawal (minor, intermediate and major).

ALCOHOL WITHDRAWAL: CLINICAL FEATURES

Withdrawal occurs in three phases:
• minor (autonomic hyperactivity)
• intermediate (autonomic hyperactivity with seizures, dysrhythmias or hallucinations)
• major (delirium tremens).

The majority of alcohol-dependent patients experience only minor withdrawal, although up to 15 per cent of alcohol-dependent patients will experience a withdrawal seizure in their lifetime.

Minor withdrawal
Patients in minor withdrawal are anxious and may have nausea and vomiting, coarse tremor, sweating, tachycardia and hypertension. The symptoms tend to appear within six to 12 hours after the last drink, or shortly after the BAC has become zero, although some patients exhibit withdrawal as the BAC declines below 90 mg% (20 mmol/L). Symptoms usually resolve within 48 to 72 hours.

Intermediate withdrawal
Patients in intermediate withdrawal experience the symptoms of minor withdrawal in addition to seizures, dysrhythmias and/or hallucinosis. Withdrawal *seizures* usually occur between 12 and 72 hours after cessation of drinking. They

are typically grand mal and non-focal. Dysrhythmias range in severity from occasional ectopic beats to atrial fibrillation and supraventricular or ventricular tachycardia. Patients with hallucinosis have auditory or visual hallucinations but they are aware of their unreal nature and remain oriented and alert.

Major withdrawal (*delirium tremens*)

Delirium tremens (DTs) is characterized by severe agitation, gross tremulousness, marked psychomotor and autonomic hyperactivity, global confusion, disorientation and auditory, visual or tactile hallucinations. DTs tend to occur five or six days after severe, untreated withdrawal. Typically, they occur in socially isolated alcoholics, in hospitalized alcoholics whose withdrawal has gone unnoticed for several days and in alcoholics with a serious illness such as pancreatitis or pneumonia. Symptoms fluctuate and are frequently worse at night. Profound autonomic hyperactivity can occur in *delerium tremens* with severe diaphoresis and vomiting, tachycardia, hypertension and fever. Sudden death can occur, presumably due to dysrhythmias caused by the sympathetic overdrive and by hypokalemia (catecholamine excess drives potassium into the cells). With prompt recognition and treatment, the mortality rate from DTs is probably less than 5 per cent (Yost, 1996).

DIAZEPAM LOADING

Many patients with minimal withdrawal do not require medication. For patients with objective signs of withdrawal, a diazepam loading protocol is recommended (see Table 4). A score of 10 or more on the CIWA scale indicates the need for diazepam.

The recommended dose is 20 mg orally q1–2h, until symptoms abate. The loading is complete when the CIWA score is less than 10 on two consecutive measurements. Some patients respond to just one or two doses. In rare cases several hundred milligrams are required. Diazepam's long half-life (40 hours) allows gradual pharmacokinetic self-tapering without the need for additional doses (although two or three 10 mg take-home doses taken q2–4h prn may be prescribed at the physician's discretion in outpatient settings).

The loading protocol has several advantages over take-home prescriptions for benzodiazepines. Patients are treated effectively and quickly, thus avoiding prolonged discomfort and hospitalization. It is safer because patients sometimes use take-home prescriptions while they are intoxicated and prolonged use of benzodiazepines can create a secondary addiction.

TABLE 4: Diazepam Loading Protocol for Alcohol Withdrawal[†],[††]

BASIC PROTOCOL	• diazepam 20 mg po q1–2h until symptoms abate *(some inpatients require several hundred mg)* • observe for 2–4 hours after last dose • take-home medication is generally not required (if take-home diazepam is necessary, give no more than 2–3 10 mg tablets) • thiamine 100 mg i.m., then 100 mg po x 3 days • do not give glucose before thiamine; may precipitate Wernicke's encephalopathy
IF HISTORY OF WITHDRAWAL SEIZURES	• diazepam 20 mg q1h for a *minimum* of 3 doses
IF INTOLERANT OF ORAL DIAZEPAM	• diazepam 2–5 mg i.v./minimum — maximum 10–20 mg q1h, or lorazepam sl
IF SEVERE LIVER DISEASE, SEVERE ASTHMA, RESPIRATORY FAILURE, ELDERLY, DEBILITATED OR LOW SERUM ALBUMIN	• lorazepam sl, po 1–2 mg q2–4h prn[†††]
IF HALLUCINOSIS	• haloperidol[††††] 2–5 mg i.m./po q1–4h — max. 5/day
ADMIT TO HOSPITAL IF	• still in withdrawal after 80 mg or more of diazepam • delirium tremens, recurrent dysrhythmias or multiple seizures • significant medical illness

[†] Adapted from A. Kalvik, P. Isaac & E. Janecek. (1995). Benzodiazepines: Treatment of anxiety, insomnia and alcohol withdrawal. *Pharmacy Connection.* September/October, 20–34.

[††] Loading protocol will not prevent seizures in patients taking large doses of benzodiazepines or barbiturates in addition to alcohol.

[†††] Note that lorazepam is a short-acting benzodiazepine. If used, the clinician is no longer employing a benzodiazepine loading protocol.

[††††] Haloperidol lowers seizure threshold. Use with caution in first 3 days — give 3 doses of diazepam 20 mg as seizure prophylaxis.

Precautions for diazepam loading

• In patients who are unable to take oral medications, diazepam may be given intravenously at a rate of 5 mg/min to a total of no more than 10–20 mg per hour. Diazepam is not well absorbed after intramuscular injection and this route should be avoided.

• Patients must be assessed prior to each dose to avoid oversedation with its risks of respiratory depression and aspiration.

• It is sometimes recommended that patients who have been given more than 200 mg of diazepam be switched to short-acting benzodiazepines to reduce the risk of oversedation as the withdrawal symptoms resolve (Fleming & Barry, 1992).

- The loading protocol will not prevent seizures in heavy drinkers who are also taking high doses of benzodiazepines or barbiturates on a daily basis (see Section 10).

- Patients with coexistent severe asthma or respiratory failure can experience respiratory depression with diazepam loading.

- In patients with compromised liver function due to cirrhosis or severe hepatitis, metabolism of diazepam may be slowed, leading to oversedation. Compromised liver function can be assumed in patients with portal hypertension, low serum albumin or prolonged prothrombin time. Diazepam may also exacerbate hepatic encephalopathy.

- Large doses of benzodiazepines given to a pregnant woman during labor may cause "floppy baby syndrome".

- Diazepam should be used with caution in cases involving elderly patients, debilitated patients and those with a low serum albumin. The half-life of diazepam can be prolonged in these patients, leading to oversedation.

Alternatives to diazepam loading

Lorazepam is a safe and effective alternative to diazepam for a pregnant woman in labor, a patient in respiratory or liver failure, elderly patients, debilitated patients and those with low serum albumin. Lorazepam has a shorter half-life and is not metabolized to an active metabolite in the liver so oversedation is less likely.

In an inpatient setting, lorazepam 1–2 mg may be administered po, sl or i.m. every two to four hours for a CIWA score of 10 or greater. Because of its shorter half-life, it cannot be used in a loading protocol and may need to be administered over several days.

TREATMENT SETTING

Office

A planned withdrawal may be undertaken in which patients are advised to stop drinking in the evening and return to the office the next morning. Patients are then monitored with the CIWA scale, loaded with diazepam as per protocol and observed for two to four hours after the last dose. If symptoms persist after three or four doses referral to the emergency department or hospital is indicated. In addition to diazepam, patients should be given thiamine, 100 mg i.m.

Withdrawal management or detoxification centre

Patients who no longer require diazepam may be sent home if a friend or relative can stay with them. If not, patients may be sent to a detoxification centre, which can provide observation, counselling and treatment planning. Non-medical detoxification centres are often not allowed to dispense benzo-diazepines. Patients should be re-examined the next day.

Hospital

Indications for hospital admission include:

- major withdrawal (i.e., DTs)
- intermediate withdrawal with persisting serious complications despite diazepam treatment (recurrent seizures or *status epilepticus,* hallucinations, dysrhythmias)
- minor withdrawal that is severe and persistent despite 60–80 mg of diazepam (severe tremor, agitation, tachycardia > 110/min)
- associated medical illness requiring treatment
- fever > 38°C
- Wernicke's encephalopathy
- physical dependence on other drugs such as benzodiazepines or barbiturates.

Hospital care should include monitoring vital signs, including cardiac monitoring if necessary, parenteral thiamine, and correction of low potassium, magnesium, phosphorus and glucose. Rehydration may be necessary. Patients should be given supportive nursing care in a dimly lit, quiet, single room, if possible.

TREATMENT OF INTERMEDIATE AND MAJOR WITHDRAWAL

Withdrawal seizures

Patients with a past or current history of withdrawal seizures should be given diazepam 20 mg q1–2h for *at least three doses,* even if their withdrawal symptoms have resolved after the first one or two doses. This should begin as early as possible in withdrawal, or when the blood alcohol concentration falls below 90 mg% (approximately 20 mmol/L). The BAC can decline as rapidly as 32 mg% (7 mmol/L) per hour in alcohol-dependent patients (18.5–21 mg% [4–4.5 mmol/L] in non-tolerant patients). Thus, patients with a BAC of 240 mg% (50 mmol/L) could begin to go into withdrawal in four to five hours and diazepam loading may be initiated at that time.

Further drug administration beyond the 60 mg for seizure prophylaxis depends on the continuing presence of withdrawal symptoms. Anticonvulsant drugs are not necessary unless patients also have idiopathic epilepsy or a structural focus.

Patients who have more than two seizures during one admission should be given a phenytoin load of 10 mg/kg, half of which can be given orally, the other half intravenously followed by 300 mg phenytoin po per day for five days. Phenytoin does not need to be continued if the seizure work-up is negative.

FIGURE B: Mild, Moderate to Severe Withdrawal

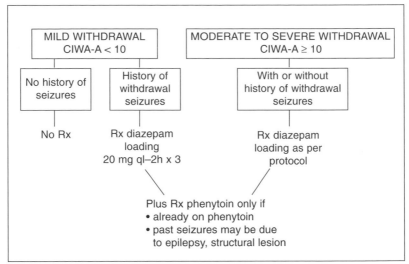

† Adapted from Devenyi & Saunders, 1986.

Status epilepticus

For *status epilepticus* give diazepam 10 mg i.v. slowly (5 mg/min), watching for respiratory depression, and also load with phenytoin. Refractory *status epilepticus* may need airway protection through general endotracheal anesthesia. Paralysis may be required to facilitate ventilation and reduce O_2 consumption. Such patients should be transferred to an intensive care unit.

Investigation of seizures

A seizure work-up is very unlikely to reveal any pathology in patients under 40 years of age who have had a typical alcohol withdrawal seizure with a normal neurological exam. Investigation (brain imaging and EEG) is recommended for:

- a first-time seizure in patients aged 40 or over
- seizures with focal features
- seizures that occur outside the usual time frame of 12 hours to four days after the last drink
- multiple seizures (more than two) or *status epilepticus*
- abnormal neurological exam.

Dysrhythmias

Most dysrhythmias subside spontaneously with resolution of the withdrawal symptoms. Paroxysmal atrial fibrillation may be treated with rapid digitalization; supraventricular tachycardia responds to verapamil. Ventricular ectopy should be treated with lidocaine if it is frequent (> 5/min), multifocal, in pairs or triplets, or is showing the "R on T" phenomenon. Since such patients are prone to sudden death, they should be monitored intensively.

Hallucinations

Hallucinations occurring in intermediate and major withdrawal may be treated with haloperidol 2–5 mg i.m. or po q2–4h (maximum five doses per day). Since haloperidol lowers the seizure threshold, diazepam 20 mg q1–2h for three doses is recommended as seizure prophylaxis. Haloperidol should be used with extra caution in the first three days of withdrawal when the seizure risk is highest.

Delirium tremens

Patients experiencing *delirium tremens* require hospital or ICU admission, monitoring of hydration status and serum electrolytes, and prompt fluid and electrolyte replacement if necessary. Cardiac monitoring may be indicated. Diazepam should be administered for autonomic hyperactivity; hundreds of milligrams may be necessary. If patients won't take diazepam orally, i.v. diazepam may be given. Haloperidol should be used for hallucinations and agitation. Intensive nursing care may be necessary; restraints should be avoided.

OTHER CLINICAL ISSUES IN MANAGING ALCOHOL WITHDRAWAL

Rehydration

Some patients need rehydration with normal saline or oral fluids. Intravenous glucose solutions are contraindicated prior to the administration of thiamine, as they can precipitate Wernicke's encephalopathy.

Thiamine

All patients should receive thiamine 100 mg i.m. Wernicke's triad of ataxia, encephalopathy and ophthalmoplegia can be difficult to diagnose in patients in withdrawal, and subtle cases can easily be missed. Usual practice calls for at least three doses of thiamine over three days. Thiamine can be safely discontinued once patients are consuming a normal diet.

Magnesium

Serum magnesium and phosphorus may be low, and should be replaced with oral solutions. Low magnesium is associated with a more severe course of withdrawal and higher mortality, although there is no clear evidence that replacement improves outcome.

3.3

ALCOHOLIC LIVER DISEASE

Florence Wong, MD, and Laurence Blendis, MD

L iver disease is the fourth most common cause of death in adults between the ages of 20 and 70 years in the United States and Canada. In most western countries, alcohol is the most common cause of chronic liver disease.

RISK FACTORS

Of chronic alcoholics, 10 to 20 per cent develop cirrhosis (Grant, Dufour & Hartford, 1988). Daily drinking carries a greater risk for developing cirrhosis than intermittent or binge drinking (i.e., drinking a large amount of alcohol in short period of time) — the type of beverage is not relevant. Men drinking more than 80 g (six standard drinks) and women drinking more than 40 g (three standard drinks) of ethanol daily over 10 years have a significant risk of developing cirrhosis (Bellentani, Saccoccio et al., 1997).

Women develop alcoholic hepatitis and cirrhosis at a younger age and after less alcohol intake. They tend to run a more severe course, with more complications, and are more likely to progress from alcoholic hepatitis to cirrhosis. Women also have a 50 per cent reduction in the activity of gastric alcohol dehydrogenase (ADH) compared with men, resulting in a diminished first passage effect and higher concentrations of alcohol in the liver (Corrao, Arico et al., 1997). All gender differences disappear after menopause.

Genetic pleomorphism of the enzymes involved in alcohol metabolism may explain the susceptibility of some individuals to liver damage (Day, Bashir et al., 1991). Nutritional deficiencies may also play a role. Animal studies have shown that rats chronically fed alcohol will not develop liver damage unless accompanied by a diet deficient in certain nutrients. However, there is a threshold of

87

alcohol consumption above which no protection will be offered by dietary supplements (Mezey, 1991).

Serological markers of hepatitis B and C infections occur in up to 30 per cent of alcoholic patients. Patients who abuse alcohol frequently also have risk factors for developing viral hepatitis. There may be an interaction between alcohol and hepatotropic viruses in producing liver injury.

SPECTRUM OF DISEASE

Fatty liver
Ethanol ingestion leads to increased triglyceride synthesis, decreased lipid oxidation and impaired secretion by the liver. This results in the accumulation of triglycerides in the hepatocytes within three to seven days of alcohol ingestion.

Patients with fatty liver are usually asymptomatic and are diagnosed incidentally only when a firm enlarged liver presents or abnormal liver function tests are reported. Sometimes it may be detected incidentally on ultrasound. Patients will present with symptoms and signs of alcoholic hepatitis or cirrhosis if these coexist with fatty liver.

Alcoholic hepatitis
When consumed in sufficient quantity, alcohol produces an inflammatory reaction that results in liver cell necrosis. Alcoholic hepatitis may occur separately or in combination with established cirrhosis. Histologically, hepatocytes are swollen and macrovesicular steatosis is usually present. Alcoholic hyaline or Mallory's bodies are common. Portal hypertension may develop as a result of the combination of hepatocyte swelling and sinusoidal collagen deposition, as well as an increased portal blood flow associated with the inflammation (Israel & Orrego, 1987). When the acute inflammation settles, a varying degree of fibrosis is seen that may eventually lead to cirrhosis.

Patients with alcoholic hepatitis usually present with a two- to three-week prodrome of fatigue, anorexia, nausea and weight loss. Clinical signs include a mild fever, tender hepatomegaly and jaundice. In the most severe case (usually following a period of binge drinking), patients are gravely ill with fever, marked jaundice, ascites and evidence of a hyperdynamic circulation such as systemic hypertension and tachycardia. Complicating hypoglycemia can precipitate coma. GI bleeding is common due to portal hypertension and the reduced ability of the liver to produce clotting factors. Signs of malnutrition are often present. Hepatic decompensation can be precipitated by vomiting, diarrhea, intercurrent infection or GI bleeding, leading to encephalopathy and liver failure.

Alcoholic hepatitis has a mortality rate of up to 50 per cent in severely decompensated and malnourished hospitalized patients (Chedid, Mendenhall et al., 1991). Patients usually deteriorate in the first few weeks, with marked jaundice being a bad prognostic sign. Assuming recovery, hepatitis may take several months to resolve.

Cirrhosis

Histologically, the cirrhosis is micronodular. The architecture is distorted and the normal relationship between the terminal hepatic vein and portal triad is disturbed. The amount of fat in the liver is variable and alcoholic hepatitis may or may not be present depending on recent alcoholic intake. Widespread pericellular fibrosis around hepatocytes is most prominent in the area around zone 3. With continued necrosis and regeneration, the cirrhosis may progress from a micro- to a macronodular pattern. Extensive fibrosis contributes to the development of portal hypertension with its attendant complications. There may be increased parenchymal iron deposition. This may be related to the iron content of beverages consumed. When marked, genetic hemochromatosis has to be excluded.

Established cirrhosis is often asymptomatic and is diagnosed incidentally in apparently well-nourished patients. Clinically, signs of chronic liver disease are present. There is palmar erythema, multiple spider nevi, and in males, gynecomastia and small testes. Hepatomegaly is often present as well as signs of portal hypertension including splenomegaly, ascites and distended abdominal wall veins. Features peculiar to alcoholic liver disease include bilateral parotid enlargement and Dupuytren's contractures. At the late stage, the right lobe of the liver may become shrunken and impalpable while the left lobe hypertrophies and is easily palpable in the epigastrium.

Evidence of alcohol damage in other organ systems such as peripheral neuropathy, memory loss and dementia from cerebral atrophy can be present. Alcoholic cirrhosis is also associated with several renal problems. These include IgA nephropathy, renal tubular acidosis and the development of hepatorenal syndrome.

DIAGNOSIS

The diagnosis of typical patients with florid alcoholic hepatitis or end-stage cirrhosis with decompensation is not difficult. However, in asymptomatic, well-nourished patients who maintain functional stability in their lives, the diagnosis of alcohol dependence and alcoholic liver disease requires a high index of suspicion on the part of the treating physician. Ultrasound can often detect a fatty liver, although it is not reliable in detecting cirrhosis. A liver biopsy is required to make a definitive diagnosis of alcoholic liver disease. Patients with fatty liver frequently have normal liver function tests, although the gamma glutamyl transpeptidase (GGT) is invariably elevated while the aminotransferases and alkaline phosphatase may be slightly increased. (See Section 1.1.)

Mild cases of alcoholic hepatitis are only recognized on liver biopsy in patients who present with a history of alcohol abuse and abnormal liver function tests.

Laboratory abnormalities that may indicate alcoholic liver disease include elevations of the aminotransferases, bilirubin, alkaline phosphatase and GGT, with the increase in GGT proportionally greater than that of alkaline phosphatase. The serum albumin level tends to decrease. The aminotransferase levels rarely exceed 300 i.u./L, except in association with acetaminophen ingestion, with the AST/ALT ratio greater than 2. Severe cases of alcoholic hepatitis can present with marked hyperbilirubinemia, with levels reaching 300 to 500 μmol/L. There is also leukocytosis of up to $20-25 \times 10^9$/L, and a prolongation of the prothrombin time that does not respond to vitamin K. Serum IgA is markedly increased, with IgG and IgM raised to a lesser extent.

Biochemical abnormalities suggestive of alcoholic cirrhosis include a low serum albumin, elevated bilirubin and elevated aminotransferases. GGT is disproportionately raised with recent alcohol ingestion. Although GGT is widely used as a screening test for alcohol abuse, its sensitivity is low (35–50 per cent) compared with questionnaires such as CAGE (see Section 1). With decompensated cirrhosis, the prothrombin time may be prolonged. Portal hypertension results in hypersplenism, leading to thrombocytopenia, anemia and leukopenia. Other non-specific serum changes include elevations in uric acid, lactate and triglycerides, and reductions in glucose and magnesium.

PROGNOSIS

Fatty liver
When fatty liver is not associated with alcoholic hepatitis the prognosis is excellent. The condition is completely reversible on cessation of alcohol. It is generally not regarded as a pre-cirrhotic lesion.

Alcoholic hepatitis
The prognosis for alcoholic hepatitis patients is variable, depending on the severity of the acute lesion and the presence or absence of underlying cirrhosis.

TABLE 5: Alcoholic Hepatitis — Bad Prognostic Indicators

- encephalopathy
- low serum albumin
- elevated serum bilirubin above 340 μmol/L
- prolonged prothrombin time to more than 8 seconds above control value

Patients with alcoholic hepatitis and encephalopathy have a one-year mortality rate of up to 50 per cent. Those without encephalopathy, but with the other bad prognostic indicators, have a one-year mortality rate of 20 per cent. In long-term follow-up of these patients there was an almost 40 per cent risk of progression to cirrhosis after a mean period of 3.3 years. Once cirrhosis is superimposed on alcoholic hepatitis, the five-year survival rate is only 26 per cent, with most of the deaths occurring in the first year after diagnosis (Chedid, Mendenhall et al., 1991).

Cirrhosis

Inactive cirrhosis without any complications is associated with a favorable prognosis, similar to that of fatty liver — especially in those who stop drinking. The five-year survival rate is reduced from 89 per cent to 68 per cent in those who continue to drink. Once complications occur, the five-year survival rate is reduced to 60 per cent in the abstainers and 34 per cent in those who continue to use alcohol.

TREATMENT

The following reviews some of the issues in the long-term outpatient management of patients with alcoholic liver disease. It does not address the acute management of complications of cirrhosis.

The most important therapeutic measure is total abstinence from alcohol. Abstinence alone has been shown to improve clinical status and survival (Orrego, Blake et al., 1987). Regular follow-up can reinforce the need for abstinence and appropriate referrals to treatment can help to maintain long-term sobriety.

Physicians should have a frank discussion with their patients about their prognosis, emphasizing that abstinence can bring about a resolution of fatty liver and alcoholic hepatitis and can reduce the morbidity and mortality associated with cirrhosis. Regular monitoring of liver transaminases is recommended and results should be shared with patients. Improved results can be a powerful reinforcement for patients attempting abstinence.

Patients with cirrhosis should be tested for hepatitis B and C as these viruses are more prevalent in alcohol-dependent patients and may act synergistically with alcohol to accelerate liver damage. Hepatotoxic medications should be used with caution and should be carefully monitored. In particular, moderate doses of acetaminophen in an alcoholic may precipitate florid alcoholic hepatitis. Therefore all patients with alcoholic liver disease should be cautioned against its regular use.

Patients with clinical or laboratory evidence of chronic alcoholic hepatitis (as evidenced by persistent elevation of AST) or cirrhosis should be referred to a hepatologist. Further investigation may reveal treatable conditions such as portal hypertension and chronic viral hepatitis.

Withdrawal
Alcoholic patients presenting with acute intoxication need to be seen safely through withdrawal. Benzodiazepines remain the treatment of choice for acute alcoholic withdrawal. (See Section 3.2, for management of withdrawal in the presence of liver disease.)

Fatty liver
Alcoholic fatty liver responds to alcohol abstinence and a nutritious diet. With this intervention, fat disappears from the liver in four to six weeks.

Alcoholic hepatitis — efficacy of corticosteroids
Therapy in acute alcoholic hepatitis has been directed towards reducing the severity of the necro-inflammatory process and preventing hepatic fibrosis. Twelve randomized, controlled trials in patients with alcoholic hepatitis have yielded the conclusion that corticosteroids are of no benefit in patients with mild to moderate alcoholic hepatitis. However, corticosteroids were noted to improve the one-month survival in a subset of patients with severe illness, manifested by encephalopathy, prolonged prothrombin time or elevated bilirubin (Ramond, Poynard & Rueff, 1992). A discriminant function of > 32 has been established as a predictor of poor prognosis and favorable response to corticosteroid therapy. Discriminant function = 4.6 x (prothrombin time - control prothrombin time) in seconds + (serum bilirubin in μmol/L ÷ 17).

Cirrhosis — use of propylthiouracil (PTU)
Because patients with alcohol-induced liver disease are in a hypermetabolic state directing treatment efforts towards reducing hypermetabolism is prudent. Propylthiouracil (PTU) has been shown to reduce the hypoxic damage in the liver of animals with an alcohol-induced hypermetabolic state exposed to low oxygen tension. By interfering with thyroid function PTU reduces the metabolic rate of the liver, thereby lowering O_2 consumption. Hypoxia in the portal triad

is felt to be an important step in the development of alcoholic cirrhosis. By reducing O_2 consumption PTU reduces hypoxia in the portal triad and slows the development of cirrhosis.

Two small studies assessing the use of PTU at a dose of 300 mg per day in patients with acute alcoholic hepatitis reported an improvement in their clinical state but not survival. In a large randomized, controlled study assessing the long-term effects of PTU in chronic alcoholic liver disease, a significantly reduced mortality in the treated group was reported (Orrego, Blake et al., 1987). Patients who benefited most were those with severe disease and who consumed the least amount of alcohol. Those who continued to drink heavily were not protected by therapy. Thus far, there have been no further double-blind, controlled trials of long-term PTU therapy. At present, PTU is not widely used in patients with chronic alcoholic liver disease. However, its theoretical advantage in reducing liver damage combined with its minimal side-effects make it a recommended treatment for patients with chronic alcoholic liver disease.

PTU occasionally causes clinical hypothyroidism. Patients on PTU should have their weight, pulse, and TSH measured on a regular basis to detect early signs of hypothyroidism. Complete blood count should also be monitored, because in rare instances PTU causes bone marrow suppression.

Cirrhosis — other approaches
The severity of protein-calorie malnutrition has been shown to correlate with the severity of liver disease and mortality. Intravenous amino acid supplements have been shown to have varying degrees of success in severely protein-malnourished patients. Oral supplementation, however, is the preferred route if the patient can tolerate a diet. Patients who receive a well-balanced diet often show improved well-being, together with improvement in laboratory parameters. However, no effect on survival has been shown with nutritional supplementation (Lieber, 1996).

Cirrhosis is an irreversible process and therapy is directed at the complications of liver failure and portal hypertension. Colchicine has been used as an antifibrotic agent without much success. Portocaval shunts will reduce the risk of bleeding from esophageal varices, but are associated with a 30 per cent incidence of hepatic encephalopathy. The recent advent of a transjugular intrahepatic portosystemic stent shunt has replaced a surgical portocaval shunt as the treatment of choice for uncontrolled esophageal varices. Hepatic encephalopathy remains a complication, but can usually be controlled with prophylactic lactulose.

Liver transplantation is being increasingly considered as a treatment option for patients with alcoholic cirrhosis who have achieved long-term sobriety. The one-year survival rate in patients transplanted for alcoholic cirrhosis is similar to that of patients transplanted for other conditions.

Prevention of encephalopathy

Patients and their families should be warned about the early signs of encephalopathy. In patients with marked deterioration in liver function, medications with sedative properties should be used with caution as they may precipitate encephalopathy. Other precipitants include infection, GI bleeding and overuse of diuretics. Some patients require a low-protein diet and lactulose to prevent the build-up of toxic ammonia derivatives.

Portal hypertension and GI bleeding

Patients with clinical or laboratory evidence of cirrhosis should have a biopsy and endoscopy to measure portal vein pressures. Beta blockers have been shown to reduce the incidence and mortality associated with bleeding esophageal varices in patients with portal hypertension (Lebrec, Poynard et al., 1988). Several clinical trials have shown that octreotide can stop initial bleeding and prevent further bleeding from esophageal varices in cirrhotic patients (Sadowski, 1997). NSAIDs should be used with considerable caution because patients with cirrhosis may have impaired hemostasis.

3.4

OTHER MEDICAL COMPLICATIONS OF ALCOHOL USE*

Peter Selby, MBBS

Alcohol consumption can affect almost every organ system. Listed below are a few pertinent conditions associated with alcohol abuse and dependence. Detailed description of these conditions is beyond the scope of this manual. For more information, standard texts in internal medicine or surgery should be consulted.

NEUROLOGICAL COMPLICATIONS RELATED TO ALCOHOL

Blackouts

A blackout is an acute reversible amnestic syndrome usually occurring at the end of an episode of heavy drinking, with no formation of long-term memory. (See Section 3.1.)

Wernicke-Korsakoff syndrome

This syndrome is characterized by Wernicke's triad (confusion, ataxia and ophthalmoplegia) and Korsakoff's psychosis (severe recent memory impairment associated with confabulation). In its most florid form the syndrome has some mortality, while subclinical forms of the disease may go unrecognized. It is caused by thiamine deficiency. The prophylactic administration of at least a single parenteral dose of thiamine (50–100 mg) is well justified in every patient sick enough to require hospital admission or outpatient medical detoxification for alcohol-related problems. Wernicke's encephalopathy is a medical emergency that usually resolves within hours after administration of intravenous thiamine. This may unmask the Korsakoff's psychosis, which does not respond as well to thiamine.

---

* Adapted from Devenyi & Saunders, 1986.

Cerebral atrophy

Cerebral atrophy in heavy alcohol users affects the cortex more than the ventricles. A certain degree of reversibility has been demonstrated with abstinence. The clinical "organic brain syndrome" that is associated with brain atrophy can range from minimal cognitive and intellectual impairment to severe dementia.

Cerebellar degeneration

Alcohol-induced degeneration primarily involves the vermis, with the main clinical correlate being ataxic gait. Other cerebellar functions such as tone and co-ordination (e.g., the finger-nose test) may be relatively preserved.

Pseudo-Parkinsonism

Pseudo-Parkinsonism in alcohol-dependent individuals has been well documented. Any or all Parkinsonian symptoms (tremor, rigidity, bradykinesia) may be present, but they resolve spontaneously with abstinence.

Peripheral neuropathy

This is also largely associated with thiamine deficiency and possibly other nutritional deficiencies. It is a symmetrical, initially distal, sensorimotor neuropathy affecting the legs more than the arms and later spreading proximally. Loss of the ankle-jerk is often an early clinical sign.

Subdural hematoma

Heavy drinkers are prone to develop acute or chronic subdural hematomas. Subdural hematomas are more likely to occur in this population than in any other and can result from relatively trivial (or unnoticed) head injury because of "stretched" subdural veins in patients with cortical atrophy. A high index of suspicion is warranted in patients with headache, intellectual deterioration, unexplained drowsiness or a bizarre neurological picture. Patients who appear more intoxicated than their BAC may suggest could have an underlying subdural hematoma, especially if there are signs of head trauma. However, signs of trauma may not be present. Symptoms can fluctuate in patients with a subdural hematoma. Signs of raised intracranial pressure are rare. A CT scan is usually diagnostic.

GASTROENTEROLOGICAL COMPLICATIONS RELATED TO ALCOHOL

Alcoholic liver disease
(See Section 3.3.)

Alcoholic gastritis and esophagitis
These conditions are responsible for dyspeptic symptoms as well as for acute and chronic blood loss. Peptic ulcer is no more common in heavy alcohol users than in the general population, but its complications may be adversely affected by alcohol. When treating dyspeptic symptoms or peptic ulcer disease in these patients, the following should be taken into consideration:

- H_2 receptor blockers should be used with caution in non-abstinent patients because they inhibit gastric alcohol dehydrogenase and lead to higher blood alcohol levels. If H_2 receptor blockers are used, then ranitidine may have some advantages over cimetidine; it is less likely to cause confusion, gynecomastia (this may be an important issue in those with alcoholic liver disease or on spironolactone therapy), and it does not inhibit hepatic microsomal enzymes (the toxicity of concurrently used drugs is not augmented).
- Proton pump inhibitors may be a better choice since they do not alter alcohol metabolism.
- Many currently available antacids have low sodium content (< 1 mg/5 mL) and are thus acceptable for patients with alcoholic liver disease who require restricted sodium intake.

Mallory-Weiss tear
This is a longitudinal tear at the gastroesophageal junction and is common in chronic heavy drinkers due to chronic vomiting. Patients present with a bout of violent vomiting followed by hematemesis.

Alcoholic pancreatitis
Although most alcoholics do not develop pancreatitis, alcohol abuse is the most common cause of pancreatitis in North America (Mergener & Baillie, 1998). This can present as acute pancreatitis or as an exacerbation of chronic pancreatitis.

A diagnosis of pancreatitis should be considered in any patients with severe acute upper abdominal pain. Pancreatic pain is typically worse in recumbency, relieved by sitting up. Rigidity is not usually marked and there is a varying degree of ileus. In the most severe cases shock, hemoconcentration, and acute renal failure may develop.

Pain relief is important in the management of acute attacks of pancreatitis. Meperidine (Demerol®) 100 mg q3–4h i.m. prn is preferable to morphine, since it is less likely to cause a spasm of the sphincter of Oddi. Fluids and electrolytes need to be replaced. Pancreatic secretions can be decreased during an acute attack by keeping the patient NPO. Pancreatic enzyme replacement therapy may be required in patients with severe exocrine insufficiency.

For the management of pain in patients with chronic pancreatitis, the clinician should prescribe opioid analgesics cautiously. Patients are at risk of developing dependence on opioid medication if there is a history of alcohol dependence. Moreover, inappropriate use of opioid medication may also precipitate a relapse to alcohol use (Miotto, Compton et al., 1996; see Section 8.3, on chronic pain).

Chronic diarrhea
This can be due to the effect of alcohol on small bowel motility and decreased water and electrolyte absorption. In patients with pancreatitis, it can also be due to fat malabsorption.

HEMATOLOGICAL COMPLICATIONS RELATED TO ALCOHOL

Anemia
The anemias in heavy users of alcohol are frequently complex, multifactorial and difficult to sort out. Alcohol *per se* can cause macrocytosis, which may confound the investigation. Iron deficiency is common, secondary to bleeding from gastritis, esophageal varices and dietary deficiency.

Anemia due to folate deficiency is quite common because of poor diet or interference by alcohol with folate absorption and utilization. Vitamin B_{12} deficiency is rare, except in advanced pancreatic disease (due to failure to split B_{12}-R protein complex). Sideroblastic anemia (ring sideroblasts in bone marrow) is attributed to inhibition of pyridoxal phosphate by alcohol. Decreased RBC survival (with or without associated leukopenia and thrombocytopenia) can be caused by hypersplenism secondary to liver disease and portal hypertension.

Anemias of any etiology, during and after investigation of the cause, should be diligently treated by trying to bring the hemoglobin (Hb) level to > 10 g/L. Especially in patients with liver disease, the restoration of Hb to acceptable levels is not only beneficial for the anemia itself but also for the liver. This is because a relative hypoxia of the liver may play a role in alcoholic liver disease.

Toxic thrombocytopenia

Toxic thrombocytopenia due to alcohol intoxication can be quite profound and occasionally symptomatic (e.g., petechiae). It is due to alcohol-induced inhibition of megakaryocyte function. In contrast to the thrombocytopenia of hypersplenism, the toxic variety is rapidly reversible with abstinence (sometimes with an "overshoot").

Leukocytosis

Leukocytosis should prompt an investigation for a focus of infection. However, alcoholic hepatitis by itself can produce leukocytosis.

ENDOCRINE AND METABOLIC COMPLICATIONS RELATED TO ALCOHOL

Sexual dysfunction

This condition commonly accompanies alcohol dependence. Hypoandrogenism in males is more common in those who have liver disease but may be caused by alcohol itself. While alcohol may remove sexual inhibitions, impotence is common.

Pseudo-Cushing syndrome

Pseudo-Cushing syndrome refers to transient cushingoid features as the result of stimulation of the pituitary-adrenal axis by prolonged and excessive use of alcohol. The syndrome disappears with abstinence.

Diabetes

Diabetes may be secondary to advanced chronic pancreatic disease. Severe liver disease may also cause glucose intolerance. Diabetes mellitus coincidental with alcohol problems may present serious management issues in non-compliant heavy users of alcohol.

Hyperuricemia

A metabolic consequence of alcoholic oxidation, hyperuricemia frequently accompanies heavy alcohol intake.

Hypoglycemia and ketoacidosis

Alcohol inhibits gluconeogenesis in the presence of starvation. This can occasionally cause symptomatic hypoglycemia requiring glucose administration. Untreated hypoglycemia causes a cessation of insulin secretion and the reproduction of counter-regulatory hormones, increasing the blood sugar and mobilizing free fatty acids, which in turn are metabolized to ketoacids. This causes an anion-gap metabolic acidosis.

99

Alcohol ketoacidosis is a mild condition in the relatively healthy individual. It may be missed because blood sugar and the clinical nitroprusside test for ketones may be normal. Alcohol ketoacidosis responds to the resumption of feeding.

CARDIOVASCULAR COMPLICATIONS RELATED TO ALCOHOL

Cardiomyopathy and dysrhythmias

Excessive alcohol consumption can depress myocardial function and produce alcoholic cardiomyopathy. Various atrial and ventricular dysrhythmias are frequently associated with excessive alcohol intake or with severe withdrawal. Thus, alcohol use must be considered in the differential diagnosis of patients presenting with otherwise unexplained heart failure or dysrhythmias. The clue to "alcoholic heart disease" is that it is associated with heavy alcohol intake, disappears with abstinence (this reversibility is lost in advanced stages) and other causes of heart disease can be reasonably excluded. Sudden death secondary to alcoholic dysrhythmias has been reported (Smith, 1995). The best treatment of alcoholic heart disease is abstinence, aided by the usual measures (e.g., verapamil for PAT, digitalization for rapid atrial fibrillation).

Hypertension

Hypertension is associated with chronic alcohol consumption in a dose-dependent manner. As people begin to consume three or more drinks per day, they are more likely to have mild to moderate elevations in blood pressure. This will often revert back to normal with abstinence. Many patients are transiently hypertensive in the alcohol withdrawal period due to excessive catecholamine release. These patients, however, usually do not require treatment for hypertension. The presence of frank hypertension past the withdrawal period should be established (and then the usual basic investigations carried out) before diagnosing essential hypertension and committing the patient to lifelong treatment.

Ischemic heart disease

There is an inverse relationship between alcohol consumption and ischemic heart disease, probably due to alcohol's effect on HDL and platelet aggregation.

Cerebrovascular accidents

There is a reduced incidence of embolic stroke but an increased risk of hemorrhagic stroke in heavy drinkers (Juvela, Hillborn & Palomaki, 1995).

Obstructive sleep apnea

Obstructive sleep apnea that is precipitated and aggravated by alcohol has been recently recognized. The periodic anoxia associated with sleep apnea can play a role in insults to the brain, liver and heart.

INFECTIONS AND ALCOHOL

Heavy drinkers have an increased incidence of all types of infections because of depressed WBC function, immunologic factors and lifestyle. Two particularly common problems deserve mention.

Pneumonia

The pneumonias are most often caused by common organisms (e.g., *Streptococcus pneumoniae*). However, bacteria that are rare pathogens in others are relatively more common causes of disease in alcohol-dependent patients, such as Klebsiella (upper lobe) and anaerobes. Aspiration pneumonias are also more common.

Bacterial peritonitis

Spontaneous bacterial peritonitis in patients with ascites is a potentially devastating complication of alcoholic liver disease. Clinical signs and symptoms are abdominal pain, tenderness, rebound tenderness and fever.

CARCINOGENIC EFFECTS OF ALCOHOL

Based on epidemiological evidence, alcohol use has been associated with a variety of carcinogenic effects. An increased incidence of breast (Smith-Warner, Spiegelman et al., 1998), mouth, pharyngeal, laryngeal and esophageal cancer and hepatoma has been reported in heavy drinkers (Kato & Nomura, 1994). While cigarette smoking is prevalent in this population, alcohol may act as a co-carcinogen.

3.5

GUIDELINES ON LOW-RISK DRINKING*

Questions are frequently asked by members of the public and by professionals on behalf of their patients or clients about the availability of guidelines on alcohol consumption, about the concept of low-risk drinking, and about whether or not alcohol is good for the heart, and if so, how much. The Addiction Research Foundation (now a division of the Centre for Addiction and Mental Health) and a number of health care partners in Ontario have reviewed the research and agreed upon a set of low-risk drinking guidelines to help answer these questions. The guidelines were developed to promote an understanding of the patterns and levels of alcohol consumption related to the *lowest risk* of adverse effects while securing the benefits derived from alcohol's protective effect against heart disease. Physicians must have a clear understanding of what constitutes low-risk drinking in order to identify and manage alcohol problems appropriately.

Consistent guidelines on low-risk drinking have a number of potential benefits. Physicians may want to provide these guidelines to patients who inquire about the health benefits of drinking or to those who have concerns about their drinking. These guidelines can:

- provide simple, concrete answers to frequently asked questions about drinking and alcohol's beneficial effects against heart disease
- help people reduce their alcohol use to a level that no longer poses a high risk to the health or social well-being of themselves or others
- guide professionals who have the power to help patients or clients change behavior
- support people who don't drink alcohol by pointing out that there are less risky alternatives to achieve a protective effect against heart disease

---

* These guidelines have been developed by the Addiction Research Foundation Division of the Centre for Addiction and Mental Health in consultation with the Canadian Centre on Substance Abuse. They have been endorsed by numerous professional health care bodies, including the College of Family Physicians of Canada.

- emphasize the distinction between alcohol consumption itself and behaviors, such as drinking and driving, that can increase the risk of harm.

Appendix 2 provides an example of how a physician could respond, using the following guidelines on low-risk drinking, to patients asking about the health benefits of drinking.

RESEARCH EVIDENCE FOR LOW-RISK DRINKING

The low-risk drinking guidelines outlined below take into account a variety of consequences of alcohol use. These include acute and chronic health effects, accidents, injuries and adverse social effects. Weekly limits were determined primarily by research evidence on long-term health effects. Daily limits were defined by two considerations: injuries and other harms linked to individual episodes of drinking, and the risk of long-term health problems.

Weekly limits
As a person's average weekly alcohol consumption increases, so does the risk of health problems, including diseases of the liver, pancreas and nervous system. In addition, there is increased risk of developing cancers of the upper respiratory and digestive systems, liver, colon and breast. For these health problems risk increases with each increase in alcohol intake and abstainers are at the lowest risk (United States Department of Health and Human Services, 1993). At the same time, alcohol decreases the risk of ischemic heart disease and stroke (Zakari, 1994). For example, Canadian men who drink fewer than 14 drinks a week on average are at lower risk of early death than men who do not drink alcohol. However, the risk of premature death begins to increase with more than 14 drinks a week for men and nine drinks a week for women (English, Holman et al., 1995). An average intake of no more than 14 drinks per week for men and nine for women does not appear to be linked to an increased overall risk of long-term health problems.

Daily limits
The number of drinks consumed in each drinking day is as important as the average number of drinks per week (Ashley, Ferrence et al., 1997). A day of heavy drinking can have several adverse consequences. One is an increase in blood pressure. In addition, as blood alcohol concentration (BAC) increases, so does the risk of accidents and injuries. For example, a driver with a BAC of 80 mg% is three times more likely to be involved in a motor vehicle crash than a driver who has not been drinking. A heavy drinking day also increases the risk of social problems related to home life, work, the law and finances. It is important to recognize that some adults who drink responsibly will exceed the

103

recommended maximum of two drinks a day on occasions such as parties or weddings. Extra caution should be taken on these occasions to avoid intoxication. Food, other drinks and safe transportation should be available, and alcohol should not be mixed with potentially hazardous activities such as sports. In the case of problem drinkers, research has shown that men who agreed to limit themselves to four drinks on drinking days and women who limited themselves to three drinks (slightly higher daily limits than the guidelines for the general public) consistently reported that they no longer had social, financial, work-related or legal problems linked to their alcohol use.

Hourly limits

The guideline of drinking no more than one drink per hour takes into account research showing that a person weighing 70 kg (154 lbs.) can eliminate roughly 8 to 10 g of absolute alcohol per hour (a standard drink is 13.6 g). It is important to note that the same amount of alcohol affects individuals differently. Absorption of alcohol can be slowed by spacing out drinks, alternating alcoholic and non-alcoholic beverages, having alcohol with food, and drinking low-alcohol beverages.

Equivalence of beverage types

These guidelines are relevant to *standard drinks* of any alcoholic beverage. A standard drink is defined as one 341 mL (12 oz.) bottle of beer (5 per cent alcohol); one 142 mL (5 oz.) glass of table wine (12 per cent alcohol); one 43 mL (1.5 oz.) shot of liquor (40 per cent alcohol); or one 85 mL (3 oz.) serving of fortified wine (18 per cent alcohol). Drinkers should pay close attention to the alcohol content of the beverage they are drinking and to the size of serving. In the case of benefits related to moderate drinking, a protective effect of alcohol against heart disease is often attributed to wine. However, the protective effect comes largely from the alcohol itself and not other ingredients (Rimm, Klatsky et al., 1996).

Protective effects

The protective effects of alcohol, outlined in the weekly limits guideline above, must be weighed against the increased risk of illness, injury and death from drinking. In Canada, the risk of death due to heart disease begins to increase at age 40–45 for men and 45–49 in women (Heart and Stroke Foundation of Canada, 1995). Above these ages, the protective effects of moderate drinking outweigh the risk of death from alcohol-related injuries. Below these ages, there is insufficient evidence to show that people achieve enough long-term benefit from alcohol use to justify the added risk. Moreover, the protective effect is achieved with an average intake of as little as one drink every other day, a level well within the recommended guidelines. There are less risky ways to protect against heart disease. These include quitting smoking, controlling blood pressure, exercising regularly and eating less fat and more fruits and vegetables.

104

Days without alcohol

An inability to go without alcohol, or a perceived need to drink daily, is a sign of potential problems. However, for an average healthy person who stays within both the daily and weekly limits, the risk of dependence is low. As well, spreading the weekly limit over seven days reduces the risk of problems. Therefore, we have not recommended a minimum number of alcohol-free days per week. Drinkers would be wise to ensure that they can comfortably go without alcohol from time to time. Those who feel they cannot go without alcohol should seek help. Also, people who have been advised by a physician or counsellor to take days off from drinking because of previous problems should follow this advice.

Drinking to cope

Drinking as a way to cope with problems or negative emotions is common among those experiencing drinking problems. However, people who drink within the recommended guidelines, enjoy good mental health and do not have a history of drinking problems are not at risk if they occasionally use alcohol to relax.

CONTRAINDICATIONS TO DRINKING

Certain health problems

The low-risk drinking guidelines may not apply in the case of certain health problems. These conditions include:

- disorders associated with increased bleeding
- recovery from an injury or operation
- gastritis, ulcers and liver disease
- uncontrolled high blood pressure
- diabetes
- depression and anxiety
- serious psychiatric illness.

Certain medications

Combining alcohol with some medications can result in serious problems. These medications include antidepressants, sedatives, sleeping pills, painkillers and heart disease medications such as anticoagulants and inotropic drugs (e.g., digitalis).

Serious personal or family drinking problems

Help for alcohol problems is available from addiction treatment agencies, physicians and mutual aid organizations such as Alcoholics Anonymous. People who have a family member with a serious drinking problem are at increased risk of problems themselves. If they follow these guidelines, they will reduce their risk

105

of problems. However, should those with a family history of alcohol problems choose to abstain or drink less, this decision should be supported. People who seek help for a drinking problem may be presented with different guidelines for alcohol use if they choose to try to cut down their drinking. For example, some guidelines developed for clinical use have higher daily limits but similar weekly limits and more strict rules about non-drinking days.

Pregnancy

Research does not show conclusively whether there is an increased risk of damage for the child of a pregnant woman who drinks within the guidelines during pregnancy. In the absence of a clear definition of risk-free levels, it is advisable not to drink any alcohol during pregnancy. Research has shown that prenatal alcohol use can cause adverse effects on the physical and mental development of the infant, and an increased risk of congenital defects. The most severe example of this, fetal alcohol syndrome, is uncommon and is found in the children of mothers with serious alcohol problems (see Section 14).

Breastfeeding

Alcohol should be avoided during breastfeeding as alcohol consumed by the mother passes readily into her milk and can affect the infant. There is some evidence that children feed less well if breast milk contains alcohol. Evidence that alcohol in breast milk can impair child development is limited, but mothers are advised not to take the risk.

Drinking and driving

Impaired driving is a major public health and safety problem. As little as one drink affects neuromotor function, judgment and the performance of skilled tasks. The risk of a motor vehicle crash increases with the increasing BAC of the driver.

When alertness is important

Studies have documented alcohol's involvement in fatal accidents and injuries related to falls, drownings, burns, wounds, hypothermia and other events occurring at home or during leisure activities. Fatal accidents are not restricted to heavy drinkers, but the risk of involvement in a fatal accident increases with every drink beyond the person's usual amount. Abstinence is advised for anyone operating machinery, responsible for public order or safety, working, studying or entering into potentially dangerous activities.

Legal and other restrictions

People in certain occupations — airline pilots, for example — may be forbidden from using any alcohol while working or before working, for safety reasons. Others are forbidden to drink by a court order. The guidelines presented above are intended for adults.

3.6

IDENTIFYING PROBLEM DRINKERS*

Meldon Kahan, MD, and Lynn Wilson, MD

A side from smoking, problem drinking is the most common substance use problem encountered by physicians. Problem drinkers are often reluctant to seek formal treatment, leaving physicians responsible for their care. Fortunately there is good evidence that problem drinkers respond to brief advice by physicians (see Section 3.7).

ALCOHOL AND ITS ASSOCIATED RISKS

Low-risk drinking guidelines

The low-risk drinking guidelines set out by the Addiction Research Foundation (now a division of the Centre for Addiction and Mental Health) recommend that men consume no more than 14 drinks per week and women no more than nine, with no more than two drinks in any one day for either sex. Physicians should be familiar with the background evidence for these recommendations. (See Section 3.5 for full description.)

Cardiovascular risks

A J-shaped risk curve describes the relationship between alcohol consumption and total cardiovascular mortality. That is, moderate ("low-risk") drinkers have a lower mortality rate than abstainers, but consumption above moderate levels is associated with increasing risk.

Alcohol exerts its cardioprotective effect by increasing HDL and inhibiting platelet aggregation (Pikaar, Wedel et al., 1987). Most of the cardioprotective effects of alcohol can be obtained from minimal consumption (e.g., one standard drink every second day). While alcohol may protect against ischemic stroke, moderate and heavy drinkers have an increased risk of hemorrhagic stroke, due

*Adapted with permission from M. Kahan. (1996). Identifying and managing problem drinkers. *Canadian Family Physician, 42*, 661-671.

in part to hypertension. Consumption of three or more drinks per day can cause elevations in both systolic and diastolic blood pressure (MacMahon, 1987).

Other risk factors

The evidence for the health benefits of moderate drinking is far less compelling for women and younger men than it is for middle-aged men. Among younger men, total mortality increases with increasing alcohol consumption, due to accidents, violence and suicide (Andreasson, Allbeck & Romelsjo, 1988). A meta-analysis of six large cohort studies demonstrated a linear relationship between current daily alcohol consumption and the risk of breast cancer. Women consuming 30 g to 60 g (two to five drinks) had a 40 per cent greater risk of developing breast cancer than abstainers. Alcohol may exert its effect by increasing the secretion of estrogen, decreasing its clearance, or by acting as a co-carcinogen (Smith-Warner, Spiegelman et al., 1998).

Because of the differential effects of alcohol on health risk, advice about safe drinking levels must be tailored to the age, sex and health profile of the individual. A lower limit is recommended for women because they are prone to develop alcoholic liver disease at lower levels of consumption than men (Tuyns & Peuignot, 1984). Pregnant patients should be advised to abstain from alcohol. Patients should be advised not to drink before driving or operating heavy machinery. Caution is advised in patients who are on medications that may interact with alcohol (such as sedatives or opioids).

Patients who abstain or drink minimally should not be advised to increase their consumption, even if they are at risk for coronary artery disease. Alcohol has powerful effects on sleep, mood and cognition, and other strategies for cardio-vascular risk reduction are safer and just as effective.

Prevalence of hazardous alcohol consumption

Studies indicate a high prevalence of alcohol consumption above the recommended limits. A survey conducted in 1989 found that 5.0 per cent of Canadian adult men reported drinking 15 to 21 drinks per week and 4.6 per cent reported drinking 22 drinks or more (Williams, Chang & Truong, 1992); 1.2 per cent of women reported drinking 15 or more drinks per week (Canadian Centre on Substance Abuse, 1994). Patients attending an outpatient medical clinic have an even higher prevalence of hazardous drinking than the general population.

Continuum of alcohol problems

Alcohol problems lie along a continuum ranging from mild to severe (see Figure B) (Skinner, 1990).

FIGURE C: Relation between Level of Alcohol Problem and Level of Intervention[†]

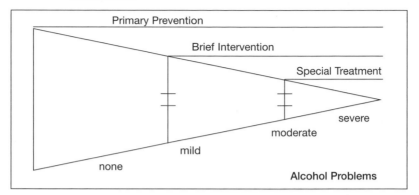

† Reproduced with permission from, H.A. Skinner. (1990). Spectrum of drinkers and intervention oppor-tunities. *Canadian Medical Association Journal, 143(10),* 1054–1059.

Problem Drinking

As illustrated above, the majority of persons with alcohol problems have problems that are not severe; these people are referred to as "problem drinkers." Problem drinkers tend to drink far less than those who are alcohol-dependent, and they often drink moderately when the occasion warrants it. They are usually intact socially, psychologically and physically. They do not perceive themselves to be "alcoholic" and are often unwilling to commit extensive time and energy to treatment.

Since it is estimated that there are at least four times as many problem drinkers as there are patients with severe alcohol dependence, the bulk of alcohol-related morbidity and mortality occurs in problem drinkers.

Problem drinking — a definition

A clinically useful definition of the problem drinker is the patient who:

*   regularly drinks above the low-risk limits of 14 drinks per week (men), nine drinks per week (women), and two drinks on a drinking day
*   may have developed a social or physical problem as a result
*   does not exhibit clinical features of severe alcohol dependence, such as pre-occupation with alcohol, withdrawal symptoms or severe social or physical consequences of alcohol use.

Some clinicians prefer to refer to problem drinkers who do not presently have an alcohol-associated problem as "at-risk" or "hazardous" drinkers.

109

Alcohol dependence

The problem drinker should be distinguished from the alcohol-dependent drinker because the treatment approaches for the two groups differ significantly. While no specific weekly limit has been established, patients with alcohol dependence typically consume 40 to 60 drinks per week or more. They rarely drink moderately (fewer than four drinks on a given occasion). Alcohol-dependent patients are often physically dependent on alcohol and undergo withdrawal on abstinence. They frequently suffer severe medical and social consequences such as cirrhosis of the liver, GI bleeds, divorce or job loss.

Assessment

Once a patient is suspected of having a drinking problem a comprehensive assessment is indicated, in order to:

* determine its severity and distinguish problem drinking from alcohol dependence (see Table 6)
* identify psychosocial problems that may require intervention
* identify potentially treatable medical and psychiatric conditions. The assessment process is described in more detail in Section 1.2.

Distinguishing problem drinking from alcohol dependence

This distinction is important because the two groups may require quite different treatment approaches. Whereas the problem drinker often responds to simple advice and brief counselling emphasizing strategies to reduce drinking, the alcohol-dependent patient usually requires more intensive treatment with abstinence as a treatment goal.

TABLE 6: Problem Drinking Versus Severe Dependence

Indication	Problem drinker	Alcohol-dependent
Withdrawal symptoms†	No	Often
Amount consumed	More than 14/week (M) More than 9/week (F)	More than 40–60/week
Drinks moderately (fewer than 4/day)	Often	Rarely
Social consequences††	Nil or mild	Often severe
Physical consequences†††	Nil or mild	Often severe
Socially stable	Usually	Often not
Neglect of major responsibilities	No	Yes

† The presence of withdrawal symptoms (tremor, morning relief drinking, seizures) should in almost all cases indicate a diagnosis of alcohol dependence.

†† Examples of mild social consequences include sporadic arguments with spouse, feeling fatigued at beginning of work week and spending less time with children. Severe consequences include threatened or actual loss of job or spouse.

††† Examples of mild physical consequences include hypertension, insomnia, fatty liver. Severe consequences include alcoholic hepatitis, GI bleeding.

110

3.7

BRIEF ADVICE PROTOCOL FOR PROBLEM DRINKERS

Meldon Kahan, MD, and Lynn Wilson, MD

A number of randomized trials have shown that physician interventions, ranging from five minutes of advice to several short counselling sessions assist in bringing about significant reductions in alcohol consumption among problem drinkers. The average reduction for male subjects is five to seven standard drinks per week, with seven to 18 per cent of subjects shifting from heavy to moderate drinking levels (Kahan, Wilson & Becker, 1995). While such reductions seem modest, they have enormous public health significance (Wallace, Cutler & Haines, 1988). One randomized trial demonstrated reductions in both hospital admissions and emergency room visits in problem drinkers receiving brief advice from their physicians (Fleming, Barry et al., 1997).

The protocol described below can be delivered in one or two sessions which may last five to 10 minutes each. Special expertise in alcohol counselling is not necessary. Physicians are also encouraged to use the Alcohol Risk Assessment and Intervention (ARAI) package, distributed by the College of Family Physicians of Canada.

INFORM PATIENTS ABOUT LOW-RISK DRINKING GUIDELINES
Included in Appendix 2 are information sheets that can be photocopied and given to patients.

SHOW PATIENTS WHERE THEIR CONSUMPTION FITS WITHIN NORTH AMERICAN NORMS
Detailed in Appendix 1 is North American epidemological information. Patients should be shown a table or graph of alcohol consumption by age and sex. This may be helpful as some patients have trouble accepting that they are drinking at hazardous levels because they do not drink more heavily than their peers.

111

OFFER INFORMATION ON THE HEALTH EFFECTS OF ALCOHOL

It is particularly helpful to relate patients' alcohol consumption to their own health problems, such as hypertension. The chronic sedative effects of alcohol should be mentioned (fatigue, depression, irritability and insomnia).

ADVISE PATIENTS ABOUT DRINKING AND DRIVING

Driving performance can be impaired at blood alcohol levels as low as 30 mg% (1.5 drinks in one hour for a man). The chance of a fatal motor vehicle accident doubles at a BAC of 50 mg% and quadruples at 80 mg% (2.5 and 4 drinks in one hour for a man, 2/3 that rate for a woman).

HAVE PATIENTS COMMIT TO A GOAL OF REDUCED DRINKING OR ABSTINENCE

The goal should be determined by patients, with some guidance by the physician. Patients should write the goals down and keep a copy available for review. Ideally, the goal should not exceed the recommended guidelines for low-risk drinking (no more than two drinks per day) (Ashley, Ferrence et al., 1997; Wilson, 1997). If patients feel that this is not a realistic goal, a more modest goal may be negotiated, aimed at avoiding overt intoxication and hazardous weekly consumption. For example, the ARAI guidelines recommend that males consume no more than four drinks per drinking occasion and females no more than three, at a rate of no more than one drink per hour (College of Family Physicians of Canada, 1994). Very heavy drinkers might find it easier to taper by 10 drinks per week until their goal is achieved.

The drinking goal should specify the maximum number of drinks to be consumed on a single occasion, the frequency of drinking and the situations in which drinking will take place. In general, patients should not drink at all in "high-risk" situations (i.e., situations in which they tend to consume large amounts of alcohol). For example, a patient may choose to have two drinks per night, three days per week, only at home, not at a bar.

IF A REDUCED DRINKING GOAL IS CHOSEN, ENSURE THAT THERE ARE NO CONTRAINDICATIONS TO DRINKING.

See table below for contraindications to drinking.

TABLE 7: Contraindications to Drinking

Physical	Social
• pregnancy • breastfeeding • active peptic ulcer or gastritis • cirrhosis of the liver • active alcoholic or viral hepatitis • pancreatitis.	Serious social consequences of any consumption (e.g, parole violation, spouse threatens separation).
Caution is required in medical conditions such as diabetes, coagulopathies, severe hypertension and seizure disorders. Alcohol can cause sedation when combined with antidepressants, benzodiazepines or opioids. It can also interact with other medications such as anticoagulants.	

REVIEW STRATEGIES TO AVOID INTOXICATION

The table below lists simple behavioral strategies designed to reduce patients' rate of alcohol consumption and avoid frank intoxication.

TABLE 8: Strategies to Avoid Intoxication

• On a drinking day, drink no more than one standard drink per hour, and no more than three drinks maximum.
• Start drinking later in the evening.
• Sip drinks, don't gulp.
• Avoid drinking on an empty stomach.
• Dilute drinks with mixer (carbonated mixers speed the absorption of alcohol and should be avoided if possible).
• Alternate alcoholic with non-alcoholic drinks.
• Place a 20-minute "time out" between the decision to drink and having a drink.

HAVE PATIENTS KEEP A DAILY RECORD OF THEIR ALCOHOL CONSUMPTION

Self-monitoring makes patients more conscious of their drinking habits, enables them to analyse their drinking patterns and triggers, and provides positive feedback for reduced drinking.

113

ORDER GGT AND MCV AT BASELINE AND FOLLOW-UP

These tests help convince patients that they are drinking at hazardous levels. They are also useful for monitoring treatment success and detecting relapse. Patients whose gamma GT decreases over time often feel pride at this evidence of their progress.

FOLLOW UP WITH REGULARLY SCHEDULED OFFICE VISITS OR PHONE CALLS

Research indicates that follow-up contact results in better treatment retention rates.

EXPLORE OTHER OPTIONS IF THE BRIEF ADVICE PROTOCOL FAILS

The physician should continue to use motivational interviewing strategies (see Section 2.5). Most jurisdictions offer treatment programs for problem drinkers. If a patient's alcohol use is causing substantial problems, referral for more intensive, abstinence-based treatment should be considered. Referral to other services may also be indicated, such as marital counselling or psychotherapy.

3.8

PHARMACOTHERAPY FOR ALCOHOL DEPENDENCE

Meldon Kahan, MD, and Lynn Wilson, MD

The identification of a neurochemical basis to alcohol and drug dependence has led to important new developments in pharmacotherapy. Despite advances, the practitioner should never view medication as the sole treatment for alcohol dependence, but as only one component of a comprehensive treatment program that includes mutual aid groups, formal treatment programs and ongoing counselling and medical care.

NALTREXONE (REVIA®)

Naltrexone, a competitive opioid antagonist, has been shown in several randomized trials to decrease the intensity and severity of binge drinking in alcohol-dependent patients engaged in formal treatment programs (Volpicelli, Alterman et al., 1992; O'Malley, Jaffe et al., 1992). It is not yet known whether non-dependent problem drinkers or patients not committed to formal treatment respond to naltrexone.

Action
The pleasurable effects of alcohol are due in part to activation of the endogenous opioid system in the brain. Naltrexone is a competitive inhibitor of endogenous opioid receptors, thus inhibiting alcohol's pleasurable effects and reducing alcohol craving. Patients often report that the reduced craving makes it easier for them to practise strategies learned in counselling.

Indications
Naltrexone is indicated as an adjunct to counselling in the treatment of alcohol dependence.

115

Dose

The standard dose is 50 mg per day. Patients who are concerned about side-effects may be started at lower doses (12.5 or 25 mg per day). Some experts recommend routinely starting at 25 mg for the first few days of treatment. The dose may be gradually increased to a maximum of 150 mg if there has been no response to the standard dose.

Duration of treatment

If no reduction in drinking occurs after four weeks on the medication, the physician should:

• Check for compliance.
• Consider more intensive counselling strategies.
• Consider a dosage increase or alternative pharmacotherapy such as disulfiram.

The effectiveness of treatment lasting more than six months has not yet been determined. Naltrexone may be discontinued after six months in patients who have a stable drinking pattern, are no longer experiencing cravings for alcohol and express confidence that they no longer need the medication. If patients are experiencing cravings or have occasional "slips," naltrexone may be continued for a longer period, accompanied by monthly reassessments and monitoring of liver transaminases.

Precautions and adverse effects

Naltrexone is generally well tolerated. It can cause mild nausea and GI upset. Anxiety and dizziness have also been reported.

Opioid withdrawal

Naltrexone renders opioid analgesics completely ineffective and will trigger a potentially severe opioid withdrawal syndrome in patients physically dependent on opioids. Patients who have been on daily opioid analgesics for two weeks or longer should discontinue the analgesics and wait seven to 10 days before starting naltrexone.

Patients with a high probability of physical dependence on opioids (e.g., patients taking heroin or high doses of potent opioids such as hydromorphone) should not receive naltrexone until they have discontinued their opioids for seven to 10 days and showed no signs of withdrawal after receiving naloxone 0.8 mg s.c. or 0.4 mg i.v.

Urgent requirement for analgesia

Patients should discontinue naltrexone three days prior to surgical procedures requiring opioid analgesics for postoperative pain control. Patients on naltrexone

116

who have an urgent requirement for analgesia should be treated with non-opioid agents if possible, such as regional anesthetics or benzodiazepine sedatives. The high doses of opioid analgesics required to overcome naltrexone blockade could cause respiratory depression. If opioid analgesia is absolutely essential, short-acting opioids with a lower risk of respiratory depression should be used. Consultation with an anesthetist is recommended.

Hepatotoxicity

Several studies have demonstrated improvement in liver enzymes in patients on naltrexone due to reductions in alcohol consumption (Volpicelli, Alterman et al., 1992; O'Malley, Jaffe et al., 1992). However, the long-term safety of using the medication to treat patients with alcoholic liver disease is not known, and patients with severe liver disease were excluded from these research trials. Naltrexone has been shown to cause reversible increases in hepatic transaminases at doses of 200–300 mg per day. The medication is contraindicated in patients with liver failure or acute hepatitis and should be used with careful monitoring in patients with any degree of liver disease.

The table below suggests a monitoring protocol for hepatotoxicity.

TABLE 9: Monitoring Protocol for Hepatic Transaminases

Baseline level	Action
< 1.5 times normal	Monthly monitoring for 3 months, less frequent monitoring thereafter
1.5–3 times normal	Repeat level in 2 weeks
> 3 times normal	Do not prescribe medication, repeat in 2 weeks
Elevated bilirubin	Do not prescribe medication

Drug interactions

Liver function should be carefully monitored when using naltrexone in combination with other potentially hepatotoxic medications (including disulfiram). Naltrexone should also be used with caution in patients who have chronic hepatitis B or C. In such patients naltrexone should be discontinued if it confers no clinical benefit or if elevations in transaminases are documented.

Alcohol withdrawal

Patients may go into unplanned withdrawal if they greatly decrease their alcohol consumption in response to naltrexone. To prevent this, patients should see their physician after a 12- to 24-hour period of abstinence. If they are in withdrawal, they should be treated with diazepam loading. The naltrexone may be started on completion of the loading.

Pregnancy

The safety of naltrexone use in pregnancy has not been established. Naltrexone should be prescribed during pregnancy only after careful consideration of the risks and benefits.

DISULFIRAM (ANTABUSE®)

Efficacy

The efficacy of disulfiram in prevention or limitation of relapse for alcohol dependence has not been demonstrated. One randomized trial found that disulfiram was no more effective than placebo or no treatment, although a subset of older, socially stable patients derived some benefit. Disulfiram may be helpful in highly motivated patients and in patients who agree to take the medication under supervision from a spouse or pharmacist (Fuller, Branchey et al., 1986).

Use in treatment

Patients should be maintained on the drug for at least four to six months, the length of time most patients need to establish a stable alcohol-free lifestyle. Disulfiram should be used in conjunction with counselling and a formal treatment program. The duration of action of disulfiram is seven days (range, two to 10). Patients should be warned to avoid medicines or food that contains alcohol.

Mechanism of action and associated risks

Disulfiram inactivates acetaldehyde dehydrogenase. The consumption of alcohol causes a build-up of toxic amounts of acetaldehyde, resulting in flushed face, headache, chest pain and vomiting. This reaction can last several hours. Most reactions are self-limiting, but occasionally they may be life-threatening, with myocardial infarction, dysrhythmias, hypotension, congestive heart failure and/or convulsions. The risk increases with the amount consumed, although fatalities have occurred after a single drink of alcohol. Patients with underlying coronary disease, cerebrovascular disease, severe pulmonary disease, seizure disorders, or those on anti-hypertensive medication are at greater risk of a severe reaction.

Side-effects

Side-effects include fatigue, impotence, peripheral neuropathy and exacerbation of depression. Disulfiram is contraindicated in patients with cirrhosis or severe alcoholic hepatitis because it can cause a toxic hepatitis. Measurement of liver transaminases is recommended at baseline, two weeks and every few months thereafter.

118

ACAMPROSATE

Acamprosate (biacetylhomotaurinate), an analogue of homocysteic acid, reduces neuronal excitability by attenuating the post-synaptic activity of excitatory amino acids such as glutamate. Neuronal hyperexcitablity may play an important role in alcohol craving, intoxication and withdrawal. In a two-year, multi-centre, randomized trial with 272 alcohol-dependent patients, acamprosate markedly increased the number of abstinent days, resulted in fewer dropouts and at the end of two years, more than twice the number of acamprosate patients remained abstinent as compared with those treated with placebo (Sass, Soyka et al., 1996).

R E F E R E N C E S

Andreasson, S., Allbeck, P. & Romelsjo, A. (1988). Alcohol and mortality among young men: Longitudinal study of Swedish conscripts. *British Medical Journal, 196,* 1021-1025.

Ashley, M.J., Ferrence, R., Room, R., Bondy, S., Rehm, J. & Single, E. (1997). Moderate drinking and health: Implications of recent evidence. *Canadian Family Physician, 43,* 687-694.

Bellentani, S., Saccoccio, G., Costa, G., Tiribelli, C., Manenti, F., Sodde, M., Saveria Croce, L., Sasso, F., Pozzato, G., Cristianini, G., Brandi, G. & the Dionysos Study Group. (1997). Drinking habits as cofactors of risk for alcohol induced liver damage. *Gut 41(6),* 845-850.

Brands, B., Sproule, B. & Marshman, J. (Eds.). (1998). *Drugs and Drug Abuse* (3rd ed.). Toronto: Addiction Research Foundation.

Canadian Centre on Substance Abuse (CCSA) and Addiction Research Foundation (ARF). (1994). *Canadian Profile: Alcohol, Tobacco and Other Drugs, 1994.* Ottawa: CCSA.

Canadian Centre on Substance Abuse and Addiction Research Foundation. (1997). *Canadian Profile: Alcohol, Tobacco and Other Drugs.* Ottawa and Toronto: Canadian Centre on Substance Abuse and Addiction Research Foundation.

Chedid, A., Mendenhall, C.L., Garside, P., French, S.W., Chen, T., & Rabin, L. (1991). Prognostic factors in alcoholic liver disease. *American Journal of Gastroenterology, 86(2),* 210-216.

College of Family Physicians of Canada. (1994). *Alcohol Risk Assessment and Intervention.* Mississauga, ON: College of Family Physicians of Canada.

Corrao, G., Arico, S., Zambon, A., Torchio, P. & Di Orio, F. (1997). Female sex and the risk of liver cirrhosis. *Scandinavian Journal Gastroenterology. 32(11),* 1174-1180.

Day, C.P., Bashir, R., James, O.F.W., Bassendine, M.F., Crabb, D.W., Thomasson, H.R., Li, T.K. & Edenberg, H.J. (1991). Investigation of the role of polymorphisms at the alcohol and aldehyde dehydrogenase loci in genetic predisposition to alcohol-related end-organ damage. *Hepatology, 14(5)*, 798-801.

Devenyi, P. & Saunders, S.J. (1986). *Physician's Handbook for Medical Management of Alcohol- and Drug-Related Problems* (1st ed.). Toronto: Addiction Research Foundation and Ontario Medical Association.

English, D., Holman, D., Milne, E., Winter, M., Hulse, G. & Codde, G. (1995). *The Quantification of Drug Caused Morbidity and Mortality in Australia.* Canberra: Commonwealth Department of Human Services and Health.

Fleming, M.F. & Barry, K.L. (Eds.). (1992). *Addictive Disorders.* St. Louis, MO: Mosby Year Book.

Fleming, M.F., Barry, K.L., Manwell, L.B., Johnson, K. & London, R. (1997). Brief physician advice for problem alcohol drinkers. *Journal of the American Medical Association, 177,* 1039-1045.

Fuller, R.K., Branchey, L., Brightwell, D.R., Derman, R.M., Emrick, C.D., Iber, F.L., James, K.E., Lacoursiere, R.B., Lee, K.K., Lowenstam, I. (1986). Disulfiram treatment of alcoholism. A Veterans Administration cooperative study. *Journal of the American Medical Association, 256(11),* 1449-1455.

Grant, B.F., Dufour, M.C. & Harford, T.C. (1998). Epidemiology of liver disease. *Seminars in Liver Disease, 8(1),* 12-25.

Heart and Stroke Foundation of Canada. (1995). *Heart Disease and Stroke in Canada 1995.* Ottawa: Heart and Stroke Foundation of Canada.

Israel, Y. & Orrego, H. (1987). Hypermetabolic state, hepatocyte expansion, and liver blood flow: An interaction triad in alcoholic liver injury. *Annals of the New York Academy of Sciences, 492,* 303-323.

Juvela, S., Hillbom, M. & Palomaki, H. (1995). Risk factors for spontaneous intracerebral hemorrhage. *Stroke, 26(9),* 1558-1564.

Kahan, M., Wilson, L. & Becker, L. (1995). Effectiveness of physician-based interventions with problem drinkers: A review. *Canadian Medical Association Journal, 152(6),* 851-859.

Kahan, M. (1996). Identifying and managing problem drinkers. *Canadian Family Physician, 42,* 661-671.

Kalvik, A., Isaac P. & Janecek E. (1995). Benzodiazepines: Treatment of anxiety, insomnia and alcohol withdrawal. *Pharmacy Connection.* September/October, 20-34.

Kato, I. & Nomura, A.M. (1994). Alcohol in the aetiology of upper aerodigestive tract cancer. *European Journal of Cancer. Part B, Oral Oncology, 30B(2),* 75-81.

Lebrec, D., Poynard, T., Capron, J.P., Hillon, P., Geoffroy, P., Roulot, D., Chaput, J.C., Rueff, B. & Benhamou, J.P. (1988). Nadolol for prophylaxis of gastrointestinal bleeding in patients with cirrhosis. A randomized trial. *Journal of Hepatology, 7(1),* 118-125.

Lieber, C. (1996). Alcohol-related liver disease. In W. Maddrey (Ed.), Gastroenterology and Hepatology, the comprehensive visual reference, *Current Medicine,* 1, 9.1-9.21.

Lowenstein, S.R. & Hunt, D. (1990). Injury prevention in primary care. *Annals of Internal Medicine, 113(4),* 261-263.

MacMahon, S. (1987). Alcohol consumption and hypertension. *Hypertension, 9,* 111-121.

Mergener, K. & Baillie, J. (1998). Acute pancreatitis. *British Medical Journal, 316(7124),* 44-48.

Mezey, E. (1991). Interaction between alcohol and nutrition in the pathogenesis of alcoholic liver disease. *Seminars in Liver Disease, 11(4),* 340-348.

Miotto, K., Compton, P., Ling, W. & Conolly, M. (1996). Diagnosing addictive disease in chronic pain patients. *Psychosomatics, 37(3),* 223-235.

O'Malley, S.S., Jaffe, A.J. Chang, G., Scottenfeld, R.S., Meyer, R.E. & Rounsaville, B. (1992). Naltrexone and coping skills therapy for alcohol dependence. *Archives of General Psychiatry, 49,* 881-887.

Orrego, H., Blake, J.E., Blendis, L.M., Compton, K.V. & Israel, Y. (1987). Longterm treatment of alcoholic liver disease with propylthiouracil. *New England Journal of Medicine, 317(23),* 1421-1427.

Pikaar, N.A., Wedel, M., van der Beek, E.J., van Dokkum, W., Kempen, H.J., Kluft, C., Ockhuizen, T. & Hermus, R.J. (1987). Effects of moderate alcohol consumption on platelet aggregation, fibrinolysis, and blood lipids. *Metabolism, 36(6),* 538-543.

Ramond, M.J., Poynard, T., Rueff, B., Mathurin, P., Theodore, C., Chaput, J.C. & Benhamou, J.P. (1992). A randomized trial of prednisolone in patients with severe alcoholic hepatitis. *New England Journal of Medicine, 326(8),* 507-512.

Rimm, E., Klatsky, A., Grobbe, D. & Stampfer, M. (1996). Review of moderate alcohol consumption and reduced risk of coronary disease: Is the effect due to beer, wine, or spirits? *British Medical Journal, 312,* 731-736.

Sadowski, D.C. (1997). Use of octreotide in the acute management of bleeding esophageal varices. *Canadian Journal of Gastroenterology, 11(4),* 339-343.

Sass, H., Soyka, M., Mann, K. & Ziegelgansberger, W. (1996). Relapse prevention by acamprosate: Results from a placebo-controlled study on alcohol dependence. *Archives of General Psychiatry, 53(8),* 673-680.

Single, E., Robson, L., Xie, X. & Rehm, J. (1996). *The Costs of Substance Use in Canada.* Ottawa: Canadian Centre on Substance Abuse.

Skinner, H.A. (1990). Spectrum of drinkers and intervention opportunities. *Canadian Medical Association Journal, 143(10),* 1054-1059.

Smith, J.W. (1995). Medical manifestations of alcoholism in the elderly. *The International Journal of the Addictions, 30(13-14),* 1749-1798.

Smith-Warner, S.A., Spiegelman, D., Yaun, S.S., van den Brandt, P.A., Folsom, A.R., Goldbohm, R.A., Graham, S., Holmberg, L., Howe, G.R., Marshall, J.R., Miller, A.B., Potter, J.D., Speizer, F.E., Willett, W.C., Wolk, A. & Hunter, D.J. (1998). Alcohol and breast cancer in women: a pooled analysis of cohort studies. *Journal of the American Medical Association, 279(7),* 535-540.

Transport Canada. (1987). *Smashed.* Ottawa: Road Safety and Motor Vehicle Regulation Directorate, Transport Canada.

Tuyns, A.J. & Peuignot, G. (1984). Greater risk of ascitic cirrhosis in females in relation to alcohol consumption. *International Journal of Epidemiology, 13(1),* 53-57.

U.S. Department of Health and Human Services. (1993). *Eighth Special Report to the U.S. Congress on Alcohol and Health from the Secretary of Health and Human Services, September 1993.* Washington, DC: National Institute of Health, National Institute on Alcohol Abuse and Alcoholism, NIH Publication No. 94-3699.

Volpicelli, J.R., Alterman, A.I., Hayashida, M. & O'Brien, C.P. (1992). Naltrexone in the treatment of alcohol dependence. *Archives of General Psychiatry, 49,* 876-880.

Wallace, P., Cutler, S. & Haines, A. (1988). Randomized controlled trial of general practitioner intervention in patients with excessive alcohol consumption. *British Medical Journal, 297,* 663-668.

Williams, B., Chang, K. & Truong, M.V. (1992). *Ontario Profile, 1992: Alcohol and Other Drugs.* Toronto: Addiction Research Foundation.

Wilson, L. (1997). Moderate drinking. *Canadian Family Physician, 43,* 592-594.

Zakhari, S. (1994). Moderate drinking and the cardiovascular system: Risk factors. *Contemporary Drug Problems, 21,* 25-44.

Nicotine

4.1 TOBACCO AND CANADIANS

4.2 TOBACCO USE AS AN ADDICTION

4.3 HUMAN PHARMACOLOGY OF NICOTINE

4.4 SMOKING CESSATION TECHNIQUES

4.5 PHARMACOTHERAPY

REFERENCES

ADDENDUM: "GUIDE YOUR PATIENTS TO A SMOKE-FREE FUTURE"

TABLES AND FIGURES

4.1

TOBACCO AND CANADIANS

Richard C. Frecker, MD, PhD

As smoking is, in the broadest sense, a public health issue, it is important to maintain a perspective on the variety of ways smoking affects whole societies, as well as the individuals within them. To provide some of that perspective, we include the following information about smoking and Canadian society.

PREVALENCE

Canadians are among the heaviest per capita tobacco consumers in the world. In 1994, 6.5 million smokers consumed an average of 17.7 cigarettes per day, for a yearly total of about 6,500 cigarettes each — in aggregate, a yearly individual dose some 100 times the mean lethal dose for humans.

The prevalence of cigarette smoking in Canada has gradually declined since the mid-1960s when 61 per cent of males and 38 per cent of females over the age of 15 smoked regularly. Important regional differences also exist in smoking prevalence among the provinces. In 1994, the prevalence of smoking in Canada nationally was 31 per cent (males 32 per cent, females 29 per cent). Prince Edward Island had the highest prevalence of current smokers (39 per cent), followed by Quebec (38 per cent). British Columbia had the lowest prevalence (25 per cent) while Ontario had a prevalence of 28 per cent.

Factors that promote smoking, especially among youths, include the extremely rapid onset of effects through inhalation (faster than by intravenous injection of comparable doses of nicotine), the long latency of harmful physical consequences and the availability of tobacco products. That said, the balance of social opinion is strongly against smoking and there is a high level of public awareness of the serious consequences of prolonged and regular use of tobacco.

CONSEQUENCES

The annual cost of cardiovascular disease, cancer and respiratory disease to Canadian society is staggering — an estimated $33 billion. Of this, $12.3 billion per year is attributable to smoking. Smoking-related illnesses generate between 5 and 8 per cent of the cost of medical prescriptions. In addition to the direct costs of treating illness, costs arise from absenteeism, accidents and fires. Another more conservative estimate of the annual economic costs of tobacco use in Canada has been calculated at $9.56 billion, or $336 per capita.

The use of nicotine, the primary psychoactive substance in tobacco, is not without hazard, especially to the cardiovascular system. Yet the primary danger to health due to both smoking and exposure to environmental tobacco smoke is represented by the inhalation of thousands of by-products of partially combusted tobacco, many of which are proven carcinogens, pro-carcinogens and potent enzyme inducers. Carbon monoxide can further compromise impaired cardiovascular function, and it plays a role in fetal growth retardation.

Adverse consequences of long-term use

In Canada, approximately 40,000 deaths each year are attributable to tobacco smoking. This represents 33 per cent of all deaths from cardiovascular disease, 83 per cent of deaths from lung cancer and more than 90 per cent of deaths from chronic obstructive lung disease (COPD). Mortality from lung cancer in women now exceeds mortality from breast cancer. This heavy loss of life is compounded by significant morbidity prior to death.

Smoking and pregnancy

Women who smoke during pregnancy have smaller babies: the risk of having a baby weighing less than 2,500 grams is increased by more than twice in mothers who smoke compared with non-smokers. Heavy smokers have a higher risk of having a low birthweight infant than do lighter smokers. Cessation of smoking during pregnancy is associated with decreased risk of having a low birthweight infant.

Environmental tobacco smoke

Environmental tobacco smoke — the smoke exhaled by the smoker plus the smoke that escapes from the cigarette ember — has been declared a Group A carcinogen in the United States. Persons in the immediate environment may inhale this smoke (passive smoking), which has been proven to have harmful effects on health. Some 300 lung cancer deaths a year in *non-smoking* Canadians are estimated to arise from the inhalation of other persons' tobacco smoke.

4.2

TOBACCO USE AS AN ADDICTION

Richard C. Frecker, MD, PhD

DEFINING TOBACCO ADDICTION

There is a decreasing emphasis on the purely pharmacological nature of addiction. Both tolerance (the need to increase dose to produce the same effects) and physical dependence (manifested by the appearance of a withdrawal syndrome following cessation of drug use) have traditionally been the pharmacological hallmarks of addiction. The following, more contemporary definition of addiction has been proposed in a report by the Royal Society of Canada (1989)*:

> Drug addiction is a strongly established pattern of behaviour characterized by (1) the repeated self-administration of a drug in amounts which reliably produce reinforcing effects, and (2) great difficulty in achieving voluntary long-term cessation of such use, even when the user is strongly motivated to stop.

The Society goes on to say:

> Cigarette smoking can, and frequently does, meet all the criteria for the proposed definition of addiction:
>
> i) It is used regularly (usually many times a day) by the majority of users, and most of those who experiment with cigarette smoking become regular daily smokers.
>
> ii) The amounts and patterns of use by regular smokers are in most cases sufficient to maintain pharmacologically significant blood levels of nicotine throughout most of the day.

*Reprinted with permission from *Tobacco, Nicotine and Addiction: A Committee Report Prepared at the Request of the Royal Society of Canada for the Health Protection Branch, Health and Welfare Canada*, Copyright 1989, Royal Society of Canada.

iii) Such nicotine levels have been shown to produce a variety of effects on the brain, altering chemical and electrophysiological aspects of brain function and producing subjective effects that the smoker recognizes, differentiates from those of other drugs and usually finds pleasurable.

iv) Sudden cessation of smoking gives rise to a withdrawal syndrome which can be alleviated by the administration of nicotine. Other drugs that act on nicotine receptors in the brain also modify smoking patterns.

v) In experimental studies, both laboratory animals and humans will expend considerable effort to self-inject nicotine intravenously in a manner similar to that shown in studies of heroin, cocaine and other drugs that are generally regarded as addicting; i.e., the effects of nicotine are clearly reinforcing.

vi) Regular cigarette smokers have great difficulty in giving up smoking, even when motivated to do so by the occurrence of respiratory, cardiovascular or other diseases caused or aggravated by smoking. Relapse rates among those who do stop smoking are high. The urge to smoke, among those who are also heavy users of alcohol or other drugs, is, in over 50% of cases, as strong as, or stronger than, the urge to use these other substances.

vii) Although much less evidence is available concerning other forms of tobacco use, including cigars and pipes, snuffs, and chewing tobacco, they are capable of giving rise to plasma nicotine concentrations as high as, or higher than, those achieved by cigarette smokers, though somewhat more slowly. The risk of addiction to these forms of tobacco use therefore warrants further study.

The Society concludes by recommending that patterns of cigarette use meeting the criteria set out above be regarded as nicotine addiction. Their analysis of tobacco smoking clearly puts it in the realm of a complex biopsychosocial phenomenon in which genetics, psychology, pharmacology and environment all interact to produce a tenacious pattern of drug use that is associated with proven and serious health consequences and extracts a heavy personal and social cost.

FAGERSTRÖM TEST FOR NICOTINE DEPENDENCE

Several questionnaires have been developed to assess the degree of tolerance to nicotine. The Fagerström Test for Nicotine Dependence, reproduced below, is a clinical measure of the degree of tolerance to nicotine and is used in predicting those who are likely to suffer significant withdrawal and those who may benefit from nicotine replacement or other pharmacotherapy. It comprises six questions that are scored zero to three. In general, a score of more than six out of 10 (the maximum) is taken to indicate significant dependence.

TABLE 1: Fagerström Test for Nicotine Dependence†

Questions	Answers	Points
How soon after you wake up do you smoke your first cigarette?	Within 5 minutes 6–30 minutes 31–60 minutes After 60 minutes	3 2 1 0
Do you find it difficult to refrain from smoking in places where it is forbidden (e.g., in church, at the library, in the cinema)?	Yes No	1 0
Which cigarette would you hate most to give up?	The first one in the morning All others	1 0
How many cigarettes a day do you smoke?	10 or fewer 11–20 21–30 31 or more	0 1 2 3
Do you smoke more frequently during the first hours after waking than during the rest of the day?	Yes No	1 0
Do you smoke if you are so ill that you are in bed most of the day?	Yes No	1 0
SCORE		

† Reproduced with permission. Copyright 1991 K.-O. Fagerström.

4.3

HUMAN PHARMACOLOGY OF NICOTINE

Richard C. Frecker, MD, PhD

PHYSIOLOGICAL EFFECTS

Pure nicotine (base) is a volatile, oily liquid that varies in color depending on its state of oxidation. Nicotine is a weak base. Figures given for its pK_a range from 8.0 (aqueous solution at 25°C) to 8.5.

The physiological effects of nicotine include small increases in heart rate, blood pressure, respiration and motor activity. Depending on the dose and circumstances of use, it may produce a range of behavioral effects, from mild stimulation and euphoria to relaxation, anxiety reduction and sedation.

For the non-smoker, a few inhaled puffs (200–300 μg of nicotine) may result in dizziness, headache, sweating, nausea, abdominal cramps and possibly vomiting or weakness. The smoke itself may produce coughing or gagging. In regular smokers, these symptoms abate with continued use as tolerance develops to the autonomic effects of the drug (such as heart rate) and certain subjective effects.

In the regular user, nicotine produces mild euphoria (or a feeling of well-being), increased arousal, enhanced ability to concentrate, relaxation and a temporary reduction in the urge to smoke. The exact mechanisms underlying the positive effects on mood remain to be elucidated, but activation (by direct or indirect means) of norepinephrine and mesolimbic dopamine may be involved. Even in established users, nicotine causes a mild increase in heart rate and blood pressure, constriction of peripheral blood vessels and lowering of skin temperature. It is also reported to decrease appetite, increase metabolic rate and lower body weight set point — effects which are sometimes sought by users for weight control and may explain part of the weight gain (often transient) experienced by many abstaining smokers.

ROUTES OF ADMINISTRATION AND DOSAGE

The usual route of administration is by smoking. When acidic tobacco cigarette smoke is inhaled, nicotine is absorbed rapidly across the membranes lining the alveoli of the lungs. However, because of the more alkaline pH of cigar and pipe smoke, nicotine from these sources is also absorbed through the membranes of the mouth and upper respiratory tract. The drug can also be absorbed through the membranes of the mouth from chewing tobacco or wet snuff and through the lining of the nose when dry snuff is used. Therapeutically, nicotine may be administered through the buccal mucosa (lining of the mouth) from nicotine polacrilex resin *(gum)*, or through the skin using a transdermal *nicotine patch* which has been designed to permit slow absorption through the intact skin.

Variables affecting absorbed dose

The combustion of tobacco produces smoke which is composed of a gas and a particulate phase. The particulate phase is the solid component of tobacco smoke that is trapped in the filters of smoking machines. The gas phase passes through these filters. Tar is the portion of the particulate phase with nicotine and water removed. Tar is formed during the combustion of tobacco products and is not present in unburned tobacco. When a cigarette is puffed, the smoker inhales mainstream smoke that passes through the cigarette. This is the main source of nicotine and other compounds for the smoker. Side-stream smoke is emitted from the end of the burning cigarette.

A smoker who uses one pack of 20 cigarettes per day will take into the body between 1.8 and 26.8 mg of nicotine (typically 16 to 20 mg), between 24 and 428 mg of tar and between 34 and 789 mg of carbon monoxide.

The actual amounts of smoke constituents reaching the bloodstream, within these wide ranges, may differ considerably from the figures reported. This is determined by the following factors: (1) the type of tobacco; (2) whether or not there is a filter; (3) the type and effectiveness of the filter; (4) the number of puffs per cigarette and the depth of inhalation; (5) the proportion of the cigarette smoked prior to its being extinguished; and, (6) the manner in which the cigarette is smoked (e.g., with low-tar/low-nicotine cigarettes, if smokers cover the small air holes in the filter with their fingers, the nicotine yield increases to a level approaching that of a regular cigarette).

Usual dose from cigarettes

A typical cigarette contains 10 to 15 mg of nicotine. However, when it is smoked in the usual manner, about 1 mg reaches the bloodstream. Yields of nicotine for different brands of cigarettes range from less than 0.1 mg to as much as 1.4 mg

131

per cigarette (constituent yields are determined under highly controlled conditions of machine smoking). Tar yields per cigarette, which correlate highly with nicotine yields, vary between 1.2 and 23.4 mg per cigarette. Different cigarettes also produce between 1.7 and 39.1 mg of carbon monoxide, a poisonous gas that impairs the oxygen-carrying capacity of the blood. Tar contributes to debilitating lung disease when chronically inhaled and contains a large number of compounds known to cause cancer in a variety of organs.

Measures of exposure

The most common measure of exposure is *number of cigarettes* smoked per day. Because of the highly variable way individuals smoke and the variety of cigarettes on the market, there is relatively poor correlation between this figure (which may range from five or 10 through 40 or more cigarettes per day) and more quantitative measures. The most accurate measure of exposure is plasma nicotine or cotinine concentration taken in the later afternoon after a regular day of smoking. Nicotine and cotinine can also be measured in saliva and urine. Terminal alveolar carbon monoxide concentrations are easy and relatively inexpensive to measure in a clinical setting and provide a useful check on self-reported smoking. Levels range from zero parts per million (ppm) in a very clean environment to baseline (non-smoking) values of seven to 10 ppm in a typical urban setting to 70 or 80 ppm in regular heavy smokers. The measurement should be done within 10 to 20 minutes after smoke was last inhaled.

Toxicology

Death directly attributable to nicotine overdose (especially as tobacco) has been reported in the past. Infants, young children and adults have been known to suffer toxic doses of nicotine through the ingestion of cigarettes and other sources of nicotine. The absorption of nicotine through the skin leading to toxic effects has also been documented. Gastric absorption is poor; acute ingestion induces vomiting through central mechanisms and nicotine absorbed from the intestinal tract is largely eliminated from the body by passage through the liver (high first-pass extraction).

The estimated lethal dose in non-tolerant adults is estimated to be about 60 mg, but much smaller amounts (2–5 mg) can cause nausea and vomiting. A few drops (0.6–0.9 mg/kg) of pure nicotine taken orally can be lethal to humans. Fatal overdose is associated with nausea, salivation, abdominal pain, sweating, headache and dizziness. Blood pressure falls and breathing becomes difficult. Death is from respiratory paralysis and may be associated with convulsions. Treatment involves gastric lavage and the infusion of activated charcoal, with support of respiration and management of shock.

Abuse liability

Nicotine is a powerful drug of addiction with a high degree of abuse liability. A significant number of those who start smoking cigarettes in their teenage years become regular, often lifelong, users. Many factors promote the initiation of smoking, including smoking by friends and family, the urge to experiment, attitudes towards smoking, academic expectations, rejection of established authority, risk taking and peer pressure. The development of tolerance to the initial negative physical effects, the early discernment of positively reinforcing effects (euphoria, stimulation, relaxation, stress reduction) and, finally, the experience of withdrawal effects during attempted cessation all act to ensure continued use.

Withdrawal syndrome

Abrupt withdrawal from regular tobacco use typically results in a withdrawal syndrome that may intensify for three to four days and persist for a week or sometimes much longer. The first symptoms to appear include irritability, restlessness, anxiety, insomnia, fatigue, lack of concentration and strong urges to smoke (cravings). The latter two symptoms may persist for weeks to months. Factors that work against successful long-term cessation include lack of personal motivation, lack of a clear strategy for quitting which includes behavioral and, where appropriate, pharmacological support, and the return to former smoking situations or relationships.

4.4

SMOKING CESSATION TECHNIQUES

Richard C. Frecker, MD, PhD

GENERAL PRINCIPLES

The busy physician needs to provide optimal and cost-effective treatment and is not always attracted to lengthy individualized therapies for smoking cessation. However, it is important to realize that 70 per cent of the general population visit their family physician each year, and in a two-year period that proportion rises to 90 per cent. The physician is, therefore, ideally situated to identify patients who are smokers and encourage them to quit. Encouragement can take many forms. It has been proven that a physician's brief advice to quit can be effective in initiating a cessation attempt. It is also useful to tie the consequences of continued smoking to a given presenting complaint (respiratory infection), symptom (cough or chest pain) or sign (altered breath sounds or hypertension). A good time to broach the matter is in the context of a lifestyle assessment.

MOTIVATING PATIENTS — STAGES OF CHANGE MODEL

When a patient is motivated to stop smoking, a number of general behavioral principles should be observed. A helpful conceptual framework is the stages of change model of Prochaska and DiClemente (1982) (see also Section 2.5). The patient is seen to be in a revolving continuum of change, starting with a state where there is no thought of quitting (precontemplation), through a state of active consideration (contemplation) when frequently risks and benefits are considered and various approaches to quitting are weighed. In the third or action phase of change, a cessation attempt is initiated, with initial success. Success may be long term, or relapse may occur and the client (after a variable time lag) re-enters the change cycle at the beginning or some point along its way. This model is useful because it allows the physician to see movement from any stage to another towards cessation as therapeutic success. This includes the frequent event of relapse, which can be seen as a useful learning experience. The patient may also be encouraged in his or her struggle towards sustained cessation in a positive way.

QUITTING VERSUS CUTTING DOWN

For the vast majority of smokers, abstinence appears to be the only reasonable treatment goal. While a small percentage (less than 5 per cent) of smokers appear able to smoke on an occasional basis, the average smoker consumes almost 20 cigarettes every day. Of those who quit successfully, even for many months, and start to use occasionally, almost all become regular heavy users once again.

QUITTING ON ONE'S OWN

It is claimed that as many as 90 per cent of smokers who are abstinent have quit "on their own." While this may have been accurate before the advent of nicotine replacement (see below), nicotine gum and the transdermal nicotine patch have given pharmacotherapy a definite edge, especially when combined with appropriate behavioral support. Abstinence rates at one year after quitting with no pharmacological or behavioral support range between 3 and 5 per cent. With comprehensive pharmacological and behavioral support for cessation, abstinence rates between 15 and 20 per cent are regularly reported, while an occasional well-controlled trial will yield results as high as 35 per cent at one year.

WINDOWS OF OPPORTUNITY

A positive non-guilt-inducing approach is most appropriate and should build on "windows of opportunity." These may be defined as circumstances or life events that sharpen the patient's focus on cessation, increase motivation to quit or provide a more supportive environment in which to quit. Such triggers to quit may include an episode of personal illness, the sickness or death of a loved one (associated with smoking), entering into a new personal relationship with a non-smoker or changing a job (especially to a non-smoking environment). Motivation to quit may relate to concerns about personal health, concern for the effects of smoking on loved ones (children or significant others), saving money, inconsistency with one's self-image (perception of being addicted or an addict), issues of locus of control and so forth. The alert physician can take these opportunities to underline the positive benefits of stopping smoking.

BEHAVIORAL TECHNIQUES

Several behavioral techniques have been employed in support of cessation attempts, many of which take the form of simple behavior modification. The essence of this technique is to suggest to the abstinent smoker a variety of diversions or coping tactics to use when experiencing the urge to smoke. Diversions may include stopping to think about what one is going to do: waiting 10 seconds (even if the cigarette is lit), making the decision to smoke a conscious rather than an automatic act, and remembering that one puff of a cigarette is just that until another has been taken (i.e., that one can stop at any point along the way). Frequently the acute urge to smoke will pass quickly. In the meantime, it may be helpful to move away from the smoking crowd, go to another room or move outdoors, or engage in a minor distracting activity (drink a glass of water, take a deep breath, talk to another person, take a brief walk, etc.). Another key feature of successful smoking cessation is to meet changing patient needs during an evolving course of treatment, possibly with changing treatment strategies.

A practical tool to aid busy physicians engaged in smoking cessation treatment is *Guide Your Patients to a Smoke-Free Future* (Canadian Council on Smoking and Health, 1994; see addendum). It provides a step-by-step overview of the program. This reference sheet offers suggestions for busy practitioners who have less than three minutes to discuss smoking with their patients.

UNPROVEN AND UNCONVENTIONAL METHODS

A variety of methods have been employed for smoking cessation for which no proof of efficacy over placebo exists in the scientific literature. These include mouthwashes or lozenges which change oral pH, leading to mild taste aversion, timing devices that monitor then disrupt smoking patterns by alternate cueing, and nicotine-free cigarettes to satisfy handling needs. The efficacy of hypnosis to motivate change is not clearly supported in the literature. While there is a possible therapeutic benefit of placebo or expectancy effects, given the more subtle and often unidentified reinforcers of abstinence that may exist in a caring treatment milieu, scientific support is required before more than casual use of such modalities can be recommended.

Acupuncture

Classical needle acupuncture has been reported as effective in some well-designed studies. However, it is important not to equate laser acupuncture performed with "cool lasers" as equivalent to needle acupuncture. There is no support from well-designed and well-conducted clinical trials to suggest the efficacy of these low-level lasers, which typically operate in the visible red region of the electromagnetic spectrum at irradiance levels below 1 mW/cm2. Such levels have not been demonstrated to result in detectable thermal or abiotic effects and are not known to modulate endorphins as some of the promotional literature claims.

4.5

PHARMACOTHERAPY

Richard C. Frecker, MD, PhD

NICOTINE REPLACEMENT

Nicotine, as it occurs naturally in tobacco, has no present medical or therapeutic use, though pure nicotine delivered in small doses has been used as an adjunct in the treatment of nicotine addiction. Compounds derived from or related to nicotine may prove to have therapeutic application in the future. The therapeutic use of nicotine for smoking cessation should be adjunctive to a program incorporating behavioral support components (individual and/or group).

Nicotine polacrilex resin (gum)

Pure nicotine has been available for therapeutic purposes for more than 10 years in Canada in the form of a chewable polacrilex resin (gum) under the trade name Nicorette®. It is available in forms containing 2 mg and 4 mg of nicotine. The 2 mg formulation is now available over the counter in Canada. For a given strength, the amount absorbed into the body depends on the pattern and duration of chewing. An appropriate technique has been specified by the manufacturer and basically involves a single "chew" followed by a period of "parking" the piece in the mouth. Too rapid chewing may lead to side-effects. The recommended maximum dose for the 4 mg polacrilex gum is 20 pieces per day, but most patients can be stabilized on 10 to 16 pieces during their first month of treatment. Treatment may be continued for as long as six months and the manufacturer recommends that the product be carried for up to three months after cessation to manage "overwhelming" urges to smoke. The 2 mg formulation is recommended for persons who are less tolerant as indicated by a score of six or less on the Fagerström tolerance questionnaire (see Table 1).

Transdermal nicotine

Since the early 1990s, nicotine patches (transdermal delivery systems) have become available from a number of manufacturers in North America. These

138

systems, while differing somewhat physiochemically and structurally, permit the absorption of small amounts of nicotine through the intact skin. The stated dose of a nicotine patch is that amount of nicotine expected to be absorbed into the bloodstream during a single application (16 or 24 hours, depending on the brand). Patches available in Canada designed to be worn day and night (24 hours) are Habitrol® (21 mg, 14 mg, 7 mg), and Nicoderm® (21 mg, 14 mg, 7 mg). One patch, Nicotrol® (15 mg, 10 mg, 5 mg), is designed to be worn only during waking hours (16 hours).

The patch is remarkably free from side-effects and its ease of use and proven efficacy have enhanced patient compliance. The most common side-effect is warmth or itch at the site of application, which should be rotated among seven or more sites. Some clinicians reserve patch treatment for persons who have relapsed from other treatment modalities, or until a heavy smoker has reduced his or her smoking to a pack a day. The best predictor of success appears to be motivation to quit, and a synergistic effect may exist between nicotine replacement and behavioral support.

A rough estimate of the dose required can be made by multiplying the number of cigarettes smoked and inhaled per day times the nicotine yield (marked on the package). In general, an established regular smoker will be started on the highest dose patch, observed for side-effects such as sleep disturbance or unpleasant dreams and weaned after each four-to-six-week period to the next lower dose, ultimately to zero. Smoking should be strongly discouraged during patch treatment, as much to extinguish smoking behavior as to avoid additive toxicological risk.

Nicotine aerosols

For some years, nicotine aerosols and sprays have been used both experimentally and therapeutically as aids to smoking cessation. While not available everywhere at the present time, their rapidity of action and the blood nicotine concentrations achieved make these products promising nicotine therapies. The comfort of use depends on a number of factors, including particle size and the physiochemical properties of the solution being aerosolized. Different methods of aerosol generation have been employed and particle sizes ranging from 0.1 to 5 microns have been reported in the scientific literature.

Safety of nicotine replacement

The question of safety often arises regarding nicotine replacement in pregnancy and in the presence of cardiovascular disease. Ideally, a woman contemplating pregnancy would have quit prior to conception. If a woman who smokes becomes pregnant and wishes to quit, the first approach should be non-pharmacological, with behavioral support of abrupt cessation or modestly rapid tapering to abstinence, depending on the severity of withdrawal experienced.

139

The nicotine patch may be used to support quitting, but the initial dose should be just sufficient to control withdrawal and the duration of treatment should be shorter than normal, with regular, ongoing behavioral support. In the case of cardiovascular disease, the literature suggests that the slowly rising and much lower levels of nicotine achieved through patch use are safer than continued smoking where much higher levels of nicotine are achieved in the coronary arteries just following inhalation (Gourlay & Benowitz, 1997). The inhalation of carbon monoxide will also further compromise oxygen-carrying capacity, which is undesirable, for example, in patients suffering from angina. In both situations concomitant smoking is strongly contraindicated.

POSSIBLE FUTURE THERAPEUTIC USES OF NICOTINE

Recently it has been suggested that the prevalence of Parkinson's disease and possibly the prevalence and severity of Alzheimer's disease may be lower in chronic smokers. This opens the possibility of an alternate therapeutic use for pure nicotine and has spurred the search for nicotine analogues that may be more specific and efficacious, while being less addictive and toxic, than nicotine itself.

OTHER PHARMACOTHERAPIES

Clonidine
Clonidine, an α-2 agonist, has a mitigating effect on the symptoms of acute nicotine withdrawal, apparently by reducing central sympathetic drive. It is not available in Canada as a transdermal patch (it is available in the United States), but the oral form may be used in incremental small doses (0.1 mg daily, up to a maximum of 0.5 mg, that may be given in two divided daily doses) for symptomatic relief. To avoid reactive hypertension the dose should be gradually tapered at the end of one to two weeks of administration. It is less efficacious than nicotine replacement for control of withdrawal and there is limited scientific support for long-term efficacy (abstinence rates at one year).

Other approaches
Various modulators of serotonin have been examined as pharmacological adjuncts for smoking cessation. The antidepressants fluoxetine (Prozac®) and sertraline (Zoloft®), and the 5-HT$_3$ agonist ondansetron (Zofran®) have not been found to be significantly superior to placebo in controlling acute nicotine withdrawal symptoms or in achieving long-term abstinence.

Among other antidepressants bupropion (Zyban®) has been shown in both immediate-release (300 mg; Ferry & Burchette, 1994) and sustained-release forms (300 mg; Hurt, Sachs et al., 1997) to have efficacy as a prescription drug for smoking cessation. The sustained-release form of bupropion is available for this indication in Canada, and since 1997 in the United States.

Bupropion acts by blocking dopamine and norepinephrine reuptake. It has been shown to relieve symptoms of nicotine withdrawal and to decrease the urge to smoke. Controlled trials suggest that it may be as effective as or more effective than the transdermal nicotine patch. Bupropion is initiated one to two weeks before the patient's intended quit date and maintained for two to three months. The initial dose is 150 mg od for three days, followed by 150 mg bid. It is contraindicated in patients with seizure disorders, a current or past history of bulimia or anorexia or patients taking MAO inhibitors or Wellbutrin®. Side-effects include insomnia and anxiety.

SUCCESSFUL CESSATION

Even with the aid of increasingly effective pharmocotherapies successful cessation most often occurs in established smokers when clear, personal reasons for quitting are present in a supportive environment, coupled to the availability of individual or group treatment. Reasons associated with successful attempts to quit often include concerns about risk to personal health or to that of family members, including the fetus, infants and young children. Successful cessation may also be associated with adopting a generally healthier lifestyle, the use of coping skills, the desire to take control (i.e., to no longer see oneself as an addict or controlled by smoking), the wish to save the money spent on tobacco and feeling confident and motivated with respect to quitting.

Dealing with relapse

Cessation attempts are characterized by relapse. A practical and humane therapeutic approach is to treat relapse as a learning event in which the predisposing factors may be identified and dealt with proactively in a subsequent cessation attempt. Inducing guilt in a patient has no part to play in treatment of nicotine addiction and positive reinforcement for incremental improvement and transient success are associated with positive outcomes.

PRIMARY PREVENTION

In the long term, the most cost-effective means of reducing the morbidity and mortality associated with cigarette smoking and other forms of tobacco use is primary prevention. A social climate in which this may be feasible and effective is evolving. Strategies may include education, legislative control of tobacco advertising and distribution, and taxation. The role of treatment will continue to

141

be prevention of progression and, regrettably, management of the tragic sequelae of chronic tobacco use. The physician is uniquely situated, through regular and extensive contact with the population of smokers, to have a major impact through education and support of patients' smoking cessation efforts.

R E F E R E N C E S

Canadian Council on Smoking and Health. (1994). *Guide Your Patients to a Smoke-Free Future.* Ottawa: Canadian Council on Smoking and Health.

Fagerström, K.-O. (1978). Measuring degree of physical dependence to tobacco smoking with reference to individualization of treatment. *Addictive Behaviors. 3(3-4)*, 235-241.

Ferry, L.H. & Burchette, R.J. (1994). Efficacy of bupropion for smoking cessation in non-depressed smokers [Abstract]. *Journal of Addictive Diseases, 13,* 249.

Gourlay, S.G. & Benowitz, N.L. (1997). Arteriovenous differences in plasma concentration of nicotine and catecholamines and related cardiovascular effects after smoking, nicotine nasal spray, and intravenous nicotine. *Clinical Pharmacology and Therapeutics, 62(4),*453-463.

Hurt R.D., Sachs, D.P.L., Glover, E.D., Offord, K.P., Johnston, J.A., Dale, L.C., Khayrallah, M.A., Schroeder, D.R., Glover, P.N., Sullivan, P., Croghan, I.T. & Sullivan, P.M. (1997). A comparison of sustained-release bupropion and placebo for smoking cessation. *New England Journal of Medicine, 337(17),* 1195-1202.

Prochaska, J.O. & DiClemente, C.C. (1982). Transtheoretical therapy: Toward a more inte-grative model of change. *Psychotherapy: Theory, Research, and Practice, 19(3),* 276-288.

Royal Society of Canada. (1989). *Tobacco, Nicotine, and Addiction: A Committee Report Prepared at the Request of the Royal Society of Canada for the Health Protection Branch, Health and Welfare Canada.* Ottawa: Royal Society of Canada.

Guide Your Patients to a Smoke-Free Future*

	PRECONTEMPLATION Not thinking about stopping	CONTEMPLATION Thinking about stopping in next 6 months	PREPARATION Planning to stop in next month	ACTION AND MAINTENANCE Have stopped smoking	SMOKING AGAIN Smoking regularly
WHEN YOU HAVE LESS THAN 3 MINUTES WITH A PATIENT TO DISCUSS SMOKING *You can choose from these suggestions.*	Label chart Ask, "How are you feeling about your smoking?"[1] Show that you understand patients' feelings.[2] Encourage patients to consider both the good things (pros) and not so good things (cons) about their smoking. Offer booklet	Label chart Ask, "What do you see as the pros and cons about stopping smoking?"[1] Reinforce patients' reasons for wanting to stop smoking.[3] Help patient identify more reasons for wanting to stop.[5] Provide booklet	Label chart and note stop smoking date "You have made an important decision."[3] Ask questions to determine nicotine dependence. Ask, "Have you decided what day you will stop?" Offer a longer visit within a few days of stop smoking date to discuss plan, especially if prescribing NRT. Provide booklet	Label chart Ask, "How are things going?"[1] Temptations? Slips? Normalize difficulties and provide encouragement and specific suggestions tailored to issues raised by patient.[3] Ask about NRT (if relevant). Offer follow-up visits or referral and continuing support. Provide booklet	Label chart Ask, "How are you feeling about stopping smoking?"[1] If discouraged, acknowledge feelings.[2] Advise that often people try several times and learn from experience with stopping before succeeding.[3] Offer to help when ready. Provide booklet Offer future visit to discuss further. RETURN TO APPROPRIATE STAGE

KEYS to EFFECTIVE COMMUNICATION

1. ASK OPEN-ENDED QUESTIONS: e.g., "How are you feeling about your smoking now?"
2. CONVEY UNDERSTANDING: e.g., "You seem concerned about the impact of your smoking on your daughter."
3. AFFIRM/ACKNOWLEDGE POSITIVELY: e.g., "Even though it's been stressful, you have been off cigarettes for two weeks; that is a major accomplishment."
4. SUMMARIZE THE KEY ISSUES: e.g., "On the one hand, smoking helps you cope with stress; on the other, you are worried about your health."
5. ENCOURAGE PATIENT TO FOCUS ON REASONS TO QUIT: e.g., "What is your most important reason for wanting to stop smoking?"

* Reprinted with permission. Copyright 1994, Canadian Council for Tobacco Control.

GUIDE YOUR PATIENTS TO A SMOKE-FREE FUTURE*
OVERALL STRATEGY

ADVISE: *"I am concerned about your smoking."* (relate to health status and risk)

ASK: *"Do you smoke?"* (all patients over 9 years of age)

YES | NO

"Good" – *"Have you ever smoked?"*

NO | YES

"When did you stop?"

<6 mo. | >6 mo.

"Are you interested in stopping smoking in the next 6 months?"

NO | YES

FOR ALL PATIENTS, PLACE LABEL OR WRITE IN VISIBLE LOCATION

ASK: *"Are you thinking about stopping in the next month?"*

NO | YES

PRECONTEMPLATION

GOAL: Help patients begin to think about stopping.

ASK: *"How are you feeling about your smoking?"*

ASK: *"How do you see the good things (pros) and not so good things (cons) about smoking?"* Convey that you understand what patient says.

ASSIST: Assure patients that you will not push stopping but want to help them understand both the pros and cons of their smoking.

Offer booklet.

CONTEMPLATION

GOAL: Help patients move toward a decision to stop in the near future.

ASK: *"How do you see the pros and cons of stopping smoking?"* Acknowledge the mixed feelings.

ADVISE: *"It's great that you are beginning to think about stopping."* Legitimize realities that patients raise about difficulties.

ASSIST: Reinforce motivation and encourage patients to focus on reasons for quitting.
Try cutting back or stopping for a day.
Provide booklet. If received before –
"Any questions?"

ARRANGE: Future visit if they want to discuss stopping smoking.

PREPARATION

GOAL: Help patients get ready and begin to use quitting skills.

ASK: *"What preparations are you making for stopping and what concerns do you have?"*

ASK: *"Are there things you can apply from previous attempts to stop smoking?"*

ADVISE: Identify barriers to stopping and elicit solutions. Encourage monitoring of smoking and scheduling of cigarettes.

ASSIST THROUGH:
- Booklet - review triggers and urges
- Action plan, e.g., realistic goals; plans for stress; lapses; rewards; and support
- Date set for stopping
- Nicotine replacement therapy (NRT) discussed, *"How much do you smoke and when is first cigarette of the day?"*
- Provide encouragement and support patients' ability to plan and stop.

ARRANGE: A follow-up visit shortly after stop smoking date. Refer to other services in the community for added support for change.

ACTION AND MAINTENANCE

GOAL: Help patients stay off tobacco and recover from slips and relapse.

ASK: *"How are you doing?"* If using NRT, check dosage and appropriate use. Ask about slips/temptations.

ADVISE: On issues raised by patient e.g., relapse prevention, weight gain, managing stressful situations. Characterize slips as learning opportunities.

ASSIST: Focus on successes and encourage the patient. Help patients reward themselves and set up helpful social supports. If patient discouraged, listen and counter with focus on successes.

ARRANGE: Future visits and referral as needed. Follow actively for 12 months.

IN CASE OF RELAPSE
i.e., back to smoking regularly:
FIND OUT PATIENT STAGE AND
CONTINUE

Sedative/ hypnotics

5.1 BARBITURATES AND OTHER SEDATIVE/HYPNOTICS

5.2 MANAGEMENT OF BENZODIAZEPINE DEPENDENCE AND WITHDRAWAL

5.1

BARBITURATES AND OTHER SEDATIVE/HYPNOTICS*

Meldon Kahan, MD

The use of barbiturates and other sedatives has been largely supplanted by the use of benzodiazepines. Fiorinal®, used in the treatment of migraine headaches, is the only barbiturate that is still frequently prescribed. Fiorinal® C ½ or Fiorinal® with codeine contains butalbital (50 mg), acetylsalicylic acid and codeine (30 mg). Fioricet® with codeine contains butalbital (50 mg), acetaminophen, and codeine (30 mg).

INTOXICATION

Barbiturates are central nervous system depressants. At low doses these drugs induce a state of relaxation and mild impairment of cognitive and motor functions. At moderate doses they induce sleep and cause a state of pleasurable intoxication. At high doses barbiturates can cause severe intoxication, coma and respiratory depression (see Table 1).

TOLERANCE

Tolerance can develop very rapidly to the sleep-inducing and mood effects of barbiturates, often within weeks of daily use. With regular use, partial tolerance to both impaired motor co-ordination and slowed reaction time appears to develop. There is a high degree of cross-tolerance among barbiturates and also between barbiturates and most other sedative/hypnotic drugs.

*Adapted from Devenyi & Saunders, 1986.

The principal toxic effect of barbiturates is respiratory depression. Tolerance to the respiratory-depressant effect develops much less rapidly than does tolerance to the psychic effects of barbiturates. Therefore the margin of safety between a lethal dose and a pleasure-producing dose decreases as the daily dose increases (Hardman, Limbird et al., 1996).

OVERDOSE

Generally, the lethal dose range is from 1 to 3 g for short-acting barbiturates (e.g., secobarbital, pentobarbital), and 5 g with the longer-acting barbiturates (e.g., phenobarbital). When used in combination with other CNS depressants such as alcohol, the lethal dose of barbiturates can be substantially lower. Acute barbiturate poisoning may be superimposed on chronic intoxication in the dependent person. These patients should be observed in the recovery phase for withdrawal.

TABLE 1: Clinical Manifestations of Acute and Chronic Barbiturate Intoxication

- lethargy
- hypotonia, dysmetria and decreased superficial reflexes
- vertigo
- ataxic gait with positive Rhomberg sign
- nystagmus, diplopia, strabismus
- slurred speech
- emotional lability

Sensation, deep tendon reflexes and pupillary reflexes are usually unaltered. The symptoms resemble those of alcohol intoxication.

WITHDRAWAL

If a chronically dependent individual stops taking the drug abruptly, there is risk of a severe and life-threatening withdrawal syndrome (Table 2). The syndrome is similar to alcohol withdrawal, though with a later onset and longer duration. As with alcohol withdrawal, barbiturate withdrawal can cause seizures, delirium, hallucinations, dysrhythmias and cardiovascular collapse.

TABLE 2: Symptoms and Signs of Barbiturate Withdrawal

Minor	Major
Onset typically 1–3 days after discontinuing sedative/hypnotics	Onset typically 2–3 days after discontinuing sedative/hypnotics (seldom occurs without preceding minor withdrawal symptoms)
Anxiety	Any or all of the signs or symptoms of minor withdrawal, plus:
Hyperreflexia	Seizures
Insomnia	Delirium
Muscle twitches	Psychosis
Restlessness	Dysrhythmias
Tremor	Hyperpyrexia
Diaphoresis	Cardiovascular collapse
Slight elevation of temperature	
Anorexia	
Nausea	
Vomiting	

Withdrawal seizures usually occur on the second or third day of withdrawal but may occur earlier or may be delayed to the seventh or eighth day. Unexplained seizures in adults should always prompt the physician to consider withdrawal from chronic barbiturate abuse. Urine and blood for drug screening will aid in making the diagnosis in patients who cannot or do not give a reliable history. Almost half of all patients who have seizures develop delirium and hyperpyrexia between the fourth to seventh day of withdrawal if not treated. The incidence of seizures, delirium and hyperpyrexia increases after continuous intoxication with large doses of barbiturates.

149

Benzodiazepines are ineffective in the management of barbiturate withdrawal seizures. Phenytoin is also ineffective and should be used only if there is a history of seizure disorder unrelated to drug abuse. Phenothiazines may lower the seizure threshold and should be avoided.

There are no reliable quantitative criteria to predict which patient is at risk of developing a severe withdrawal reaction. As a general guide, count on this risk in any patient who has taken the equivalent of 500 mg/day of a short- or intermediate-acting barbiturate (e.g., secobarbital or butalbital) for at least a month. Since histories are seldom clear-cut or reliable, gross over- as well as understatement of dosages may be reported.

Abrupt withdrawal in a chronically dependent individual is dangerous and contraindicated. The decision, however, about who is or who is not chronically dependent and therefore at risk for severe withdrawal is often based on clinical judgment and sometimes on guesswork. Since our current suggested treatment method of *phenobarbital loading* entails little danger of overdosing, we recommend that the physician, if in doubt, err on the side of treating. The purpose of phenobarbital loading is to mildly intoxicate the patient in order to prevent major withdrawal reactions *before* they occur. The criteria in the table below can be used as a guide.

TABLE 3: Criteria for Phenobarbital Loading†

1. Barbiturate dose > 500 mg/day
2. Seizures
3. Delirium
4. History of seizures or delirium when withdrawing from the same type and amount of drug
5. Evidence of withdrawal: anxiety, restlessness, insomnia, nausea and vomiting, tremor, diaphoresis, confusion, hallucination, hyperreflexia

† Because patients are sometimes unable to quantify precisely their daily barbiturate dose, it is safest to use phenobarbital loading if they meet any one of criteria 2 through 5, even if the physician cannot obtain a clear history of daily use >500 mg per day.

Another criterion for phenobarbital loading is clinical tolerance with "toxic" drug levels. For example, a patient with a butalbital level above 40 μmol/L who is alert and shows no signs of intoxication probably has a high degree of physical dependence and is at risk for serious withdrawal on abrupt cessation of the drug.

TABLE 4: Advantages of Phenobarbital Loading

- effective
- safe
- simple and objective
- no reinforcement of drug-taking behavior
- shorter period of medical supervision
- slow rate of elimination of phenobarbital (average half-life 86 hours)
  - minimizes fluctuation in clinical status
  - can be used to reassure patient (and physician)
- loading dose of phenobarbital indicates the degree of physical dependence
- phenobarbital has:
  - low abuse potential
  - wide margin of safety
  - superior anticonvulsant properties

INSTRUCTIONS FOR PHENOBARBITAL LOADING

Phenobarbital loading is to be done only in a medically supervised inpatient setting. After completion of the loading, patients should remain in hospital until they are alert and can safely return home.

A drug screen should be carried out, if possible, before phenobarbital loading. The blood drug screen should include a quantitative level of the barbiturate of abuse. The blood level of the drug(s) of abuse should be correlated with the patient's clinical status. Lack of intoxication with a toxic blood level indicates tolerance and the likelihood of a withdrawal syndrome with abstinence. Urine drug screening should also be carried out to detect other drugs of abuse such as benzodiazepines and opioids (see Section 10).

Begin loading when the barbiturate level is below "toxic" value (e.g., 40 for butalbital). If a level is not available, begin loading when the patient shows no signs of barbiturate intoxication and has not taken any barbiturates for at least 12 hours. Loading should begin promptly if the patient has symptoms or signs of barbiturate withdrawal.

Oral loading

Give 120 mg phenobarbital orally every hour (1.8 mg/kg) in a patient of normal weight (70 kg). Clinically assess the patient every hour or prior to each oral dose.

151

Discontinue phenobarbital when patient exhibits three or more of the following signs: asleep but able to be wakened, nystagmus, dysarthria, ataxia, drowsiness or emotional lability. In our experience, no supplementary doses of phenobarbital will be needed once this end-point has been reached.

Continuous i.v. method

Give 2.4 mg/kg per hour (concentration 10 mg/mL N saline) to obtain the same end-point as with oral administration. If patient is in major withdrawal, initially give phenobarbital 1.75 mg/kg i.v. over five minutes and then the continuous infusion. The intravenous method is used if oral administration is impossible, contraindicated, or if the situation is medically urgent such as in the case of seizures or delirium.

POLYSUBSTANCE WITHDRAWAL

For patients with a combined sedative/hypnotic and opioid dependence, treatment of barbiturate withdrawal takes precedence because it has the greatest risk of serious complications. Fortunately, phenobarbital is effective for alcohol and benzodiazepine withdrawal, and the general sedative effects of phenobarbital will partially relieve symptoms of opioid withdrawal (see also Section 10).

OUTPATIENT PHENOBARBITAL TAPERING

While patients on barbiturate doses of less than 500 mg per day are unlikely to experience major withdrawal, they may experience minor withdrawal symptoms such as anxiety and insomnia if they have taken more than 100–200 mg daily for at least a month. Such patients may be tapered as outpatients if they are medically stable, are not abusing alcohol or other substances and are reliable and unlikely to access barbiturates from other doctors or the street.

Patients may be tapered with their usual barbiturate or switched to the equivalent dose of phenobarbital. The former approach avoids the problem of establishing the equivalent phenobarbital dose. However, phenobarbital is an ideal tapering agent because of its long half-life and low abuse potential. Benzodiazepines are not effective in treating barbiturate withdrawal. If the patient takes barbiturates intermittently or only takes small doses (less than 200 mg daily), the drug may safely be stopped without tapering.

Phenobarbital equivalence

With outpatient tapering, the patient's drug of choice is first converted to the equivalent dose of phenobarbital (see Table 5). For example, patients taking 8 Fiorinal®

or Fioricet® tablets a day (containing a total daily dose of 400 mg of butalbital) would be given 60 mg of phenobarbital bid. The dose may then be decreased by 15 mg every three or four days so that the taper is completed in several weeks.

TABLE 5: Barbiturate and Sedative/Hypnotic Equivalence†

Drug	Equivalence to 30 mg phenobarbital††
AMOBARBITAL	100 mg
BUTABARBITAL	100 mg
BUTALBITAL	100 mg
PENTOBARBITAL	100 mg
SECOBARBITAL	100 mg
CHLORAL HYDRATE	500 mg
ETHYCHLORVYNOL (PLACIDYL®)	500 mg
MEPROBAMATE (MILTOWN®)	1200 mg

† Adapted from Wesson, Smith & Ling, 1994.
†† This equivalence table is based on clinical experience, not on pharmacological testing, so the clinician should not place undue faith in it. Upward or downward titration of dose will frequently be required to avoid sedation or difficult withdrawal symptoms. Since outpatient tapering is indicated for patients taking less than 500 mg of barbiturates per day, phenobarbital doses of greater than 150 mg per day should not be necessary. Careful monitoring is required to avoid oversedation, especially in the elderly.

Non-barbiturate sedatives/hypnotics

Non-barbiturate sedatives/hypnotics such as chloral hydrate and meprobamate involve the same risks of withdrawal as barbiturates and should be managed in the same manner. Table 5 lists equivalent doses. A patient chronically taking 5 capsules (2500 mg) of chloral hydrate daily is at risk for serious withdrawal if the drug is stopped suddenly.

5.2

MANAGEMENT OF BENZODIAZEPINE DEPENDENCE AND WITHDRAWAL

Nicholas Pimlott, MD, PhD, and Meldon Kahan, MD

EPIDEMIOLOGY

Benzodiazepines are among the most commonly prescribed drugs. The annual prevalence of use was 8 per cent in the United States in 1990. Most patients take benzodiazepines for only brief periods. Overall, in the past two decades there has been a shift in prescribing away from long-acting sedatives towards short-acting hypnotics. Rates of use increase with age such that the elderly receive a disproportionately large number of benzodiazepine prescriptions (Woods and Winger, 1995).

THERAPEUTIC USES OF BENZODIAZEPINES

Some controversy surrounds the appropriate use and effectiveness of benzo-diazepines. The most common indications, and some alternatives to benzo-diazepine use, are summarized below.

Anxiety disorders

Panic disorder may respond to short-term treatment with short-acting benzo-diazepines such as clonazepam and alprazolam, although long-term use may result in problems with dependence and difficulty with discontinuation. For this reason, selective serotonin reuptake inhibitors (SSRIs) are often recommended as the first line of treatment.

Similarly, benzodiazepines are used to treat acute and chronic *generalized anxiety disorder.* Benzodiazepines are best used intermittently during periods of severe anxiety symptoms, at the lowest possible dose for the shortest possible time. Some of these patients may have other underlying psychiatric disorders or personality disorders and may be at risk for benzodiazepine dependence. SSRIs may also be effective in treating generalized anxiety disorder and social phobia.

Buspirone (Buspar®) is a useful alternative to benzodiazepines in patients who require pharmacotherapy for generalized anxiety disorder, particularly for patients who have a history of alcohol or drug dependence. Controlled trials indicate that it may be as effective as diazepam in the treatment of generalized anxiety disorder. Buspirone has little or no dependence liability since it takes one or two weeks to exert a psychoactive effect, has no immediate reinforcing properties and is not associated with a withdrawal syndrome. Patients who have taken benzodiazepines in the past generally prefer them over buspirone. Buspirone is not effective in the treatment of benzodiazepine withdrawal.

Depression and other mood disorders
Benzodiazepines are often combined with antidepressants in patients with depression and prominent anxiety symptoms, and are used as an adjunct to lithium in bipolar affective disorder when anxiety symptoms are prominent. However, caution is warranted in the use of benzodiazepines with depressed patients. In common with other sedatives such as alcohol and barbiturates, benzodiazepines may cause or exacerbate symptoms of depression, particularly in higher doses over a prolonged period. Benzodiazepines may be used as adjuncts to neuroleptics in treating patients with schizophrenia who do not respond to neuroleptics alone.

Insomnia and other sleep disorders
Short-acting benzodiazepines are used to treat transient insomnia. It is recommended that they be prescribed at the lowest effective dose for a limited time, typically three weeks or less. Benzodiazepines suppress both deep and REM stages of sleep. Daily use for more than three weeks can cause rebound insomnia characterized by vivid dreams and a fitful, unsatisfying sleep. Rebound insomnia can take several weeks to resolve.

Sedatives/hypnotics such as chloral hydrate are sometimes used in the treatment of insomnia. Chloral hydrate has pharmacological properties and side-effects similar to barbiturates and has no clinical advantage over benzodiazepines. Tricyclic antidepressants and phenothiazines are also sometimes used to treat insomnia. Although these agents do not cause significant physical or psychological dependence, they carry a greater risk of overdose and medical complications such as dysrhythmias. Other medications used to treat insomnia include L-tryptophan, antihistamines and melatonin.

Zopiclone (Imovane®) has been marketed as a "non-addictive" alternative to benzodiazepines in the management of sleep disorders. Zopiclone is a cyclopyrolone derivative and is structurally unrelated to existing hypnotics. The pharmacological profile of zopiclone is similar to that of benzodiazepines. As with short-acting benzodiazepines, it should be prescribed for short-term use. The

155

problems associated with its use are similar to those associated with short-acting benzodiazepine hypnotics, including dependence and withdrawal.

Benzodiazepines are also used in the treatment of parasomnias including periodic restless leg movements, sleepwalking and night terrors. Careful diagnostic evaluation, including a sleep study, is needed since treatment is usually long term.

Alcohol withdrawal and seizure disorders

Benzodiazepines are used in the management of acute alcohol withdrawal and in the acute management of *status epilepticus* (see Section 3.2).

SAFE PRESCRIBING OF BENZODIAZEPINES

The following protocol is suggested to ensure safe and appropriate prescribing of benzodiazepines:

ENSURE ACCURATE DIAGNOSIS OF THE UNDERLYING PROBLEM

In the case of *insomnia,* a careful sleep history is indicated to assess the pattern of sleep and to identify physical and psychiatric causes of sleep disturbance. Daytime napping and going to bed early in the evening may cause sleep difficulties at night. Bedtime activities such as reading or watching television can also disturb sleep. Physical causes of insomnia include excess caffeine and alcohol use, medications such as beta blockers, cardiorespiratory conditions causing dyspnea or palpitations, prostatism, restless leg syndrome and chronic pain conditions such as osteoarthritis. Psychiatric causes include depression and anxiety disorders.

In the case of *anxiety,* a psychiatric history will often identify potentially treatable causes of anxiety such as panic disorder, substance abuse, depression, obsessive-compulsive disorder, psychosis and post-traumatic stress disorder. Mixed anxiety/depression syndromes are common. Benzodiazepines are sometimes inappropriately prescribed to anxious patients with an undiagnosed depression.

In older patients with new onset of anxiety, the physician should search for possible organic causes including early dementia, hyperthyroidism and cardiorespiratory conditions. In all patients, a psychosocial history should be undertaken to identify factors that may be amenable to counselling, such as spousal abuse or job dissatisfaction.

CONSIDER NON-PHARMACOLOGICAL APPROACHES FIRST

In the case of insomnia education regarding good "sleep hygiene" should be attempted before using hypnotic medications. Non-drug management of insomnia has been shown to be effective (Morin, Culbert & Schwartz, 1994; Guilleminault, Clerk et al., 1995). In many cases, simple education and reassurance will suffice. For example, many of the sleep changes in aging patients are common and normal and do not result in daytime dysfunction. The table below lists some simple behavioral strategies to deal with insomnia.

TABLE 6: Sleep Hygiene

- Avoid excess alcohol.
- Avoid tea, coffee and cola, especially in the evening.
- Exercise regularly, but avoid intense exercise before bed.
- Do not overeat before going to bed.
- Use the bedroom for sleep and sex only, not for reading, television, etc.
- See your doctor about physical symptoms that are keeping you awake, such as pain, frequent urination, etc.
- If you are having trouble sleeping, get up and do something else for 15–20 minutes (other than watching television), then return to bed.
- Don't take daytime naps or go to bed before 9–10 pm.

When treating anxiety, there is mounting evidence that counselling and cognitive therapy are effective in the treatment of depression and anxiety disorders (Enright, 1997). Physicians should always attempt to combine pharmacotherapy with appropriate counselling and referral in the treatment of chronic insomnia and anxiety.

TAKE A CAREFUL DRUG AND ALCOHOL HISTORY AND PRESCRIBE CAUTIOUSLY TO HIGH-RISK PATIENTS

Patients with a prior or current history of drug and/or alcohol problems are at highest risk of benzodiazepine misuse. For such patients, buspirone or SSRIs are the agents of choice. If benzodiazepines are used, those with a lower dependence liability (such as oxazepam or chlordiazepoxide) should be chosen over benzodiazepines with higher dependence liability (such as diazepam, alprazolam or lorazepam).

Treatment contracts are helpful in minimizing abuse and preventing behaviors such as "running out early" and double-doctoring (see Addendum 2 of

157

Section 8 for a sample contract). Other safeguards include dispensing medications for short periods only, careful monitoring of amounts dispensed over time and avoidance of phone repeats (see Section 17).

TAKE A CAREFUL MEDICAL/PSYCHIATRIC HISTORY TO DETECT PATIENTS AT RISK FOR ADVERSE REACTIONS

Benzodiazepines can decrease respiratory drive and cause potentially fatal hypoxia in patients with sleep apnea or chronic obstructive lung disease. Benzodiazepines sometimes cause paradoxical excitement in psychotic patients or patients with personality disorders.

CHOOSE THE LOWEST EFFECTIVE DOSE FOR THE SHORTEST PERIOD OF TIME

If after consideration of the above a benzodiazepine is to be prescribed, choose the lowest effective dose for the shortest period of time and carefully monitor use. Keep in mind that both anxiety and insomnia wax and wane with time and spontaneous improvement of anxiety is common.

AVOID BENZODIAZEPINES IN PREGNANCY

It is not clear whether benzodiazepines alone are teratogenic or have an adverse effect on outcomes during pregnancy. Teratogenicity after heavy maternal benzodiazepine use occurs with multiple alcohol and substance abuse exposure. Heavy use of benzodiazepines during or just prior to labor may result in "floppy baby syndrome."

BE PARTICULARLY CAUTIOUS IN PRESCRIBING BENZODIAZEPINES TO THE ELDERLY; AVOID LONG-ACTING BENZODIAZEPINES IF POSSIBLE AND INITIATE TREATMENT AT ONE HALF THE USUAL ADULT DOSE

As indicated in the first section, the elderly receive a disproportionately large number of prescriptions for benzodiazepines and are at special risk for adverse reactions to these medications. The half-life of benzodiazepines can be prolonged in the elderly, who are at greater risk for CNS side-effects such as *impaired recall, confusion and sedation.* Epidemiological studies indicate an increased risk of falls and hip fractures in seniors taking benzodiazepines, particularly long-acting benzodiazepines such as diazepam and chlordiazepoxide. Benzodiazepines alone may contribute to risk, but those patients at greatest risk are more likely to be taking other psychoactive drugs and to have significant co-existing medical illness. There is also recent evidence that long-acting benzodiazepine use in the elderly increases the risk of motor vehicle accidents.

USE CAUTION IN COMBINING BENZODIAZEPINES WITH OTHER PSYCHOACTIVE MEDICATIONS

Benzodiazepines in combination with other psychoactive medications can cause increased fatigue, depression, confusion and trauma from accidents and falls. Potentially inappropriate combinations include concurrent use of two different benzodiazepines, or benzodiazepines plus barbiturates, opioid analgesics, tricyclic antidepressants or antipsychotics.

WARN PATIENTS ABOUT DRIVING

All patients should be warned about potential impairment in their ability to drive, operate machinery or perform other complex psychomotor tasks. Risk is probably greatest in the first few days or weeks of treatment, and in combination with alcohol or other psychoactive agents.

ABUSE AND DEPENDENCE

There are widely different views regarding the issue of benzodiazepine dependence and abuse. Woods and his colleagues (1988) have challenged the view that benzodiazepines are like other drugs of abuse. They have advocated a *therapeutic use model* wherein these medications are usually used appropriately for the treatment of conditions for which they are effective. The *abuse model* represents the hypothesis that much of the use of benzodiazepines is for purposes other than those for which the drug was prescribed. The therapeutic use model appears to be supported by epidemiological data, as most patients take benzodiazepines for appropriate indications.

Many individuals who use benzodiazepines as prescribed may develop physical but not psychological dependence and may not meet the criteria for abuse and dependence as discussed below. Individuals at greatest risk for abuse and inappropriate use are those with a history of alcohol abuse or dependence, other drug abuse or addiction (usually polysubstance). Moderate drinkers (11–12 drinks/ week) may also be at higher risk for abuse (Woods & Winger, 1995).

159

There are at least four circumstances when urging patients to stop taking benzodiazepines is clearly justified (DuPont, 1990):

• where there is active chemical dependence or regular illicit drug use of any kind
• where there is use of benzodiazepines in excess of the usual recommended dose for the treatment of anxiety
• where there is a poor therapeutic response to the drug
• where there is evidence of toxic effects including sedation, impairment, treatment-related depression and other psychiatric conditions.

Periodic attempts at tapering are recommended even for patients who do not meet the above criteria. Patients sometimes find that discontinuing benzodiazepines makes them feel more alert, energetic and clear-thinking with less emotional blunting and a greater range of positive emotions.

BENZODIAZEPINE WITHDRAWAL SYNDROMES

Acute sedative/hypnotic withdrawal

This is seen in those who use both therapeutic and high doses of benzodiazepines usually over prolonged periods (greater than two weeks). For those taking short-acting benzodiazepines (SABs) the onset of withdrawal symptoms is within one or two days of cessation, whereas the onset of withdrawal symptoms is within two to four days for those taking long-acting benzodiazepines (LABs). In either case, symptoms peak within five to seven days of cessation and may last up to two weeks.

The most common symptoms of acute withdrawal are anxiety, agitation, insomnia, vivid dreams or nightmares, anorexia and tremulousness (see Table 7). Common but less frequent symptoms include vomiting, depersonalization, blurred vision and visual and auditory hypersensitivity. Less common, but by no means rare, are withdrawal seizures. Serious but rare complications include delirium, hallucinations and dysrhythmias.

The severity of the withdrawal symptoms is in general, but not always, proportional to the amount of drug taken, the duration of use, the use of SABs and the severity of the underlying anxiety disorders.

TABLE 7: Benzodiazepine Anxiolytic Discontinuance Symptoms†

Very frequent	Common but less frequent	Uncommon
Anxiety	Nausea	Psychosis
Insomnia	Coryza	Seizures
Restlessness	Diaphoresis	Persistent tinnitus
Agitation	Lethargy	Confusion
Irritability	Hyperacusis	Paranoid delusions
Muscle tension	Aches and pains	Hallucinations
	Blurred vision	
	Depression	
	Nightmares	
	Hyperreflexia	
	Ataxia	

† Reprinted with permission from *Benzodiazepine Dependence, Toxicity and Abuse: A Task Force Report of the American Psychiatric Association.* Copyright 1990, American Psychiatric Association.

Rebound anxiety and symptom recurrence

Withdrawal symptoms should be distinguished from "rebound anxiety" and symptom recurrence (Table 8). Rebound anxiety is a temporary intensification of anxiety that occurs upon abrupt cessation of benzodiazepines. Recurrence is a return of the symptoms for which benzodiazepines were originally prescribed. Withdrawal is a neurological phenomenon that can be distinguished from rebound or recurrence by the presence of neurological symptoms such as tinnitus, auditory and visual dysperceptions and depersonalization.

TABLE 8: Symptoms of Benzodiazepine Discontinuance Syndrome†

Symptom category	Type of symptoms	Severity compared with original symptoms	Course
REBOUND	Same as original	More	Rapid onset and temporary
RECURRENCE	Same as original	Same	Very gradual onset; does not disappear with time

Table 8 continued

Symptom category	Type of symptoms	Severity compared with original symptoms	Course
WITHDRAWAL	New symptoms	Variable	Occurs early or late; lasts 2–4 weeks (occasionally longer)

† Reprinted with permission from *Benzodiazepine Dependence, Toxicity, and Abuse: A Task Force Report of the American Psychiatric Association.* Copyright 1990, American Psychiatric Association.

Subacute, prolonged withdrawal

This is seen in those who use both therapeutic and high doses of benzo-diazepines. For both SABs and LABs the duration of symptoms may vary from several weeks up to one year (possibly longer). The most common symptoms include anxiety, insomnia, tachycardia, muscle spasms and paresthesias. The key feature of symptoms is the fluctuating level of severity. Patients report feeling "fragile," with a heightened emotional response to daily events or thoughts.

There is controversy as to whether this pattern represents withdrawal or the re-emergence of anxiety symptoms. Patients with this pattern should be assessed in more detail with respect to the possibility of an underlying anxiety disorder. Psychiatric consultation is probably appropriate.

MANAGEMENT OF BENZODIAZEPINE WITHDRAWAL

There are two cardinal principles that must be kept in mind when treating ben-zodiazepine abuse:

- Benzodiazepines should never be abruptly stopped unless serious complica-tions warrant immediate discontinuation.
- Withdrawal from benzodiazepines should be slow and gradual.

Graded reduction of current benzodiazepine

This approach may be especially useful in the primary care setting and is best undertaken in those who (1) take only benzodiazepines, and (2) have become dependent while taking doses within the therapeutic range. It is recommended that the dose be tapered by about 10 to 15 per cent per week over about six to 12 weeks (Landry, Smith et al., 1992). Faster reductions (e.g., four weeks) should be accompanied by more frequent physician follow-up. Symptoms

162

persisting beyond 12 weeks may represent an underlying anxiety disorder or other disorders, and appropriate psychiatric referral may be indicated.

Substitution of a long-acting benzodiazepine

This approach can also be used in the primary-care, outpatient setting and allows a more gradual reduction of dose with fewer withdrawal symptoms (Landry, Smith et al., 1992).

Diazepam and chlordiazepoxide are the two most common drugs used for substitution and withdrawal. Chlordiazepoxide may have less street value and a lower abuse potential than diazepam and therefore may be a better choice in some circumstances. However, chlordiazepoxide has a shorter half-life and a more variable absorption than diazepam. The equivalency of these two drugs versus other benzodiazepines can be calculated from the table below.

TABLE 9: Approximate Oral Benzodiazepine Equivalence[†]

Drug	Equivalence to 5 mg diazepam (mg)[††]
Alprazolam (Xanax®)	0.5
Bromazepam (Lectopam®)	3 –6
Chlordiazepoxide (Librium®)	10 –25
Clonazepam (Rivotril®, Klonopin®)	0.5–1
Clorazepate (Tranxene®, Gen-XENE®)	7.5
Flurazepam (Dalmane®)	15
Lorazepam (Ativan®)	0.5–1
Nitrazepam (Mogadon®)	5 –10
Oxazepam (Serax®)	15
Temazepam (Restoril®)	10 –15
Triazolam (Halcion®)[†††]	0.25

[†] Adapted from Kalvik, Isaac & Janecek, 1995 and Canadian Pharmacists Association, 1999.
[††] Equivalences are approximate. Careful monitoring is required to avoid oversedation, especially in the elderly. **These equivalences should be used only as a general guide for the initiation of tapering because they are based on clinical indication (sleep/anxiety) rather than doses used for withdrawal.**
[†††] Equivalency uncertain.

It should be noted that equivalences are approximate. If the patient reports over-sedation on the new medication, the dose should be lowered. If the patient reports significant withdrawal symptoms, the dose may be increased. If a range of equivalences are listed, as in the above table, it is safer to place the patient on a more conservative initial dose (the midpoint or lower end of the range).

Patients on alprazolam or triazolam should be tapered with those drugs or with the equivalent dose of clonazepam. The equivalent dose of diazepam has not yet been established and diazepam may not be effective in treating withdrawal from these agents.

Substitution and graded withdrawal typically should be carried out over a period of six to 12 weeks depending upon the amount and duration of drug use. A patient who has taken therapeutic doses over one or two months may be successfully tapered in two or three weeks. A patient taking high doses or using benzodiazepines for a number of years may require a much longer taper. The dose should be tapered at a rate of 10 to 15 per cent per week (2–5 mg of diazepam per week for patients on therapeutic doses). If severe withdrawal symptoms occur during the taper, the dose may be increased and the taper prolonged. Because patients typically report that the final stages of the taper are the most difficult, the taper may need to be slowed near the end. A tapering protocol is included in the Addendum to this chapter.

Patients should be advised to not miss doses or prolong the interval between doses, as this may create anxiety. Scheduled rather than prn dosing should be used to minimize the reinforcing effects of benzodiazepines. A treatment contract is sometimes helpful, specifying that replacement doses will not be given if the patient takes extra doses. If the patient has been known to take more medication than prescribed or to access medication from other sources, daily or weekly dispensing is recommended.

Tapering patients with mixed anxiety and depression
Patients with severe anxiety or mixed anxiety and depression should be tapered slowly and carefully with close follow-up and monitoring for suicidal ideation. If symptoms worsen significantly, the taper should be halted or reversed. Psychiatric consultation and follow-up may be indicated before initiating the taper.

Supportive counselling during tapering
Close and consistent follow-up is required to ensure the success of tapering. Patients should be encouraged to note positive effects of the taper, such as feeling more alert and energetic. Stress management techniques and cognitive-behavioral therapy are often helpful. Underlying psychosocial causes of anxiety

such as marital discord should be identified and the patient and physician should negotiate a strategy and timetable for dealing with them.

End-point of the taper

For patients on therapeutic doses of benzodiazepines with no obvious adverse effects, tapering should be viewed as a therapeutic trial to establish the ongoing need for benzodiazepines, to determine the lowest effective dose, and to determine if the patient actually feels and functions better without the medication. If patients find the taper difficult despite supportive counselling and adjustments to the taper rate, the physician may choose to end the taper and maintain the patient at the lowest comfortable dose. Patients who have been abusing benzodiazepines or show clear signs of psychological dependence (i.e., taking doses in excess of those prescribed, accessing multiple sources of the drug, experiencing frequent bouts of intoxication and withdrawal) should be weaned off the medication and encouraged to enter a drug treatment program. If this is not possible, patients should be referred to an addiction medicine specialist before they are maintained chronically on benzodiazepines.

Tapering benzodiazepine hypnotics

Patients who only use benzodiazepines for sleep should not be switched to diazepam because it may cause daytime sedation. Instead they should be tapered with the drug they currently use, or switched to the equivalent dose of another benzodiazepine with a short or intermediate half-life such as oxazepam. Patients taking triazolam for sleep should not be switched to a benzodiazepine other than clonazepam. Once they have been tapered to the minimal daily dose, they may be switched to intermittent dosing for several weeks: for example, five doses per week, then three, then one.

Management of high-dose benzodiazepine withdrawal

High-dose benzodiazepine use often occurs in patients who are actively abusing benzodiazepines and other substances through double-doctoring and buying drugs off the street. These patients are often difficult to manage because of an unreliable dose/duration history and because of mixed anxiolytic/hypnotic abuse. They are best cared for by addiction specialists, preferably in an inpatient setting. Readers are referred to a review of the subject by Alexander and Perry (1991).

As a general guide, patients taking the equivalent of 50 mg of diazepam or more per day consistently over a period of weeks or months are at risk for seizures, psychosis or delirium if their dose is stopped suddenly. The Addendum summarizes a tapering protocol for high-dose users.

Equivalent diazepam dose > 100 mg

Patients taking more than 100 mg diazepam or its equivalent per day should be admitted (preferably in an inpatient alcohol and other drug program) and given half to two-thirds the equivalent diazepam dose in a tid-qid schedule. For example, lorazepam 1 mg is equivalent to 5–10 mg of diazepam. The equivalent diazepam dose of a patient taking 20 mg of lorazepam per day is approximately 150 mg (the midpoint of the range). The initial diazepam dose should therefore be 75 mg (half to two-thirds the equivalent dose). Additional doses may be administered as needed. If the patient experienced significant withdrawal on the initial dose, the next day the dose should be increased by 10–30 mg.

The dose should then be tapered by no more than 10 per cent per day (usually in the range of 5–15 mg). Once a safer dose is reached (50 mg or less), the taper may be continued on an outpatient basis.

Equivalent diazepam dose 50–100 mg

Patients taking between 50 and 100 mg per day should receive inpatient care if possible, preferably in a formal alcohol and drug treatment program. They can be treated as outpatients if they are medically and psychiatrically stable, are not combining benzodiazepines with other substances such as alcohol or opioids and are reliable and unlikely to access benzodiazepines from the street or other doctors. The equivalent diazepam dose should not be reduced by half, because prn dosing is not practical on an outpatient basis. However, an upper limit of 75 mg diazepam per day is suggested as an initial dose, with daily assessment for the first few days to titrate the dose. Daily or biweekly dispensing and frequent follow-up is suggested. Patients should be tapered by 5 mg every 3–4 days at doses above 50 mg, and 5 mg per week at lower doses. The taper may need to be slowed at doses below 20 mg.

Prognosis

Results of studies conducted in the past five years indicate that in the short term, patients discontinued from SABs are more likely to relapse than users of LABs. In the long term, success rates may be similar. Unlike detoxified, abstinent alcoholics, patients discontinued from benzodiazepines express little or no "craving" to resume use of these drugs.

R E F E R E N C E S

Alexander, B. & Perry, P.J. (1991). Detoxification from benzodiazepines: Schedules and strategies. *Journal of Substance Abuse Treatment, 8(1-2)*, 9-17.

Canadian Pharmaceutical Association. (1999). *CPS Compendium of Pharmaceuticals and Specialties (34th ed.)*. Ottawa: Canadian Pharmaceutical Association.

Devenyi, P. & Saunders, S.J. (1986). *Physician's Handbook for Medical Management of Alcohol- and Drug-Related Problems (1st ed.).* Toronto: Addiction Research Foundation and Ontario Medical Association.

DuPont, R.L. (1990). A physician's guide to discontinuing benzodiazepine therapy. *Western Journal of Medicine, 152(5),* 600-603.

Enright, S.J. (1997). Cognitive behaviour therapy clinical applications. *British Medical Journal, 314(7097),* 1811-1816.

Guilleminault, C., Clerk, A., Black, J., Labanowski, M., Pelayo, R. & Claman, D. (1995). Non-drug treatment trials in psychophysiologic insomnia. *Archives of Internal Medicine, 155(8),* 838-844.

Hardman, J.G., Limbird, L.E., Molinoff, P.B., Ruddon, R.W. & Gilman, A.G. (Eds.). (1996). *Goodman and Gilman's The Pharmacological Basis of Therapeutics (9th ed.).* New York: Pergamon Press.

Kalvik, A., Isaac, P. & Janecek, E. (1995). Benzodiazepines: Treatment of anxiety, insomnia and alcohol withdrawal. *Pharmacy Connection, 2(5),* 20-35.

Landry, M.J., Smith, D.E., McDuff, D.R. & Baughmann, O.L. (1992). Benzodiazepine dependence and withdrawal: Identification and medical management. *Journal of the American Board of Family Practice, 5(2),* 167-175.

Morin, C.M., Culbert, J.P. & Schwartz, S.M. (1994). Non-pharmacologic interventions for insomnia: A meta-analysis of treatment efficacy. *American Journal of Psychiatry, 151(8),* 1172-1180.

Sellers, E.M. (1990). *Benzodiazepine Dependence, Toxicity, and Abuse: A Task Force Report of the American Psychiatric Association.* Washington, DC: American Psychiatric Association.

Smith, D.E. & Wesson, D.R. (1983). Benzodiazepine dependency syndromes. *Journal of Psychoactive Drugs, 15(8),* 85-95.

Wesson, D.R., Smith, D.E. & Ling, W. (1994). Management of multiple drug/alcohol intoxication and withdrawal. In N.S. Miller (Ed.) *Principles of Addiction Medicine.* Chevy Chase, MD: American Society of Addiction Medicine.

Woods, J.H., Katz, J.L. & Winger, G. (1988). Use and abuse of benzodiazepines: Issues relevant to prescribing. *Journal of the American Medical Association, 260(23),* 3476-3480.

Woods, J.H. & Winger, G. (1995). Current benzodiazepine issues. *Psychopharmacology, 118(2),* 107-115.

167

ADDENDUM

DIAZEPAM TAPERING FOR

BENZODIAZEPINE WITHDRAWAL[†]

I.	
For patients taking < 50 mg/day diazepam equivalent Outpatient protocol:	• Convert to equivalent dose of diazepam (maximum 50 mg/day) in divided doses. • Taper by 5 mg per week. • Adjust initial dose and rate of taper according to symptoms. • May need to slow taper at doses below 20 mg. • Dispense daily, biweekly or weekly depending on dose and patient reliability.
II.	
For patients taking 50–100 mg/day diazepam equivalent **Inpatient preferable but outpatient possible if:** • not physically dependent on other drugs • medically, psychiatrically stable • unlikely to access benzo-diazepines from other sources.	• Convert to equivalent diazepam dose (maximum 75 mg/day) on divided doses. • Daily dosage titration for first few days to avoid sedation or significant withdrawal. • Taper by 5 mg every 3–4 days at doses above 50mg, then 5mg per week. • Adjust rate of taper according to symptoms; may need a slow taper at doses below 20 mg. • Dispense daily, weekly or biweekly depending on dose and patient reliability.
III.	
If _typical_ daily use over past 2 months is equivalent to diazepam 100 mg or more:	• Consider hospitalization and addiction medicine consult. • Start taper at one-half to two-thirds the equivalent diazepam dose. • Administer tid-qid. • If significant withdrawal on this dose, increase total dose by 10–30 mg the next day. • May give prn diazepam 10–20 mg 1–3 times per day for acute withdrawal.[††] • Hold diazepam and decrease daily dose if drowsiness or sedation.

Diazepam Tapering for Benzodiazepine Withdrawal (continued)

	• Taper by 5–15 mg per day as inpatient (taper by no more than 10% of daily dose; slow taper as dose decreases). • May switch to outpatient protocol at doses less than 50 mg. • Adjust initial dose and rate of taper according to symptoms.
IV. **For patients on alprazolam or triazolam:**	• Taper with alprazolam and triazolam, or equivalent dose of clonazepam.†††

  † Patients using benzodiazepines in a dose equivalent to diazepam 50mg/day are at higher risk for seizures, psychosis or delirium if their dose is stopped abruptly. The risk is greater with use of benzodiazepines with a short half-life.

 †† Acute withdrawal consists of severe anxiety, insomnia, and signs of autonomic hyperactivity (tremor, sweating, tachycardia, hypertension).

††† Diazepam may not be effective for alprazolam or triazolam withdrawal — equivalent diazepam dose is uncertain.

Stimulants

6.1 COCAINE

CONTENTS/SECTION 6

173

6.1

COCAINE

Douglas L. Gourlay, MSc, MD

GENERAL DESCRIPTION

Cocaine is a CNS stimulant with local anesthetic properties. It is prepared from the leaves of the *Erythroxylum coca* bush, found primarily in Peru and Bolivia. Native people have chewed coca leaves as a stimulant for centuries. Coca paste, a crude extract made from the leaves, is readily available in South America. This paste, containing cocaine sulfate, is usually smoked. Through purification the hydrochloride salt of cocaine is formed. In this form it is smuggled into and sold illicitly in North America and elsewhere. Further steps may then be taken to convert the cocaine salt into cocaine alkaloid, the so-called freebase form of cocaine. The cocaine alkaloid, when combined with sodium bicarbonate forms "crack" cocaine. This name is derived from the crackling sounds made by the material as it is heated and smoked.

Indications

The medical uses for cocaine have steadily declined as clinicians have become aware of dependency risk, abuse by health care professionals and diversion of the drug for "street use." Currently, there is no legitimate use for the parenteral form of cocaine in clinical medicine. Cocaine is still used as a topical local anesthetic/vasoconstrictor, primarily in otolaryngology and clinical procedures involving instrumentation of the upper airway. Even within these limited areas combinations of a local anesthetic such as bupivicaine with a vasoconstrictor such as epinephrine are replacing cocaine preparations.

Trade names

Cocaine is marketed for medical use in non-sterile aqueous preparations of 4 and 10 per cent (PMS-Cocaine Hydrochloride®). Cocaine hydrochloride is also available as a fine chemical from various sources.

Street names
- Cocaine hydrochloride: Blow, C, Coke, Flake, Snow, Stardust
- Freebase cocaine: Crack, Rock, Freebase
- Cocaine hydrochloride plus heroin: Dynamite, Speedball
- Crack impregnated with heroin: Moon Rock
- Crack impregnated with PCP: Space Cadet, Tragic Magic

PHARMACOLOGICAL ACTIONS

Cocaine affects several neurotransmitters in the brain. Dopamine, serotonin and epinephrine are the primary transmitters involved. Cocaine has a direct effect at the synaptic junction resulting in an increase in quantity and extended duration of action for dopamine. This occurs through reuptake inhibition of dopamine at the presynaptic nerve terminal. The resulting dopamine depletion leads to upregulation of the postsynaptic dopamine receptors. Transmission of dopamine within the mesolimbic and mesocortical areas is also enhanced (Miller, Gold et al., 1989). Dopamine depletion may explain the dysphoria experienced by chronic cocaine abusers. As well, dopamine has a direct effect on the release of presynaptic catecholamines, which is thought to account for the acute psychomotor stimulant effects of both cocaine and amphetamines.

PHARMACOKINETIC EFFECTS

Routes of administration
The method of cocaine use affects its pharmacokinetics. Cocaine enters the cerebral circulation fastest (about 6 to 8 seconds) after smoking. The intravenous route takes longer, reflecting the transit time through the pulmonary and systemic circulations.

Nasal insufflation (snorting) produces euphoria in three to five minutes, with peak cocaine levels in 30 to 60 minutes. Estimates of bioavailability of snorted cocaine range from 20 to 60 per cent. Absorption by the mucosal route is self-limited due to the drug's vasoconstrictive effects. Compared with intravenous levels, the potency of a dose of snorted cocaine is approximately 60 per cent.

Half-life, excretion and metabolites
The biological half-life of cocaine in the blood is approximately one hour. Regardless of route, urinary excretion of cocaine and its metabolites occurs within 24 hours of administration. Less than 5 per cent of cocaine appears unchanged in the urine. Benzoylecognine and ecognine methyl ester, with half-lives of approximately six and four hours respectively, account for more than

80 per cent of known cocaine metabolites. Benzoylecognine results from spontaneous non-enzymatic hydrolysis of cocaine. It can be found in the urine at concentrations nearly 50 to 100 times that of cocaine. Less than 10 per cent of cocaine is N-demethylated by the liver into norcocaine, a potentially toxic metabolite.

PATTERNS OF USE

Typically, cocaine use begins with intranasal administration in quantities of less than one gram of varying degrees of purity (0–50 per cent cocaine hydrochloride "cut" with a variety of adulterants). As tolerance develops the amount used generally increases to several grams. With ongoing heavy use, users often switch to large amounts of smoked "crack" or freebase cocaine. The speed of onset of the drug effect varies, depending on the route of administration (seconds for smoked and parenteral cocaine, five to 20 minutes for intranasal cocaine, and 20 to 60 minutes for oral administration). The intensity of the "high" is related in part to speed of onset — regular users report a 10-fold increase for smoked or i.v. use over intranasal absorption.

Cocaine differs from other drugs of abuse in that it is typically used episodically in heavy binges rather than daily. Users average one to seven binges per week, each lasting several hours to several days. This is usually followed by several days of abstinence. Initially, the user feels intense euphoria, with a sense of alertness, well-being and self-confidence. The user may become loquacious and full of energy, with a heightened sense of all pleasurable experiences. As use progresses, tolerance develops to the euphoric effects, while the negative effects increase. Chronic use leads to a state of agitation, anxiety and even panic attacks. The abuser loses concentration and libido and may exhibit stereotyped movements, teeth and jaw grinding and pacing. The abuser is hyperactive, with pressured speech and labile affect. There may be psychotic symptoms similar to paranoid schizophrenia.

Physical signs of intoxication are those of increased sympathetic tone and include dilated pupils, increased blood pressure, heart rate and respiratory rate. At toxic doses, the risk of seizures, cardiac dysrhythmias, hyperthermic crisis and shock are greatly increased.

EPIDEMIOLOGY

In 1996 the *National Household Survey on Drug Abuse,* which reports on drug use in the United States, found that 10.3 per cent of the total population had used cocaine at some point in their lifetimes. This represents 12.8 per cent of the male population and 8 per cent of the female population. Use in the past year was reported by 2.5 per cent of males and 1.3 per cent of females. Lifetime use of crack cocaine was reported by 2.2 per cent of the total population. Of males, 2.8 per cent report ever having used crack, while 1.6 per cent of females report ever having used crack. Use of crack in the past year was reported by 0.8 per cent of males and 0.5 per cent of females in the United States (Substance Abuse and Mental Health Services Administration, 1998).

The rates of lifetime use in Canada are much lower than in the United States. In 1994, 4.9 per cent of males over 15 and 2.7 per cent of females over 15 reported using cocaine in their lifetimes. Use of cocaine in the past year was reported by 0.8 per cent of Canadian males over 15, and by 0.5 per cent of Canadian females over 15 (Canadian Centre on Substance Abuse, 1997).

TREATMENT OF STIMULANT ABUSE

As with all rational treatment plans, therapy for stimulant abuse begins with careful diagnosis. Loss of control, use despite harm and preoccupation with getting and using the drug are all key. Once a diagnosis is made, treatment options fall into two groups: inpatient and community-based outpatient programs. There is some debate over which is preferable.

The American Society of Addiction Medicine Placement Criteria is of some help. In general terms, the lack of medical risk secondary to abrupt discontinuation of stimulants makes initial treatment on an outpatient basis reasonable. In cocaine dependency treatment, behavioral approaches dominate after initial symptomatic medical management. Treatment must address environmental issues as reinforcers of drug use or abstinence.

COCAINE WITHDRAWAL — SYMPTOMS AND MANAGEMENT

Triphasic abstinence syndrome

The common withdrawal symptoms observed with cocaine are largely psychological. Although there are no gross physiological changes as seen with alcohol or opioid withdrawal, a triphasic abstinence syndrome has been observed in some, but not all patients.

* *Phase 1:* "The Crash." This occurs immediately after the effects of the last dose of cocaine wear off, and lasts up to four days. There is a profound

decrease in mood and energy. The intensity of this phase is proportional to the speed of onset of the drug, smoking being more intense than nasal insufflation. Drug cravings, agitation, anxiety and paranoia peak, followed by decreased cravings, hyperphagia and hypersomnia. During this time, sedative drugs are often taken by the individual to decrease the agitation and anxiety.

- *Phase 2:* Withdrawal Dysphoria. This is a period of prolonged dysphoria, anhedonia, lack of motivation and markedly increased craving for the drug, lasting one to 10 weeks. Abusers are at greatest risk of relapse during this period. The effects of cocaine (euphoria and cessation of dysphoria) reinforce relapse.

- *Phase 3:* Extinction. During this period, craving becomes episodic and gradually extinguishes over time. The duration of this phase is indefinite.

This triphasic withdrawal phenomenon seems to be less commonly observed in inpatient than in outpatient settings. This may in part be due to the reduction of cues associated with drug use in the inpatient environment.

Management of withdrawal

Management of cocaine withdrawal is primarily supportive. Physiological changes occurring during acute toxic overdoses are usually short-lived providing that the absorption of cocaine is stopped. Table 1 below outlines the supportive treatment for cocaine toxicity. The patient who is qualitatively or quantitatively deficient in plasma cholinesterase may be at particular risk for sudden death. This may be due to a toxic buildup of cocaine secondary to inhibition of its primary metabolic pathway (Hoffman, Henry et al., 1992).

EVALUATION IN EMERGENCY SETTING

Presenting symptoms of patients in the emergency department are often variable. In the voluntary patient, evaluation is usually straightforward. Evaluation of the individual presenting for involuntary treatment may, however, be quite complicated. Assessment of physical appearance, mental state and vital signs combined with an abbreviated medical exam will help with the initial triage. Autonomic instability, hyperthermia and pupillary dilation with lateralizing findings demand immediate medical intervention to prevent further deterioration and possible death. Patients without such findings may be better served in an emergency psychiatric setting.

The possibility of coexisting medical conditions such as HIV infection and nutritional deficiency should also be addressed. While urine toxicology may provide useful information with respect to drug use, appropriate medical/psychiatric management must begin immediately.

179

ACUTE MEDICAL MANAGEMENT

In the treatment of acute cocaine intoxication, maintenance of basic life support is the first concern. A patent airway, adequate ventilation and effective circulation are paramount. Close monitoring of vital signs and neurological status will enable the treatment team to institute appropriate care. Hyperthermia must be aggressively managed to limit this potentially life-threatening complication of cocaine toxicity.

Seizures
Cocaine-induced seizures are best managed with i.v. diazepam. In the case of intractable seizures, it may be advantageous to secure the airway with endotracheal intubation. Adequate treatment of the seizures may require the addition of phenytoin or a short-acting barbiturate such as pentobarbital sodium. It must be remembered that paralysis of the patient with non-depolarizing muscle relaxants to facilitate ventilation does not stop seizure activity.

Hypertension and cardiac arrhythmias
Treatment of cocaine-induced hypertension and cardiac arrhythmias is somewhat controversial. The use of beta-adrenergic blockers, such as propranolol, alone may result in a paradoxical increase in blood pressure secondary to unopposed alpha-adrenergic activity. The use of a potent competitive alpha-adrenergic agent such as phentolamine (2–10 mg i.v. over 10 minutes) will reduce blood pressure through vasodilation. In more severe cases, a sodium nitroprusside drip may be required. Beta-adrenergic blockade has been used successfully to treat stimulant-related tachycardia and hypertension. Typical doses have been propanolol 1 mg i.v. every 2 minutes to a total of 8 mg. To date, there have been no large case studies or controlled clinical trials to compare vasodilation with beta-adrenergic blockade in terms of either safety or efficacy in treatment of cocaine-induced hypertension.

Other clinical issues
Efforts should be made to ensure that there is not ongoing drug absorption. In cases of oral ingestion, nasogastric lavage with or without activated charcoal is indicated. Failure to respond to treatment may indicate the presence of secreted drug in one or more body cavities (see body packing later in this chapter). Urgent surgical removal of drug packs may be lifesaving. Unlike the case with amphetamines, acidification of the urine does little to increase renal clearance of cocaine.

As with any medical emergency, other causes for clinical findings must be considered. Urine and blood toxicology may indicate the presence of other drugs of abuse that the patient had been unwilling/unable to divulge. Intoxication/withdrawal from these other drugs may confuse the clinical picture and lead to misdiagnosis of potentially treatable conditions. Commonly abused drugs used with cocaine include the benzodiazepines, alcohol and opioids.

180

TREATMENT OF LIFE-THREATENING INTOXICATION

Beginning with basic supportive management (airway and circulatory stabilization, an i.v. of dextrose in water, thiamine 100 mg i.v. ± naloxone 2 mg i.v. as indicated), specific crisis management can begin.

In general, the standard therapy for acute cocaine intoxication relies on treatment of cardiac/hemodynamic instability, sedation and cooling. Muscle paralysis may also be of added benefit in helping to control hyperthermia. The table below outlines treatment approaches to life-threatening cocaine intoxication.

TABLE 1: Systems Approach to Life-Threatening Cocaine Intoxication

CVS HYPERTENSION	• Vasodilation: nitroprusside, phentolamine, nifedipine • Beta blockers: propanolol, labetalol (beta blocker with alpha-adrenergic activity) may be superior to propanolol due to the theoretical risk of unopposed beta blockade with propanolol leading to hypertensive crisis
MYOCARDIAL ISCHEMIA	• Nitrates, calcium channel blockers
TACHYARRHYTHMIAS	• Atrial: observation, propanolol, verapamil • Ventricular: propanolol, lidocaine[†], other antiarrhythmics
CNS AGITATION/CONVULSIONS	• Sedation (diazepam) → anticonvulsants (phenobarbital ± phenytoin) → general anesthesia ± paralysis
HYPERTHERMIA	• Control agitation, seizures, initiate rapid cooling
Psychiatric SEDATION	• Benzodiazepines, antipsychotics[†]
Renal ACUTE TUBULAR NECROSIS (MYOGLOBINURIC RENAL FAILURE SECONDARY TO RHABDOMYOLYSIS):	• Treat with forced alkaline diuresis, including careful fluid and electrolyte imbalance treatment.

† Use with caution in acute cocaine intoxication owing to seizure threshold-lowering properties.

181

Psychiatric Complications

From all evidence available, cocaine-induced neuropsychiatric disease is on the rise. Cocaine may be more toxic to the CNS than any other recreationally abused drug currently available (Galanter, Egelko et al., 1992; Bunt, Galanter et al., 1990). Permanent neurological damage is thought to be due, in part, to the vasoconstrictive properties of cocaine. The effect of cocaine intoxication is highly dose-dependent. At lower doses, cocaine use is said to be a pleasurable experience. At higher doses, dysphoria predominates. Routes of administration also influence the subjective effects of cocaine use. Initial effects at low dose include elation, euphoria and overconfidence. Intravenous and "freebase" users report a brief but euphoric cocaine "rush" followed by a longer lasting pleasurable "high." At higher doses, anxiety, dysphoria, affective instability and paranoia predominate. Chronic cocaine abuse at high doses leads to a paranoid state that may be indistinguishable from a schizophreniform psychosis. Autonomic instability, hyperthermia and a catatonic state often precede seizures and death. CNS damage due to stroke may result from such instability.

Cocaine-associated mood disorders

Cocaine abusers may present with a wide range of symptoms suggestive of a variety of affective disorders. Manic and mixed bipolar states should be considered in the patient who appears thin and reports disruption in eating and sleep cycles. Patients presenting in the first phase of cocaine withdrawal, "the crash," may report anhedonia, anxiety, dysphoria and anergia. Suicidal ideation and residual paranoia may also be present. Rapid resolution or improvement of these symptoms after three to four days of confirmed abstinence helps to differentiate "crash" symptoms from a major depressive disorder. However, patients in the second phase of withdrawal, and chronic daily cocaine users who are not currently abstaining, may also present with a clinical picture similar to a major depressive disorder. Symptom improvement should occur within several weeks of abstinence.

Cocaine-associated psychotic disorders

Chronic stimulant abuse can lead to the development of a paranoid psychosis. Paranoid psychotic episodes induced by cocaine may resemble psychotic disorders ranging from delusional disorders to schizophrenia-like illness. Generally, the cocaine-induced psychotic state lacks the formal thought disturbance typically present with psychotic disorders. Most patients retain a high degree of organized thinking and abstract reasoning. Reports of illusions and misperceptions, as well as rudimentary and non-bizarre delusions, will often be present. Less commonly, patients may report frank auditory, visual, olfactory or tactile hallucinations with fixed and highly developed delusions. Cognition remains intact while insight and judgment are severely impaired. In cases of chronic, high-dose intoxications, psychosis may persist for periods of several days to weeks. Psychosis associated with acute intoxication at low doses usually resolves in a matter of hours to days if abstinence is maintained. Of the various types of delusional disorders, the persecutory, jealous and somatic types predominate. With chronic abuse, a somatic delusional disorder known as parasitosis (formication) or cocaine "bugs" can occur. This is often preceded by visual hallucinations known as "snow lights," or as formed geometrical figures.

Cocaine-associated organic mental disorders

Given the widespread use and abuse of recreational drugs, physicians should include substance intoxication and withdrawal in the differential diagnosis of acute mental status changes. When evaluating a state of hyperarousal, intoxication by other stimulants, hallucinogens and phencyclidine (PCP), as well as withdrawal from CNS depressants, must be considered.

Cocaine-induced delirium usually begins with the acute onset of paranoia followed by bizarre and violent behavior. Disorientation and cognitive impairment along with disturbances in attention and perception also occur. Hyperthermia, mydriasis and autonomic instability leading to respiratory collapse may occur suddenly and without warning.

Cocaine-induced delirium resembles that caused by anticholinergic drugs and PCP. Cocaine delirium differs from anticholinergic toxicity by the presence of excess perspiration. PCP toxicity is characterized by the presence of lateral nystagmus.

CARDIOVASCULAR COMPLICATIONS

Cocaine intoxication can manifest itself in a variety of life-threatening conditions. The cardiovascular system is particularly vulnerable due to cocaine's inhibition of norepinephrine reuptake at the nerve terminal. The resulting vasoconstriction leads to hypertension and increased cardiac workload. Cases of Prinzmetal angina and myocardial infarction secondary to direct coronary vasoconstriction have been reported in the literature.

Cocaine is also arrhythmogenic, either due to direct cardiac toxicity or through cardiac sensitization by catecholamines. The spectrum of rhythm changes range from asystole to ventricular fibrillation. In the young, otherwise healthy user, it is not uncommon to find evidence of past cardiac damage. In the older user with documented cardiac disease, the consequences of use can be devastating. Cases of congestive heart failure and accelerated atherosclerosis presumably secondary to chronic cocaine intoxication have been reported (Karch & Billingham, 1988).

183

NEUROLOGICAL COMPLICATIONS

Seizures

Animal studies have shown a strong correlation between seizures and cocaine-induced death. Hyperthermia and hyperthermia-induced seizures were the main causes of death while cardiovascular mechanisms were less important. A suggested mechanism was a lowering of the seizure threshold by the local anesthetic properties of cocaine.

Typically, cocaine-induced seizures are generalized, though focal seizures also occur. In the case of generalized seizures, the diagnosis is often clear while the complex behaviors accompanying partial complex seizures can sometimes be mistaken for psychosis. EEG and CT scans can verify the clinical impression and rule out structural causes. Benzodiazepines and/or phenobarbital should be used to treat *status epilepticus,* which is a rare complication of cocaine intoxication.

Brain hemorrhage and stroke

Sudden intracranial bleeds have been described as a complication of cocaine abuse. Usually they develop severe headache of sudden onset with or without associated focal neurological deficits. Rarely, subarachnoid hemorrhage presenting as a confusional state mimics psychiatric illness. While the mechanisms involved in cocaine-induced brain hemorrhage are complex, angiography has shown that an underlying AV malformation or aneurysm is present in half these cases. Hypertension is presumed to have led to hemorrhage in abnormal vessels.

PREGNANCY AND COCAINE USE

The low molecular weight of cocaine, and its high solubility in water and lipids, results in rapid placental transfer. Reduced plasma cholinesterase activity due to fetal immaturity may allow for toxic cocaine accumulation in the fetus (Chasnoff, Lewis & Squires, 1987).

Obstetrical complications include increased rates of spontaneous abortion due to increased uterine contractility and *abruptio placentae.* The latter is most likely due to increased blood pressure and vasoconstriction resulting in decreased uterine blood flow and decreased oxygen transfer.

Adverse perinatal effects include prematurity and intrauterine growth retardation (MacGregor, Keith et al., 1987; Chouteau, Namerow & Leppert, 1988). Some studies have found that the prevalence of congenital defects in cocaine-abusing women is increased over that of the general population (Platt, 1997)

184

although other studies found no association (Kaltenbach & Finnegan, 1997). However some of these studies did not adequately control for other essential factors (alcohol, smoking, nutrition and prenatal care). One case control study found that cocaine-exposed children adopted at birth had lower scores on language tests at school age compared with control children matched for mother's IQ and socioeconomic status. However, the study did not control for intrauterine exposure to alcohol and tobacco (Nulman, Rovet et al., 1994). The term "cocaine baby" is more a lay term than a medical entity. Maternal cocaine use in the nursing mother has resulted in acute cocaine intoxication in the infant. For this reason, breastfeeding by the cocaine-using mother is contraindicated (Chasnoff, Lewis & Squires, 1987).

IDENTIFICATION OF COCAINE ABUSERS

As with most drugs of abuse, there is no "typical" cocaine abuser profile. Asking specific questions, in a non-judgmental fashion, about drugs of abuse will give the practitioner a clearer insight into a patient's problem. General questions will not draw out information about specific drugs of abuse due to embarrassment or fear of legal consequences. Collateral information from a friend or spouse is often very helpful.

Cocaine users often present in the emergency room with manifestations of toxicity in the target end organs. Cardiac symptoms, including chest pain in an otherwise healthy young person, are a typical presentation of acute cocaine toxicity. Likewise sudden onset headache, acute psychiatric symptoms, or other neurological manifestations are commonly seen in cocaine overdose. In an outpatient clinic, or in a family practice office, signs and symptoms consistent with chronic use are more common. These would include weight loss, depression, needle marks, nasal septal perforation, chronic rhinitis and addiction to other drugs. It is important to remember that addiction is often polysubstance in nature. It is often helpful to broaden the search when evidence of addiction to one substance is detected.

BODY PACKING AND BODY STUFFING

Body packing and body stuffing syndromes pose a difficult challenge in the diagnosis and treatment of these patients.

Body packers ("mules") are individuals who smuggle drugs by means of carefully constructed double-, triple- or even quadruple-layered packages (often condoms) that are then swallowed or inserted in the vagina or rectum. Although rare, these packs can rupture or leak, leading to catastrophic overdose. Patients are usually followed radiologically in an intensive care setting until the packets are expelled. Obstruction at the gastric outlet or splenic flexure or a sudden change in the clinical picture may necessitate surgical intervention.

Body stuffing is a variation of body packing. Body stuffers typically ingest illegal drugs to conceal evidence from the authorities. Unlike the body packer, the body stuffer does not have the time to take the elaborate precautions to seal these drugs and so absorption is common. Treatment implications are numerous. Activated charcoal with gastric lavage is often effective.

Since many cocaine users who experience life-threatening complications die within minutes after using cocaine, most never arrive in the emergency department. The patient who arrives alive in the ER should survive if supportive measures are taken quickly and effectively.

PHARMACOTHERAPEUTIC APPROACHES TO TREATMENT FOR DEPENDENCE

Research into pharmacological treatment of cocaine dependency has yielded few positive results. In general terms, Kosten and his colleagues (1988,1989) have described two strategies. The *clinical rationale* is based largely on the observation that the withdrawal picture in cocaine is depressive in nature. This has led to the use of antidepressive medications for the treatment of cocaine dependency. The *neurochemical rationale,* which deals with the impact of cocaine on the dopamine reward systems of the brain, has led to the search for substances that either substitute for cocaine, act as blocking agents to cocaine, or are able to reverse the neurochemical changes that result from cocaine use.

Weiss and Mirin (1990) have proposed four classes for pharmacological agents useful in cocaine dependency. The first are agents that block the effects of cocaine, such as euphoria. Blocking agents include antidepressants (imipramine, trazodone), dopamine agonists (e.g., bromocriptine, neuroleptics such as haloperidol) and even buprenorphine and lithium as evidenced from animal studies. They have also proposed the use of aversive agents, or drugs that when taken with cocaine lead to a toxic reaction. To date, the only drug in this category is the MAOI phenelzine. The use of aversive agents in this context, however, is contraindicated due to potentially life-threatening consequences. The use of cocaine while taking phenelzine may lead to a severe toxic reaction. A similar agent in the treatment of alcoholism is disulfiram (Antabuse®). Another approach they propose is drugs to treat premorbid coexisting psychiatric conditions such as antidepressive drugs, lithium for bipolar disorder and

186

methylphenidate (Ritalin®) or magnesium pemoline for attention deficit disorder. Lastly they propose the use of drugs that treat cocaine-induced states, including withdrawal and craving. Desipramine, bromocriptine, amantadine, imipramine and flupenthixol have all been shown to have some efficacy, but to what degree is unknown.

Another promising area of research involves the manipulation of an individual's immune system such that it attacks cocaine in the bloodstream before it crosses the blood-brain barrier. The resultant cocaine complex becomes too large to cross into the brain and is therefore unable to reduce the central effects typically seen in cocaine use. This approach may prove able to protect the brain's chemistry from the effects of cocaine such as dopamine depletion, receptor upregulation and stimulation of the dopamine reward centre.

6.2

AMPHETAMINES*

Douglas L. Gourlay, MSc, MD

GENERAL DESCRIPTION

As a group, the amphetamines act as CNS stimulants. Typically, their use produces transient effects such as wakefulness, alertness, increased availability of energy, anorexia and a general sense of well-being.

Although initially used for their decongestant properties, amphetamines gradually became used for a variety of other medical complaints including obesity, narcolepsy and attention-deficit hyperactivity disorder (ADHD). Tolerance to desired effects, physical and psychological dependence, unwanted appetite suppression and psychological dependency have led to the realization that the risks associated with use outweigh the perceived therapeutic advantage.

At high doses, this group of drugs can lead to a toxic psychosis characterized by hallucinations and paranoid delusions often accompanied by aggressive or violent behavior. Amphetamine abuse has declined from its peak in the 1960s. A specific form of amphetamine, however, crystal methamphetamine, or "ice," has been reported since the mid-1980s. In this smokable form, a very rapid onset of drug action is achieved without the injection-related risk. This profile, along with its low cost, make the "ice" form of methamphetamine comparable to the "crack" form of cocaine.

Other drugs related to amphetamines, so-called designer drugs, continue to be used. These include MDA (methyldioxyamphetamine), MDMA (methyenedioxymethamphetamine; see Section 6.4) and PMA (para-methoxyamphetamine). These drugs have both hallucinogenic and stimulant properties.

---

*Adapted from Brands, Sproule & Marshman, 1998.

Indications

The medical indications for amphetamines have become very limited but include:

- narcolepsy — amphetamine or dextroamphetamine in total daily dose of 5–60 mg/day.
- ADHD — as above in total daily dose of 2.5–40 mg/day.

Source and form

These drugs are produced through chemical synthesis by the pharmaceutical industry and in illicit "basement" laboratories. Amphetamines can be made simply and cheaply in a two-step synthesis (Leukart reaction) in clandestine labs.

Pharmaceutical preparations of amphetamine and d-amphetamine are white, odorless, crystalline powders with a bitter taste. They are soluble in water and slightly soluble in alcohol. Methamphetamine (not legally available in Canada) differs from the above in that it is freely soluble in both water and alcohol. Illicit products vary from a fine to a coarse powder, to crystals or "chunks." Whitish in color, the product is often packaged loose, in capsules or as tablets. Crystal methamphetamine resembles glass slivers or very clear rock salt.

Doses

Daily doses for heavy users can vary considerably from 250 mg to more than 1,000 mg per day. Although commonly taken by mouth, injected or smoked, amphetamines can also be sniffed or snorted.

NEUROPHARMACOLOGY

The amphetamines are indirect catecholamine agonists. Amphetamine use increases the release of newly synthesized (as opposed to stored) norepinephrine and dopamine. High doses of amphetamine decrease tyrosine hydroxylase activity in the neostriatum and substantia nigra regions of the brain. Also, at high doses amphetamine releases 5-hydroxytryptamine and may affect serotonergic receptors.

These synthesis-sensitive mechanisms can be contrasted with other stimulants, such as methylphenidate and cocaine, that act on stored pools rather than newly synthesized pools of catecholamines. The effect of amphetamine action on the dopamine system is interesting in that it is not stereospecific: the l and d forms of amphetamine are equipotent in reuptake inhibition of dopamine. Amphetamine affects the norepinephrine system in a similar fashion, although these receptors are more sensitive to structural changes in the parent drug. The

189

beta-phenethylamine and alpha-methyl structures are key to much of the observed action of amphetamine. Changes to these structures form the basis for the so-called designer drug class stemming from the amphetamine root.

EFFECTS OF USE

In acute and subchronic cases, amphetamines exhibit several effects, including:

- locomotor stimulation
- stereotypy induction
- aggression
- anorexia.

Short-term low-dose effects
Short-term low-dose effects include the following:

- *CNS, behavioral, subjective*: overstimulation, restlessness, dizziness, insomnia, euphoria, dysphoria, mild confusion, tremor, panic and/or psychotic episodes (rarely); reduction of appetite, dilated pupils, increased talkativeness, alertness and energy; reduction of fatigue and drowsiness, general increase in psychomotor activity, a heightened sense of well-being; improved performance on fatigue-impaired simple mental tasks
- *Cardiovascular*: palpitations, tachycardia (may be preceded by a brief bradycardia), irregular heartbeat, headache, hypertension
- *Respiratory*: tachypnea and deepening of breaths.

Long-term effects
Long-term effects include:

- chronic sleep disturbances including insomnia, frequent nocturnal awakening and poor quality sleep
- anxiety and tension states
- anorexia leading to nutritional deficiency
- cardiovascular symptoms as seen with short-term use.

Regular high-dose use can lead to paranoid thinking, severe agitation, repetitious behavior (stereotypy) and, in the extreme, a prolonged amphetamine psychosis.

Regular use of amphetamines often leads chronic abusers to combat drug-related effects with other drugs such as cannabis, alcohol, benzodiazepines, other sedative/hypnotics and opioids. Polydrug abuse is common.

Indirect effects related to contamination of the drug through improper manufacture or the addition of adulterants can lead to serious complications for the drug user. Frequent i.v. drug injection and sharing of needles expose the user to serious infections such as viral hepatitis, septicemia, bacterial endocarditis and HIV. Abscesses at the site of injection and general thrombophlebitic/embolic sequelae are also risks of chronic i.v. drug use (see also Section 12).

The euphoria and other mood-elevating effects of amphetamines are subject to rapid tolerance. So-called runs of amphetamine use seem to result from the user's attempts to achieve the pleasurable effects of the initial injection. While tolerance to the pleasurable effects of the drug occurs rapidly, there does not seem to be any degree of tolerance to the psychosis-producing effects of the amphetamines.

Lethality

The use of amphetamines can lead to death in several ways. Intravenous use of as little as 120 mg of amphetamine has resulted in death. However, the lethal dose varies widely and non-tolerant persons have survived doses of 400 to 500 mg.

Death results from cerebrovascular accidents, cardiac failure, hyperthermia, seizures and coma. Indirect causes of death include the numerous violent accidents, homicides and suicides that have been attributed, at least in part, to the use of stimulant drugs such as amphetamines.

IDENTIFICATION OF AMPHETAMINE ABUSERS

While there is no specific user profile for amphetamine abusers, the reader should refer to the information included in the preceding chapter on identifying cocaine abusers.

TREATMENT FOR AMPHETAMINE INTOXICATION

Patients intoxicated with amphetamines may present with anxiety, agitation, paranoid delusions and hallucinations. In the case of significant overdose, they may present with seizures and hyperthermia. Patients often respond to a quiet room and calm reassurance. Marked anxiety and agitation can be treated with short-acting benzodiazepines such as sublingual lorazepam. Psychotic symptoms can be treated with neuroleptics, although caution is needed as they can lower the seizure threshold. Hyperthermic patients require aggressive management, up to and including established protocols for malignant hyperthermia. Persisting seizures should be treated with anti-epileptics.

191

6.3

METHYLPHENIDATE

Yasemin Ikizler, MD

GENERAL DESCRIPTION

Methylphenidate (Ritalin®) is an amphetamine-like stimulant. When used inappropriately the effects are similar to cocaine and amphetamines. For this reason methylphenidate has an abuse potential similar to cocaine and amphetamines. Tolerance and dependence does occur. Therefore methylphenidate must be recognized as being a potentially abused prescription drug.

Indications
There are legitimate indications for the prescription of methylphenidate, including attention-deficit hyperactivity disorder (ADHD) and narcolepsy. The therapeutic doses for these conditions are 5–10 mg po tid and 20–60 mg od, respectively. Efficacy for ADHD is well established and safety is supported by five decades of clinical experience. Methylphenidate and dextroamphetamine are the drugs of choice for ADHD. Methylphenidate is an *adjunctive* treatment. Other components of treatment must include teaching of parenting skills, social skills teaching and assistance with classroom management. When prescribed appropriately for these two indications, methylphenidate has a therapeutic effect and abuse is not common.

Street names
Children's cocaine, poor man's cocaine, rits, uppers.

Routes of administration
The most obvious route of administration is oral ingestion. Because methylphenidate is water-soluble it can be administered intravenously. There are also reports in the literature of intranasal administration of crushed tablets. Individuals who are heavily dependent on methylphenidate report using several hundred milligrams of the substance on a daily basis.

192

ADVERSE EFFECTS

Adverse effects of methylphenidate at therapeutic doses ($\leq$ 60 mg/day) include upset stomach, headache, decreased appetite, dizziness, nervousness, euphoria and insomnia. Tics and depression can be exacerbated. Rebound effects can occur when the medication wears off. Drug holidays are recommended on a yearly basis.

Effects of greater than therapeutic doses (> 60 mg/day) of methylphenidate over short time periods include hyperactivity, excitation, agitation, muscle twitching, confusion, hallucinations, paranoid thinking, pupillary dilation, flushing, increased blood pressure, increased pulse rate, dryness of mouth, vomiting, fever and sweating. Hazardous doses of methylphenidate may result in delirium, convulsions and possibly coma.

After long-term abuse of high doses of methylphenidate, a state similar to amphetamine psychosis can occur. The condition resolves itself with cessation of methylphenidate use.

Other medical complications

Other medical complications of methylphenidate abuse include stroke, hyperthermia, hypertension and seizures. Individuals may also develop pulmonary talcosis as a result of injecting insoluble binding agents such as talc, cornstarch or cellulose which are found in the methylphenidate tablets. Microscopic pulmonary emboli result. The inflammatory reaction then leads to pulmonary talcosis, interstitial fibrosis, emphysema, pulmonary hypertension and respiratory failure.

MANAGEMENT OF ACUTE INTOXICATION

Management of acute methylphenidate intoxication is supportive in nature. No pharmacotherapy specific to methylphenidate use exists. Maintenance of hydration and the correction of electrolyte imbalances are important. Short-term use of an antipsychotic medication may be necessary in situations of acute psychosis. Referral to an addiction treatment specialist is important to prevent relapse and provide support.

ABUSE

One common scenario of methylphenidate abuse occurs when parents of children with ADHD abuse their children's prescribed medication. This scenario is common when the parents have a history of drug and/or alcohol problems.

193

Abuse of methylphenidate by children and adolescents with ADHD is possible if the individual has a history of drug or alcohol abuse. Fortunately, this is not common. Two consistent characteristics of individuals who abuse methylphenidate are their older ages and long histories of polysubstance abuse. There have been media reports of methylphenidate abuse by adolescents who obtain the medication from peers who have been prescribed methylphenidate. The source of methylphenidate in all of these cases is almost exclusively through diversion of prescriptions. Patients have reported that physicians often seem to be unaware of the abuse potential of methylphenidate. As a result of this, patients report that obtaining prescriptions is fairly easy.

There has been controversy in the literature about whether children with ADHD are more prone to substance abuse problems. To date, the literature presents no evidence that the use of stimulants in the treatment of ADHD leads to future substance abuse. In fact, the belief that there is a correlation between methylphenidate treatment for ADHD and future substance abuse can create a barrier to individuals with ADHD who require treatment for substance use problems. Case reports in the literature indicate that individuals with concurrent diagnoses are more successful in recovery from drug and alcohol problems when their underlying concurrent disorder is treated. Therefore, treatment of ADHD with methylphenidate in carefully selected individuals may be appropriate even in the context of chemical dependency. A recent study found that appropriate treatment of ADHD in adolescence resulted in an 85 per cent reduction in risk for future substance abuse (Biederman, Wilens et al, 1999). Further research is needed in this area.

A history of substance abuse does not exclude methylphenidate as a treatment option for ADHD. The physician must be aware of the abuse potential, be able to recognize and manage drug-seeking behavior and be able to diagnose and manage the problems of chemical dependency.

S U G G E S T E D   R E A D I N G

Elia, J., Ambrosini, P.J. & Rapoport, J.L. (1999). Treatment of attention-deficit-hyperactivity disorder. *New England Journal of Medicine, 340(10)*, 780–788.

Zametkin, A.J. & Ernst, M. (1999). Problems in the management of attention-deficit-hyperactivity disorder. *New England Journal of Medicine, 340(1)*, 40–46.

6.4

MDMA

Douglas L. Gourlay, MSc, MD

GENERAL DESCRIPTION

The drug 3,4-methylenedioxymethamphetamine (MDMA) is often referred to as a "designer amphetamine." It has gained popularity in North America with young people, particularly at parties known as "raves." It was first synthesized in 1912 as an appetite suppressant and was also used briefly as an adjunct to psychotherapy due to its reported ability to "break down barriers" to intimacy in couples therapy. It became a restricted drug in Canada in 1976, and with its increased popularity among American youth, it was given a "most dangerous drug" classification (Schedule 1) in 1985.

Indications
There are no current clinical indications for the use of MDMA. It is produced in limited quantities in research laboratories and on a large scale in clandestine drug labs.

Street names
Ecstasy, XTC, Adam, Euphoria, X, MDM, M&M, Rave, Hug Drug.

NEUROPHARMACOLOGY

MDMA has a variety of psychoactive properties. Affecting both the dopaminergic and serotonergic systems, it is an amphetamine-like drug that is usually taken orally. Users typically report tachycardia, increased blood pressure, anorexia, decreased fatigue, mood elevation, and jaw clenching or bruxisms. Frank hallucinations are rarely, if ever, reported. The desired effects for which the drug is taken include euphoria, heightened sensuality, and enhanced feelings of closeness, affection and ease of communication. Users also report a decrease in

195

feelings of self-consciousness and embarrassment. Some of these effects are mediated by displacement of dopamine and norepinephrine. It has been suggested that displacement of serotonin and the resultant increased availability at the synapses may underlie the positive feelings surrounding MDMA use.

Adverse effects include unstable gait, fatigue and nausea. The effects of the drug typically last from four to six hours after a single oral dose of approximately 100 mg.

Neurotoxicity

Neurotoxicity has been studied in both primate and non-primate models. Despite exaggerated doses in excess of typical doses of 1–2 mg/kg, evidence of toxicity is limited. There are dose-related reductions in both brain serotonin (5-HT) and 5-hydroxyindoleacetic acid (5-HIAA). There is a diminution of 5-HT uptake sites and a decreased activity of tryptophan hydroxylase, which is a necessary enzyme for serotonin synthesis. This neurotoxicity has also been seen with other serotonin displacers including MDA, methamphetamine and the appetite suppressant fenfluramine.

General toxicity

Reports in the United Kingdom suggest a myriad of systemic toxic effects from use of MDMA. These include cardiac dysrhythmias, aplastic anemia and hepatotoxicity. Reports of extreme hyperthermia and dehydration leading to rhabdomyolysis, disseminated intravascular coagulopathy (DIC), acute renal failure and death have come from the United Kingdom but not the United States or Holland. The practice of "raves" and the intense physical activity in hot crowded halls may have played a significant role in these more serious complications of MDMA use. In the UK, it is common to advise youth to remain well hydrated and to avoid overheated, crowded dance halls.

EFFECTS OF LONG-TERM USE

Although not well studied, long-term users of MDMA report increased physical discomfort (hangover) as well as weight loss, exhaustion, "flashbacks," irritability, paranoia, depression, psychosis and loss of desired effect. Symptoms can be short-lived, associated largely with acute dosing, to longer-lasting (weeks to months) residual effects. Little is known about the tolerance and dependency of chronic use of MDMA but it would seem that tolerance, at least to the positive effects of the drug, develops quickly. It has been shown to lead to self-administration in animal models, supporting its addictive potential.

In general terms, MDMA should not be thought of as a benign recreational drug. Its inherent reinforcing nature and rapid tolerance gives it a clear potential as a drug of abuse. Whether the drug itself is causative in the reported deaths and serious medical complications, or whether the harm is due to a combination of factors between the drug and its manner of use, is not clear. It is clear, however, that the increased use of this drug has resulted in significant morbidity.

R E F E R E N C E S

Azmitia, E.C. & Whitaker-Azmitia, P.M. (1991). Awakening the sleeping giant: Anatomy and plasticity of the brain serotonergic system. *Journal of Clinical Psychiatry, 52(suppl)*, 4-16.

Battaglia, G., Yeh, S.U. & DeSouza, E.B. (1988). MDMA-induced neurotoxicity: Parameters of degeneration and recovery of brain serotonin neurons. *Pharmacology, Biochemistry and Behavior, 29(2)*, 269-274.

Brands, B., Sproule, B. & Marshman, J.A. (Eds.). (1998). *Drugs and Drug Abuse* (3rd ed.). Toronto: Addiction Research Foundation.

Brody, S., Krause, C., Veit, R. & Rau, H. (1998). Cardiovascular autonomic dysregulation in users of MDMA ("Ecstasy"). *Psychopharmacology, 136(4)*, 390-393.

Bunt, G., Galanter, M., Lifshutz, H. & Castaneda, R. (1990). Cocaine/"crack" dependence among psychiatric inpatients. *American Journal of Psychiatry, 147*, 1542-1546.

Canadian Centre on Substance Abuse and Addiction Research Foundation. (1997). *Canadian Profile: Alcohol, Tobacco and Other Drugs, 1997*. Ottawa: CCSA.

Chasnoff, I.J., Lewis, D.E. & Squires, L. (1987). Cocaine intoxication in a breast-fed infant. *Pediatrics, 80*, 836-838.

Chouteau, M., Namerow, P.B. & Leppert, P. (1988). The effect of cocaine abuse on birth weight and gestational age. *Obstetrics and Gynecology, 72*, 351-354.

Cole, T.B. (1996). Identifying substance abusers at preschool age. *Journal of the American Medical Association, 275*, 1391-1392.

Cuomo, M.J., Dyment, P.G. & Gammino, V.M. (1994). Increasing use of "ecstacy" (MDMA) and other hallucinogens on a college campus. *Journal of the American College Health Association, 42(6)*, 271-274.

Elia, J. (1993). Drug treatment for hyperactive children: Therapeutic guidelines. *Drugs, 46*, 863-871.

Elk, C. (1996). MDMA (Ecstacy): Useful information for health professionals involved in drug education programs. *Journal of Drug Education, 26(4)*, 349-356.

Erickson, P.G., Adlaf, E.M., Smart, R.G. & Murray, G.F. (1994). *The Steel Drug: Cocaine and Crack in Perspective*. Toronto: Maxwell Macmillan.

Fineschi, V. & Masti, A. (1996). Fatal poisoning by MDMA (ecstasy) and MDEA: A case report. *International Journal of Legal Medicine, 108(50)*, 272-275.

Galanter, M., Egelko, S., De Leon, G., Rohrs, C. & Franco, H. (1992). Crack/cocaine abusers in the general hospital: Assessment and initiation of care. *American Journal of Psychiatry, 149*, 810-815.

Hoffman, R.S., Henry, G.C., Howland, M.A., Weisman, R.S., Weil, L. & Goldfrank, L.R. (1992). Association between life-threatening cocaine toxicity and plasma cholinesterase activity. *Annals of Emergency Medicine, 21*, 247-253.

Jaffe, S.L. (1991). Intranasal abuse of prescribed methylphenidate by an alcohol and drug-abusing adolescent with ADHD. *Journal of the American Academy of Child and Adolescent Psychiatry, 30*, 773-775.

Kaltenback, K. & Finnegan, L. (1998). Prevention and treatment issues for pregnant cocaine-dependent women and their infants. In J.A. Harvey, B.E. Kosofsky et al. (Eds.), *Cocaine: Effects on the Developing Brain. Annals of the New York Academy of Sciences, 846* (pp 329-334). New York: New York Academy of Sciences.

Karch, S.B. & Billingham, M.E. (1988). The pathology and etiology of cocaine-induced heart disease. *Archive of Pathology and Laboratory Medicine,112(3)*, 225-230.

Kosten, T.R., Kleber, H.D. & Morgan, C. (1989). Treatment of cocaine abuse with buprenorphine. *Biological Psychiatry, 26(6)*, 637-639.

Kosten, T.R., Schumann, B. & Wright, D. (1988). Bromocriptine treatment of cocaine abuse in patients maintained on methadone. *American Journal of Psychiatry, 145(3)*, 381-382.

Lowinson, J.H., Ruiz, P., Millman, R.B. & Langrod, J. (Eds.). (1996). *Substance Abuse: A Comprehensive Textbook* (3rd ed.). Baltimore, MD: Williams and Wilkins.

MacGregor, S.N., Keith, L.G, Chasnoff, I.J., Rosner, M.A., Chisum, G.M., Shaw, P. & Minogue, J.P. (1987). Cocaine use during pregnancy: Adverse perinatal outcome. *American Journal of Obstetrics & Gynecology, 157,* 686-690.

Miller, N.S., Gold, M.S. & Millman, R.L. (1989). Cocaine. *American Family Physician, 39(2),* 115-120.

Milroy, C.M. & Smith, C.L. (1996). Pathology of deaths associated with "ecstasy" and "eve" misuse. *Journal of Clinical Pathology, 49(2),* 149-153.

Nulman, I., Rovet, J., Altmann, D., Bradley, C., Einarson, T. & Koren, G. (1994). Neurodevelopment of adopted children exposed *in utero* to cocaine. *Canadian Medical Association Journal, 151(11),* 1591-1597.

Padley, S.P., Adler, B.D., Staples, C.A., Miller, R.R. & Miller, N.L. (1993). Pulmonary talcosis: CT findings in three cases. *Radiology, 186,* 125-127.

Parran, T.V., Jr. & Jasinski, D.R. (1991). Intravenous methylphenidate abuse: Prototype for prescription drug abuse. *Archives of Internal Medicine, 151,* 781-783.

Platt, J.J. (1997). *Cocaine Addiction: Theory, Research and Treatment.* Cambridge, MA: Harvard University Press.

Safer, D.J. & Krager, J.M. (1992). Effect of a media blitz and a threatened lawsuit on stimulant treatment. *Journal of the American Medical Association, 268,* 1004-1007.

Schubiner, H., Tzelepis, A., Isaacson, J.H., Warbasse, L.H., Zacharek, M. & Musial, J. (1995). The dual diagnosis of attention-deficit/hyperactivity disorder and substance abuse: Case reports and literature review. *Journal of Clinical Psychiatry, 56,* 146-150.

Substance Abuse and Mental Health Services Administration. (1998). *National Household Survey on Drug Abuse: Main Findings 1996.* Rockville, MD: Substance Abuse and Mental Health Services Administration.

Weinmann, W. & Bohnert, M. (1998). Lethal monointoxication by overdosage of MDEA. *Forensic Science International, 91(2),* 91-101.

Weiss, R.D. & Mirin, S.M. (1990). Psychological and pharmacological treatment strategies in cocaine dependence. *Annals of Clinical Psychiatry, 2(4),* 239-243.

Hallucinogens

7.1   CANNABIS

7.2   LSD

7.3   PHENCYCLIDINE (PCP)

7.1

CANNABIS

Thea Weisdorf, MD

GENERAL DESCRIPTION

Drug source
Marijuana, hashish and hashish oil are obtained from the plant *Cannabis sativa*, which grows in both tropical and temperate climates. The principal psychoactive constituent of this plant is delta-9-tetrahydrocannabinol (THC), a hallucinogenic substance.

Medical uses
There are no widely accepted medical uses. However, marijuana, THC and structurally similar synthetic chemicals are under study in the treatment of epilepsy, wide-angle glaucoma, anorexia nervosa and asthma, for relief of nausea and vomiting produced by anticancer therapy, and as an appetite stimulant in HIV/AIDS.

THC, available as dronabinol (Marinol®), is used to treat nausea and vomiting caused by cancer chemotherapy. A related synthetic compound, nabilone (Cesamet®), is also available for this purpose.

Street names
Bhang, Colombian, ganja, grass, hemp, joint, pot, reefer.

Physical appearance
Marijuana is prepared from the dried flowering tops and leaves of the harvested plant and may range in color from greyish-green to greenish-brown. The THC content in marijuana depends on the growing conditions, the genetic characteristics of the plant and the proportions of flowering parts, lower leaves, upper leaves, stems and seeds in the marijuana preparation. Hydroponic growth of cloned material from high potency plants may yield concentrations of THC as high as 10 per cent or more.

203

Hashish consists of dried cannabis resin and compressed flowers, ranging in color from light ochre brown to almost black. It is sold on the street in the form of hard chunks or cubes. The THC content of hashish sold in North America may be as high as 15 per cent.

Cannabis oil is a viscous, highly potent substance obtained by extracting the cannabinoids from hashish with an organic solvent and concentrating the filtered extract. The concentration of THC in hashish oil is generally from 10 to 20 per cent, although samples containing 70 per cent have been confiscated (Brands, Sproule & Marshman, 1998).

Routes of administration

Almost all possible routes of administration have been used, but by far the most common method is smoking (inhaling) a hand-rolled "joint" resembling a cigarette. Cannabis, particularly hashish, may be cooked or baked in food. The oral dose must be three to five times greater than the smoked dose to produce the equivalent intensity of effect. Very rarely, extracts of cannabis have been injected, usually resulting in unpleasant side-effects, such as pain and inflammation at the injection site, and toxic systemic effects.

TOLERANCE, DEPENDENCE AND POTENTIAL FOR ABUSE

Frequent and longer-term regular administration of high daily doses of cannabis results in less sensitivity to the desired effects. Additionally, clinical observations suggest that tolerance develops. Therefore, regular high-dose smokers must increase their daily dose to achieve the desired intensity of the psychoactive effects.

With regular high-dose use, tolerance develops to some of the other effects of cannabis: rapid heart rate, impaired performance on psychomotor tasks and other forms of cognitive impairment.

Psychological dependence on cannabis can develop with regular use. Indicators of psychological dependence include a persistent craving for its psychoactive effects, the central role it can take on in the user's life and the anxiety and feelings of panic if the drug is temporarily unavailable.

Similarly, with regular use, physical dependence may develop. Abrupt termination of use can produce a mild withdrawal syndrome, with symptoms including sleep disturbances, irritability, loss of appetite and weight, nervousness, anxiety, sweating and upset stomach. This typically lasts for less than a week, although sleep disturbances may persist. It has been suggested that in adolescent heavy users it is the withdrawal symptoms and not the psychological drug craving that contributes to the persistent use of cannabis or reinstitution of drug use despite motivation to stop (Duffy & Milin, 1996).

Cannabis and other subsequent substance use

While there is a statistical association between the use of cannabis and subsequent use of other substances, the reason for that link is less clear. It is unlikely that the use of cannabis in itself leads to use of other illicit drugs. For example, while roughly one in four Canadians has used cannabis at some point in their lives, only 4 per cent have used crack or powder cocaine (Canadian Centre on Substance Abuse & Addiction Research Foundation, 1997). A more likely explanation is that cannabis use may be one of several social and cultural factors associated with the use of other illicit drugs.

EPIDEMIOLOGY

In 1989, Health and Welfare Canada conducted a national telephone survey of 11,634 persons aged 15 years and older, and found that 23 per cent of the sample reported they had used cannabis at least once in their lifetimes, with higher rates among males than females across all age groups. Prevalence of lifetime use declined with age, from a high of 43 per cent among those aged 20–24 to 10 per cent among those aged 45–54 and 2 per cent among those aged 55–64.

Several surveys of the prevalence of marijuana use in high-school students have shown a consistent increase through the 1970s followed by a stabilization and decline in the 1980s. More recent surveys indicate a resurgence of use in the 1990s. Although marijuana use by Canadian high-school students in Ontario increased from 1989 to 1995, a recent study found that the level of use remained unchanged from 1995 to 1997 (Adlaf, Ivis & Smart, 1997).

HEALTH EFFECTS

Short-term use — low to moderate doses

• CNS, behavioral, subjective (some or all may occur): disinhibition and garrulousness; relaxation and drowsiness; general feeling of well-being; distortions of the perception of time, body image and distance; increased auditory and visual acuity; enhanced tactile, olfactory, kinesthetic and gustatory senses; spontaneous laughter; mild impairment of recent memory and concentration; mild confusion and disorientation; reduced attention span; impaired ability to process information; impaired balance and stability when standing; decreased

205

muscle strength and hand steadiness; impaired ability to perform complex motor tasks; fearfulness and anxiety; mild paranoia.

• Cardiovascular: increased heart rate; increased peripheral blood flow; rapid fall in blood pressure when changing from lying to sitting/standing; reddening of the eyes.

• Respiratory: irritation of respiratory mucosal membranes; bronchodilation.

• Gastrointestinal: increased appetite; dryness of mouth and throat.

Short-term use — higher doses

Intensification of the low-dose effects as well as:

• CNS, behavioral, subjective: synesthesias (melding of one sensory modality with another); pseudohallucinations; impaired judgment; slowed reaction time; impairment of simple motor task performance; confusion; true hallucinations, delusions and feelings of depersonalization; pronounced paranoia, agitation and panicky feelings (Brands, Sproule & Marshman, 1998).

A recent study has highlighted that the existence of individual vulnerabilities such as a personal or family history of schizophrenia is adversely affected by cannabis use (Hall, Solowij & Lemon, 1994). Cannabis use has been shown to negatively affect schizophrenia in the following ways: lower age of onset, more severe clinical disability, poorer therapeutic response, higher rate of recurrences and increased demand for services (Allebeck, Adamsson et al., 1993; Negrete, Knapp et al., 1986; Martinez-Arevalo, Calcedo Ordonez et al., 1994).

Long-term use

• Psychological: Occasional and more regular low-dose use (smoking one marijuana cigarette one or two times a week) probably does not significantly affect normal psychological functioning in healthy adults.

• Controversy abounds regarding the association between those individuals who are regular high-dose users and significant psychological adjustment problems. One pattern of behavior frequently described is the chronic intoxication state referred to as "amotivational syndrome," which is characterized by lethargy, emotional apathy, mental slowing, impairment of memory, and reduced ability to plan and carry out complex activities and long-term plans (Millman & Sbriglio, 1986). It has yet to be firmly established whether a causal relationship exists between amotivational syndrome and heavy cannabis use or whether the syndrome arises from the combination of a preexisting disposition of the user to the symptoms described, reinforced by chronic heavy use.

206

- It is fairly well established that certain symptoms do appear in chronic heavy cannabis users. The most important of these are memory and concentration impairment. Other symptoms described include a gradual loss of pleasurable effects from smoking the drug and a gradual shift towards undesirable effects such as despondency, depersonalization, poor sexual performance and less satisfying sleep (Weller & Halikas, 1982; Halikas, Weller et al., 1985).

- Respiratory: Heavy cannabis users will experience increased episodes of bronchitis, asthma and sore throats. Cannabis, when smoked, yields more tar than strong brands of tobacco. This, in conjunction with the fact that the user generally inhales more deeply and holds cannabis smoke in the lungs for much longer periods per puff, intensifies the adverse effects.

- Endocrine and reproductive: Long-term studies are again conflicting, yet it is generally accepted that there are disruptions in hormonal balance and a decrease in sperm count in adult users. However, there appears to be little or no substantial effect on fertility. What has not yet been proven is whether even temporary endocrine disturbances may produce permanent impairment of development in adolescents if occurring at a critical stage in maturation.

- Immunologic: Many animal studies confirm that cannabinoids suppress both cellular and humoral components of immune responses. These findings have been inconsistent in human studies (Brands, Sproule & Marshman, 1998).

- Fetal and newborn effects: Some discrepancy prevails among studies, but evidence exists on the following detrimental effects of *in utero* exposure to cannabis on fetal and postnatal development: significantly lower birthweights and babies who were smaller for a given gestational age (Hingson, Zuckerman et al., 1986; Hatch & Bracken, 1986); greater frequency of protracted or precipitate labor and more evidence of fetal distress (Greenland, Staisch et al., 1982); more irritability and less responsiveness to light stimuli (Fried, 1982); and a higher incidence of minor anomalies (O'Connell & Fried, 1984; Hingson, Zuckerman et al., 1986).

TREATMENT FOR CANNABIS ABUSE

Few studies exist on the treatment of marijuana-related problems. Many subjects report an interest in treatment aimed at cessation of use, but few report participating in prior treatment (Rainone, Deren et al., 1987; Roffman & Barnhart, 1987). Some have promoted adaptations of 12-step approaches to the treatment of marijuana dependence (Miller, Gold & Pottash, 1989; Zweben & O'Connell, 1988). Marlatt and Gordon's (1980, 1985) relapse prevention treatment model

207

promotes the belief that addiction or dependence is primarily a learned behavior and that relapse is a failure of behavioral and cognitive coping skills rather than a physiologically based loss of control over substance use. No one model has proven to be superior and much study is needed in this area.

7.2

LSD

Douglas L. Gourlay, MSc, MD

GENERAL DESCRIPTION

LSD (lysergic acid diethylamide) was first synthesized by Albert Hofmann in 1938 at the Sandoz laboratory in Basel, Switzerland. It was not until the spring of 1943 that its psychedelic properties were realized. LSD is the most powerful of the known hallucinogens.

Indications

There are no medical indications for the use of LSD. Although a very small amount of the drug is produced legally for research purposes, LSD is typically produced in illicit drug laboratories.

Street names

Acid, barrels, blotters, California sunshine, cube, domes, flats, frogs, lids, wedges, windowpane. In combination with MDMA ("ecstasy"; see drug information sheet on ecstasy in Appendix 3) the term "candy-flipping" has been used. Note that PCP is often contained as an adulterant in LSD sold on the street. In some cases, PCP itself is passed on the street as LSD.

NEUROPHARMACOLOGY

Clinical research has indicated that LSD may exert its effects by interacting with serotonin receptors. There also is evidence that LSD binds to dopamine receptors.

EFFECTS OF LSD

In doses as small as 25–50 μg LSD can produce mild changes in perception, mood and thought. At higher doses, the effects become more intense and at 100 μg may include visual "pseudohallucinations" and distortions that the subject usually knows to be unreal. Synesthesia, the confusion of the senses, can be experienced by users who believe that they are able to "see" music or "hear" visual patterns. There may be a loss of boundary between self and the environment, with a distortion of body image, space and time. Time is often said to pass very slowly during the period of drug effect. A sense of gaining great insight into oneself may occur, although feelings of alienation from self and surroundings may also occur. The term "trip" describes the sense of wonder and joy that may occur. The perception of adverse experiences, a so-called bad trip, may occur even in those who have previously had pleasant experiences using the drug.

Psychiatric effects

There have been reports of severe psychotic episodes that may last beyond the normal elimination period for the drug. The psychotic state may include bizarre behavior, delusional thinking, terror and true hallucinations (which the user believes to be real), in contrast to the previously mentioned "pseudohallucinations." In the case of persistent psychosis, it would appear that LSD had unmasked rather than caused a schizophrenic state. Flashbacks (Hallucinogen Persisting Perception Disorder [HPPD], a DSM-IV diagnosis) may be experienced by some users for months or years after last use. As with many other hallucinogens, LSD cannot be taken for more than a few days before it loses its psychic potency. Tolerance to these effects develops quickly, though there is no evidence of physical dependence.

Acute use

With short-term use, CNS effects predominate. Early effects may include numbness, muscle weakness, muscle twitching, hyperreflexia, tremulousness and impairment of co-ordination and motor skills. There may be anxiety or exhilaration, and, although rare, frank seizures have been reported.

Onset of action is usually 30 to 40 minutes after the oral administration of LSD. The magnitude of the effect is dependent on both the dose and the setting in which the drug is taken. The user's expectation, past drug experience and underlying personality play essential roles. It is interesting that even within the same user, subsequent drug experience may be quite different. These effects typically subside within six to eight hours.

Chronic use

In the context of chronic use, several effects have been described. Flashbacks (HPPD) may be the most frequently reported phenomenon associated with LSD use, and although they are not common, frequent users of LSD are said to be at greater risk of flashbacks. There is no evidence of organic brain damage or that those who experience flashbacks are more psychologically disturbed than those who do not. Visual flashbacks are most commonly described although other senses are represented to a lesser extent.

An "amotivational syndrome" has been described in some chronic LSD users. Apathy and decreasing interest in the users' environment may in fact represent effects of the lifestyle adopted by many members of the drug culture and not be clearly "caused" by the use of LSD.

Both one-time users and chronic users of LSD have developed persistent psychotic states. In many respects, this psychosis resembles a paranoid schizophrenia characterized by true hallucinations, delusional thinking and bizarre behavior. Whether LSD plays a causal role in this persistent psychosis or simply unmasks a latent psychotic state is not clear.

Other effects
Physical effects that are described are largely sympathetically mediated and occur from 15 to 45 minutes after ingesting LSD. Increased blood pressure and heart rate, rapid and deepened breathing, nausea and vomiting, suppression of appetite and hyperthermia have all been observed.

Initial concerns of chromosomal damage in some laboratory studies have not been proven. There does seem to be an increased risk of spontaneous abortion and congenital abnormalities in fetuses of mothers who regularly used LSD during pregnancy. However, the use of other drugs during pregnancy by the women confounds any attempts at proving a causal relationship.

TREATMENT FOR LSD ABUSE

While there is no specific treatment agreed upon for hallucinogen abuse, several points must be kept in mind. There are no specific pharmacological agents targeted towards treating hallucinogen abuse. Patients who exhibit a concurrent psychiatric disorder need appropriate management of the psychiatric problem while addressing the substance use issues. The primary treatment modality is often behavioral in nature using such techniques as cognitive and guided self-change strategies. Outpatient programs offer the individual the ability to address drug use problems in a more natural setting than that experienced in the residential treatment setting. In persons who have failed at outpatient treatment, residential and therapeutic community approaches may be beneficial.

The use of LSD is not particularly reinforcing; users must "learn" to enjoy it. While there is no evidence of withdrawal or abstinence syndrome, there does seem to be a psychological dependence among some users. "Use despite harm" and preoccupation with getting and using this drug do meet the psychological criteria for addiction. Although a drug with low intrinsic lethality, LSD has caused accidental death, homicide and death by suicide during its use. As the most powerful member of the hallucinogen group, LSD remains a concern.

7.3

PHENCYCLIDINE (PCP)

Douglas L. Gourlay, MSc, MD

GENERAL DESCRIPTION

Phencyclidine (1-1(phenylcyclohexyl) piperidine; PCP; "angel dust") was developed in the mid-1950s by Parke-Davis. It was marketed under the trade name Sernyl® for use as a general anesthetic agent. As an anesthetic it had a number of unique and promising properties: it lacked the cardiovascular depressant effects of typical anesthetics at typical clinical doses; and, it induced a unique anesthetic state characterized by generalized catatonia, flat face, open mouth and a fixed staring gaze. There was no overt loss of consciousness as observed with typical general anesthetics but rather a "dissociative state" apart from the environment. For this reason, phencyclidine and the related compounds cylcohexamine and ketamine were classed as dissociative anesthetics.

Several of PCP's properties, however, led to its discontinuation in clinical use in humans. Severe intraoperative reactions including agitation and hallucinations, and emergence phenomena such as frank psychotic states that persisted in some cases for one hour to 10 days were observed. For these reasons, clinical use of phencyclidine and the related compound cyclohexamine was abandoned in 1965. Only the less potent drug ketamine continues to be used in clinical operative anesthesia.

It is interesting that substances with such clear negative and aversive behavioral properties should become drugs of abuse. In fact, much of the PCP ingested in the mid-1960s and 1970s was mixed with other drugs of abuse. During the last half of 1970 and beyond, a steady increase in the purity of PCP was noted. PCP had become a drug of choice for many individuals.

Indications
While not used clinically in humans, PCP continues to be used in veterinary medicine. For this reason, PCP continues to be available for illicit diversion.

213

Ketamine, however, remains a drug of use in anesthesia, particularly for children, in trauma cases where hemodynamic stability is difficult to maintain, and as a sedative for use in repetitive but painful procedures such as burn debridement.

Intravenous low-dose ketamine for sedation is of the order of 0.2–0.5 mg/kg body weight, while anesthetic doses are typically 1–2 mg/ kg. A feature of ketamine that is of particular use is its analgesic effect. This effect is seen with low-dose ketamine and typically persists after the patient regains consciousness. Amnesia lasts for approximately one hour after apparent recovery.

Street names
Amoeba, angel dust, animal tranquillizer, cadillac, crystal, crystal joint, CJ, DOA (dead on arrival), dust, elephant tranquillizer, goon, hog, horse tranquillizer, killer weed, KJ, lovely, mist, PCP, peace, peace pill, PeaCe Pill, peace weed, rocket fuel, scuffle, seams, sheet, snorts, supergrass, super kools, superweed, surfer, synthetic THC.

METHOD OF USE

The typical method of use is by snorting or smoking. This gives the user better control over the drug dose as compared with the oral form. Chronic users take from 100 mg to 1 g within a 24-hour period. The effects last between four and six hours followed by a longer "coming down" period. The drug is usually used in a social setting and its use crosses all socioeconomic boundaries. Chronic users show persistent cognitive and memory problems, speech difficulties, mood disorders, loss of purposeful activities and weight loss. This may last for a year or more after last use. In extreme cases, chronic users may develop paranoia and violent behavior with auditory hallucinations.

EPIDEMIOLOGY

As recently as 1997, data from the United States indicated that, of the total population, 0.2 per cent tried PCP in the previous year. This can be compared with annual use rates for marijuana, cocaine, crack and inhalants of 9.0 per cent, 1.9 per cent, 0.6 per cent and 1.1 per cent, respectively (Substance Abuse and Mental Health Services Administration, 1998). In 1997, 2 per cent of Ontario students between grades 7 and 13 indicated that they had used PCP in the previous year (Adlaf, Ivis & Smart, 1997).

214

NEUROPHARMACOLOGY

Depending on the dose, dissociative anesthetics can produce an excited or a cataleptoid state. The dissociative anesthetics alter a large variety of brain neurotransmitter functions, including dopamine, acetylcholine, serotonin, and the ion channel associated with N-methyl-D-aspartate (NMDA) receptors of glutamic acid. For this reason, a reversal agent for the effects of this group of compounds is unlikely to be found.

The volume of distribution is high and is present in different body tissues for varying periods. Some have suggested that phencyclidine may remain in some body fluid samples for up to two weeks. There appears to be significant variability in phencyclidine biotransformation. Both genetic and environmental factors seem to be implicated.

Neurotoxicity
Human data relating to neurotoxicity is limited. At the lower doses associated with behavioral studies there does not appear to be any significant long-lasting neurotoxicity. At abuse-level doses (5 to 50 mg/kg) PCP induces neuronal vacuolization, especially in the posterior cingulate/retrosplenial cortex. These same effects are seen with other congeners such as ketamine, indicating that the mechanism involved may be NMDA receptor-mediated.

Effects of long-term use
There is evidence for tolerance to the behavioral effects of PCP in animals, but this has not been sufficiently studied in humans. Signs of PCP withdrawal include somnolence, tremor, seizures, diarrhea, piloerection, bruxism and vocalizations. There is clear evidence of continued self-administration in animals supporting the reinforcing, and addictive, properties of PCP and related compounds.

PCP INTOXICATION — TREATMENT ISSUES

A particular feature of PCP intoxication is nystagmus. Horizontal, vertical and rotatory nystagmus has been observed. This feature often helps to distinguish PCP intoxication from other psychotic states. Some of the observed neurological signs are dose-dependent neuronal hyperexcitability, including increased deep tendon reflexes and seizure states. The latter can be generalized or focal, likely based on cerebral vasoconstriction. Seizures are managed with intravenous benzodiazepines.

215

Behavioral toxicity with PCP results from the disinhibition that follows administration of this family of drugs. Unpredictable, distorted, even violent reactions to environmental stimuli often accompany the PCP-caused disruption of sensory input.

Treatment of PCP intoxication

No drug at present can be called a "PCP antagonist." Any drug that would competitively bind to the PCP receptor in the NMDA channel would itself block the NMDA receptor-mediated ion fluxes. Certain treatment modalities however can reduce the effects of this drug.

The use of activated charcoal in the stomach has been shown to bind PCP and decrease its toxic effects. The proposed mechanism relies on the trapping of ionized PCP in the stomach. Since the volume of distribution for this drug is so great, neither hemodialysis nor hemoperfusion can significantly promote drug clearance. It should be remembered that the oral route of absorption for PCP is extremely unpredictable. A prolonged period of observation is mandatory before concluding that no life-threatening complications will ensue.

Therapy directed at specific drug-related effects should be started. Haloperidol has been the neuroleptic of choice, but neuroleptics with few anticholinergic properties may be used. Autonomic instability as observed with atropine-like toxicity can lead to severe hyperthermia, resulting in death. Cardiovascular toxicity includes mild to severe hypertension that is dose-dependent. The mechanism of action is through both catecholamine reuptake blockade and direct release of catecholamines by PCP. This may be so severe as to lead to hypertensive crisis and CNS complications. At significant doses, and in combination with other physiologically debilitating states, myocardial depression ultimately occurs, often with hemodynamic collapse. In the final analysis, supportive care directed at specific signs and symptoms must be undertaken to limit the toxic effects of these drugs.

Treatment of chronic PCP use

The treatment of the chronic phencyclidine abuser is difficult. As a management issue, acute phencyclidine intoxication demonstrates the importance of classical supportive treatment measures. After recovery from the acute intoxication, it is very important that follow-up psychiatric, social and educational therapies are begun to reduce the risk of relapse.

R E F E R E N C E S

Adlaf, E.M., Ivis, F.J. & Smart, R.G. (1997). *Ontario Student Drug Use Survey: 1977-1997.* Toronto: Addiction Research Foundation.

Allebeck, P., Adamsson, C., Engstrom, A. & Rydberg, U. (1993). Cannabis and schizophrenia: A longitudinal study of cases treated in Stockholm County. *Acta Psychiatrica Scandinavica, 88,* 21-24.

Brands, B., Sproule, B. & Marshman, J.A. (Eds.). (1998). *Drugs and Drug Abuse* (3rd ed.). Toronto: Addiction Research Foundation.

Canadian Centre on Substance Abuse & Addiction Research Foundation. (1997). *Canadian Profile: Alcohol, Tobacco & Other Drugs.* Canadian Centre on Substance Abuse & Addiction Research Foundation.

Duffy, A. & Milin, R. (1996). Case study: Withdrawal syndrome in adolescent chronic cannabis users. *Journal of the American Academy of Child and Adolescent Psychiatry, 35(12),* 1618-1621.

Fried, P.A. (1982). Marihuana use by pregnant women and effects on offspring: An update. *Neurobehavioral Toxicology and Teratology, 4(4),* 451-454.

Greenland, F., Staisch, K.J., Brown, N. & Gross, S.J. (1982). Effects of marijuana on human pregnancy, labor, and delivery. *Neurobehavioral Toxicology and Teratology, 4(4),* 447-450.

Halikas, J.A., Weller, R.A., Morse, C.L., Hoffmann, R.G. (1985). A longitudinal study of marijuana effects. *International Journal of the Addictions, 20,* 701-711.

Hall, W., Solowij, N. & Lemon, J. (1994). *The Health and Psychological Consequences of Cannabis Use* (National Drug Strategy Monograph Series No. 25). Canberra: Australian Government Publishing Service.

Hatch, E.E., Bracken M.B. (1986). Effect of marijuana use in pregnancy on fetal growth. *American Journal of Epidemiology, 124,* 986-993.

Hingson R., Zuckerman B., Amaro H., Frank, D.A., Kayne, H., Sorenson, J.R., Mitchell, J., Parker, S., Morelock, S. & Timperi, R. (1986). Maternal marijuana use and neonatal outcome: Uncertainty posed by self-reports. *American Journal of Public Health, 76,* 667-669.

Kalant, H., Corrigall, W.A., Hall, W. & Smart, R.G. (Eds.). (1999). *The Health Effects of Cannabis.* Toronto: Centre for Addiction and Mental Health.

Marlatt, GA. & Gordon, J.R. (1980). Determinants of relapse: Implications for the maintenance of behavior change. In P.O. Davidson & S.M. Davidson (Eds.), *Behavioral Medicine: Changing Health Lifestyles*. New York: Brunner/Mazel.

Marlatt, G.A. & Gordon, J.R. (1985). *Relapse Prevention: Maintenance Strategies in the Treatment of Addictive Behaviors*. New York: Guilford Press.

Martinez-Arevalo, M.J., Calcedo Ordonez, A. & Varo Prieto, J.R. (1994). Cannabis consumption as prognostic factor in schizophrenia. *British Journal of Psychiatry, 164*, 679-681.

Miller, N.S., Gold, M.S. & Pottash, A.C. (1989). A 12-step treatment approach for marijuana (cannabis) dependence. *Journal of Substance Abuse Treatment, 6*, 241-250.

Millman, R.B. & Sbriglio, R. (1986). Patterns of use and psychopathology in chronic marijuana users. *Psychiatric Clinics of North America, 9(3)*, 533-545.

Negrete, J.C, Knapp, W.P., Douglas, D.E. & Smith, W.B. (1986). Cannabis affects the severity of schizophrenia: Results of a clinical survey. *Psychological Medicine, 16*, 515-520.

O'Connell, C.M. & Fried, P.A. (1984). An investigation of prenatal cannabis exposure and minor physical anomalies in a low risk population. *Neurobehavioral Toxicology and Teratology, 6*, 345-350.

Rainone, G.A., Deren, S., Kleinman, P.H. & Wish, E.D. (1987). Heavy marijuana users not in treatment: The continuing search for the "pure" marijuana user. *Journal of Psychoactive Drugs, 19(4)*, 353-359.

Roffman, R.A. & Barnhart, R. (1987). Assessing need for marijuana dependence treatment through an anonymous telephone interview. *International Journal of the Addictions, 22(7)*, 639-651.

Substance Abuse and Mental Health Services Administration. (1998). *National Household Survey On Drug Abuse: Population Estimates 1997*. Rockville, MD: Substance Abuse and Mental Health Services Administration.

Weller, R.A. & Halikas, J.A. (1982). Change in effects from marijuana: A five- to six-year follow-up. *Journal of Clinical Psychiatry, 43*, 362-365.

218

Zukin, S.R., Sloboda, Z. & Javitt, D.C. (1997). Phencyclidine (PCP). In J.H. Lowinson, P. Ruiz, R.B.Millman & J.G. Langrod (Eds.), *Substance Abuse: A Comprehensive Text* (3rd ed.). Baltimore: Williams and Wilkins.

Zweben, J.E. & O'Connell, K. (1988). Strategies for breaking marijuana dependence. *Journal of Psychoactive Drugs, 20,* 121-127.

Opioids

8.1 INTOXICATION, OVERDOSE AND WITHDRAWAL

8.2 METHADONE TREATMENT FOR OPIOID DEPENDENCE

8.3 PREVENTION, DIAGNOSIS AND TREATMENT OF OPIOID DEPENDENCE IN PATIENTS WITH CHRONIC NON-MALIGNANT PAIN

TABLES AND FIGURES

8.1

INTOXICATION, OVERDOSE AND WITHDRAWAL*

Meldon Kahan, MD, and David C. Marsh, MD

PHARMACOLOGY

Opioids act by attaching to endogenous opioid receptors in the brain. They are used as analgesics, antitussives and acute antidyspneics for pulmonary edema. Their psychoactive effects range from a mild mood-levelling effect (codeine) to a profound euphoria and sense of inner peace (heroin). The analgesic and psychoactive duration of action for heroin and most prescription opioids ranges from three to six hours. Long-acting preparations (MS Contin®, Oramorph SR® and Codeine Contin®) induce analgesia for up to 12 hours.

ADVERSE EFFECTS

Common physical symptoms
Common physical symptoms include sweating, nausea and constipation.

Narcotic bowel syndrome
Narcotic bowel syndrome is characterized by bloating and vague abdominal discomfort. Physical exam and investigations are negative, except for dilated bowel (with no obstruction) on two views of the abdomen. Treatment consists of tapering and discontinuing the opioid.

Medication-induced headaches
Medication-induced headaches should be considered in patients with migraine who report a greatly increased headache frequency since starting mixed opioid/non-opioid analgesics such as Tylenol® #3. Most patients improve on cessation of the analgesic.

---

*Adapted in part from Kahan, Wilson et al., 1996.

Fatigue and confusion

Fatigue and confusion are found particularly in the elderly during initial titration of dose. Older people tend to be more sensitive to the sedative effects of opioids, so caution is needed when prescribing.

Cognitive impairment

Some studies have suggested that long-term opioid use causes subtle neuropsychiatric impairment (Portenoy & Payne, 1996). However, these studies did not control for other factors and the issue remains in dispute. Studies of patients on long-term methadone have not found evidence of cognitive impairment.

Respiratory depression

Respiratory depression can occur in patients who are given large doses of opioids in the initial titration phase, especially if they have chronic obstructive pulmonary disease or sleep apnea. Risk is increased with benzodiazepine use.

Reproductive and endocrine effects

Opioids can cause impotence in men due to suppression of testosterone production. Opioids can also cause menstrual irregularities in women. Pregnant women who are physically dependent on opioids can have adverse reproductive effects, including spontaneous abortion and premature labor if they undergo withdrawal. The newborns of physically dependent women can also experience withdrawal, characterized by poor feeding, irritability, sweating and diarrhea. Severe, untreated neonatal withdrawal can result in seizures and death (see also Section 8.2).

TOLERANCE

Tolerance to the analgesic effects of opioids develops very slowly. Patients taking opioid analgesics for chronic pain are often able to remain on the same dose for years. However, tolerance to the psychoactive effects of opioids develops quickly, forcing patients who are seeking the mood-altering effects of opioids to rapidly escalate their dose. Highly tolerant patients often consume opioids in amounts that would be fatal in non-tolerant patients. Those tolerant patients do not get "high" but rather take the drug to ward off withdrawal symptoms.

OVERDOSE

The purity of street heroin has increased dramatically in recent years. It was reported that in 1995 in the United States the average purity of heroin seized in

East Coast cities was between 40 per cent and 90 per cent (Office of National Drug Control Policy, 1995). Patients who have taken an opioid overdose appear drowsy, "nodding off" as if falling asleep. They have pinpoint pupils and shallow breathing, with a respiratory rate of less than 12 per minute. They may also be bradycardic and cyanotic.

Such patients should be referred urgently to the emergency department for a naloxone infusion and possibly airway protection and intubation. It is prudent to have naloxone available in the office. The administration of naloxone 0.4–2.0 mg i.v. will rouse the patient temporarily, although repeat injections may be needed until the patient reaches the emergency department.

Nalmefene, a long-acting oral opioid antagonist, obviates the need for repeated injections. However, nalmefene will put the patient in prolonged withdrawal, and its role in the treatment of overdose in opioid-dependent individuals has not been established. (Nalmefene is not currently available in Canada.)

The drowsy-but-conscious patient

Opioid-dependent patients presenting with drowsiness, slurred speech or ataxia are often, but not always, intoxicated on alcohol, sedative/hypnotics, heroin or other drugs. Incorrectly assuming a patient is intoxicated can have serious, sometimes fatal consequences. To avoid this error, be on guard when the patient's drowsiness or ataxia is greater than one would expect, given the amount of drug the patient admits to taking. Such patients could be suffering from head trauma, toxic blood levels of medications that can mimic illicit drug intoxication, such as lithium or phenytoin, or a medical condition that could mimic intoxication, such as diabetes.

The physician should inquire about trauma and recent use of medications. An examination should be conducted, including vital signs, a search for signs of trauma, and a brief cardiovascular and neurological exam (looking for ataxia and focal neurological signs). Blood and urine drug screens, therapeutic blood levels of medications if indicated, and CBC, electrolytes and blood glucose should also be ordered. If the patient remains drowsy and ataxic he or she should be referred to a hospital emergency department for observation and possible naloxone administration.

227

OPIOID WITHDRAWAL

Individuals who ingest, inject or inhale opioid agonists on a regular basis quickly develop signs of physical dependence, including tolerance and withdrawal. Over time many opioid-dependent patients will continue to use, more to relieve the discomfort of withdrawal than for any associated euphoria. It is essential for the clinician to have a full understanding of the signs and symptoms of opioid withdrawal as an aid in the detection and diagnosis of opioid dependence. For the many patients for whom methadone maintenance therapy is not indicated, management of withdrawal is the first stage of treatment.

Signs and symptoms of withdrawal

The signs and symptoms of opioid withdrawal are due to overactivity of the sympathetic nervous system. See the table below for DSM-IV criteria for diagnosis of Opioid Withdrawal.

TABLE 1: DSM-IV Diagnostic Criteria for Opioid Withdrawal†

A. Either of the following:
1) cessation of (or reduction in) opioid use that has been heavy and prolonged (several weeks or longer)
2) administration of an opioid antagonist after a period of opioid use

B. Three (or more) of the following, developing within minutes to several days after Criterion A:
1) dysphoric mood
2) nausea or vomiting
3) muscle aches
4) lacrimation or rhinorrhea
5) pupillary dilation, piloerection, or sweating
6) diarrhea
7) yawning
8) fever
9) insomnia

C. The symptoms in Criterion B cause clinically significant distress or impairment in social, occupational, or other important areas of functioning.

D. The symptoms are not due to a general medical condition and are not better accounted for by another mental disorder.

† Reprinted with permission from *Diagnostic and Statistical Manual of Mental Disorders* (4th ed.). Copyright 1994, American Psychiatric Association.

Opioid withdrawal is characterized by intense anxiety and craving for opioids. Subjective symptoms include restlessness, insomnia, fatigue and myalgias. Objective signs resemble a bad case of the flu affecting the respiratory and GI tract; lacrimation, rhinorrhea and dilated pupils; vomiting and diarrhea; tachycardia and hypertension; sweating, chills and piloerection. Unlike withdrawal from sedative/hypnotics, opioid withdrawal is not accompanied by serious medical complications, except in pregnant women and neonates.

The time course of opioid withdrawal is related to the elimination half-life of the agonist being used. For agents with a short half-life such as heroin, morphine, codeine or oxycodone, withdrawal begins within hours of cessation or reduction in use. The administration of an opioid antagonist such as naloxone or naltrexone to an opioid-dependent patient will abruptly precipitate withdrawal of particularly severe intensity.

Withdrawal symptoms peak in intensity within two to three days after the last use and largely resolve by five days. Some patients are symptomatic for up to 10 days. Patients may experience insomnia and dysphoria for months afterwards, perhaps because of suppression of endorphins or a structural derangement of the opioid receptor system (Zweben & Payte, 1990).

Assessment of withdrawal

Since many opioid users also take large doses of alcohol, sedative/hypnotics or cocaine, a careful drug history should be taken (see Section 1.2). A brief mental status exam also should be conducted, inquiring specifically about suicidal ideation. Opioid users may experience suicidal ideation due to the dysphoria associated with withdrawal and the serious personal difficulties they face. Women should be asked about use of birth control, and a BHCG should be ordered if pregnancy is a possibility. Since withdrawal can be dangerous for the fetus, pregnant patients should be placed on methadone.

The general demeanor of the patient should be assessed; the patient in withdrawal appears uncomfortable and restless. The patient should be examined for signs of autonomic hyperactivity, including dilated pupils, tachycardia, hypertension, goose bumps, tremor, sweating, yawning, lacrimation and active bowel sounds.

Routine investigations include CBC, LFTs, HIV and hepatitis B and C serology.

229

MANAGEMENT OF WITHDRAWAL

General principles

Detoxification should always be combined with a drug rehabilitation program, since detoxification alone rarely results in long-term abstinence. Detoxification is a necessary first step for individuals for whom methadone maintenance therapy is not appropriate, not desired or not available. Physicians can work together with the patients' friends or family to make the experience easier to endure and thus improve opioid-dependent patients' chances of avoiding early relapse. From here these individuals can begin to engage in other forms of treatment which can help them rebuild their lives without drug dependence.

Three commonly used therapies for opioid withdrawal are tapering doses of methadone, tapering doses of prescription opioids and clonidine. Inpatient admission should be considered for patients who are medically or psychiatrically ill or about to be admitted to a rehabilitation program.

Management of withdrawal

Physicians can provide several interventions to assist their patients to cope with opioid withdrawal. In all cases it is advisable to provide symptomatic pharmacological treatments in the form of an antiemetic (dimenhydrinate 50 mg po q6h prn for nausea and vomiting), a non-steroidal anti-inflammatory agent (ibuprofen 200–400 mg po qid prn for muscle, joint or back pain) and an antidiarrheal agent (loperamide 4 mg initially followed by 2 mg po after each loose stool to a maximum 16 mg per 24 hours). Physicians may choose to prescribe a short course of benzodiazepines to relieve insomnia in inpatients undergoing opioid withdrawal. This should be undertaken with caution because of the common occurrence of sedative abuse and dependence among opioid-dependent individuals. Ensure a supportive environment including the provision of adequate oral hydration, warm clothing and blankets for chills, hot baths, supportive and encouraging caregivers and, most importantly, the absence of cues for drug use.

Clonidine detoxification

Clonidine has been shown to be more effective than placebo in suppressing withdrawal symptoms (Jasinski, Johnson & Kocher 1985), although it is probably less effective than methadone. It does, however, avoid the problem of drug-seeking and double-doctoring. Clonidine is thought to act by central inhibition of the hypernoradrenergic state that occurs in opioid withdrawal.

For outpatients, a test dose of clonidine 0.1 mg po should be given. If the patient's blood pressure remains above 90/60 mm Hg after one hour, an initial dose of 0.1 mg tid-qid prn may be prescribed. If necessary, this may be increased to 0.2 mg tid-qid prn the following day, although the risk of symptomatic hypotension increases with this dose. After five days of regular use, clonidine may be continued on an as-needed basis for an additional three to five days. Patients who use clonidine daily for two weeks or more risk rebound hypertension if the drug is stopped abruptly.

Patients requiring larger doses of clonidine should be admitted to hospital. For inpatients whose blood pressure and sedation can be monitored more closely, clonidine doses of 0.2–0.3 mg po every six hours can be administered up to a daily maximum of 1–2 mg. The dose should be withheld if the patient is symptom-free or the BP is less than 90/60 mm Hg. Clonidine protocols for outpatients and inpatients are presented in the table below.

TABLE 2: Clonidine Protocol for Opioid Withdrawal

Outpatient	Clonidine 0.1 mg tid-qid; warn about symptoms of postural hypotension and drowsiness. May increase to 0.2 mg tid-qid after first day (but risk of hypotension increases). Continue qid for 3–5 days then prn for 3–5 more days. Additional treatment options: naproxen (Naprosyn®), acetaminophen, loperamide, dimenhydrinate, diazepam 10 mg hs.
Inpatient	Check BP prior to each dose. Hold if BP < 90/60 or marked postural drop. May increase to 0.3 mg qid.

Patients should be warned about the side-effects of clonidine, particularly postural hypotension, sedation and dry mouth. They should be advised not to drive a motor vehicle if clonidine induces drowsiness. They should also be clearly warned of the dangers of life-threatening hypotension should they inject heroin while taking moderate or high doses of clonidine. There have been case reports of deaths in patients taking hot baths while on clonidine, presumably because of peripheral vasodilation leading to severe hypotension.

Inpatient methadone detoxification

Methadone is known to be a safe and effective treatment for opioid withdrawal. The provision of methadone in hospital can help convince a seriously ill heroin user to stay in hospital and complete treatment. During the first two to three days of admission, methadone is given in doses of 5–15 mg q6h prn, depending on the severity of the withdrawal symptoms (to a maximum of 40–50 mg over 24 hours). On the subsequent day, two-thirds of the previous day's total dose may be given with one to three 5 mg prn doses. The dose is then

231

tapered by 5–10 mg per day (unless the patient is to be transferred to a methadone program). Methadone doses should be withheld and close observation is recommended if the patient appears drowsy (adapted from Devenyi & Saunders, 1986).

In Canada, physicians can obtain an emergency authorization to prescribe methadone in a hospital setting by calling the Bureau of Drug Surveillance, Health Canada.

Outpatient methadone detoxification

Outpatient detoxification should be completed over a period of one to three months, to a maximum of six months. The general principles of methadone dosing, as outlined below, apply to outpatient detoxification. Begin with a safe initial dose of 15–30 mg, and titrate upwards by 10–15 mg every five days. Once the optimal dose is reached, the patient is then tapered at a rate of 5 mg every three to 14 days. The rate of the taper is determined by the completion date agreed upon by physician and patient, and patient symptoms and drug use. The taper may be slowed when the dose reaches 20 mg. Urine drug screening and counselling should be continued throughout the taper.

Tapering with opioids other than methadone

Clonidine and methadone are the preferred agents for opioid detoxification. Outpatient tapering with opioids is usually reserved for patients with true chronic pain, or for patients addicted to mild opioid analgesics such as over-the-counter codeine. Tapering with opioids is risky because it is very difficult to prevent patients from double-doctoring. Also, tapering sometimes elicits drug-seeking behavior ("You're taking me down too fast"), and patients on a slow taper may delay seeking treatment and counselling. Therefore, outpatient tapering should only be done if the physician has a long-standing relationship with the patient and is fairly certain that the risk of double-doctoring is minimal (see also Section 17).

Outpatient tapering should not be attempted unless the patient gives consent to contact all other physicians who have been involved in their care. Daily or weekly dispensing of the medication is recommended. Urine drug screening is advised, although it will only detect double-doctoring if the patient uses an opioid different than the one prescribed for the detoxification. Patients should be referred to a drug rehabilitation program.

Codeine is the preferred agent for outpatient tapering. For example, a patient taking 20 tablets of acetaminophen 325 mg + codeine 8 mg (e.g., Tylenol #1®) daily could be safely and conveniently tapered with acetaminophen 325 mg + codeine 30 mg (Tylenol #3®) starting at 4 tablets per day. Short-acting opioids

232

with a high dependence liability, such as oxycodone or hydromorphone, should not be used for tapering. Patients addicted to large doses of potent opioids are unlikely to respond to codeine and should be treated with clonidine or methadone instead. If these treatments are unavailable, ineffective or cause unacceptable side-effects, tapering with long-acting morphine may be considered. (See Section 8.3 for a detailed description of a morphine tapering protocol.)

The taper should be completed within two to eight weeks. Scheduled (q4–6h) rather than prn dosing is recommended. Tapering with sustained-release codeine (Codeine Contin®) could make for a smoother and more comfortable withdrawal, but the dose of this formulation (50 mg) may make tapering impractical.

When switching a patient from one opioid to another, remember that the patient may not be fully tolerant to the new opioid, so the dose of the new opioid should be only one-half the equianalgesic dose of the original opioid (see Section 8.3 for a more complete description of tapering).

Pregnancy
Pregnant opioid-dependent patients should be referred to a specialized centre. To prevent withdrawal symptoms, the patient is usually placed on methadone (a long-acting oral opioid) for the duration of the pregnancy. The newborn is admitted to a nursery for close observation and given oral morphine as needed (see Section 8.2).

8.2

METHADONE TREATMENT FOR OPIOID DEPENDENCE*

Meldon Kahan, MD, Bruna Brands, PhD, and Douglas Gourlay, MD

GENERAL INFORMATION

Methadone is an oral opioid with a long duration of action. In appropriate doses, methadone relieves symptoms of opioid withdrawal and reduces cravings for opioids for 24 to 36 hours, without causing sedation or euphoria. This allows individuals to function normally and to perform mental and physical tasks without impairment. In addition, in adequate doses methadone "blocks" the euphoric effects of self-administered illicit opioids (cross-tolerance). Randomized trials and large prospective studies have shown that methadone maintenance treatment reduces illicit drug use, needle sharing and the social costs and health risks associated with heroin addiction (Simpson & Sells, 1982; Ball & Ross, 1991).

Pharmacology

Methadone is a μ agonist with pharmacological properties similar to those of morphine. It is well absorbed from the GI tract following oral administration and can be detected in plasma within 30 minutes. Peak concentrations occur in two to four hours and approximately 90 per cent is bound to plasma proteins. Methadone undergoes biotransformation in the liver to pyrrolidines and pyrroline, which are excreted in the urine and bile. After repeated administration, methadone accumulates in the tissues. When methadone is discontinued, small amounts are released from these storage sites and it is believed that this process is responsible for the mild but protracted abstinence syndrome (Reisine & Pasternak, 1996). Side-effects include constipation, sweating and erectile dysfunction. Higher doses can cause sedation and respiratory depression (see Section 8.1).

---

* The following chapter provides a general overview for the use of methadone in the treatment of opioid dependence. For a comprehensive review, the reader is referred to *Methadone Maintenance: A Physician's Guide to Treatment* (Brands & Brands, 1998).

234

Barbiturates, rifampin, anticonvulsants (such as carbamazepine and phenytoin) and chronic alcohol use may increase methadone metabolism through enzyme induction, resulting in higher methadone dose requirements. Opioid antagonists such as naloxone and naltrexone and opioid agonist-antagonists such as pentazocine can precipitate acute opioid withdrawal in patients maintained on methadone.

CANDIDATES FOR METHADONE TREATMENT

Candidates for methadone maintenance must meet DSM-IV criteria for Opioid Dependence (see Introduction, for DSM-IV criteria for Substance Dependence and above Table 1 for DSM-IV diagnostic criteria for Opioid Withdrawal). Typically, patients present with a long history of opioid use, physical dependence on opioids and failure with other forms of treatment. Patients who have used heroin for less than a year, or who have never received other forms of treatment, are often advised to consider alternative treatments first. (For more detailed information on assessment and other issues, the physician is directed to Brands & Brands, *Methadone Maintenance: A Physician's Guide to Treatment,* 1998.)

Assessment

All patients must undergo a comprehensive medical and psychosocial assessment prior to starting methadone (see Section 1). Opioid-dependent patients have a high prevalence of psychiatric disorders such as anxiety, depression and suicidal ideation, and psychosocial problems such as current or past abuse, in addition to medical problems such as hepatitis C.

Since methadone patients develop a physical dependence on methadone, it can be very difficult to discontinue. Moreover, patients who are not tolerant to opioids are at risk of potentially fatal overdose if started on methadone. Therefore, it is essential that the physician establish a diagnosis of opioid dependence prior to starting methadone. This can be determined through the patient's history, physical examination (signs of withdrawal or intoxication, and needle "track" marks) and laboratory tests (urine drug screens positive for opioids; see Section 1).

Information should be obtained from previous physicians and treatment providers. If the patient has previously been treated with methadone, knowledge of that experience is particularly helpful in developing a treatment plan for the patient.

Treatment agreement

Prior to starting methadone, the patient should sign a treatment agreement. The physician should carefully review the benefits and side-effects of methadone with the patient. (Some patients are surprised to hear that they will develop a physical dependence to methadone.) The physician's expectations of the patient should also be clearly stated, including frequency of urine drug screens, office visits and counselling or psychotherapy sessions. Consequences of breaking the agreement should be explicitly stated. (See Addendum 1 for a sample methadone maintenance treatment agreement.)

DOSAGE GUIDELINES

Methadone is administered once daily in 100 cc of orange drink under the supervision of a nurse or pharmacist.

Initial dose

All new patients should be started on an initial dose of 15–30 mg methadone (Drummer, Opeskin et al., 1992). Patients who report very heavy opioid use do not always require high doses of methadone, so it is unsafe to exceed these guidelines. Starting doses of 40 mg or more have led to deaths after three days of treatment (Caplehorn, 1998). A single day's maintenance dose of methadone (50–100 mg) can be lethal to non-tolerant adults (Harding-Pink, 1993).

Optimal dose

The optimal methadone dose relieves withdrawal symptoms and drug cravings without sedation or other side-effects. For most patients, this dose ranges from 50 to 120 mg per day, although some patients do well on doses as low as 20–30 mg. Research suggests that higher methadone doses (greater than 60 mg per day) are more effective than lower doses at retaining patients in treatment and decreasing heroin use (Strain, Stitzer et al., 1993; Caplehorn & Bell, 1991). The optimal dose can be established within two to six weeks for most patients.

Although concern is sometimes expressed that patients on higher maintenance doses, and who wish to discontinue methadone, will have greater difficulty in successfully tapering from methadone, there is little empirical evidence to support this view. Regardless of the dose at the start of the taper, patients typically experience their worst withdrawal symptoms at doses below 20 or 30 mg (Bell, Seres et al., 1988).

Guidelines for dosage adjustment

The majority of patients can be stabilized on methadone within two to six weeks of initiating methadone treatment. Each dose adjustment should be in the range of 5–15 mg of methadone, depending on the severity and daily duration of the patient's withdrawal symptoms or drug cravings. Patients in the first week of treatment who show overt physical signs of withdrawal (such as vomiting, piloerection or sweating) should have a dose increase on the same day if possible. Otherwise, dose adjustments should be made no more frequently than every three to four days, since it takes five days for plasma levels of methadone to reach a steady state. *Because of its long half-life, frequent dosage increases can cause an accumulation of methadone in the serum, causing overdose one to two weeks after treatment initiation* (Caplehorn, 1998). Concurrent use of sedatives and opioids, or illnesses such as pneumonia, may increase the likelihood of overdose. Once a daily dose of 60–80 mg has been reached, the rate and amount of dosage adjustment should be decreased somewhat, to no more than 5–10 mg every one to two weeks.

Assessing dose adequacy
Dosage adjustment is based primarily on patients' self-reports of withdrawal symptoms. Objective signs of withdrawal usually disappear after the first few weeks of methadone treatment. Drug cravings and persistent opioid use may also indicate the need for a dose increase, even in the absence of withdrawal symptoms.

One simple way to assess the adequacy of the dose is to ask the patient how long it "lasts" — that is, its duration of action in relieving withdrawal symptoms. The optimal dose is one that is effective throughout the night, although patients often report mild withdrawal symptoms in the morning.

Dose adjustments should not be used to reward or punish patients (Payte & Khuri, 1992). As with other medications, the balance between the desired effect and adverse effects should be the physician's prime consideration.

Some therapists and physicians express concern that granting dosage increases too readily will enable patients to acquire unnecessarily large doses. Research does not support this concern. Resnick, Butler and Washton (1982) found that patients who were allowed to self-adjust their methadone doses made only moderate adjustments, well below the maximum attainable dose.

Preventing methadone overdose
Methadone overdoses are generally due to overaggressive prescribing in the first few weeks of treatment, before the patient is fully tolerant (Caplehorn, 1998; Drummond, Opeskin et al., 1992). Overdoses can be avoided by observing the following guidelines:

• Resist pressure to rapidly increase the dose. Patients should be forewarned that dosage titration usually takes two to six weeks.
• Avoid prescribing opioids, benzodiazepines or other drugs with sedative properties.

237

- Warn patients that they risk overdosing if they take additional opioids, even if they use amounts that were previously well tolerated.
- Be particularly cautious in prescribing methadone to elderly patients and those with lung disease.
- Do not prescribe take-home doses of methadone (carries) until the patient is stable.
- When patients become eligible for take-home doses, instruct them to store their medication safely (i.e., in a *locked* container in the refrigerator, away from the reach of children).

A 10–20 mg dose of methadone can be fatal to a child (Aronow, Paul et al., 1972). Doses routinely prescribed in a methadone program may be fatal if ingested by a non-tolerant adult (Harding-Pink, 1993).

- Remember that patients may quickly lose tolerance to their usual methadone dose when regular administration is reduced or interrupted. Be particularly aware of the following circumstances:

  - Incarceration in a facility that does not provide methadone. These patients are particularly at risk for overdose when they are released. Such patients should be started at a substantially lower initial dose and titrated slowly upwards to their previous methadone level.

  - Diversion of methadone take-home doses. Patients who do not drink all of their prescribed dose may gradually lose tolerance for this dose level. If they suddenly resume taking all of their prescribed dose, they may be at risk of overdose.

Long-term opioid users sometimes view mild opioid intoxication as a normal and desirable mental state and expect to achieve that state with methadone. The patient may therefore request dosage increases even as family members report that methadone makes the patient appear drowsy. Overprescribing in this circumstance can be avoided by obtaining corroborating information from the patient's family, and by assessing the patient when the peak effect of methadone is reached, two to four hours after dosing. Careful patient education is also important.

METHADONE TREATMENT DURING PREGNANCY AND LACTATION

Birth control
Female heroin users frequently experience reduced fertility and oligomenorrhea or amenorrhea (Finnegan, 1980). As a result, some women are convinced that

they do not need birth control. On starting methadone, their cycles typically become more regular and they become more fertile. It is important to initiate birth control measures at this time.

Rationale for methadone treatment during pregnancy

Pregnant heroin-dependent women have a high infant mortality rate, due primarily to high rates of prematurity and low birthweight (Finnegan, 1978). Low birthweight has been attributed to the direct effects of heroin on the fetus, as well as poor nutrition, smoking and inadequate prenatal care. Withdrawal from opioids can trigger uterine contractions that can lead to spontaneous abortion in the first trimester and premature labor in the third trimester. Withdrawal from opioids has also been linked with fetal death, especially if it occurs during labor (Ward, Mattick & Hall, 1992).

Women on stable doses of methadone receive better prenatal care, better nutrition and are far less likely to experience opioid withdrawal than women using heroin (Kaltenbach & Finnegan, 1992). As a result, pregnant women on methadone have lower rates of prematurity, higher birthweight infants and lower infant mortality than heroin users not on methadone (Deren, 1986).

Pregnant heroin-dependent women often have multiple psychosocial and medical problems, in addition to being at high risk for maternal and neonatal complications. As outlined below, methadone itself is not without risks when taken during pregnancy. For these reasons, the prescribing of methadone during pregnancy is best undertaken by experienced physicians working in a comprehensive treatment program.

Neonatal abstinence syndrome

Methadone readily crosses the placenta. Of neonates exposed to methadone or heroin, 60 to 80 per cent experience a withdrawal syndrome characterized by irritability, sleep disturbances, tremors, poor feeding, vomiting, sneezing, yawning and fever. Seizures can occur, and untreated withdrawal can lead to dehydration and death. The withdrawal usually begins within 24 to 72 hours of birth, but late presentations have been reported (Kandall & Gartner, 1972). Symptoms may last for several weeks or months. A clear relationship has not been established between maternal methadone dose and the severity of infant withdrawal (Finnegan, 1991). No long-term sequelae have been demonstrated.

Neonates born to women physically dependent on opioids should be observed closely in hospital for at least five days. They generally require care in a higher-level nursery (level 2) or neonatal intensive care unit, under the care of a neonatologist experienced in the assessment and treatment of withdrawal.

Morphine, phenobarbital or paregoric (camphorated tincture of opium) may be used to control withdrawal symptoms (Hoegerman & Schnoll, 1991). Morphine is the treatment of choice. Paregoric has adulterants, such as camphor, that confer no clinical benefit, and phenobarbital may not prevent seizures as effectively as opioids (Kandall, Doberczak et al., 1983). However, phenobarbital may be the preferred agent for treating withdrawal in neonates born to women physically dependent on both opioids and alcohol or sedatives.

A 21-item neonatal assessment form (Neonatal Abstinence Scoring System) has been developed to grade the severity of neonatal withdrawal (Finnegan, 1986). Scoring should be initiated within two hours of admission to the nursery, and continued for at least five days, even if scores are low. The scale should be administered every four hours. If the score is eight or greater, it should be given every two hours. An item is scored if it occurs at any time within the four-hour interval. An average score of eight or more for the past three consecutive readings indicates the need for pharmacotherapy. Dosing is given according to a standard protocol. The stabilizing dose should be maintained for five days, then slowly tapered. Scoring should be continued for at least three to five days after the morphine or paregoric is discontinued.

Some newborns are still in mild withdrawal when discharged to the care of their mothers. Mothers should be instructed that giving their newborns even a small dose of methadone can cause a fatal overdose.

Symptoms similar to neonatal withdrawal can occur with hypoglycemia, hypocalcemia, hypomagnesia, sepsis, intracranial hemorrhage and hypothermia. These conditions should be excluded before initiating therapy. A urine drug screen should be obtained from the neonate on admission.

Effects of methadone on the fetus and the infant
A number of prospective studies have shown that infants of women on methadone have lower birthweights and head circumferences than infants of non-drug-using women (Doberczak, Thornton, et al., 1987). The differences were generally modest and tended to resolve within one to two years. Longitudinal studies on the neurological and developmental effects of methadone have had inconsistent results. Some studies documented lower scores on measures of psychomotor development. There is also evidence to suggest an increased incidence of strabismus in infants born to women receiving methadone (Johnson, 1984).

Dose adjustments during pregnancy
Prior to initiating methadone, the patient should be informed of the possible effects of methadone on the fetus and the neonate. Inpatient admission is

recommended to initiate methadone treatment (Finnegan, 1991). At the first sign of withdrawal, 10–15 mg is given, followed by 5 mg q4-6h if withdrawal symptoms continue (to a maximum of 40 mg). The next day, the previous day's total dose is given, followed by up to three supplemental 5 mg q6h doses if necessary. Methadone should be withheld if drowsiness or other signs of opioid intoxication are observed. The dose is considered stable if no additional medication is required over a 24-hour period. Most patients are discharged on 35–60 mg/day. For patients who refuse inpatient admission, outpatient stabilization may be attempted using the above regimen on a day basis. This should be done only as a last resort and only if withdrawal is mild or moderate.

The need for subsequent dosage increases should be carefully assessed and given in increments of no more than 5–10 mg. Patients experiencing significant withdrawal symptoms or who continue to use heroin should be offered a dose increase. There is insufficient data on the effects of high doses of methadone on fetal growth and development. Methadone doses should be titrated carefully during pregnancy, and a daily dose of 80 mg should be exceeded only if clearly indicated. It is probable, however, that the known risks of continued nonprescribed opioid use outweigh the potential risks of a higher dose of methadone.

Dosage increases

Small dosage increases are sometimes necessary in the latter part of pregnancy. The rate of metabolism of methadone appears to increase in the third trimester, resulting in lower serum methadone levels (Pond, Kreck et al., 1985). If the patient requires more than 100 mg per day, twice daily dosing may be beneficial, to compensate for the reduction in drug half-life.

Tapering during pregnancy

Tapering should be avoided if possible, but if the patient insists, the safest time to taper is between 14 and 32 weeks when the risk of spontaneous abortion or premature labor is at its lowest. The patient should be tapered by no more than 5 mg every two weeks, and the taper should be put on hold if the patient experiences significant withdrawal symptoms. Dosage decrements of 1–2 mg at a time are recommended.

Breast-feeding

Methadone enters the breast milk, although infants probably ingest very small quantities (0.01 to 0.03 mg per day; Pond, Kreck et al., 1985) which are unlikely to be clinically significant. Nursing is felt to be relatively safe in women whose methadone dose is 20 mg or less. For patients on higher doses, infant exposure can be minimized by nursing just prior to taking methadone. Levels of methadone in breast milk peak at two to four hours after ingestion, so nursing should be avoided if possible during this time period. Weaning the baby or

241

discontinuing methadone is recommended at three to six months, when the baby is growing quickly and consuming large volumes of breast milk. Women using cocaine or abusing alcohol in the post-partum period should be discouraged from breast-feeding, as these drugs enter breast milk.

Hepatitis C

A large proportion of methadone patients have hepatitis C. Pregnant women should be informed of the risks of *in utero* transmission of hepatitis C to the neonates. One study found that 11 of 131 pregnant women positive for hepatitis C RNA had infants infected at birth. There was no evidence of transmission through breast-feeding, although the power of the study was limited (Resti, Azzari, et al.,1998).

HIV

All pregnant women should be offered an HIV test. HIV-positive women should be treated with zidovudine (AZT®). Several studies have shown reduced rates of vertical transmission of HIV with the different regimens of AZT administered to the mother and neonate (Connor, Sperling et al., 1994; Sperling, Shapiro et al., 1996). Elective Cesarean sections in HIV-positive women have also been shown to reduce vertical transmission of HIV by 50 per cent (International Perinatal HIV Group, 1999).

COUNSELLING

Counselling is an essential component of methadone treatment. Observational studies have shown that patients in methadone programs with a strong orientation towards counselling have significantly less drug use than patients in programs lacking such an orientation (Ball & Ross, 1991).

URINE DRUG SCREENS

Urine drug screens should be collected at least twice per week for the first eight weeks. Thereafter, patients who are stable, with minimal or no drug use, should have urine testing every one to two weeks, preferably at random. Urine drug screens should be supervised by a lab attendant if possible.* If this is not feasible, routine temperature testing is recomended. See Section 1.3 for information on the number of days that drugs are detectable by urine drug screening. Variations in detection times can occur, reflecting the amount of drug ingested, the amount of fluid consumed and individual drug metabolism. Urine

---

* In Ontario, physicians should refer to the *Methadone Maintenance Guidelines* (College of Physicians and Surgeons of Ontario, 1996) for more details.

specimens should be tested for methadone, methadone metabolite, cocaine, benzoylecognine, opiates, monoacetylmorphine (MAM, a metabolite of heroin) and benzodiazepines. (See Section 1.3 for further details.)

Tampering

Some patients may tamper with their urines by surreptitiously pouring into the specimen bottle a clean urine sample from another patient or by diluting the urine specimen with toilet water or other fluids. *In vivo* dilution of the urine sample is accomplished by water loading or diuretics.

When tampering is suspected, the urine sample (50cc) should be temperature-tested within four minutes of collection, using an electronic thermometer or temperature strips affixed to the outside of the urine collection container. The normal temperature range is 32°C to 38°C. Urine temperatures outside of this range can be considered as "passed" or "substituted" samples.

CARRY OR TAKE-HOME MEDICATION

While "carries" (take-home doses of methadone) pose a risk of drug diversion and overdose, they are a powerful incentive for behavioral change. Carry privileges may be granted for patients who have been on methadone for three months or more and are stable, with minimal or no unauthorized drug use (College of Physicians and Surgeons of Ontario, 1996). Temporary suspension of carry privileges should be considered for sustained use of unauthorized drugs or non-compliance with the program rules (such as failure to comply with the urine drug screen schedule).

MANAGEMENT OF CONTINUED DRUG USE

During the first two or three months of methadone treatment (the "stabilization" period), opioid use should not lead to discharge. The patient may not have had enough time to complete the requisite lifestyle changes, such as dropping contacts with drug users. Patients who regularly use opioids beyond the stabilization period should be offered counselling and one or two dosage increases of 15 mg (in case the methadone dose is not adequate).

Cocaine, alcohol and benzodiazepines are the most commonly abused drugs among methadone patients. If the drug use causes significant medical, social or psychiatric problems and counselling does not lead to substantial reductions in use, referral to a formal treatment program should be considered. Many outpatient and day programs and a few inpatient programs will accept patients on methadone.

Some methadone providers discharge patients for continued use of unauthorized drugs. Others employ a "harm-reduction" approach, in which patients who use illicit drugs are maintained on methadone as long as they derive overall benefit from treatment (i.e., decreased drug use and improved psychosocial functioning). While the issue is controversial, the harm-reduction approach is probably more effective at retaining patients in treatment and reducing rates of criminal activity.

MANAGEMENT OF PAIN IN METHADONE-TREATED PATIENTS

In general, pain in opioid-dependent patients is poorly managed. Unreasonable fear of worsening underlying addiction by aggressive pain management has led to relapse in many opioid-dependent individuals. When both pain and opioid dependence are present, it is important to determine which is dominant, and then to aggressively assess and treat that problem.

Acute Pain
Patients on a stable dose of methadone, whether for pain management or for the treatment of opioid dependence, may develop tolerance to the drug's analgesic effects. Because of this, and possible cross-tolerance to other opioids, it has been suggested that these patients may require more frequent doses of opioids than non-methadone patients for the treatment of acute pain (Payte & Khuri, 1992). Patients who are not yet on a stable dose of methadone may have incomplete tolerance and may therefore be at risk for overdose if given additional opioids. The use of short-acting opioids with a high dependence liability, such as oxycodone (e.g., Percocet®, Percodan®, Roxicodene®, and Tylox®) should be discouraged. Patients should be cautioned against using mixed agonist/antagonist agents (e.g., pentazocine; Talwin®, Talacen®) due to the risk of precipitating acute withdrawal.

Chronic Pain
Methadone maintenance patients who report chronic pain require a careful, comprehensive assessment and possible referral to a specialist in pain and addiction medicine. In general, non-opioid treatment modalities should be employed first, with chronic use of other opioids avoided unless there is a compelling rationale for their use. Methadone itself is an effective analgesic but requires multiple daily dosing. This fact makes the use of methadone for pain problematic in terms of compliance with carry guidelines (College of Physicians and Surgeons of Ontario, 1996), and supervised dispensing.

In the case of problems related to pain and chemical dependency, it is important to determine which element is dominant at the time of assessment. Aggressively assessing and treating pain in a methadone maintenance patient is unlikely to lead to a satisfactory outcome if resolution of the pain problem will lead to interruption of the supply of opioids, which may be the primary drug of choice in that patient.

Ideally, all opioids prescribed to a given patient should be prescribed by a single practitioner. In Canada, any person obtaining prescription opioids from a doctor must disclose any recent (within the past 30 days) opioid prescriptions (including methadone) obtained from other practitioners. Failure to do so is an indictable criminal offense (double doctoring).

Psychiatric Disorders and Benzodiazepine Use

Opioid-dependent individuals have a high prevalence of affective and anxiety disorders and the identification of those conditions is extremely important. If left untreated, patients may use alcohol, or prescription and illicit drugs, as a form of symptom control. Opioid users are also at high risk for developing cross-dependence on benzodiazepines. Periodic attempts should be made to wean patients placed on benzodiazepine therapy. Benzodiazepines with a high dependence liability, such as diazepam, lorazepam or alprazolam, should be avoided.

Completion of Treatment

The ideal candidate for discharge is socially stable, has developed supportive relationships with non-drug users, has discovered alternative ways of dealing with the precipitants to drug use and is confident and motivated to taper off methadone. Patients who are doing well and do not wish to discontinue methadone should not be pressured to do so. Observational studies suggest that patients remaining in treatment for two to three years or longer have a better outcome than those in treatment for shorter periods. This effect persists even after they leave methadone treatment.

245

TAPERING DURING VOLUNTARY WITHDRAWAL FROM METHADONE

Methadone tapering is associated with insomnia, depression and anxiety, sometimes lasting for months after completion of the taper. Slow tapers (5 mg per week or less) have been shown to be more successful than rapid tapers (Senay, Dorus et al., 1977). The pace of the taper should be determined by the patient, and should be halted or reversed at the patient's request. Tapering may have to proceed more slowly when the dose descends below 20 mg. Tapering should be put on hold or reversed if the patient experiences severe withdrawal symptoms, drug cravings or drug use.

8.3

PREVENTION, DIAGNOSIS AND TREATMENT OF OPIOID DEPENDENCE IN PATIENTS WITH CHRONIC NON-MALIGNANT PAIN*

Meldon Kahan, MD, Lynn Wilson, MD, and Douglas Gourlay, MD

RISK OF OPIOID DEPENDENCE IN CHRONIC PAIN PATIENTS

The long-term prescribing of opioids for patients with chronic non-malignant pain poses a difficult dilemma for many physicians. They feel they must respond to the patient's distress, yet they wish to avoid iatrogenic addiction or legal problems. This section briefly reviews the prevention, assessment and treatment of opioid dependence in patients with chronic pain.

Tolerance to the analgesic effects of opioids develops very slowly and patients are often able to remain on the same dose for years. Furthermore, most patients do not experience euphoria or other reinforcing effects with opioids. A number of large surveys of patients with acute and chronic pain have found that the majority of patients do not abuse or become psychologically dependent on opioids (Portenoy, 1996).

Occasionally, patients with a true organic pain condition do develop psychological dependence on prescription opioids. That is, they use the drug not only for its analgesic effect but for its psychic effects as well. Tolerance to the psychic effects of opioids develops quickly, forcing the patient to seek increasing doses of the drug. Such patients often have a prior history of addiction to opioids, alcohol or other drugs.

ASSESSMENT

A careful assessment of chronic non-malignant pain is essential for the development of an effective management plan. The steps for conducting a comprehensive assessment are listed in the table below.

*Adapted from Kahan, Wilson et al., 1996.

TABLE 3: Assessment of Chronic Non-Malignant Pain

- Establish a diagnosis and rule out other serious causes of pain.
- Assess the degree of distress and functional disability caused by the pain.
- Identify aggravating and relieving factors.
- Conduct a mental status examination.
- Take an alcohol and drug history.
- Inquire about psychosocial status.
- Obtain records from previous physicians.
- Conduct a detailed physical examination.
- Request a consultation.
- Know the strengths and limitations of your consultants.

MANAGEMENT OF THE CHRONIC PAIN PATIENT

Comprehensive treatment plan

A systematic, comprehensive plan should evolve from the assessment. The plan may involve several consultants and caregivers, including pain specialists, physiotherapists and psychiatrists. A variety of treatment modalities may be employed.

The goal of treatment is to improve patients' physical, psychological and social functioning and comfort level. Physicians should look beyond a narrow focus on the elimination of pain through medication and examine strategies to help patients improve their psychological and behavioral responses to pain. Exclusive focus on analgesic medication may actually reinforce pain behavior (Moulin, Iezzi et al., 1996). The components of a comprehensive treatment plan should include the following:

LIFESTYLE MODIFICATION

Exercise, weight loss, regular sleep, decreased caffeine and alcohol intake and regular meals can benefit patients with chronic back pain and headache. Simple lifestyle adjustments such as regulating work hours or getting assistance with housework may also be helpful.

SUPPORTIVE COUNSELLING AND PSYCHOTHERAPY

Counselling approaches that may benefit chronic pain patients include:

(a) *General supportive therapy,* consisting of empathic listening, reinforcement of coping strategies and practical advice when requested by the patient.

(b) *Cognitive behavioral therapy,* in which patients analyse the negative thoughts that accompany their pain and learn to view their pain differently. Addressing cognitive distortions helps patients generate alternative ways of dealing with their pain. Cognitive behavioral therapy has been shown to be of benefit in patients with chronic pain (Enright, 1997).

(c) *Solution-focused therapy,* in which patients focus on solutions and coping strategies rather than problems. For example, the patient may be asked, "Tell me about the times when your pain is 5 out of 10 instead of 8 out of 10. What are you doing at those times?" When solutions are identified, the patient is asked to use those behaviors more frequently.

TREAT UNDERLYING PSYCHIATRIC DISORDERS

Disorders such as depression and anxiety may contribute to the patient's perception of pain.

TRY NON-OPIOID TREATMENTS FIRST

Non-opioid treatment should always be tried first before making a long-term therapeutic commitment to opioid therapy.

See Section 8.1 for a discussion of the adverse effects of opioids, including tolerance, overdose and withdrawal.

EFFECTIVENESS OF OPIOIDS IN TREATING CHRONIC PAIN

To date, only a few randomized placebo-controlled trials have been conducted on the efficacy of opioids in treating chronic pain. One trial (Arkinstall, Sandler et al., 1995) found a 30 per cent decrease in pain intensity and pain-related disability in patients with musculoskeletal pain receiving sustained-release codeine. Almost all of the patients were already on long-term opioid treatment, making interpretation of the study difficult. Another trial (Moulin, Iezzi et al., 1996) found that patients with musculoskeletal pain who had not responded to codeine, anti-inflammatories or antidepressants had a 15 per cent reduction in pain intensity when placed on sustained-release morphine. No reduction in disability was observed. A third trial (Watson & Babul, 1998) found that oxycodone reduced neuropathic pain from post-therapeutic neuralgia. These trials suggest that opioids confer a modest reduction in perceived pain intensity in patients with chronic musculoskeletal or neuropathic pain, but that the effectiveness of opioids in reducing disability is not certain.

Role of opioids in treating different types of pain

Below, Table 4 summarizes the role of opioid treatment according to the type of pain. Opioids are most effective for nociceptive pain. The WHO analgesic ladder should be followed (acetaminophen and NSAIDs should be tried first, followed by codeine preparations). Significant pathology should be documented before prescribing opioids.

Neuropathic pain often fails to respond to opioids, although some patients derive definite benefit. Because neuropathic pain is relatively unresponsive to opioids, larger doses may be necessary, which can produce unacceptable side-effects. First-line drugs for neuropathic pain include tricyclic antidepressants, anticonvulsants such as gabapentin (Neurontin®) and membrane stabilizers.

Opioids have no role in the treatment of isolated tension headaches or pain of psychogenic or of unknown origin such as fibromyalgia. A number of other medications are effective both acutely and prophylactically for migraine headaches and these should be tried before opioids are used. Regular use of mixed opioid/non-opioid analgesics in the treatment of migraine headaches can cause medication-induced headaches. Butorphanol should be used only for infrequent, severe attacks. Demerol® should only be used in the treatment of migraine headaches when all other treatments have failed.

TABLE 4: Role of Opioid Analgesics in Treating Different Types of Pain

	Nociceptive pain	Neuropathic pain	Visceral pain	Psycho-genic pain of uncertain origin	Headache[†]
Examples	Severe degenera-tive changes (multilevel or joint)	Diabetic neuropathy, causalgia, central pain (stroke, spinal cord injury)	Chronic pancreatitis, Crohn's	Somato-form pain disorder, depression (conversion disorder), fibromyalgia	Tension, migraine

Table 4 continued

	Nociceptive pain	Neuropathic pain	Visceral pain	Psycho-genic pain of uncertain origin	Headache[†]
First-line medications	WHO analgesic ladder: Acetaminophen, NSAIDs	Tricyclic antidepressants, anticonvulsants, (e.g., gabapentin), membrane stabilizers	Smooth muscle relaxants, antacids, H_2 blockers		Prophylactic: Beta blockers, calcium channel blockers Chronic: tricylic antidepressants, antiepileptics, NSAIDs Acute: NSAIDs DHE, sumatriptan, ketorolac, chlorpromazine, dexamethasone
Effectiveness of opioids in therapy	Of value	Limited but definite value in selected cases	Limited value	No value	Tension: Rarely indicated Migraine: Limited value
Place in therapy	Use only when other medications have failed	Use only when other medications have failed	Use only when other medications have failed	Not indicated	Use only when other medications have failed

Table 4 continued

	Nociceptive pain	Neuropathic pain	Visceral pain	Psycho-genic pain of uncertain origin	Headache[†]
Caveats	Document significant organic pathology before long-term prescribing.	Opioids less effective in neuro-pathic pain. Higher doses may be required but dosing limited by side-effects. Follow Alberta Guidelines for Management of Chronic Non-Malignant Pain.[††]			Use combination medications (e.g., Tylenol #3) only intermittently for short periods. Short-acting analgesics are a major cause of rebound headache. Butorphanol only for infrequent, severe attacks when other treatments have failed. Demerol® only as last resort.

[†] Pryse-Phillips, Dodick et al., 1997.
[††] College of Physicians and Surgeons of Alberta, 1993. See Addendum 3.

Before prescribing opioids, physicians need to define and prioritize targets for treatment, bearing in mind that most chronic pain syndromes have a mix of mechanisms and that psychiatric comorbidity is common. For example, in a depressed patient with diabetic neuropathy, treatment should be targeted towards depression, insomnia and neuropathic pain. Tricyclic antidepressants would be the treatment of choice, because they are effective for all three targets.

Prescribing Opioids to the Chronic Pain Patient

Opioids should be used only after an adequate trial of non-opioid analgesics and after other treatment modalities have failed to significantly improve the patient's pain. Keep in mind that treatment success is measured by diminished pain and improved psychosocial functioning, not by the complete absence of pain, which is an unrealistic goal in most cases. Use opioids with particular caution in patients who have a history of substance abuse. (For a quick summary see Addendum 2: "Do's" and "Don'ts" of Prescribing Opioids for Chronic Non-Malignant Pain, at the end of this section. Also consult the detailed Guidelines for Management of Chronic Non-Malignant Pain policy of the Alberta College of Physicians and Surgeons, included as Addendum 3.)

Summarized below is a protocol for prescribing opioids to the chronic pain patient.

TABLE 5: Prescribing Opioids to Chronic Pain Patients

1. Screen for alcohol and drug problems.
2. Obtain informed consent.
3. Avoid prescribing parenteral opioids.
4. Avoid prescribing short-acting opioids with a high dependence liability.
5. Avoid prescribing benzodiazepines and other sedatives.
6. Use the WHO analgesic ladder, begin with ASA/acetaminophen/codeine combinations.
7. Add morphine only after failure of an adequate trial of codeine combinations.
8. Discontinue opioids if there is no analgesic response.
9. Switch the patient to a long-acting opioid preparation (e.g., MS Contin®).
10. Use rescue doses sparingly.
11. Refer the patient for consultation or transfer of care prior to long-term opioid treatment.
12. Monitor for adverse effects of chronic opioid administration.
13. Contact other physicians involved in the patient's care to clarify which physician will be responsible for prescribing opioids.
14. Implement a treatment contract.
15. Keep an opioid prescription flow chart.
16. Assess the patient frequently, monitoring and charting changes in functional status, analgesia, adverse effects and behaviors suggestive of dependence. Alter the treatment plan accordingly.
17. Periodically reassess the need for opioids.

1. SCREEN FOR ALCOHOL OR DRUG PROBLEMS

Physicians should screen for current or past alcohol and drug problems before initiating long-term opioid therapy (see Section 1). Opioids should be used with caution if the patient scores positive on the CAGE questionnaire or reports heavy alcohol consumption. Caution is also required when prescribing opioids to patients who report current or past heavy use of prescription, over-the-counter or street drugs.

2. OBTAIN INFORMED CONSENT

Review potential side-effects (see Section 8.1), including the small risk of physical and psychological dependence and the reproductive effects.

3. AVOID PRESCRIBING PARENTERAL OPIOIDS

Because parenteral opioids are more potent than oral opioids, patients who self-administer subcutaneous or intramuscular opioids are at greater risk for overdose, dependence and other adverse effects.

4. AVOID PRESCRIBING SHORT-ACTING OPIOIDS WITH A HIGH DEPENDENCE LIABILITY

Examples include: Fiorinal C^1/$_4$, C^1/$_2$®, Percocet® and Dilaudid®. Demerol® and Leritine® should be avoided because they are very short-acting and they can cause an accumulation of the toxic metabolite normeperidine, which has neurotoxicity (causing seizures and delerium).

TABLE 6: Commonly Prescribed Short-Acting Opioids with a High Dependence Liability

Opioid or other psychoactive agent	Trade name
Anileridine	Leritine
Butalbital[†] ± codeine	Fiorinal, Fiorinal C^1/$_4$, C^1/$_2$
Hydromorphone	Dilaudid, Dilaudid-HP, PMS-Hydromorphone, Hydrostat
Hydrocodone	Anexsia, Calmydone, Hycodan, Hycomine, Hydrocet Lortab Mercodol, Novahistex DH Expectorant, Robidone, Solucodan, Triaminic Expectorant DH, Vasofrinic DH, Vicodin

† Butalbital is a barbiturate that has a high abuse liability and is used as a short-acting analgesic.

Table 6 continued

Opioid or other psychoactive agent	Trade name
Meperidine	Demerol, Mepergan
Morphine sulphate or morphine hydrocholoride	Astramorph, Infumorph MISR, Morphitec, M.O.S., Roxanol, Roxanal 100, Statex
Oxycodone	Percocet, Endocet, Percodan, Tylox, Roxicodone
Propoxyphene	Davocet, Darvon, Wygesic

5. AVOID PRESCRIBING BENZODIAZEPINES AND OTHER SEDATIVES

The combination of benzodiazepines and opioids may cause confusion, fatigue, falls and motor vehicle accidents (particularly in the elderly). They may also cause physical and psychological dependence in higher doses and in susceptible individuals.

6. USE THE WHO ANALGESIC LADDER

Begin with ASA/acetaminophen/codeine combinations. The majority of patients requiring opioid analgesics can be managed with these medications. To avoid acetaminophen toxicity, no more than 4 g should be taken in one day; lower doses are recommended for heavy drinkers and patients with viral hepatitis.

7. ADD MORPHINE ONLY AFTER FAILURE OF AN ADEQUATE TRIAL OF CODEINE COMBINATIONS

The Alberta College of Physicians and Surgeons Guidelines (1993) recommend titrating initially with morphine syrup 10 mg every 4 hours, increasing the dose once or twice weekly as needed. Slow and careful titration is recommended to avoid sedation and respiratory depression. Doses above 300 mg per day are rarely necessary. Substantially lower initial doses are suggested for elderly or debilitated patients, those with respiratory disease, and those on medications that may interact with morphine.

8. DISCONTINUE OPIOIDS IF THERE IS NO ANALGESIC RESPONSE

Patients should experience a graded analgesic response to dosage increases. If no analgesic benefit is observed, the patient's underlying pain condition may not be responsive to opioids and they should be discontinued.

9. SWITCH THE PATIENT TO A LONG-ACTING OPIOID PREPARATION

Once an effective dose is established, the patient can then be switched to the equivalent dose of a long-acting opioid preparation such as MS Contin®, Codeine Contin® or the transdermal fentanyl patch. Long-acting opioids are less likely to cause rebound pain or withdrawal symptoms than shorter-acting agents.

10. USE RESCUE DOSES SPARINGLY

Wherever possible, opioid doses should be "time dependent" (scheduled) rather than "pain contingent" (prn). Particularly for musculoskeletal pain, reliance on rescue doses may actually undermine the patient's use of lifestyle modification, exercises and behavioral techniques to prevent and manage exacerbations of pain. If rescue doses are necessary, they should be limited if possible to no more than four to six doses per month (Portenoy & Payne, 1996). Alternatively, patients may be instructed to take one or two extra doses in a given day if needed, as long as they reduce the total dosage by an equivalent amount on the following day.

11. REFER THE PATIENT FOR CONSULTATION OR TRANSFER OF CARE PRIOR TO LONG-TERM OPIOID TREATMENT

Physicians who feel uncomfortable with the dose or duration of the patient's opioid use may choose to refer the patient to a physician or clinic with greater experience in the management of chronic pain. The guidelines of the Corporation professionelle des médecines du Québec (1991) recommend that physicians who administer opioids to patients with chronic non-malignant pain for more than eight weeks "secure another physician's opinion before continuing such therapy."

12. MONITOR FOR ADVERSE EFFECTS OF CHRONIC OPIOID ADMINISTRATION

See Section 8.1 (above).

13. CONTACT OTHER PHYSICIANS INVOLVED IN THE PATIENT'S CARE TO CLARIFY WHICH PHYSICIAN WILL BE RESPONSIBLE FOR PRESCRIBING OPIOIDS

This will help to avoid confusion and double-doctoring.

14. IMPLEMENT A TREATMENT CONTRACT (SEE ADDENDUM 4 AT THE END OF THIS SECTION)

Physicians should make liberal use of treatment contracts with patients who are chronically prescribed opioids. The conditions of the contract should include:

- the maximum amount of opioids to be dispensed per week or month
- an agreement that the patient will not seek opioids from any other source, including over-the-counter medications, friends or relatives, or another physician. (All physicians involved in the patient's care should agree on who will be the opioid-prescribing physician.)
- an agreement that opioids will not be dispensed early if the patient "loses" the medication or uses more than prescribed
- the consequences of breaking the contract. (The physician may decide to cease writing narcotic prescriptions or end the physician-patient relationship.)

15. KEEP AN OPIOID PRESCRIPTION FLOW CHART (SEE ADDENDUM 5 AT THE END OF THIS SECTION)

Trends towards increased opioid use can be detected by using a separate flow chart for narcotic prescriptions, specifying the date and number of tablets dispensed.

16. ASSESS THE PATIENT FREQUENTLY. RECORD CHANGES IN FUNCTIONAL STATUS, ANALGESIA, ADVERSE EFFECTS AND BEHAVIORS SUGGESTIVE OF DEPENDENCE

Alter the treatment plan accordingly. The patient should have regular follow-up visits, particularly in the early stages of treatment.

17. PERIODICALLY REASSESS THE NEED FOR OPIOIDS

Indications for discontinuing opioids include: no benefit in analgesia or functional status, severe adverse effects and multiple episodes of behaviors suggestive of dependence (see Table 7). Furthermore, patients' pain waxes and wanes with time and frequently patients will tolerate dosage reductions with little difficulty.

METHADONE FOR THE MANAGEMENT OF CHRONIC PAIN

While the primary indication for methadone is the treatment of opioid dependence, it is also being used with increasing frequency in the treatment of patients with chronic pain. Owing to its N-methyl-D-aspartate (NMDA) receptor antagonist properties, methadone may be particularly useful in the treatment of neuropathic pain. However, because experience with and knowledge about the analgesic properties of methadone are still emerging, and because its long half-life can cause drug accumulation and toxicity, methadone should be used as an analgesic with caution, and only after standard opioid and non-opioid treatments have failed. Likewise, methadone should only be prescribed by physicians experienced in its use. Like other opioids, methadone should be used for analgesia with particular caution in patients who have a prior or current history of alcohol or drug dependence.

Methadone's duration of analgesic action is only 6–8 hours (compared with 14 to 40 hours for suppression of opioid withdrawal symptoms), so it must typically be administered three or more times daily. Patients must be started on a low initial dose (no more than 2.5 mg tid if they are not already on opioids; no more than 5 mg tid if they are taking opioids). The dose should be titrated upwards in small increments (typically not more than 5 mg per dose) every five to seven days. In the case of those patients who are using significant amounts of other potent opioids, this regime may be increased as the other opioid is being tapered during the crossover period. Physicians are cautioned to watch for signs of accumulation and toxicity even in those who are clearly tolerant to other potent opioids as there is often incomplete cross-tolerance between methadone and other opioids. Patients and family members should be advised to watch closely for sedation, and to contact a physician immediately should it occur. Use of alcohol and other sedatives should be avoided if possible during the initial titration.

It is not uncommon for patients to require small quantities of short-acting opioids for breakthrough pain. In cases where significant medical illness (i.e. COPD) or advanced age coexist with pain, inpatient admission for dose titration or crossover may be prudent. Consultation with practitioners experienced in the use of methadone for pain management is strongly recommended.

OPIOID DEPENDENCE IN THE CHRONIC PAIN PATIENT

Behaviors suggesting opioid dependence

The behaviors outlined in the table below suggest the development of opioid dependence in the chronic pain patient. Some of these behaviors are displayed by patients whose pain has been inadequately treated, a phenomenon known as "pseudoaddiction." The behaviors have been divided into "less suggestive" and "more suggestive" of opioid dependence. Physicians need to interpret worrisome behaviors in context. One unsanctioned dosage escalation or "lost" script is less predictive of addiction than multiple episodes.

TABLE 7: Behaviors Suggesting Opioid Dependence†

Less suggestive of opioid dependence:

- The patient requests opioids in amounts well in excess of that required by other patients with a similar condition.
- The patient requests escalating doses.
- The patient occasionally takes more opioids than were prescribed.
- The patient occasionally requests scripts early, claiming to have lost the script.
- The patient occasionally seeks scripts from another physician, takes over-the-counter opioids or "borrows" from a friend or family member.
- The patient is reluctant to try non-opioid alternatives and consistently reports that they do not help.
- The patient is addicted to alcohol or other drugs.

Strongly suggestive of opioid dependence:

- The patient repeatedly takes a higher opioid dose than prescribed by the physician.
- On multiple occasions, the patient requests scripts early, using a variety of excuses.
- The patient frequently threatens or harasses the physician or his/her staff in order to obtain opioids.
- The patient regularly attempts to obtain opioids from other sources, including friends and family, buying from the street, and other doctors (often without informing them of previous opioid use).
- The patient alters, steals or sells scripts.
- The patient injects oral opioid preparations.
- The patient shows deterioration in functional status (e.g., loss of job, family dysfunction).
- The patient shows signs of opioid intoxication (e.g., drowsiness, pinpoint pupils).
- The patient has symptoms or signs of opioid withdrawal.

---

† Adapted from Portenoy, 1996.

259

ASSESSMENT OF CHRONIC PAIN PATIENTS SUSPECTED OF OPIOID DEPENDENCE

The physician should carefully assess patients suspected to be opioid dependent. The physician should ask about the pattern of opioid use (looking in particular for an escalating pattern), effectiveness and adverse effects of opioids and current and past alcohol and drug use. The physician should also inquire about the psychic effects of the opioid. Patients who report that they sometimes take the drug to relax or worry less are acknowledging some degree of psychological dependence. Similarly, physical dependence can be determined by asking about withdrawal symptoms such as insomnia, myalgia or dysphoria as the opioid "wears off," and about drug use to avoid withdrawal symptoms.

The physician should also ask whether the patient has concerns about his or her opioid use, or if anyone else has expressed concerns about the patient's opioid use. Psychiatric symptoms should be elicited. Depression, suicidal ideation, anxiety, insomnia and fatigue are common among patients dependent on opioids. The patient's level of functioning should be determined. The patient should be asked about behaviors suggestive of dependence, such as double-doctoring, altering scripts or purchasing opioids from family, friends or the street.

TABLE 8: Detecting Signs and Symptoms of Opioid Dependence

- Ask about the pattern of opioid use.
- Ask about the effectiveness and adverse effects of opioids.
- Ask about current and past alcohol and drug use.
- Inquire about the psychic effects of the opioids.
- Ask about problems related to opioid use.
- Inquire about withdrawal symptoms.
- Inquire about psychiatric symptomatology.
- Inquire about psychosocial status before and after starting opioids.
- Ask about double-doctoring, altering of prescriptions and other behaviors indicative of addiction.
- Conduct a physical examination and appropriate laboratory tests.
- Order a urine drug screen and laboratory markers for alcohol abuse, hepatitis and HIV infection.
- Obtain corroborating information from the patient's spouse and previous physician.

Confirmation of assessment

Since some opioid-dependent patients will deny that they misuse the drug for fear of being "cut off," it is essential that the physician look for objective evidence of dependence by conducting a physical examination and obtaining a urine drug screen. During the physical examination, a search should be made for track marks and signs of opioid intoxication or withdrawal. A urine drug screen will detect all the common drugs of abuse (see Section 1). CBC, liver transaminases and hepatitis screen are recommended to look for alcohol abuse and viral hepatitis. HIV testing should be offered. Finally, corroborating information should be obtained from the patient's spouse and previous physician. The spouse is often the first person to notice signs of dependence such as fatigue, irritability, opioid intoxication and increasing social isolation. Since a diagnosis of dependence sometimes becomes apparent only over a long period of time, the previous physician may provide valuable information concerning the patient's pattern of behavior.

MANAGEMENT OF CHRONIC PAIN PATIENTS WHO ARE OPIOID DEPENDENT

The chronic pain patient who is opioid dependent presents a considerable challenge to the physician. Depression, anxiety and insomnia, the sympathetic overdrive associated with opioid withdrawal and non-compliance with treatment plans all contribute to the opioid-dependent patient's perception of pain (Savage, 1994). The following protocol is recommended.

TAPERING

A consultation should be obtained from a pain specialist or addiction medicine specialist. The patient should be tapered slowly with methadone or long-acting morphine (see below for dosage calculations). The taper should be completed within two weeks to three months. Patients are often afraid that their pain will worsen during a taper, but case series suggest that the pain remains stable or improves (Savage, 1994). This is probably because the patients are less depressed, their functional status improves and they experience less opioid withdrawal. Tapering is contraindicated in pregnancy. Pregnant opioid-dependent patients should be placed on methadone maintenance treatment.

Tapering with an opioid is *only* recommended for patients with confirmed chronic organic pain who are also opioid dependent. It is not recommended for drug-seeking patients who do not have chronic organic pain but make false or deliberately exaggerated claims of pain in order to acquire opioids. Tapering such patients poses the risk of double-doctoring. Distinguishing

261

the opioid-dependent chronic pain patient from the drug-seeker may be difficult. For this reason, consultation with an addiction medicine physician or pain specialist is recommended.

Note: As a general rule, tapering should not be attempted unless the physician knows the patient well and feels that the risk of double doctoring is minimal.

Frequent follow-up visits are recommended during the taper. The patient should be encouraged to look for positive effects of tapering, including greater energy, more stable mood and less pain. While withdrawal may be uncomfortable, it is not life-threatening and the patient should be encouraged to persist in the taper. Other pain management modalities should be employed during tapering. If the tapering has failed or is not indicated (as in a drug-seeking patient), the opioid should be stopped. Clonidine can be used to treat withdrawal symptoms.

Periodic urine drug screens can be helpful in detecting unauthorized drug use. A treatment contract should be implemented, specifying that replacement doses will not be given if the tapering dose is used up too quickly. Finally, an inpatient or outpatient drug and alcohol treatment program is recommended to address the patient's opioid dependence.

DOSAGE ADJUSTMENT DURING TAPERING

Since short-acting opioids may be more likely to cause withdrawal and rebound pain with tapering, patients should be switched to methadone or long-acting morphine (see Table 9 below). Since the dose comparisons in Table 9 are based on analgesic equivalences, not psychoactive effects, upwards or downwards titration may be needed. Published tables show a large variation in suggested equivalences.

The initial conversion should be no more than half the calculated amount, to a maximum of 80 mg of morphine. This will minimize the risk of opioid overdose since patients may not be fully tolerant to morphine. The morphine should then be adjusted until the patient is reasonably comfortable and tapered by no more than 10 per cent every four to seven days. The taper should be completed within two to four months. Some flexibility in dosage adjustment will be necessary in response to the patient's pain or withdrawal symptoms.

EXAMPLE OF TAPERING

A patient taking 30 tablets of Percocet® per day (150 mg of oxycodone) should be switched to half the calculated amount of morphine (75 mg of morphine, given as 15 mg q4h for 5 doses/day). If the patient suffers withdrawal symptoms, the dose can be adjusted upwards by 5 or 10 mg per day until a maximum dose of 150 mg is reached. The patient should be switched to an equivalent dose of MS Contin® (e.g., 75 mg bid if the final required dose of morphine is 150 mg/day) and tapered by 10 per cent (15 mg) once or twice per week.

TABLE 9: Equianalgesic Opioid Doses†

Opioid	Approximate equianalgesic oral dose	Approximate equianalgesic parenteral dose
Morphine	30 mg q3–4h (around-the-clock dosing, i.e. chronic use) 60 mg q3–4h (single dose or intermittent dosing)	10 mg q3–4h
Codeine	130 mg q3–4h	75 mg q3–4h
Oxycodone (Percocet®)	30 mg q3–4h	Not available
Meperidine (Demerol®)	300 mg q2–3h	100 mg q3h
Hydrocodone	30 mg q3–4h	Not available
Hydromorphone (Dilaudid®)	7.5 mg q3–4h	1.5 mg q3–4h
Methadone	20 mg q6–8h	10 mg q6–8h

† Adapted from Savage, 1994.

Note: Published tables vary in the suggested doses that are equianalgesic to morphine. Clinical response is the criterion that must be applied for each patient: titration to clinical response is necessary. Because there is not complete cross-tolerance among these drugs, it is usually necessary to use a lower than equianalgesic dose when changing drugs, and to re-titrate to the response (Panel on Acute Pain Guidelines, 1992).

Caution: Recommended doses do not apply to patients with renal or hepatic insufficiency or other conditions affecting drug metabolism and kinetics (Panel on Acute Pain Guidelines, 1992).

IF THE TAPER FAILS

If the patient refuses to taper off opioids or breaks the treatment contract, the physician is under no obligation to continue prescribing opioids and may request that the patient find another doctor. If the patient is able to taper to a lower dose and finds it difficult to taper further, the physician must reassess the treatment plan. The physician may choose to maintain the patient at the lower dose if it is more consistent with usual practice, if the treatment contract has been followed and if the patient reports an improvement in mood and functional status.

Chronic opioid therapy and clinical uncertainty

Many physicians have patients who have been maintained on therapeutic doses of opioids for long periods without exhibiting clinical features of dependence and without apparent adverse effects. Such patients can pose a dilemma for physicians if the need or indication for such opioid treatment is uncertain. A typical example would be the patient who has taken two to three oxycodone tablets per day for years for mild osteoarthritis. In such patients, a therapeutic trial of tapering is warranted, in order to establish the need for ongoing opioid therapy and to rule out subtle adverse effects. Patients who are tapered off opioids sometimes report that they feel more alert and energetic without any increase in pain.

The tapering should be done slowly, over weeks or months. Switching to long-acting morphine during the taper is usually not necessary if the patient is taking small or moderate doses of opioids. Supportive counselling and non-opioid treatments should be tried during the taper. The taper should be halted or reversed if the patient's pain becomes worse. Sometimes tapering establishes the patient on a lower effective dose.

PAIN MANAGEMENT IN THE RECOVERING SUBSTANCE USER

Several authors have addressed the many issues associated with the assessment and treatment of pain in those patients in recovery (Wesson, Ling et al., 1993; Miotto, Compton et al. 1996). While an in-depth discussion of this topic is beyond the scope of this handbook, several key points should be made.

First, addiction and chronic pain are not binary processes; they may coexist in patients, either concurrently or consecutively. Having a pain problem does not prevent a predisposition to addiction from expressing itself, nor does having a history of addiction prevent the development of chronic pain. Having both does, however, complicate the assessment and management of each problem.

264

Second, for most people in recovery the fear of relapse is very real — often to the point where they endure chronic pain rather than seeking effective treatment. This is less obvious for those whose drug of choice was other than opioids. For people with alcohol problems, the risks associated with prescribed opioids are often minimized by both the patient and the prescribing physician. Thus, both under-medication and over-medication of patients in recovery can lead to relapse. In fact, untreated pain is a commonly identified trigger to relapse. The person in recovery not only deserves adequate pain relief, they need it in order to reduce the risk of relapse to drugs or alcohol.

Third, the aggressive assessment and treatment of pain among patients in recovery, by a physician who is knowledgeable about both addiction and pain management, is associated with the best outcome. To ignore pain is to leave a major trigger to relapse unattended.

In general, it is best to avoid prescribing short-acting, highly reinforcing drugs for the chronic management of pain. This is also true when managing chronic pain in patients in recovery. It is appropriate, however, to provide a small amount of short-acting opioid for breakthrough pain management. Should breakthrough medication become regularly used, it should be replaced with a long-acting drug, given in accordance with accepted dosing intervals for the agent used. A small amount of short-acting medication for breakthrough should remain part of the daily dosing schedule. If the dose appears to be escalating, organic causes should be explored first before the escalation is assumed to result from an underlying addictive process. Careful behavioral contracts regarding self-escalation of dose, lost prescriptions and early prescription refills can be helpful. These contracts may be either informally noted in the chart, or formally signed by the patient and clinician.

Physicians should encourage patients who participate in a 12-step recovery program to continue working toward their recovery. Many patients find that the 12-step philosophy of "powerlessness" over a substance of abuse also applies to chronic pain. For patients with chronic pain who are in recovery from an addiction, the 12 steps may offer a complementary source of support.

R E F E R E N C E S

Arkinstall, W., Sandler, A., Goughnour, B., Babul, N. & Harsanyi, Z., Darke, A.C. (1995). Efficacy of controlled-release codeine in chronic non-malignant pain: A randomized, placebo-controlled clinical trial. *Pain, 62*(2), 169-178.

Aronow, R., Paul, S.D. & Woolley, P.V. (1972). Childhood poisoning: An unfortunate consequence of methadone availability. *Journal of the American Medical Association, 219*(3), 321-324.

Ball, J.C. & Ross, A. (1991). *The Effectiveness of Methadone Maintenance Treatment: Patients, Programs, Services, and Outcome.* New York: Springer-Verlag.

Bell, J., Seres, V., Bowron., Lewis, J. & Batey, R. (1988). The use of serum methadone levels in patients receiving methadone maintenance. *Clinical Pharmacology and Therapeutics, 43*(6), 623-629.

Brands, B. & Brands, J. (Eds.). (1998). *Methadone Maintenance: A Physician's Guide to Treatment.* Toronto: Addiction Research Foundation.

Caplehorn, J.R.M. (1998). Deaths in the first two weeks of maintenance treatment in NSW in 1994: Identifying cases of iatrogenic methadone toxicity. *Drug and Alcohol Review,* 17, 9-17.

Caplehorn, J.R.& Bell, J. (1991). Methadone dosage and retention of patients in maintenance treatment. *Medical Journal of Australia, 154*(3), 195-199.

College of Physicians and Surgeons of Alberta. (1993). *Guidelines for Management of Chronic Non-malignant Pain.* Edmonton, AB: College of Physicians and Surgeons of Alberta.

College of Physicians and Surgeons of Ontario. (1996). *Methadone Maintenance Guidelines.* Toronto: College of Physicians and Surgeons of Ontario; Addiction Research Foundation; Ontario College of Pharmacists.

Connor, E.M., Sperling, R.S., Gelber, R., Kiselev, P., Scott, G. & O'Sullivan, M.J., (1994). Reduction of maternal-infant transmission of human immunodeficiency virus type 1 with zidovudine treatment. *New England Journal of Medicine, 331*(18), 1173-1180.

Corporation professionelle des médecines du Québec. (1991). *Pain Treatment Centres.* Montreal: Corporation professionelle des médecines du Québec.

Deren, S. (1986). Children of substance abusers: A review of the literature. *Journal of Substance Abuse Treatment, 3,* 77-94.

Devenyi, P. & Saunders, S.J. (1986). *Physicians' Handbook for Medical Management of Alcohol- and Drug-related Problems.* Toronto: Addiction Research Foundation and Ontario Medical Association.

Doberczak, T.M., Thorton, J.C., Bernstein, J. & Kandall, S.R. (1987). Impact of maternal drug dependency on birth weight and head circumference of offspring. *American Journal of Diseases of Children, 141*(11), 1163-1167.

266

Drummer, O.H., Opeskin, K., Syrjanen, M. & Cordner, S.M. (1992). Methadone toxicity causing death in ten subjects starting on a methadone maintenance program. *American Journal of Forensic Medicine and Pathology, 13(4)*, 346-350.

Enright, S.J. (1997). Cognitive behaviour therapy — clinical applications. British Medical *Journal, 314(7097)*, 1811-1816.

Finnegan, L.P. (1978). Management of pregnant drug-dependent women. *Annals of the New York Academy of Sciences, 311,* 135-146.

Finnegan, L.P. (1980). *Drug Dependency in Pregnancy: Clinical Management of Mother and Child.* London: Castle House.

Finnegan, L.P. (1986). Neonatal abstinence syndrome: Assessment and pharmacotherapy. In F.F. Rubaltelli & B. Granati (Eds.), *Neonatal Therapy: An Update.* New York: Elsevier.

Finnegan, L.P. (1991) Treatment issues for opioid-dependent women during the perinatal period. *Journal of Psychoactive Drugs, 23(2),* 191-201.

Harding-Pink, D. (1993). Methadone: one person's maintenance dose is another's poison. *The Lancet, 341,* 665-666

Hoegerman, G. & Schnoll, S. (1991). Narcotic use in pregnancy. *Clinics in Perinatology, 18(1),* 67-73.

International Perinatal HIV Group. (1999). The mode of delivery and the risk of vertical transmission of human immunodeficiency virus type 1 — a meta analysis of 15 prospective cohort studies. *New England Journal of Medicine, 340(13),* 977-87.

Jasinski, D.R., Johnson, R.E. & Kocher, T.R. (1985). Clonidine in morphine withdrawal: Differential effects on signs and symptoms. *Archives of General Psychiatry, 42(11),* 1063-1066.

Judson, B.A, Ortiz, S., Crouse, L., Carney, T.M. & Goldstein, A. (1980). A follow-up study of heroin addicts five years after first admission to a methadone treatment program. *Drug and Alcohol Dependence, 6(5),* 295-313.

Kahan, M., Wilson, L., Mailis, A. & Davis, D. (1996). *Appropriate Prescribing of Narcotic Analgesics.* Toronto: College of Physicians and Surgeons of Ontario.

Kaltenbach, K. & Finnegan, L.P. (1992). Methadone maintenance during pregnancy: Implications for perinatal and developmental outcome. In T.G. Sonderegger (Ed.), *Perinatal Substance Abuse: Research Findings and Clinical Implications.* Baltimore: Johns Hopkins University Press.

267

Kandall, S.R., Doberczak, T.M., Mauer, K.R., Strashun, R.H. & Korts, D.C. (1983). Opiate v CNS depressant therapy in neonatal drug abstinence syndrome. *American Journal of Diseases of Children, 137(4),* 378-382.

Kandall, S.R. & Gartner, L.M. (1972). Late presentations of drug withdrawal symptoms in newborns. *American Journal of Diseases of Children, 127,* 58-61.

Miotto, K., Compton, P., Ling, W. & Conolly, M. (1996). Diagnosing addictive disease in chronic pain patients. *Psychosomatics, 37,* 223-235.

Moulin, D.E., Iezzi, A., Amireh, R., Sparpe, W.K., Boyd, D. & Merskey H. (1996). Randomised trial of oral morphine for chronic non-cancer pain. *Lancet, 347(8995),* 143-147.

Newman, R.G. & Whitehall, W.B. (1979). Double-blind comparison of methadone and placebo maintenance treatments of narcotic addicts in Hong Kong. *Lancet, 2(8141),* 485-488

Office of National Drug Control Policy. (1995). *Pulse Check: National Trends in Drug Abuse.* Washington, D.C.: Office of National Drug Control Policy.

Panel on Acute Pain Guidelines. (1992). *Acute Pain Management: Operative or Medical Procedures and Trauma.* Rockville MD: Agency for Health Care Policy Research.

Payte, J.T. & Khuri, E.T. (1992). Principles of methadone dose determination. In *State Methadone Treatment Guidelines.* Washington, DC: Office for Treatment Improvement, Alcohol, Drug Abuse, and Mental Health Administration, Public Health Service, US Dept. of Health and Human Services. Rockville, MD: Center for Substance Abuse Treatment.

Pond, S.M., Kreck, M.J., Tong, T.G., Raghjunath, J. & Benowitz, N.L. (1985). Altered methadone pharmacokinetics in methadone-maintained pregnant women. *Journal of Pharmacology and Experimental Therapeutics, 233(1),* 1-6.

Portenoy, R.K. (1996). Opioid therapy for chronic nonmalignant pain: A review of the critical issues. *Journal of Pain & Symptom Management, 11(4),* 203-217.

Portenoy, R.K. & Payne, R. (1996). Acute and chronic pain. In: J.H. Lowinson, P. Ruiz, R.B. Millman & J. Langrod (Eds.), *Substance Abuse: A Comprehensive Textbook.* Baltimore, MD: Williams & Wilkins.

Pryse-Phillips, W.E.M., Dodick, D.W., Edmeads, J.G., et al. (1997). Guidelines for the diagnosis and management of migraine in clinical practice. *Canadian Medical Association Journal, 156,* 1273-1287.

Reisine, T. & Pasternak, G. (1996). Opioid analgesics and antagonists. In J.G. Hardman, L.E. Limbird, P.B. Molinoff, R.W. Ruddon & A.G. Gilman (Eds.), *Goodman and Gilman's The Pharmacological Basis of Therapeutics* (9th ed.). New York: Macmillan.

Resnick, R.B., Butler, P. & Washton, A.M. (1982). Patient self-adjustment of methadone maintenance dose. *NIDA Research Monograph, 41,* 327-330.

Resti, M., Azzari, C., Mannelli, F., Moriondo, M., Novembre, E., de Martino, M. & Vierucci, A. (1998). Mother to child transmission of hepatitis C virus: Prospective study of risk factors and timing of infection in children born to women seronegative for HIV-1. Tuscany Study Group on Hepatitis C Virus Infection. *BMJ, 317(7156),* 437-441.

Savage, S.R. (1994). Management of acute and chronic pain and cancer pain in the addicted patient. In N.S. Miller (Ed.), *Principles of Addiction Medicine.* Chevy Chase, MD: American Society of Addiction Medicine.

Senay, E.C., Dorus, W., Goldberg, F. & Thornton, W. (1977). Withdrawal from methadone maintenance: Rate of withdrawal and expectation. *Archives of General Psychiatry, 34(3),* 361-367.

Simpson, D.D. & Sells, S.B. (1982). Effectiveness of treatment for drug abuse: An overview of DARP research program. *Advances in Alcohol and Substance Abuse, 2(1),* 7-29.

Sperling, R.S., Shapiro, D.E., Coombs, R.W., Todd, J.A,, Herman, S.A. & McSherry, G.D. (1996). Maternal viral load, zidovudine treatment and the risk of transmission of human immunodeficiency virus type 1 from mother to infant: Pediatric AIDS Clinical Trials Group Protocol 076 Study Group. *New England Journal of Medicine, 335(22),* 1621-1629.

Strain, E.C., Stitzer, M.L., Liebson, I.A., & Bigelow, G.E. (1993). Dose-response effects of methadone in the treatment of opioid dependence. *Annals of Internal Medicine, 119(1),* 23-27.

Ward, J., Mattick, R.P. & Hall, W. (1992). *Key Issues in Methadone Maintenance Treatment.* Kensington, NSW: New South Wales University Press.

Watson, C.P. & Babul, N. (1998). Efficacy of oxycodone in neuropathic pain: A randomized trial in post-herpetic neuralgia. *Neurology, 50,* 837-841.

Wesson, D.R., Ling, W. and Smith, D.E. (1993). Prescription of opioids for treatment of pain in patients with addictive disease. Journal of Pain Symptom Management, 8(5), 289-296.

Zweben, J.E.& Payte, J.T. (1990). Methadone maintenance in the treatment of opioid dependence. A current perspective. *Western Journal of Medicine, 152(5),* 588-599.

ADDENDUM 1

SAMPLE METHADONE MAINTENANCE TREATMENT AGREEMENT*

Client Name:_____ File No.: _____

Opiate Dependence Treatment Program
Methadone Treatment Agreement

I _____ agree to enter into a program of methadone mainte-
nance treatment offered by the Opiate Dependence Program at the Centre for Addiction and
Mental Health (CAMH). This treatment program is specifically designed to help me deal with my
problems of opiate dependence, and will assist me in dealing with the psychological and social
difficulties which often accompany problems of addiction. The main purpose of this program is
to help me make positive changes in my life related to my use of opiates and other substances.

I am seeking help with reducing or stopping harmful use of illicit drugs and of substances like
alcohol and prescription drugs. I am interested in gaining assistance in overcoming my problems
with drug use and any associated psychosocial difficulties.

I understand that the Opiate Treatment Program offers a range of services in conjunction with
methadone maintenance treatment which can assist me in achieving my goals. Medical care pertinent to my methadone treatment will be provided. In addition, a range of counselling services
are encouraged and available on a voluntary basis. Counselling options include support groups,
relapse prevention groups, individual counselling, crisis support and assistance with addressing
any specific concrete needs that I have such as financing, housing and referrals to other
community services.

I understand that this treatment is likely to help me but I cannot be guaranteed that the treatment will work in my individual case. If treatment is not proving effective, other clinical care will
be discussed with me.

I understand that as a participant in this treatment program I am agreeing to the following:

1. Methadone Treatment

Methadone is an opiate and as such its prescribing and dispensing are regulated by a number of
legal guidelines. I understand that my receipt of methadone depends upon the following.

- I agree to pick up my medication during pharmacy dispensing hours and to take the medicine according to the pharmacist's directions. Dispensing hours are listed in the Methadone
  Treatment handbook.

- I agree to notify program staff of all prescription and non-prescription medications that I am
  taking. I will bring my prescriptions or medication bottles to the CAMH pharmacy so that the
  exact drug and dosage can be noted. The treatment team will advise me in consultation with
  my prescribing physician of any drugs that I am taking that are inconsistent with my treatment plan and I will refrain from taking them while I am receiving treatment on this program.

Addendum 1 continued

- I understand that on some days I may be required to leave a supervised urine sample before obtaining my methadone dose. If I am unable to provide the required sample, staff may ask me to wait. Upon providing the urine sample a medication slip will be given to me that I can take to pharmacy to pick up my methadone. I understand that tampering with urine samples is a serious program violation.

- I understand that as I progress in the program I may request methadone carries or community pharmacy pick-ups which reduces the number of days I have to attend the clinic. (Please refer to the Methadone Treatment handbook for details.)

- I understand that I may request to have my methadone dose reduced or increased at any time by making a request in writing to the program staff.

- Methadone is prescribed for my personal use only and I will use it as prescribed. I will present a picture identification card (as issued by CAMH) to the pharmacy staff when I pick up my methadone dose. Sharing, selling or distributing methadone is illegal and considered a serious program violation.

- When I work to improve my situation, I realize that achieving lasting change is challenging. To help me keep on track with my targeted goals I am aware that the treatment team will provide checks to ensure that I am taking my methadone and that I am providing my own urine samples. To enable the treatment team to ensure that I am drinking my methadone and that I am providing valid urine samples I agree to have a harmless clinical marker placed in my methadone dose from time to time.

2. **Initial Assessment/Treatment Progress Reviews**

- I understand that upon entry to the program I will receive an initial comprehensive assessment that will be used to help me develop a personal action plan based on my specific needs and goals. In the event that I am unable to attend the scheduled initial assessment meetings, I will notify the program's staff as soon as possible, preferably at least 24 hours in advance. Program staff will demonstrate the same courtesy if they are unable to attend a scheduled session.

- I will be offered a range of counselling options that I can elect to engage in. I understand that continued eligibility in most counselling services depends on regular attendance.

- I understand that I will be expected to attend periodic meetings (once every three months during the first year on the program) to have my methadone prescription renewed and to review my treatment progress.

3. **Medical Care**

- I will be provided with an initial assessment by a physician affiliated with the program. This assessment is for the purpose of determining if methadone is appropriate and safe for me. I agree to be reassessed by a program physician at least annually for continuance in methadone maintenance treatment.

- I understand that CAMH is a specialized addictions service and not a family practice clinic. It is my responsibility to have a family physician in the community. I agree to sign a consent form allowing my family physician and CAMH staff to exchange medical information relevant to my care. A copy of this form with be sent to my family physician. I understand that if I do not have a family physician, the clinic staff will assist me in finding one.

- If another physician or dentist proposes to prescribe opioids (i.e., narcotics) to me I will inform him or her that I am receiving methadone. It is dangerous and illegal to obtain a narcotic prescription from a physician or dentist without informing him or her that I have obtained another prescription narcotic (including methadone) within the past 30 days.

271

---

4. Clinic Environment

- I understand that CAMH is committed to maintaining a clinic environment that is safe for clients, visitors and staff and to maintaining positive, respectful behavior between people which does not include threats, violence or destructive behavior. I agree to uphold these standards.

- I understand that if I have any concerns, I may approach staff immediately. If I am not satisfied with the response I receive, I understand that there is a problem resolution procedure outlined in the Methadone Treatment handbook.

5. Confidentiality

- My privacy will be respected. Confidentiality of my CAMH health record will be protected in the same way that it is in other health facilities. No release of information from my health record will be given without my written consent or as required by law.

- I understand that in certain situations the treatment team may be required by law to give out information without my consent. This involves situations where the treatment team perceives my behavior to be a potential risk to myself or to other people (such as when child neglect or abuse is suspected).

- Because my participation in the program will bring me into contact with other opiate users, I expect other clients to be respectful of my rights, confidentiality and treatment goals, and I will respect the rights, confidentiality and treatment goals of other clients.

My signature below indicates that I have discussed this treatment agreement with a counsellor and understand and agree to all of the above. Should I fail to meet my responsibilities as a participant in this program I understand that this will result in a reassessment of the treatment plan and a consideration of my continued involvement in the program.

Witness	Signature
	Name
	Address
	Date

I have been informed about methadone and have had an opportunity to ask questions and have my questions answered. I understand that I can ask the pharmacy at any time about methadone or other medications.

Signature of Client	Date
Signature of Pharmacist	Date

---

*This sample agreement was developed as part of an ongoing methadone dissemination project being undertaken by the Centre for Addiction and Mental Health. It is intended to be used the by the Centre's methadone maintenance treatment program. When the Methadone Maintenance handbook is completed, that resource will be provided to patients when treatment is initiated. The handbook will give patients an overview of the treatment, answer frequently asked questions and clearly state the rights and responsibilities of methadone maintenance treatment patients.

ADDENDUM 2

"DOS" AND "DON'TS" OF PRESCRIBING OPIOIDS FOR CHRONIC NON-MALIGNANT PAIN

DO

- Take a careful history and physical examination; make a diagnosis.
- Screen for current and past alcohol and drug problems.
- Try non-opioid medications and adjuvant treatments first.
- Focus on improving function, not complete pain relief.
- Obtain a consultation before starting long-term opioid treatment.
- Titrate opioids carefully, looking for analgesic effectiveness, functional status and adverse effects.
- Switch to a long-acting opioid.
- Implement a treatment contract with your patient.
- Keep an opioid prescription flow sheet on the patient's chart.
- Reassess the patient at least every six to eight weeks.
- Put the number of tablets to be dispensed both in words and numerals.

DON'T

- Prescribe large amounts of short-acting opioids.
- Renew an opioid prescription earlier than the stated time on the contract.
- Prescribe injectable opioids.
- Prescribe two different opioids at the same time.
- Prescribe opioid-containing cough syrups (check the CPS for the "N" in the diamond).
- Provide long-term opioid prescriptions to new patients.
- Prescribe benzodiazepines and opioids concurrently.

ADDENDUM 3

GUIDELINES FOR MANAGEMENT OF CHRONIC NON-MALIGNANT PAIN*

The College of Physicians and Surgeons of Alberta recognizes the important role served by physicians in relieving pain and suffering. While endeavoring to offer the best care possible, one is also compelled to do no harm. In no area of the practice of medicine is this dichotomy more plainly faced than in the assessment and management of chronic non-malignant pain.

The scope of the problem of chronic non-malignant pain is staggering; the cost of annual lost productivity due to chronic pain in North America is measured in the billions of dollars. Other less easily measured parameters such as failed marriage or poor quality of life underscore the gravity of the situation.

The chronic non-malignant pain patient population is heterogeneous. A rational understanding for the likely mechanisms of pain is a requisite for developing an effective clinical approach. Comprehensive evaluation of such patients should provide reasonable clinical hypotheses about the pathophysiological processes that are contributing to the pain (nociceptive, neuropathic and/or psychological). For example, chronic back pain in some patients may be associated with spondylolisthesis, osteoporotic collapse or some other discrete organic lesion, and in other patients may be associated with clearly demonstrable organic disease on imaging procedures while not fulfilling criteria for a discrete diagnosis.

In some patients the important therapeutic issues relate to the identifiable organic process and in others, to the degree of disability and associated psychological issues. There is a large group of patients with a form of chronic non-malignant pain which is best described as idiopathic, i.e., pain that is perceived by the clinician to be excessive for the degree of organic pathology evident.

---

* A policy of the College of Physicians and Surgeons of Alberta. Reprinted with permission. Copyright 1993, College and Physicians of Alberta.

274

Some of those patients may have a primary psychological cause for the pain, but unless a strong case for this can be made, the patient's pain is best termed idiopathic and the potential for possible organic processes left open.

Impeccable management of post-surgical acute pain or acute pain following accidents, will not only reduce immediate patient morbidity, but will also lower the risk of the patient developing a chronic non-malignant pain syndrome. Guidelines for the management of acute surgical pain have been published, most recently by the US Department of Health and Human Services. Further information can be obtained from this office.

There is usually no easy solution to offer to patients with chronic non-malignant pain. Standard advice on management includes the following:

1. Take a complete pain history and physical examination.
Assessment of physical function and evaluation of disability are important.

2. Assess for the possibility of coexistent depression, sleep disorder, personality disorder, poorly developed coping skills, and level of social function.
These issues are addressed as separate from the medical condition causing the pain; sometimes pain cannot be changed but a person's response to a difficult situation can be.

3. Obtain all relevant documentation concerning prior investigations and consultations.
Consider whether a new diagnosis may be present (e.g., newly extruded disc in a patient with chronic back pain), and arrange any further tests or consultation needed to assess the condition. The goal is to complete the evaluation in order to help the patient focus on getting better.

4. Consider in what way the patient can become empowered to get better.
The treatment of chronic non-malignant pain is dedicated to two goals: enhanced function (broadly defined to include physical, psychological and social function), and improved comfort.

The appropriate therapeutic paradigm for most patients with non-malignant pain is derived from a rehabilitative model, rather than an acute medical model. Once it is clear that pain will not be eliminated by treatment of an underlying cause, clinicians should no longer draw out the evaluation or repeatedly attempt useless trials of primary therapy; the emphasis of intervention is towards the goals of functional restoration and symptomatic relief.

275

Non-medical analgesic interventions can include a regular exercise program and weight loss for back pain, or improved sleep or dietary habits in chronic daily headache. Other non-medical interventions can include psychological interventions such as behavioral or cognitive approaches, TENS (available through a physiotherapist), or guidance in carrying out daily functions (available through an occupational therapist). Even when there is limited therapy for the disease or the pain, patients are often comforted by the offer to continue care and support. Functional improvement is defined as fewer days off work, return to work, greater social interaction, improved marital relations, or amelioration in other clearly definable activities.

5. Long-term treatment with analgesic medication should be administered if analgesics result in relief of pain, functional improvement, or both.

If relief of pain without functional improvement occurs, the former benefit should clearly exceed any identifiable adverse effect in order to justify long-term analgesic use. Analgesic medications should initially include the non-opioid analgesics or the adjuvant analgesics. Long-term therapy with one or more agents within these two general categories continues to be the preferred pharmacotherapeutic approach in patients with chronic non-malignant pain (in contrast to those with cancer pain). Long-term use of non-pharmacological analgesic approaches should be considered, and these include anesthetic, neurostimulatory, and other approaches.

6. Opioids are not first-line drugs in management of chronic non-malignant pain but are occasionally helpful.

One must carefully weigh the benefit and potential problems associated with such medications when used long term.

The college acknowledges the difficulty inherent in dealing with chronic non-malignant pain. The purpose of the Triplicate Prescription Program is to prevent patients from seeking opioids from multiple physicians, and it should not discourage physicians from their usual practice of quality medical care.

In highly unusual circumstances, physicians may elect not to carry a triplicate prescription pad. In other settings, however, the college strongly endorses the appropriate use of opioid analgesics, according to the judgment of the attending physician.

7. A multidisciplinary team approach is optimal.

276

GUIDELINES FOR OPIOID USE IN CHRONIC NON-MALIGNANT PAIN

1. The underlying medical diagnosis causing the pain should be established, and the pain should appear to be commensurate with the diagnosis. For example, the physician should determine whether the painful process is somatic in origin (eg, chronic osteomyelitis), visceral (eg, chronic pancreatitis), or neuropathic (eg, post-herpetic neuralgia). Patients with idiopathic pain are not excluded from a trial of opioids. Rather, the clinician should exercise particular caution in those patients whose pain is idiopathic or appears to be primarily determined by psychological factors.

2. A history of recent or remote substance abuse is a relatively strong contra-indication; the available evidence suggests that chronic opioid therapy should be considered only under the most extraordinary circumstances in such patients.

3. An adequate trial of non-opioid analgesics and adjuvant analgesics should have been carried out without success.

4. One physician only should prescribe opioids.

5. In order to start a patient on an opioid, the principles of the World Health Organization "analgesic ladder" should be employed. Patients first should be started on opioids in combination with non-steroidal anti-inflammatory drugs or acetaminophen. Opinion concerning opioid therapy is evolving and the decision to rely on combination products or other products prior to considering trials of morphine or similar opioids is arbitrary and based on convention, rather than pharmacological principles.

    Fixed combinations of acetaminophen with oxycodone (Percocet®) or codeine (Tylenol #3®) are commonly used. No greater than 12 tablets of the above preparations may be taken per day because of risk of acetaminophen toxicity. Fixed combination preparations are fairly safe but usually need to be administered every four to six hours.

    The role for agonist-antagonist or partial agonist opioids, e.g., pentazocine (Talwin®), is less clear. Experience with long-term opioid therapy, as conducted in the cancer population, has been almost exclusively with pure agonist opioids, and on this basis they are preferred over agonist-antagonist or partial agonist opioids. Meperidine (Demerol®) has relatively poor oral bioavailability, is short-acting, and can be associated with accumulation of a toxic metabolite, normeperidine. Anileridine (Leritine®) is chemically

277

related to meperidine. The use of these two opioids in management of chronic pain syndromes is not recommended.

6. Treatment of pain with opioids is actually a treatment trial, and like all therapeutic trials, may be effective or ineffective. Effective therapy may be defined as identification of a dose associated with meaningful partial analgesia and no adverse effects severe enough to compromise comfort or function. This dose must be one at which the clinician can comfortably maintain the patient given the clinician's level of experience and training. Opioids almost always need to be titrated upwards, and effective doses are commonly higher than the starting dose. Personal discomfort by the physician at the apparent level of opioid requirement is a valid reason not to proceed, and may warrant the referral of the patient to a physician who has more expertise in chronic pain management.

7. If a fixed combination preparation of an opioid and non-opioid analgesic is not satisfactory, then the patient may be tried on oral morphine. The syrup preparation is convenient for titration purposes, and is recommended. We advise starting at 10 mg by mouth every four hours. The dose should be increased once or twice weekly by 25–50%. Increased doses should be accompanied by increased analgesic effect, although doses of oral morphine (or its equivalent) above 300 mg daily are unusual but not contraindicated in chronic non-malignant pain.

    If the short-acting morphine preparation is useful and there are no features suggesting abuse, the patient should then be switched to a long-acting (q8h or q12h) morphine preparation.

    The physician should watch for apparent drug-related behaviors. Behaviors which could be used to label a patient as an abuser exist on a continuum, and pain-relief-seeking behavior can be mistaken for drug-seeking behavior. The clinician will need to monitor carefully for evidence of psychological dependency and drug abuse. Some behaviors which provide compelling evidence of abuse include the selling of prescription drugs, covertly obtaining prescription medications from more than one physician, concurrent abuse of related illicit drugs, repeated unsanctioned dose escalations despite warnings, and events such as prescription "loss." Other signs of compulsive drug use may be more subtle, including the use of the opioid to treat symptoms other than pain, frequent visits to emergency rooms, and hoarding of drugs obtained from routine prescriptions. Relapse after withdrawal is a feature of addiction that is difficult to interpret in the context of chronic non-malignant pain, as relapse of pain (and the re-institution of opioid therapy) can be rationally anticipated to occur sometimes.

8. Parenteral dosing of opioids to treat chronic non-malignant pain should be strongly discouraged, and daily i.m. injections abhorred.

9. There should be an agreement between the patient and the prescribing physician which clearly delineates that there is to be no unsanctioned dose escalation, no selling of opioids, no injecting of opioids, no seeking of opioids from another physician and no hoarding of opioids. This contract should clearly define consequences of violation, which include a non-negotiable end to the prescribing relationship between the physician and the patient. If the patient sees another physician to obtain opioids for any reason (such as when the primary physician is not available), then the primary physician should be informed by the patient at the first reasonable opportunity. If warranted, this contract should be in writing. Otherwise, documentation of a verbal agreement in the physician's records is sufficient.

10. The patient should be seen and assessed at least every nine weeks and more frequently if needed (e.g., if there is a history of previous substance abuse). The clinician should specifically evaluate the patient for several distinct aspects of therapy at each visit, including:

    - analgesic efficacy,
    - adverse pharmacological events,
    - function (physical and psychological), and
    - the occurrence of apparent drug abuse-related behaviors (see above).

    Documentation is very important with this therapy and physicians should keep careful records that include reference to these various aspects of therapy. Once a regular dose of opioid is established, the patient should not request a refill of the prescription earlier than the established duration for the prescription.

11. Flares of pain can be treated with small extra doses of opioid by mouth; each monthly prescription should include a few extra doses for this purpose.

    The goal of chronic opioid therapy is not the elimination of pain (which may be impossible) but rather to control pain to a tolerable level; there is a clear emphasis on level of function of the patient in his social, work, and personal life.

    Addiction is quite distinct from tolerance and physical dependence; true addiction resulting from appropriate medicinal use of opioids is extremely uncommon. The clinician must monitor for the possibility that opioids are

279

contributing to disability, impairing function directly, or producing adverse pharmacological effects that lead to impaired function.

(a) **Addiction** is a state where a person takes a medication for its psychic effect, not for its pain-relieving effect, and is characterized by loss of control, compulsive drug use, and continued drug use despite its harm. Tolerance and physical dependency are different phenomena and can develop in patients who consume opioids chronically, are also part of the symptom complex of addiction, but of themselves are not pathognomonic of addiction.

(b) **Tolerance** is a poorly understood phenomenon characterized by the need for higher doses to maintain opioid effects. Clinical experience in patients with chronic non-malignant pain managed with long-term use of opioids indicates that tolerance does occur initially but tends to be less of an issue over the course of many years.

(c) **Physical dependence** is a response to a drug characterized by the occurrence of an abstinence syndrome on abrupt dose reduction or administration of an antagonist.

More frequently seen is chronic pain syndrome, whereby a patient takes a large variety of medications with questionable benefit, and uses drugs inappropriately as part of the behavioral disturbances that characterize this state. Other behavioral traits of chronic non-malignant pain syndrome include physical inactivity, inability to work, and social isolation. Analgesic medications should only be used in this setting as part of a carefully controlled overall pain management program.

These guidelines are intended as a framework for medical decision making in the treatment of chronic non-malignant pain, and as an overview of a current management rationale for this difficult medical problem.

The College of Physicians and Surgeons of Alberta gratefully acknowledges the helpful advice of Dr. Russell K. Portenoy in the preparation of the document.

ADDENDUM 5

OPIOID PRESCRIPTION FLOW SHEET

Patient Name: _____

Chart Number: _____

Prescribing Physician: _____

DATE	MEDICATION	DOSE	DIRECTION	NUMBER DISPENSED	COMMENTS

ADDENDUM 4

TREATMENT CONTRACT FOR USE OF OPIOIDS IN MANAGING CHRONIC PAIN

I understand that I am receiving an opioid medication from Dr. _____
to treat my pain condition, and I agree to the following conditions under which
this medication is prescribed:

I will not seek opioid medications from another physician. Only
Dr. _____ will prescribe opioids for me.

I will not take opioids in larger amounts or more frequently than is prescribed
by Dr. _____.

I will not give or sell my medication to anyone else, including family members
nor will I accept any opioid medication from anyone else.

I will not use over-the-counter opioid medications such as 222® or Tylenol #1®

I understand that if my prescription runs out early for any reason (for example
if I lose the medication or take more than prescribed), Dr. _____
will not prescribe extra medications for me. I will have to wait until the next
script is due.

I understand that if I break these conditions, Dr. _____
may choose to cease writing opioid prescriptions for me.

Patient's signature: _____

Physician's signature: _____

Date: _____

2

Other Frequently Abused Substances

SECTION 9

9.1

ANABOLIC STEROIDS

Bruna Brands, PhD, and Meldon Kahan, MD

GENERAL DESCRIPTION

Anabolic steroids (testosterone and its synthetic derivatives) are typically used by athletes to enhance performance and increase muscle bulk, and by adolescent males to improve their appearance (Strauss, 1989; Yesalis, Streit et al., 1989). Doses used by weightlifters and body builders are often 10 to 100 times higher than therapeutic doses (Rogol & Yesalis, 1992). Rather than regular daily dosing, users frequently ingest combinations of steroids in complex dosing patterns called "cycling" (alternating periods of use with periods of abstinence), "pyramiding" (variation of cycling that involves building up to a peak dose followed by tapering) or "stacking" (use of multiple steroids in both injectable and oral forms).

ADVERSE EFFECTS

Psychiatric
Individuals taking high doses of anabolic steroids commonly develop symptoms of aggression ("steroid rage"), depression or anxiety (Pope and Katz, 1994). Case reports of psychosis, such as paranoid delusions and mania have also been reported. Symptoms generally resolve quickly with abstinence.

Cardiovascular
Anabolic steroids adversely affect the serum lipid profile. They lower the HDL:LDL ratio, thereby increasing the risk of coronary artery disease. However, these changes are reversible on cessation of steroid use (Brukner & Khan, 1993). Although studies are inconclusive, steroids may be thrombogenic and directly toxic to the myocardium. Case reports have linked steroid use with myocardial infarctions, cerebrovascular accidents and pulmonary emboli.

Endocrine

Women may experience irregular menses and masculinizing effects such as acne. Men can develop testicular atrophy and gynecomastia, due to metabolism of testosterone to estrogen. Gynecomastia is not always reversible. Steroids can cause premature closure of the epiphyses in adolescents.

Hepatic

Steroids cause elevations in liver transaminases, toxic hepatitis and hepatocellular carcinoma. Steroid users sharing needles are at risk for viral hepatitis and HIV infection.

DEPENDENCE

Steroids can induce euphoria, perhaps through endogenous opioid release in the CNS (Kashkin and Kleber,1989). It appears that dependence (according to DSM-IIIR criteria) to anabolic steroids does occur (Brower, Blow et al, 1989). Case reports describe steroid users who have features of dependence such as preoccupation with acquiring and using the drug, escalating use, continued use despite knowledge of harm and withdrawal on cessation of use. Abrupt cessation of steroids in heavy users appears to cause a syndrome similar to opioid withdrawal (Tennant et al., 1988), with depression, insomnia, myalgia and flu-like symptoms.

IDENTIFICATION AND MANAGEMENT

Adolescents and young adults engaged in high-risk athletic activities such as weightlifting, football, or competitive track or swimming should be asked about steroid use. The physician might lead into a discussion about steroid use by asking about use of performance aids such as protein supplements, and if any of the patient's acquaintances use steroids.

Physicians should be alert to common symptoms and signs of steroid abuse. Common symptoms include appetite changes, menstrual abnormalities, muscle aches and changes in libido. Physical signs include acne, marked increases in muscle bulk, needle marks in the deltoid, and hirsutism and deepened voice in females. Psychiatric presentations include irritability, aggressiveness, depression, delusions and mania.

Laboratory abnormalities include elevated liver transaminases (although GGT is unaffected), CPK, hematocrit and hemoglobin (due to erythropoiesis), and decreased LH and FSH. Testosterone will be increased if exogenous testosterone is used, or decreased if other steroids are used. Note that intensive weightlifting can cause elevations in ALT, AST and CPK even without steroid use (Brower, 1992).

MANAGEMENT OF WITHDRAWAL

The major risks associated with withdrawal are relapse and suicidal ideation. Patients in withdrawal should receive supportive counselling and assessment for suicidal risk. Pharmacotherapy for steroid withdrawal has not been studied. Symptomatic treatment may be indicated, such as NSAIDs for myalgias or headache.

TREATMENT

Patients in whom steroid use is identified or suspected should be informed of the health risks, and advised to limit contact with athletes who use steroids or gyms where steroids are accessible. While formal treatment programs for steroid users are very rare, patients should receive ongoing counselling that addresses issues such as self-esteem and body image. Patients should be counselled on alternatives to steroids for fitness and body building. Referral to a nutritionist or fitness expert may be helpful. Adolescents should be warned that steroid use might stunt growth. Needle users should be tested for HIV and hepatitis, and warned about the risks of sharing needles. When treating males physicians should consider ordering a sperm count test. An abnormal test result may act as a motivating factor (NIDA, 1991).

9.2

DIMENHYDRINATE

Yasemin Ikizler, MD

THERAPEUTIC USES

Dimenhydrinate is a histamine antagonist with sedative and anticholinergic properties. It is a non-prescription medication. Histamine antagonists act as CNS depressants. Both dimenhydrinate (Gravol®) and the active moiety of dimenhydrinate, diphenhydramine (e.g., Benadryl®), have high CNS-depressant potential.

Indications

Dimenhydrinate is used for the treatment and prevention of nausea, vomiting or vertigo associated with motion sickness. Therapeutic doses are from 50–100 mg every four to six hours, to a maximum of 400 mg in a 24-hour period. Dimenhydrinate is taken orally and can be administered intramuscularly and intravenously. The active moiety of dimenhydrinate, diphenhydramine, is used for allergic conditions.

ADVERSE EFFECTS

At therapeutic doses, dimenhydrinate can cause drowsiness, dizziness, mild impairment of concentration, impaired co-ordination, excitation, nervousness and dry mouth.

ABUSE

There are numerous reports of abuse of dimenhydrinate by adolescents who may use it to obtain hallucinogenic-like effects. Case reports claim that doses as high as 750 mg/day have been abused by adolescents (Gardner & Kutcher, 1993;

Rowe, Vergee & Koren, 1997). Individuals may use dimenhydrinate when their drug of choice is not available. Adults are known to chronically abuse high doses of dimenhydrinate to enhance the effects of alcohol and other drugs of abuse. Dimenhydrinate is also misused as a sleep aid. Because of the anorexic and emetic properties (at high doses) of dimenhydrinate, one author speculated on the abuse potential in individuals with eating disorders (Young, Boyd & Kreeft, 1988). Psychiatric patients, including those with schizophrenia, have been reported to abuse dimenhydrinate (Bartlik, Galanter & Angrist, 1989).

Individuals abusing dimenhydrinate usually take it orally. However, there are reports of adolescents crushing the tablets and snorting the powder. Adolescents also report adding the powder to marijuana. Dimenhydrinate is attractive to them because the drug is inexpensive, legal and easily accessible from pharmacies. Doses of 400 mg of dimenhydrinate and 500 mg of diphenhydramine can produce intoxication (Isaac, 1996).

Case reports indicate that with chronic abuse individuals may experience confusion, inattentiveness, depressed mood, loss of energy, difficulty thinking, difficulty socializing and working, vomiting and urinary retention.

TOLERANCE, DEPENDENCE AND WITHDRAWAL

Case reports support claims of the development of tolerance, dependence and withdrawal with daily use of dimenhydrinate (Craig & Mellor, 1990; Bartlik, Galanter & Angrist, 1989). Also reported are individuals escalating their daily doses of dimenhydrinate and developing tolerance to doses that would ordinarily produce coma in acute situations.

A withdrawal syndrome does not occur in all individuals and does not appear to be life-threatening. Patients can be tapered or stop their use abruptly. Case reports have documented a variety of physical signs and symptoms that occur during withdrawal, including nausea, vomiting and diarrhea, mild irritability, difficulty thinking clearly, excitability, increased pulse, elevated blood pressure, mydriasis and extreme malaise. The duration of withdrawal is usually seven to 10 days.

TOXIC EFFECTS

At higher than therapeutic doses both dimenhydrinate and diphenhydramine cause vomiting, ataxia, excitement, seizures (especially in children), thought disorder, visual, auditory and tactile hallucinations, ideas of reference and persecution, amnesia, delirium, hypotension and cardiac arrhythmias. Psychotic symptoms resolve within one to two days following discontinuation of the drug. Fortunately, fatalities are rare. They are usually associated with the ingestion of very high doses, especially when combined with alcohol or other substances of abuse. One case report describes the death of a 14-year-old girl following intentional ingestion of 7.5 grams of diphenhydramine (Krenzelok, Anderson & Angrist, 1982). Fatal doses of dimenhydrinate are between 25 mg/kg and 250 mg/kg body weight.

9.3

INHALANTS

Luis Fornazzari, MD

DEFINITIONS

Inhalants are a heterogeneous class of volatile, highly addictive solvents, that are self-administered for their psychoactive properties. Inhalants may be "sniffed" (inhaled directly from a container), "huffed" (when a rag soaked in the substance is held to the face) or "bagged" (a bag is held to the mouth). In some cases the substance is sprayed directly into the mouth.

These volatile solvents are found in numerous products used in the home, industry, construction and in agriculture. None of these products have been formulated for human consumption or use (see table below).

TABLE 1: Volatile Compounds That May Be Abused by Inhalation[†]

Aliphatic Hydrocarbons	Iso-butane, n-butane, n-hexane, propane
Aromatic Hydrocarbons	Toluene, xylene
Mixed Hydrocarbons	Gasoline
Ketones	Acetone, butanone, methyl iso-butyl ketone
Halogenated Compounds	Bromochlorodifluoromethane, chlorodifluoromethane, chloroform, dichlorofluoromethane, dichloromethane, enflurane, halothane, tetrachloroethylene, trichlorofluoromethane
Anesthetic Gases	Nitrous oxide
Room Odorizers	(Iso)amyl nitrite, (iso)butyl nitrite

† Adapted with permission from J. Ramsey, H.R. Anderson, K. Bloor & R.J. Flanagan. (1989). An introduction to the practice, prevalence and chemical toxicity of volatile substance abuse. *Human Toxicology, 8*(4), 261-269.

EPIDEMIOLOGY

Inhalant abuse is a worldwide problem that is more extensive than most clinicians realize. It affects mostly young adolescents from disadvantaged groups of the population (Kozel, Sloboda et al., 1995). The typical inhalant user is poor, comes from a broken home where alcohol and drugs are used and does poorly at school. Inhalant users come from both inner cities and remote rural areas (Beauvais & La Boeuff, 1985; Padilla, Padilla et al., 1979). In Canada, an ongoing survey of the student population in the province of Ontario found that 4.2 per cent of the students aged 12 to 15 years had used solvents at least once during the year (Adlaf, Ivis et al., 1997). A 1994 survey found that 0.1 per cent of Canadians aged 15 years or older reported solvent use in the past year. Levels of solvent use are considerably higher among homeless and disadvantaged youth. Surveys of street youth in three Canadian cities between 1989 and 1992 found that between 8 and 17 per cent reported past year solvent use (Canadian Centre on Substance Abuse & Addiction Research Foundation, 1997).

There are no data on deaths linked to inhalant use in Canada or the United States. British data indicate that 50 per cent of fatalities among young inhalant users were due to inhalation of gas fuels (butane). The rest of the cases were equally due to aerosols (fluorocarbons), solvents in adhesives and other solvents (trichloroethane, toluene) (Anderson, 1990). The direct causes of death are related to the cardiotoxic properties of solvents or to respiratory depression. Indirect causes of death include, or are due to, aspiration (e.g., vomit), suffocation (e.g., bag left over face), trauma and a shock syndrome due to hypothermia or hyperthermia (Garriott, 1992; Taylor & Norman, 1995).

CLINICAL PRESENTATION

Transient and chronic users

Sharp and Rosenberg (1997) classified solvent abusers as either transient or chronic users. Transient users are those who use inhalants for a short time, either with a friend (socially) or alone. This group is usually young, between 10 and 16 years of age, with school difficulties (often due to Attention Deficit/Hyperactivity Disorder) and with minor legal problems. Chronic solvent abusers are older, between 20 and 30 years of age. Generally they inhale with friends, but also use alone. Typically, they have been using solvents for at least five years and show symptoms and signs of brain impairment. Common characteristics of the chronic user include poor social skills and legal problems, problems that are accentuated by the fact that they frequently leave school early in high school.

Acute intoxication occurs three to five minutes after inhalation (10 to 15 breaths are sufficient) and the euphoric effect may last between three and six hours. The very high lipid solubility of the solvents is responsible for the rapid absorption from the lungs. The main symptoms observed are:

• Euphoria
• Agitation
• Irritability
• Disinhibition
• Mental status alteration, involving transient psychotic symptoms such as delusions, hallucinations and self-reference ideation (true paranoia).

All these behavioral symptoms are responsible for the aggression, violence and the accident-prone behaviors experienced by solvent abusers (Benignus, 1981; Reese & Kimbrough, 1993; Remington & Hoffman, 1984; Goldbloom & Chouinard, 1985).

First-time users often present with gastrointestinal symptoms such as nausea, vomiting and abdominal cramps. Chronic users can experience withdrawal manifested as GI symptoms, intention tremor and malaise (Brands, Sproule & Marshman, 1998; Rosenberg, 1992).

CLINICAL FINDINGS IN CHRONIC USERS — CNS COMPLICATIONS

Chronic solvent users commonly experience general physical impairment and several neurological symptoms. CNS complications include the following clinical presentations:

Acute encephalopathy
Acute encephalopathy is expressed clinically as a global cognitive impairment with fluctuating levels of consciousness and is specifically characterized by inattention. If the patient continues to inhale the substance, encephalopathy may progress to coma (Burns & Currie, 1995; Brady & Torzillo, 1994).

Chronic neurological deficit
Chronic neurological deficit consists of progressive cortical and subcortical symptoms. They generally occur after years of daily use. Associative cortex functions are frequently affected and characterized by executive dysfunctions and immediate, recent, remote and procedural memory impairment. Difficulties with visual and constructive abilities are also a frequent finding.

293

Cranial nerve involvement

Abnormal eye movements are observed, varying from mild to severe nystagmus, including the opsoclonus type. Cranial nerve involvement can also cause optic neuropathy, trigeminal and cochleovestibular abnormalities. Anecdotal findings suggest that olfactory dysfunction is present early in this condition. From the standpoint of deterrence, it is important to evaluate this finding because the choice of the solvent used is related to its euphoriant effect and not to the odor per se.

Motor impairment

Motor impairment with pan-cerebellar ataxia is a debilitating complication. This may or may not be associated with myoclonus, particularly in gasoline and petroleum abusers. Inhalation of gasoline, which contains n-hexane and methylketone can cause peripheral neuropathy of the axonal type (Fornazzari, Wilkinson et al., 1983; Sharp & Rosenberg, 1997; Lazar, Ho et al., 1983). A rather severe complication occurs in those inhaling petroleum (e.g., diesel fuel) due to its lead content. Apart from the frequent development of neuro-pathy and the associated paralysis of both lower limbs, these individuals are admitted to emergency departments with severe encephalopathy generally associated with a poor prognosis. This problem affects mostly remote areas and aboriginal populations in North America and Australia (Burns, Currie et al., 1994; Beauvais & Oetting, 1987).

CLINICAL FINDINGS IN CHRONIC USERS — SYSTEMIC COMPLICATIONS

Practically speaking, almost every system in the body is affected by solvent use. The most severe findings are well documented in the renal, hepatic, respiratory, cardiovascular and hematological systems.

Renal system

The most serious metabolic abnormality observed in chronic solvent abusers is a tubular acidosis of the distal type with an associated hyperchloremic metabolic acidosis and hypokalemia and hypocalcemia. A proximal tubular acidosis is also present, but less frequently. This is responsible for the wasting of amino acids and the loss of albumin and other proteins. With repetitive metabolic insults, other organs are affected. A severe acidosis of the cerebrospinal fluid has been reported in chronic abusers, associated with cognitive impairment and cortical and subcortical atrophy on CT scans of the brain (Fornazzari, Wilkinson et al., 1983). The nephrotoxicity affects both mothers abusing solvents and their fetuses who may have findings compatible with nephrotoxicity (Batlle, Sabatini & Kurtzman, 1988; Carlisle, Donnelly et al., 1991; Daniell, Crouser & Rosenstock, 1988; Lindemann, 1991).

Hepatic system

Solvent mixtures are responsible for the reversible hepatotoxicity frequently found in chronic users. The hepatic damage is potentiated by the abuse of alcohol as in the "painting solvent syndrome" described in the Scandinavian countries (Stewart & Witts, 1993; Cordes, Brown & Quinn, 1988; Dossing, 1986).

Pulmonary toxicity

Pulmonary hypertension, acute respiratory distress, increased airway resistance or residual volume and restricted ventilation are all complications associated with solvent abuse. They tend to be reversible but the frequent association with smoking may aggravate the condition (Reyes de la Rocha, Brown & Fortenberry, 1987; Schikler, Lane et al., 1984).

Cardiovascular toxicity

Ventricular fibrillation, cardiac arrhythmias and acute cardiomyopathy are frequent causes of sudden death. (Boon, 1987; Cunningham, Dalzell et al., 1987; Wiseman & Banim, 1987).

Hematological disorders

Methylene chloride-containing substances produce high levels of carboxyhemoglobin which may result in brain dysfunction and/or brain damage and death. Mixtures such as gasoline, thinners, varnish and removers that contain benzene are signalled as causing severe blood dyscrasias such as aplastic anemias and acute leukemias (Barrowcliff & Knell, 1979; Austin, Delzell et al., 1988).

NEONATAL SYNDROME

Some evidence is accumulating in relation to a "fetal solvent syndrome" in women who abuse solvents during pregnancy. It shares features with "fetal alcohol syndrome," perhaps due to the concurrent use of alcohol and solvents. The cases reported are usually stillborn babies with microcephaly, severe dysmorphic features and severe CNS malformations (Hersh, Podruch et al., 1985; Pearson, Hoyme et al., 1994).

TREATMENT

Perhaps more than with any other form of substance abuse, prevention is central to reducing the harm associated with inhalant abuse.

Acute solvent intoxication

Life-protective measures should be used as soon as cardiorespiratory difficulties are suspected in a young adolescent using solvents. These are crucial steps, because cardiac complications are likely the main cause of death.

Because we do not know of any antidote for solvent intoxication, good emergency procedures with rapid correction of blood and electrolyte imbalance are mandatory. Judicious use of benzodiazepines could be used in the rare case of agitation.

Chronic solvent abuse

Any intervention must consider the time it takes for solvents to leave fat tissue, particularly in the brain. There are suggestions that at least 14 days are necessary for an adequate detoxification. This is the amount of time that it takes for the brain to be free of the effects of the solvents and their metabolites (Watson, 1999).

There are no antidotes to decrease the symptoms of withdrawal, such as nausea, postural and intention tremors, abdominal cramps, severe anorexia and intense craving for solvents.

Most inpatient treatment programs use behavioral and cognitive approaches to support patients during withdrawal and prevent relapse. Following withdrawal management, patients should be referred to addiction treatment and/or continuing care programs.

R E F E R E N C E S

Adlaf, E.M., Ivis, E.J., Smart, R.G. & Walsh, G.W. (1997). *Ontario Student Drug Use Survey: 1977-1997.* Toronto: Addiction Research Foundation.

Anderson, H.R. (1990). Increase in deaths from deliberate inhalation of fuel gases and pressurised aerosols. *BMJ (Clinical Research Ed.), 301(6742),* 41.

Austin, H., Delzell, E. & Cole, P. (1988). Benzene and leukemia: A review of the literature and a risk assessment. *American Journal of Epidemiology, 127(3),* 419-439.

Barrowcliff, D.F. & Knell, A.J. (1979). Cerebral damage due to endogenous chronic carbon monoxide poisoning caused by exposure to methylene chloride. *Journal of the Society of Occupational Medicine, 29(1),* 12-14.

Bartlik, B., Galanter, M. & Angrist, B. (1989). Dimenhydrinate addiction in a schizo-phrenic woman. (Letter to the editor). *Journal of Clinical Psychiatry, 50(12)*, 476.

Batlle, D.C., Sabatini, S. & Kurtzman, N.A. (1988). On the mechanism of toluene-induced renal tubular acidosis. *Nephron, 49(3)*, 210-218.

Beauvais, F. & Oetting, E.R. (1987). Toward a clear definition of inhalant abuse. *International Journal of the Addictions, 22(8)*, 779-784.

Beauvais, F. & La Boeuff, S. (1985). Drug and alcohol abuse intervention in American Indian communities. *International Journal of the Addictions, 20(1)*, 139-171.

Benignus, V.A. (1981). Health effects of toluene: A review. *Neurotoxicology, 2(3)*, 567-588.

Boon, N.A. (1987). Solvent abuse and the heart. *BMJ (Clinical Research Ed.), 294(6574)*, 722.

Brady, M. & Torzillo, P. (1994). Petrol sniffing down the track. *Medical Journal of Australia, 160(4)*, 176-177.

Brands, B., Sproule, B. & Marshman, B. (Eds.). (1998). *Drugs and Drug Abuse* (3rd ed.). Toronto: Addiction Research Foundation.

Brower, K.J., Blow, F.C., Beresford, T.P. & Fuelling, C. (1989). Anabolic-androgenic steroid dependence. *Journal of Clinical Psychiatry, 50(1)*, 31-33.

Brower, K.J. (1992). Clinical assessment and treatment of anabolic steroid users. *Psychiatric Annals, 22(1)* 35-40.

Brukner, P. & Khan, K. (1993). *Clinical Sports Medicine*. Sydney: McGraw-Hill.

Burns, C.B. & Currie, B. (1995). The efficacy of chelation therapy and factors influencing mortality in lead intoxicated petrol sniffers. *Australian and New Zealand Journal of Medicine, 25(3)*, 197-203.

Burns, C., Currie, B., Currie, J. & Marruff, P. (1994). Petrol sniffing down the track. *Medical Journal of Australia, 160(11)*, 729-730.

Canadian Centre for Substance Abuse & Addiction Research Foundation. (1997). *Canadian Profile: Alcohol, Tobacco and Other Drugs*. Toronto: Canadian Centre for Substance Abuse and Addiction Research Foundation.

297

Carlisle, E.J., Donnelly, S.M., Vasuvattakul, S., Kamel, K.S., Tobe, S. & Halperin, M.L. (1991). Glue sniffing and distal renal tubular acidosis: Sticking to the facts. *Journal of the American Society of Nephrology, 1*(8), 1019-1027.

Cordes, D.H., Brown, W.D. & Quinn, K.M. (1988). Chemically induced hepatitis after inhaling organic solvents. *Western Journal of Medicine, 148*(4), 458-460.

Craig, D.F. & Mellor, C.S. (1990). Dimenhydrinate dependence and withdrawal. *Canadian Medical Association Journal, 142,* 970-973.

Cunningham, S.R., Dalzell, G.W., McGirr, P. & Khan, M.N. (1987). Myocardial infarction and primary ventricular fibrillation after glue sniffing. *BMJ (Clinical Research Ed.), 294*(6574), 739-740.

Daniell, W.E., Couser, W.G. & Rosenstock, L. (1988). Occupational solvent exposure and glomerulonephritis. *Journal of the American Medical Association, 259*(15), 2280-2283.

Dossing, M. (1986). Occupational toxic liver damage. *Journal of Hepatology, 3*(1), 131-135.

Fornazzari, L., Wilkinson, D.A., Kapur, B.M. & Carlen, P.L. (1983). Cerebellar, cortical and functional impairment in toluene abusers. *Acta Neurologica Scandinavica, 67*(6), 319-329.

Gardner, D.M. & Kutcher, S. (1993). Dimenhydrinate abuse among adolescents. *Canadian Journal of Psychiatry, 38,* 113-116.

Garriott, J.C. (1992). Death among inhalant abusers. In C.W. Sharp, F. Beauvais & R. Spence (Eds.), *Inhalant Abuse: A Volatile Research Agenda.* NIDA Research Monograph 129. Rockville, MD: NIDA.

Goldbloom, D. & Chouinard, G. (1985). Schizophreniform psychosis associated with chronic industrial toluene exposure: Case report. *Journal of Clinical Psychiatry, 46*(8), 350-351.

Hersh, J.H., Podruch, P.E., Rogers, G. & Weisskopf, B. (1985). Toluene embryopathy. *Journal of Pediatrics, 106*(6), 922-927.

Isaac, P. (1996). High on dimenhydrinate. *Pharmacy Practice, 12,* 28.

Kashkin, K.B. & Kleber, H.D. (1989). Hooked on hormones? An anabolic steroid addiction hypothesis. *Journal of the American Medical Association, 262*(22), 2048-2049.

Kozel, N., Sloboda, Z. et al. (1995). Epidemiology of inhalant abuse: An international perspective. NIDA research monograph series #1148, NIH publications 95-3831 . Washington DC: National Institutes of Health.

Krenzelok, E.P., Anderson, G.M. & Angrist, B. (1982). Massive diphenhydramine overdose resulting in death. *Annals of Emergency Medicine, 11(4),* 212-213.

Lazar R.B., Ho, S.U., Melen, O. & Daghestani, A.N. (1983). Multifocal central nervous system damage caused by toluene abuse. *Neurology, 33(10),* 1337-1340.

Lindemann, R. (1991). Congenital renal tubular dysfunction associated with maternal sniffing of organic solvents. *Acta Paediatrica Scandinavica, 80(8-9),* 882-884.

National Institute on Drug Abuse. (1991). *Anabolic Steroids: A Threat to the Body and the Mind.* Rockville, MD: NIDA.

Pearson, M.A., Hoyme, H.E., Seaver, L.H. & Rimsza, M.E. (1994). Toluene embryopathy: Delineation of the phenotype and comparison with fetal alcohol syndrome. *Pediatrics, 93(2),* 211-215.

Pope, H.G. & Katz, D.L. (1994). Psychiatric and medical effects of anabolic steroid use. A controlled study of 160 athletes. *Archives of General Psychiatry, 51(5),* 375-382.

Ramsey, J., Anderson, H.R., Bloor, K. & Flanagan, R.J. (1989). An introduction to the practice, prevalence and chemical toxicity of volatile substance abuse. *Human Toxicology, 8(4),* 261-269.

Reese, E. & Kimbrough, R.D. (1993). Acute toxicity of gasoline and some additives. *Environmental Health Perspectives, 101 (suppl 6),* 115-131.

Remington, G. & Hoffman, B.F. (1984). Gas sniffing as a form of substance abuse. *Canadian Journal of Psychiatry, 29(1),* 31-35.

Reyes de la Rocha, S., Brown, M.A. & Fortenberry, J.D. (1987). Pulmonary function abnormalities in intentional spray paint inhalation. *Chest, 92(1),* 100-104.

Rogol, A.D. & Yesalis, C.E. (1992). Clinical review 31: Anabolic-androgenic steroids and athletes: What are the issues? *Journal of Clinical Endocrinology and Metabolism, 74(3),* 465-469.

Rosenberg, N.L. (1992). Neurotoxicology. In J.B. Sullivan & G.R. Krieger (Eds.). *Hazardous Material Toxicology.* Baltimore: Williams & Wilkins.

Rowe, C. Verjee, Z. & Koren, G. (1997). Adolescent dimenhydrinate abuse: Resurgence of an old problem. *Journal of Adolescent Health, 21(1),* 47-49.

Schikler, K.N., Lane, E.E. Seitz, K. & Collins, W.M. (1984). Solvent abuse associated pulmonary abnormalities. *Advances in Alcohol and Substance Abuse, 3(3),* 75-81.

Sharp, C.W. & Rosenberg, N.L. (1997). Inhalants. In J.H. Lowinson, P. Ruiz & J.G. Langrod, (Eds.). *Substance Abuse: A Comprehensive Textbook*. (3rd ed.). Baltimore: Williams and Wilkins.

Stewart, A. & Witts, L.J. (1993). Chronic carbon tetrachloride intoxication, 1944 (classical article). *British Journal of Industrial Medicine, 50(1),* 8-18.

Strauss, R.H. (1989). High school kids: Looking better, living worse? *The Physician and Sports Medicine, 17(2),* 35.

Taylor, J.C., Norman, et al. (1995). Trends in death associated with abuse of volatile substances, 1971-1993. Report 8. London: St George's Hospital Medical School, June.

Tennant, F., Black, F.L. & Voy, R.O. (1988). Anabolic steroid dependence with opioid-type features. *New England Journal of Medicine, 319 (9),* 578.

Watson, J. (1999). Conversation with author, Toronto, ON.

Wiseman, M.N. & Banim, S. (1987). "Glue sniffer's" heart? *BMJ (Clinical Research Ed.), 294(6574),* 739.

Yesalis, C.E., Streit, A.L., Vicary, J.R., Friedl, K.E., Brannon, D. & Buckley, W. (1989). Anabolic steroid use: Indications of habituation among adolescents. *Journal of Drug Education, 19(2),* 103-116.

Young, G.B., Boyd, D. & Kreeft, J. (1988). Dimenhydrinate: Evidence for dependence and tolerance. *Canadian Medical Association Journal, 138,* 437-438.

300

Polysubstance Abuse

10 POLYSUBSTANCE ABUSE

10

POLYSUBSTANCE ABUSE

Meldon Kahan, MD

Assessment

Polysubstance use is extremely common. Patients dependent on more than one substance generally have a poorer prognosis than patients dependent on only one drug, even when other factors are similar between the two groups.

In the assessment of polydrug users it is important to keep in mind that patients may not view every substance being used as problematic. Furthermore, patients may be very honest about their consumption of one drug but may minimize or hide their use of other substances. The reason may be shame or fear of repercussions, or they may feel that their use of other substances is not problematic and does not merit discussion. For example, a woman might be forthcoming about her use of prescription benzodiazepines but hide her use of alcohol. Because such situations are common, physicians should take a comprehensive alcohol and drug history of all patients being treated for their substance use (see also Section 1).

Treatment Goals

Sometimes polysubstance users are dependent on one drug but use other substances in moderation, leading both patients and caregivers to focus exclusively on the primary drug of abuse. While this may be appropriate, careful assessment will often reveal that the secondary drug triggers cravings for the primary drug, or its use places patients in situations where they are exposed to the primary drug. Furthermore, the secondary drug sometimes causes unrecognized problems such as fatigue, insomnia or depression. As a general rule, therefore, the patient should aim for abstinence from all substances.

MANAGEMENT OF WITHDRAWAL

The various protocols in polysubstance withdrawal management are briefly summarized in Table 1. The cardinal principles in managing withdrawal are:

- The substance posing the greatest risk of serious withdrawal should receive priority. (A patient on high doses of barbiturates and opioids, for example, should be treated with phenobarbital loading first.)
- Equivalent doses are approximate and wide ranges are reported in the literature. Careful titration is required to avoid oversedation or significant withdrawal.
- When combining drugs such as phenobarbital, diazepam and clonidine, watch for oversedation and use conservative doses.
- When in doubt, consult with an addiction medicine specialist.

For an example of polysubstance withdrawal management, consider a patient taking daily doses of 20 mg of Ativan®, 20 capsules of Fiorinal®, 12 Tylenol #3® and six alcoholic drinks. Butalbital withdrawal poses the greatest risk for the patient, followed by lorazepam, alcohol and codeine. The patient should be admitted and receive phenobarbital loading, which will prevent serious withdrawal from butalbital, lorazepam and alcohol (phenobarbital is the "universal drug" for treating withdrawal). Small doses of clonidine may be added to relieve opioid withdrawal symptoms, although it should not be prescribed until the phenobarbital load is completed and the patient is alert.

Once the phenobarbital load has been completed, the patient is no longer at risk for severe benzodiazepine withdrawal but may experience a subacute, prolonged withdrawal as described in Section 5.2. This can be managed by inpatient or outpatient tapering with an initial diazepam dose of no more than $1/2$ to $1/3$ the equivalent lorazepam dose (in this case, the equivalent diazepam dose is approximately 150 mg of diazepam, so an initial daily dose of 50 mg should be sufficient). The taper should not start until the patient is alert and fully recovered from the phenobarbital load. The taper may then proceed following the protocol outlined in Section 5.2.

TABLE 1: Management of Polysubstance Withdrawal

Co-occurring substances		Protocol
Alcohol withdrawal and ...	benzodiazepine withdrawal	*Day 1:* diazepam loading (for alcohol withdrawal).†
		Day 2 and on: diazepam tapering (for benzodiazepine withdrawal).
	barbiturate withdrawal (daily dose 500 mg or more)	Phenobarbital loading.
	barbiturate withdrawal (daily dose 200–450 mg)	*Outpatient:* *Day 1:* diazepam loading (for alcohol withdrawal)
		then: phenobarbital tapering (after diazepam load completed and patient alert).
		Inpatient: Phenobarbital loading.
	opioid withdrawal	*First:* diazepam loading
		then: clonidine after loading completed (for alcohol withdrawal)
Benzodiazepine withdrawal and ...	barbiturate withdrawal (daily dose 500 mg or more)	*Day 1:* phenobarbital loading
		then: diazepam tapering when load completed and patient alert (start at $1/3$ to $1/2$ the equivalent diazepam dose).
	barbiturate withdrawal (daily dose 200–450 mg)	*If diazepam equivalent < 50 mg/day:* phenobarbital tapering.
		If patient has significant withdrawal symptoms, physician may need to titrate dose upwards or add small dose of diazepam, e.g., 5 mg tid.
		If diazepam equivalent > 50 mg/day: diazepam tapering as per high-dose protocol.

305

Table 1 continued

Co-occurring substances		Protocol
Benzozdiazepine withdrawal and...	barbiturate withdrawal (daily dose 200–450 mg) (continued)	If patient has significant withdrawal symptoms, physician may need to titrate dose upwards or add small dose of phenobarbital, e.g., 15 mg bid. If barbiturate dose 350–450 mg, consider phenobarbital tapering concurrently but use conservative doses and watch for oversedation (see example††).
	opioid withdrawal	Diazepam tapering and clonidine (lower doses may be required — both diazepam and clonidine are sedating).
Opioid withdrawal and ...	barbiturate withdrawal (daily dose 500 mg or more)	*Day 1:* phenobarbital loading *then:* clonidine when load complete, patient is alert and has symptoms of opioid withdrawal.
	barbiturate withdrawal (daily dose 200–450 mg)	Phenobarbital tapering and clonidine (watch for sedation).

† Diazepam should be used with caution in elderly patients, debilitated patients and those with a low serum albumin. The half-life of diazepam can be prolonged in these patients, leading to oversedation. Lorazepam is a safe and effective alternative for these patients because it has a shorter half-life and is not metabolized to an active metabolite in the liver. Therefore, it is less likely to cause oversedation. Lorazepam is given in a dose of 1–2 mg every 2 to 4 hours for CIWA greater than 10. It can be administered orally, intramuscularly or sublingually. Because of its shorter half-life, it cannot be used as a loading protocol but must be administered for the full duration of withdrawal.

†† Consider a patient on six Fiorinal® and 225 mg of oxazepam per day. The equivalent phenobarbital and diazepam doses are 90 mg and 75 mg respectively. Start tapering with phenobarbital 30 mg tid and diazepam 45 mg per day.

Emergency Management of Intoxications and Overdoses

11   EMERGENCY MANAGEMENT OF INTOXICATIONS AND OVERDOSES

11

EMERGENCY MANAGEMENT OF INTOXICATIONS AND OVERDOSES

Margaret Thompson, MD

INTOXICATION AND OVERDOSE

Intoxication is defined as the intake of a quantity of a substance that exceeds individual tolerance and produces behavioral and/or physical abnormalities. There is obviously an element of relativity in this definition.

The term "overdose" implies that the person has ingested a drug quantity that is higher than the recommended normal or therapeutic dose and that also exceeds his or her tolerance. The term is used here in a broader context that includes poisonings with substances that do not have therapeutic uses and therefore have no "normal" dose.

The information provided here is not meant to give guidelines that are comprehensive for the management of overdoses and poisonings. The physician must rely on other resources. A few basic points and reminders are offered pertaining to any intoxication and to common drugs of abuse.

MANAGEMENT OF INTOXICATION AND OVERDOSE

The intoxicated patient should be treated as a critically ill patient. Attention must be paid to establishing and maintaining the patient's airway, breathing and circulation. This may require intubation, mechanical ventilation, intravenous access and inotropic support. The intoxicated patient may also have suffered some traumatic event as a result of alteration in mentation. Depending on circumstances, protecting the cervical spine must be considered.

Drug therapy may also include ACLS (Advanced Cardiac Life Support) protocols and/or the administration of universal antidotes of oxygen, thiamine

(100 mg i.v.), glucose (0.5–1.0 g/kg i.v.) and naloxone (see Opioid Overdose below). Neither flumazenil nor physostigmine are considered universal antidotes because their margin of safety is narrow.

Blood samples should be sent for hematology, coagulation studies, electrolytes, urea, glucose, measured serum osmolarity, arterial blood gases, ASA and acetaminophen levels as a minimum. Specific levels of toxicologic importance include methanol and ethylene glycol determinations. Many other therapeutic drug levels can be monitored. General drug screens are available (see Section 1). When dealing with a patient who is a substance user, knowledge of these levels will not change the acute management of the patient. Therefore, drug screens are not necessary or recommended.

For all practical purposes, decontamination of the gastrointestinal (GI) tract is currently limited to the administration of activated charcoal without sorbitol at a dose of 1 g/kg body weight or, if known, 10 g/g drug ingested. Repeated doses may be of benefit for specific intoxicants.

Determining full vital signs and performing a physical examination are mandatory, and are directed at identifying specific toxidromes or alternative explanations for patient presentations. Alternative explanations may include meningitis, structural CNS lesions, sepsis and seizures. Generally, the drug-abusing or intoxicated patient is not regarded as a reliable historian. This is especially relevant with regard to the street source of the substance. The unsuspecting user may have used a drug substituted or cut with another. Common alterations include haloperidol for street diazepam (resulting in dystonia), phencyclidine (PCP) contamination of marijuana (causing opisthotonos), and lidocaine dilution of cocaine (producing seizures).

Specific antidotes are available for some intoxicants, such as naloxone for opioids and flumazenil for benzodiazepines.

Patients must be continually reassessed. Continuous monitoring of oxygen saturation, blood pressure, cardiac activity and level of consciousness are the minimum in managing these patients. Other investigations include trauma series radiographs, urinary output and pH, abdominal flat plates, etc., as indicated.

ACETAMINOPHEN OVERDOSE

A discussion of acetaminophen toxicity is included in this section because many narcotic preparations are available in combination with acetaminophen.

Acetaminophen (N-acetyl-*p*-aminophenol [APAP]) is primarily metabolized in the liver by glucuronidation, sulphation or by the formation of a free epoxide radical which requires glutathione (GSH) for detoxification. If inadequate reagents are available for the two former reactions as a result of these pathways being overwhelmed by the overdose, a more toxic metabolite is formed from the parent APAP. Similarly, if inadequate GSH stores are present, centrilobular hepatic necrosis occurs, which can lead to complete destruction of the liver — a condition that is more likely to occur in the malnourished patient. This pathway is also inducible, making the alcoholic or barbiturate user more susceptible to hepatic injury. The toxic free radical can be formed in the kidney. In rare cases the patient who experiences an APAP overdose develops renal failure. Both hepatic and renal necrosis are fully reversible if treated in a timely fashion.

TREATMENT OF APAP TOXICITY WITH N-ACETYLCYSTEINE (NAC)

N-acetylcysteine (NAC) is available as a specific antidote for APAP toxicity. It acts to prevent or reverse the damage secondary to the free radical intermediate. Early, it can be a GSH precursor (GSH itself will not cross the cell membrane), or it may replace GSH. NAC provides free sulphur so that the formerly overwhelmed sulphation pathway becomes active. Given late (i.e., beyond the traditional 10- to 12-hour mark), it becomes a non-specific inhibitor of inflammation. There is now evidence that administration of NAC many hours following the acute overdose may be beneficial, even after hepatotoxicity has occurred (Tucker, 1998).

NAC is most effective if given early after a toxic ingestion of APAP. The therapeutic dose of APAP is 10–15 mg/kg every four hours. A single dose of APAP of 140 mg/kg (or 6 g) is potentially hepatotoxic and should be treated with a full course of intravenous or oral NAC if serum levels are unavailable. If serum levels can be obtained in a timely fashion, the determination of those requiring full antidote treatment is made by comparing patient serum (APAP) with the Rumack-Matthew acetaminophen nomogram (Figure A).

311

When using the Rumack-Matthew acetaminophen nomogram, the following points should be kept in mind:

- The nomogram is valid only for those ingesting a single overdose of regular APAP at a known time.
- The serum APAP level must be taken at least four hours after the ingestion to allow complete absorption and distribution of APAP to have occurred.
- The nomogram is not valid and is as yet untested for the new extended-release preparation.

Figure A: Rumack-Matthew Nomogram for Assessing Potential Toxicity of Acetaminophen Overdose from Drug Plasma Levels†

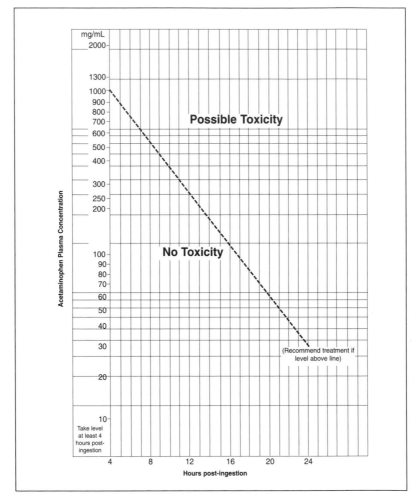

† Reprinted with permission from B.H. Rumack & H. Matthew. (1975). Copyright 1975.

N-acetylcysteine (NAC) Loading Protocol

EARLY PRESENTATION

If a patient presents within 10–12 hours following a toxic ingestion, the 20-hour intravenous NAC protocol is acceptable treatment.

Loading dose (LD): 150 mg/kg in D5W over 20 minutes;
followed by: 50 mg/kg in D5W (500 cc) over four hours;
then: 100 mg/kg in D5W (1,000 cc) over 16 hours.

Urticaria or bronchospasm that may develop during the loading will respond to slowing the rate of infusion and/or giving diphenhydramine or salbutamol as the clinical condition dictates.

LATE PRESENTATION

The late presentation (>10–12 hours post-ingestion) of a toxic APAP dose requires the full 72-hour oral NAC treatment of 150 mg/kg po LD, followed by 17 doses of 70 mg/kg every four hours, each dose being suspended in juice. (This protocol is also more appropriate for the pediatric patient under age 5 when fluid overload is a concern.) As with any oral overdose, initial charcoal decontamination should occur even if the oral NAC route is to be used.

MODIFIED DOSING SCHEDULE

A modified intravenous dosing schedule can be used for those presenting after 10–12 hours, but before 24 hours.

Loading dose: 150 mg/kg i.v. over one hour
followed by: 14 doses (q4h) 70 mg/kg i.v. each dose over one hour.

For those who present with staggered ingestions, ingestions of extended-release preparations or later than 24 hours, other recommendations may be provided by local poison information centres.

Alcohol (Including Ethanol, Ethylene Glycol and Methanol) Intoxication and Poisoning

Ethanol intoxication

The management of ethanol (ethyl alcohol) intoxication is dealt with in detail in Section 3 of this manual and is presented in this section only in comparison with other alcohol intoxication.

313

Acute clinical presentation of ethanol intoxication includes CNS disinhibition, then depression, pupillary constriction and arterial dilation manifesting as conjunctional injection, hypotension, tachycardia and potentially hypothermia. Absorption of ethanol from the GI tract is usually rapid. Distribution is in plasma-free water and across the blood-brain barrier. Little ethanol is excreted unchanged by the kidney. Most ethanol is metabolized in the liver by the enzyme alcohol dehydrogenase (ADH) to non-toxic CO_2 and water. No metabolic derangement, except perhaps respiratory acidosis secondary to CNS depression, occurs due to acute ethanol intoxication alone.

Methanol and ethylene glycol

When ethyl alcohol is unavailable to the chronic abuser, dangerous but accessible over-the-counter ethanol substitutes may be used. Both methanol (also known as methyl alcohol or wood alcohol), found in antifreeze, windshield washer fluid, cleaning products, etc., and ethylene glycol, found in antifreeze and coolants, cause the same level of CNS disinhibition and depression as does ethanol. Usual lethal ingestions of methanol (100 per cent) are 0.5 cc/kg and of ethylene glycol (100 per cent), 1.0–1.5 cc/kg. Clinical presentation of acute intoxication is virtually indistinguishable. Similarly, they share the same absorption and distribution characteristics as ethyl alcohol. Indeed, because of such small volumes of distribution, dialysis is an effective therapeutic manoeuvre for the removal of all three alcohols.

In their native state (i.e., as an alcohol), neither methanol nor ethylene glycol is dangerous. The intermediate and end-products of ADH metabolism cause the blindness and renal failure associated with methanol and ethylene glycol ingestion respectively, as well as the metabolic acidosis. ADH, which metabolizes ethyl alcohol to CO_2 and H_2O, is relatively inefficient at metabolizing the other alcohols. Metabolic derangements may not be seen until long after ingestion, hence the classic increased osmolar gap metabolic acidosis attributed to these intoxications.

In interpreting blood work in these situations, however, there are several caveats to be exercised.

- Methyl and ethyl alcohols and ethylene glycol all contribute to an increased osmolar gap once absorbed (increased osmolar gap may be missed if ingestion was minutes before) but before metabolism (metabolic end-products CO_2, formate and oxalate of ethanol, methanol and ethylene glycol respectively are *not* osmotically active particles).
- Calculated serum osmolality = 2Na + BUN + glucose. This is an estimate only. Osmolar gap = (measured - calculated) serum osmolality. Hence, the osmolar gap is an estimate as well and has a wide range of normal, from -10 to +10 mOsm/L.

- Metabolic acidosis may not develop until hours after ingestion. The serum half-life for methanol is 24 to 30 hours, and for ethylene glycol it is three to 17 hours. Because ADH prefers to metabolize ethanol first the half-life is even further prolonged for both substitute alcohols if ethyl alcohol has been co-ingested. If all native alcohol has been metabolized the osmolar gap will no longer be elevated.

TREATMENT PROTOCOL FOR METHANOL AND ETHYLENE GLYCOL INTOXICATION

The treatment for methanol and ethylene glycol intoxications is, first, supportive. Large doses of bicarbonate, to correct profound metabolic acidosis, may be necessary. There is probably little role for decontamination. Additives in most methanol and ethylene glycol-containing products are nauseating and the patient may well have vomited already. Charcoal binding to alcohols is of such low affinity that no benefit occurs to justify the risks of its administration.

ETHANOL LOADING
Because ADH preferentially metabolizes ethanol, ethyl alcohol in doses large enough to completely saturate ADH (serum ethanol concentrations at least = 23 mmol/L) is immediate therapy to block the formation of meta-bolites. Remember that binding to ADH is competitive. To completely block methanol or ethylene glycol metabolism, blood alcohol concentrations (BACs) must be at least $1/10$ that of the other alcohol. A BAC of 23 mmol/L can usually be achieved in a chronic drinker with an LD of 10 cc 10 per cent ethanol/kg i.v. bolus and a maintenance of 1.5–2.0 cc/kg per hr 10 per cent ethanol, or 1 cc/kg per hr 10 per cent ethanol in the novice.

PROMOTE ALTERNATE METABOLISM
Metabolic pathways for both methanol and ethylene glycol to non-toxic products do exist. Giving folic acid (50 mg i.v. q4h) for methanol intoxica-tion and thiamine (100 mg i.v. q6h) with pyridoxine (50 mg i.v. q6h) for eth-ylene glycol ingestions may promote alternate metabolism/breakdown.

HEMODIALYSIS
Hemodialysis of methanol and ethylene glycol is indicated for:
- levels of 16 mmol/L methanol and 8 mmol/L ethylene glycol
- metabolic acidosis (toxic metabolites are dialyzable)
- evidence of end-organ damage (visual impairment, renal failure or crystalluria)
- history of ingestion of potentially lethal amounts and no levels available.

315

4-METHYLPYRAZOLE

An oral ADH blocker, 4-methylpyrazole (4-mp), is now approved and available for the treatment of ethylene glycol intoxication. In some circumstances the use of this agent may obviate the need for alcohol therapy in the future. Slow elimination of unmetabolized methanol and ethylene glycol by the kidneys and lungs would then occur until cleared from the body.

ASA OVERDOSE

ASA (acetylsalicylic acid) toxicology is reviewed here because many over-the-counter and prescription analgesics, anti-inflammatories and cold preparations include salicylates. Like APAP, ASA is found in combination with the opioids codeine and oxycodone.

TABLE 1: Signs of Salicylate Overdose

CNS	• direct respiratory centre stimulation ⇒ respiratory alkalosis (early) • tinnitus (early) • cerebral edema ⇒ seizures, coma
METABOLIC	• uncoupling oxidative phosphorylation ⇒ metabolic acidosis ⇒ hyperthermia ⇒ tachycardia ⇒ hyperventilation
HEPATIC	• inhibition of vitamin K-dependent factor VII production ⇒ coagulation abnormalities • hyper/hypoglycemia (various mechanisms) • potentially linked with Reye's syndrome
GI	• direct irritation
GU	• delay in onset of labor, postmaturity • premature closure of the ductus arteriosus
HEMATOLOGICAL	• platelet adhesiveness

GI absorption of ASA in overdose may be delayed for several reasons including availability of delayed-release and buffered preparations as well as the potential formation of concretions. The implication is that repeated doses of charcoal may be necessary and beneficial for adequate GI decontamination. Similarly, serial ASA levels are important for adequate monitoring of absorption and treatment.

Hemodialysis

ASA is distributed in plasma water and is amenable to hemodialysis. As serum pH falls with increased ASA toxicity, ASA distributes more widely and becomes more toxic. Serum alkalinization helps prevent ASA from crossing the blood-brain barrier.

At low ASA concentrations, there is some hepatic metabolism. As ASA levels rise, metabolism is overwhelmed and ASA excretion is renal. Urine alkalinization allows ASA to be trapped in the urine, leading to increased elimination. Adequate urine volumes to allow renal elimination of ASA are necessary. The replacement of fluid losses secondary to nausea/vomiting/hyperventilation and hyperthermia will require saline boluses. However, continued diuresis is dangerous in the setting of pulmonary and cerebral edema.

TABLE 2: Achieving Urine Alkalinization†

When serum pH is	And urine pH is	Then give NaCO$_3$	U/O
alkali	alkali	2 amps in 1 L D5W$\frac{1}{4}$NS	2–3 cc/kg per hr
alkali	acid	3 amps in 1 L D5W$\frac{1}{4}$NS	
acid	acid	4 amps in 1 L D5W	

† Note that failure to adequately alkalinize urine may occur when serum K$^+$ levels are low, because H$^+$ will be exchanged for K$^+$ at the renal tubular level; K$^+$ replacement may be considered.

Indications for hemodialysis include:

- ASA > 5 mmol/L in chronic intoxication; > 9 mmol/L in acute
- history of ingestion of ASA > 500 mg/kg
- inability to adequately alkalinize urine
- rising ASA or falling serum pH despite two hours of aggressive decontamination and alkalinization
- evidence of end-organ damage (CNS, pulmonary edema, metabolic acidosis, etc.) that precludes aggressive alkalinization.

317

Unlike the Rumack-Matthew nomogram for APAP toxicity (Figure A), the Done nomogram for salicylate toxicity provides no therapeutic direction. The Done nomogram only predicts toxicity and should not be relied upon (Dugandzic, Tierney et al., 1989).

BENZODIAZEPINE INTOXICATION AND OVERDOSE

Acute intoxication with benzodiazepines alone is rarely life-threatening. Presentation is similar to that of acute alcohol intoxication, with disinhibition, decreased level of consciousness, miosis and nystagmus. Massive overdoses, or in combination with other sedatives, have caused deep coma and cardiovascular collapse, even leading to death. The mainstay of therapy is supportive.

Benzodiazepines work at specific receptors in the CNS and peripheral nervous systems potentiating the effect of the inhibitory neurotransmitters, GABA and glycine respectively.

Flumazenil

Flumazenil is a competitive benzodiazepine antagonist acting in the CNS only. Its use should be restricted to the reversal of *iatrogenic* benzodiazepine sedation. There is *no* indication for its use in the setting of a coma of unknown etiology or known benzodiazepine overdose. Patients who may be benzodiazepine-dependent are at risk for severe symptoms of benzodiazepine withdrawal and the precipitation of seizures when given flumazenil. The pharmacokinetics of flumazenil lead to its effects lasting as long as 60 minutes. During this time the use of antiseizure medications may not be beneficial. In addition, flumazenil is contraindicated in the setting of tricyclic antidepressant overdoses. Death has been reported after the administration of flumazenil in the resuscitation of those with coma of unknown etiology and mixed overdoses where tricyclic toxicity was eventually identified as a component of the presentation.

OPIOID OVERDOSE

Endogenous opioids, known as beta-endorphins, interact and cause their effects by stimulating opioid receptors in the CNS and spinal cord. Stimulation of these receptors induces euphoria and blocks pain. Naturally occurring opioids and the synthetic opioids likewise stimulate these receptors.

The classic opioid overdose toxidrome is characterized by miosis and respiratory and CNS depression. Other possible presentations of acute intoxication include hypotension, bradycardia, hypothermia, seizures (from metabolites of specific opioids), pulmonary edema and death. Opioid overdose is a medical emergency as compared with opioid withdrawal, which is at the most uncomfortable. The exception to this is the passively exposed neonate who may develop withdrawal seizures (see Section 8.2).

In the addict, sudden withdrawal can precipitate violent behavior and the risk of elopement from medical care. For this reason, treatment of opioid overdose with the competitive antagonist naloxone should be titrated to effect. A judicious approach is to give doses of 0.01 mg/kg to those whose clinical presentation is suggestive of opioid abuse. If a physical examination reveals signs of chronic dependence such as track marks, even lower doses may be appropriate. If the initial dose is ineffectual, 10 times the original dose (i.e., 0.1 mg/kg) could be given safely as a repeat bolus. Some opioids bind the opioid receptors particularly tightly and higher doses of the antagonist are required to competitively block receptors. If a clinical effect is achieved secondary to the naloxone, an intravenous infusion of $2/3$ of the effective "wake-up" dose per hour is appropriate maintenance therapy. The desired therapeutic end-point is adequate respiratory drive. As the parent or offending opioid is metabolized, the rate of this infusion can be titrated down to achieve this effect.

With few exceptions, most naturally occurring opioids and synthetic opioids have much longer durations than naloxone. Even for those with shorter half-lives (e.g., fentanyl, heroin, meperidine and pentazocine) absorption may continue if decontamination has not been addressed. If the patient has eloped from medical care under the influence of naloxone, which then is metabolized while the opioid agonist is still active, the patient will again lapse into unresponsiveness. There are those, as well, who believe that all heroin overdoses should be admitted to hospital because of the risk of latent non-cardiogenic pulmonary edema in this population. Patient compliance with this approach is understandably poor.

TRICYCLIC ANTIDEPRESSANT OVERDOSE

Because there are a number of patients with concurrent diagnoses of substance dependence and depression, physicians are likely to encounter many dependent patients who use tricyclic antidepressants (TCAs). With the introduction of selective serotonin reuptake inhibitors (SSRIs) for the treatment of depression, the use of TCAs is falling out of favor. Nevertheless, there is the rare patient who experiences solely the central antimuscarinic effects of the TCAs (i.e., disinhibition and hallucinations) and who may abuse them for this reason. The TCAs also serve as a model for understanding the adverse effects and treatment of intoxications from diphenhydramine, skeletal muscle relaxants and even cocaine.

319

There are several mechanisms by which TCAs cause toxicity. TCAs have anticholinergic (specifically antimuscarinic) effects, acting at central and post-synaptic peripheral receptors, causing hallucinations, mydriasis, vasodilation, lack of sweating, tachycardia, decreased bowel motility and urinary retention. They stimulate release of norepinephrine from nerve terminals, producing tachycardias, arrhythmias and hypertension, and then depletion of norepinephrine by preventing its reuptake by pre-synaptic nerve terminals, making it accessible to degradation. The effect is cardiovascular collapse. Sodium channel blockade of the myocardial cell results in cardiac conduction blockade and bradyarrhythmias as well as decreased cardiac output and subsequent hypotension. Other effects on serotonin and histamine receptors may be responsible for the therapeutic benefits of relieving depression.

The mainstay of therapy is supportive. Intravenous access is of utmost importance because sudden deterioration of clinical status is usual. Hypotension must be treated with intravenous fluid boluses first, and then sodium bicarbonate boluses. The aim is not to alkalinize the serum or urine but to present sodium in high concentrations to the myocardial cell in order to overcome the sodium channel blockade and increase cardiac rate and inotropy. Inotropes (dopamine, dobutamine, noradrenaline, etc.) may be required. Because of the known depletion of norepinephrine, it makes theoretical sense to use noradrenaline as the inotrope of choice. Other inotropes have been found to be effective in adequate doses. Tachyarrhythmias (i.e., ventricular tachycardia and fibrillation) should be treated as per ACLS, with the notable exception that sodium bicarbonate boluses should be used early in the resuscitation, for the reasons noted above. Bradyarrhythmias and widened QRS complexes greater than 0.16 msec should also be treated with sodium bicarbonate boluses. The end-point for bicarbonate treatment is the resolution of the hypotension, arrhythmia or shortening of the QRS complex. Therapeutic effect will be seen within minutes. Care must be taken not to exceed a serum pH of 7.55. Again, there is *no* role for sodium bicarbonate infusions or prophylaxis.

Seizures should be treated like any toxic seizure. Benzodiazepines are the drug of first choice. Physicians should be aware that arrhythmias often follow a seizure secondary to lactic acidosis. It is thought that more free drug is available to the myocardium when the serum is acidic.

R E F E R E N C E S

Dugandzic, R.M., Tierney, M.G., Dickinson, G.E., Dolan, M.C. & McKnight, D.R. (1989). Evaluation of the validity of the Done nomogram in the management of acute salicylate intoxication. *Annals of Emergency Medicine, 18(11)*, 1186-1190.

Rumack, B.H., Matthew, H. (1975). Acetaminophen poisoning and toxicity. *Pediatrics, 55(6)*, 871-876

Tucker, J.R. (1998). Late-presenting acute acetaminophen toxicity and the role of N-acetyl-cysteine. *Pediatric Emergency Care, 14(6)*, 424-426.

S U G G E S T E D   R E A D I N G

Ellenhorn, M.J. (1997). *Ellenhorn's Medical Toxicology: Diagnosis and Treatment of Human Poisoning*, 2nd ed. Baltimore, MD: Williams and Wilkins.

Goldfrank, L.R., Flomenbaum, N.E., Lewin, N.A., Weisman, R.S., Howland, M.A. & Hoffman, R.S. (1998). *Goldfrank's Toxicologic Emergencies*, 6th ed. Norwalk, CO: Appleton and Lange.

Complications of Injection Drug Use

12.1 PREVENTION AND MANAGEMENT OF INFECTIOUS COMPLICATIONS IN INJECTION DRUG USERS

12.2 VIRAL HEPATITIS

12.3 HIV AND SUBSTANCE USE

REFERENCES

TABLES AND FIGURES

12.1

PREVENTION AND MANAGEMENT OF INFECTIOUS COMPLICATIONS IN INJECTION DRUG USERS

Meldon Kahan, MD

INFECTION CONTROL STRATEGIES: OVERVIEW

Office-based interventions

Injection drug users have an extremely high prevalence of hepatitis C (see Section 8.2), and HIV seroprevalence rates have shown alarming increases in many jurisdictions (Remis, Millson & Major, 1997). Physicians have a key role in the prevention, detection and management of these and other infectious complications such as sexually transmitted diseases and endocarditis. Harm-reduction strategies, such as advice on needle sharing, are a key component of infection control in patients who continue to use illicit drugs. The following protocol is suggested for the management of patients who are injection drug users.

TABLE 1: Summary of Infection Control Strategies

• Advise all patients about the risks of needle sharing, how to acquire new needles and how to clean needles.
• Order hepatitis B serology on all patients, and immunize susceptible patients and contacts.
• Order hepatitis C serology on all patients.
• Monitor transaminases every two to six months in hepatitis-C-positive patients. Refer to a hepatologist if ALT is 1.5 to 2 times normal on two or more occasions.
• Order HIV serology every six months.
• Provide methadone treatment to HIV-positive opioid users.
• Screen for sexually transmitted diseases.
• Counsel on safe sex.
• Screen for TB.
• Be alert for other infectious complications, e.g., endocarditis, cellulitis.

EXPLAIN THE RISKS OF NEEDLE SHARING

Injection drug users should be advised of the risks of needle sharing. In an Australian study (Wolk, Wodak et al., 1990), 80 per cent of a sample of methadone patients admitted to needle sharing during their current period of drug use, even though 99 per cent were aware that needle sharing can transmit HIV.

Patients should be advised that spoons and filters (used to mix and purify drug solutions) are sources of virus transmission when shared. Physicians also need to address the myth that it is safe to share needles with close friends or sexual partners. Patients should be advised to return used needles to an exchange program for safe disposal.

ADVISE PATIENTS OF ACCESS TO NEW SYRINGES

One of the major reasons given by addicts for sharing needles is the difficulty in obtaining sterile equipment (Metzger, Woody et al., 1991) and the refusal of pharmacists to sell needles (Coates, Rankin et al., 1992). In Canada, the Ontario College of Pharmacists encourages the sale of needles by pharmacists to injection drug users. Needle and syringe exchange programs exist in most large cities.

SHOW PATIENTS HOW TO CLEAN NEEDLES

The physician should explain how to clean needles using household bleach.

- Fill the syringe with bleach twice, then fill with tap water two or more times. Some patients are concerned that the bleach will enter their veins; reassure them on this point.
- Warn patients that cleaning used needles with bleach does not always eradicate the hepatitis virus.
- Emphasize that acquisition of new needles is preferable to cleaning and reusing used ones.

Some physicians are uncomfortable with this advice, feeling that it encourages needle use. The message, however, is not that clean needle use is acceptable, only that it is preferable to dirty needle use. This is similar to the message given to heavy drinkers: Don't drink; but if you do, at least don't drive.

ORDER HEPATITIS B SEROLOGY AND LIVER TRANSAMINASES ON ALL PATIENTS, AND IMMUNIZE SUSCEPTIBLE CONTACTS

Patients who are susceptible to hepatitis B (i.e., seronegative for both the surface antigen and the surface antibody) should be offered immunization. The recommended schedule is at initial point of contact with physician, one month and 6 months. With drug-using patients, some flexibility in dosage schedule may be required. Patients with hepatitis C should also be offered immunization for hepatitis B at their first visit (Wong, Wreghitt & Alexander, 1996).

ORDER HEPATITIS C SEROLOGY ON ALL PATIENTS. IF POSITIVE, MONITOR LIVER TRANSAMINASES EVERY TWO TO SIX MONTHS, AND REFER IF ALT IS 1.5–2X NORMAL ON TWO OR MORE OCCASIONS

Elevated transaminases should be monitored every two to three months. Normal transaminases should be checked every six months. Patients should be referred to a hepatologist if their ALT remains above 1.5–2 times normal for two measurements, or if they have signs of liver disease on physical examination. Some hepatologists routinely order an abdominal ultrasound. Patients with hepatitis C are at increased risk of fulminant hepatitis due to hepatitis A virus superinfection. Therefore, all susceptible patients with hepatitis C should be offered hepatitis A immunization (Vento, Garofano et al., 1998).

Interferon has been shown to return ALT to normal in about 50 per cent of cases. Of these cases, 50 per cent will relapse, giving an overall cure rate of 25–30 per cent (Davis, Balart et al., 1989; Di Bisceglie, Martin et al., 1989; Shindo, Di Bisceglie et al., 1991). Despite the low cure rate, a trial of interferon is reasonable given the high probability of developing serious liver disease.

ADVISE HEPATITIS B AND C PATIENTS ABOUT THE RISK TO CONTACTS

Sexual transmission of hepatitis C appears to be infrequent (Osmond, Padian et al., 1993). The U.S. Public Health Service (1991) recommends that hepatitis C virus (HCV) carriers avoid multiple sexual partners, practise safe sex to reduce contact with blood and body fluids, and inform prospective sexual partners of their HCV status. Testing exposed partners for HCV is also suggested, and carriers should be advised to avoid sharing toothbrushes or other objects contaminated with blood (e.g., razors).

Similar precautions are recommended for hepatitis B carriers. In addition, household members and sexual partners of hepatitis B carriers should be tested and immunized if susceptible.

SCREEN INJECTION DRUG USERS FOR HIV EVERY SIX MONTHS

Patients who have shared needles since 1978 should be tested for HIV. Pre- and post-test counselling should be done. Because many injection drug users do not have permanent housing, careful follow-up arrangements are needed to inform patients of the result. Also, patients who are depressed or suicidal may need to have the test deferred.

PROVIDE METHADONE TREATMENT TO HIV-POSITIVE OPIOID USERS

HIV-positive patients should be fast-tracked for admission to methadone treatment programs in order to ensure proper medical care and decrease the risk of transmission. Patients entering methadone treatment markedly reduce their rate of needle use and needle sharing (Ball & Ross, 1991).

ADVISE ABOUT SAFE SEX, AND SCREEN FOR STDS

Unsafe sexual practices, such as multiple sexual partners and unprotected intercourse, are common among injection drug users (Wolk, Wodak et al., 1990). Both men and women should be advised about condom use. Sexually active women should be screened yearly for gonorrhea and chlamydia. Carcinoma of the cervix and pelvic inflammatory disease must be considered when women present with discharge or abdominal pain.

PROVIDE ROUTINE TB SKIN TESTING

Chest X-ray and TB skin testing should be considered for injection drug users who present with fever or a chronic cough.

ACUTE INFECTIOUS COMPLICATIONS

Acute hepatitis

Patients with acute hepatitis present with malaise, myalgias, fever, right upper quadrant pain and jaundice. Care is supportive. Hospitalization is not necessary unless patients develop laboratory evidence of severe hepatic dysfunction (markedly elevated PT, decreased albumin), clinical signs of hepatic failure (encephalopathy) or dehydration from profuse vomiting. Sometimes an admission for a rest and drug detoxification is indicated if patients feel quite ill.

Fever NYD

Fever with no obvious source is another common presentation of injection drug users. One study found that 11 per cent of injection drug users who presented to an emergency room with fever from no obvious source turned out to have a major illness, usually bacteremia (Samet, Shevitz et al., 1990). The only significant clinical and laboratory predictors of major illness were fever greater than 38.8°C, last i.v. drug use within five days and proteinuria. White blood cell count was not predictive.

Investigations should include CBC, urinalysis and culture, chest X-ray and blood culture. Injection drug users with fever NYD should be hospitalized pending blood culture results, unless the fever is less than 38.5°C, the patients do not look ill and they can be contacted within the following 48 hours if the culture comes back positive.

Endocarditis

Right-sided (tricuspid valve) endocarditis is more common than mitral valve endocarditis in injection drug users. Often patients with right-sided endocarditis do not have the classic signs of endocarditis, such as a new heart murmur. They may present only with fever NYD. Prompt recognition and treatment will prevent valvular damage and other complications.

12.2

VIRAL HEPATITIS

Morris Sherman, MB, BCh, PhD

INCIDENCE AND TRANSMISSION

Viral hepatitis is a common problem in patients with addictions, with hepatitis B and C being the most common infections in this group. Studies have indicated that among injection drug users (IDUs), hepatitis C infection occurs in about 65 to 80 per cent (Zeldis, Jain et al., 1992; van den Hoek, van Haastrecht et al., 1990). Contamination of shared needles and syringes is the likely route of infection. Hepatitis C is also more prevalent in IDUs who use needle exchanges. This is due to contamination of drug-use paraphernalia apart from needles and syringes. Many patients are not aware that sharing of spoons and filters can also transmit disease. Infection with hepatitis C virus (HCV) is also more common in nasal cocaine users. The inhaled cocaine causes irritation to the nasal mucosa, with bleeding. The contaminated straw used to inhale the cocaine may be shared by other users, with transmission of disease.

Hepatitis B infection is less common than hepatitis C infection in IDUs, with about 60 per cent of IDUs having been infected with hepatitis B (Garfein, Vlahov et al., 1996). The majority recover completely and become immune. About 3 to 6 per cent of IDUs are hepatitis B carriers. Transmission of hepatitis B by nasal cocaine probably also occurs, but because the prevalence of active hepatitis B infection is much lower than that of active hepatitis C, this is a less obvious source of infection.

Alcoholics also have a higher than expected prevalence of both hepatitis B and hepatitis C. Presumably this is also related to past IDU and to unprotected sex, which is seen in this population.

SCREENING FOR VIRAL HEPATITIS

Screening for viral hepatitis has two components. First, patients need to be screened for the presence of hepatitis virus infection, and second, patients with viral hepatitis need to be screened for the presence of liver disease. All patients who have been or are currently using intravenous substances of abuse or nasal cocaine, as well as all alcoholics, should be tested for hepatitis B and hepatitis C infection.

Screening tests

The most appropriate test for hepatitis B is the hepatitis B surface antigen (HBsAg). If this is negative, the antibodies to the surface antigen (anti-HBs) should be measured. Those who are negative for both HBsAg and anti-HBs require immunization. Those who are anti-HBs-positive do not require immunization.

The screening test for hepatitis C is the anti-HCV assay. Most patients in whom this test is positive will be infected, particularly if there is a risk factor such as IDU. However, a small proportion will have normal liver enzymes and may have cleared the virus. Unfortunately, there is no certain way of assessing viral clearance. A positive hepatitis C RNA test confirms the presence of the hepatitis C virus. However, a negative RNA test does not exclude chronic hepatitis C infection.

TABLE 2: Hepatitis B and C Serology

	HBsAg	Anti-HBc		Anti-HBs	HBeAg	Anti-HBe	Anti-HCV	HCV-RNA
		IgM	IgG					
ACUTE HBV	+	+	-	-	+	-		
EARLY RESOLUTION "WINDOW PERIOD"	-	-	+	-	-	-		
CONVALESCENT HBV	-	-	+	+	-	+/-		
VACCINATED WITH HBsAG	-	-	-	+	-	-		
CHRONIC HBV (CARRIER)	+	-	+/-	-	+/-	+/-		
HETEROTYPIC HBV (RARE)	+	+/-	+/-	+	+/-	+/-		
HEPATITIS C	-	-	-	-	-	-	+/-	+/-

Screening for liver disease includes measurement of the transaminases (AST and ALT), measurements of liver function (albumin, bilirubin and INR) and screening tests for portal hypertension (CBC: a low platelet or white cell count or a normocytic anemia may indicate hypersplenism due to portal hypertension). Elevated transaminases indicate hepatic inflammation but do not provide information about liver function or the presence of cirrhosis.

Liver function tests, if abnormal, suggest cirrhosis, but may also be abnormal in acute hepatitis with liver failure. Portal hypertension only develops in advanced cirrhosis. Thus mild degrees of cirrhosis may be impossible to diagnose without a biopsy.

MANAGING HEPATITIS B

In the vast majority of infected adult IDUs the initial infection is asymptomatic. A minority of infected individuals become jaundiced. The majority of acute infections clear within six months, with the development of immunity. Fewer than five per cent of acute hepatitis B infections in otherwise healthy young adults become chronic (Tassopoulos, Papaevangelou et al., 1987). There are two patterns of disease in chronic carriers. One group will develop only mild hepatitis and will seroconvert from e antigen (HBeAg) positive to anti-HBe-positive early in the course of the disease, with remission of hepatic inflammation. However, the majority of adult-acquired infections will result in ongoing active hepatitis of varying degrees of severity. Most patients with chronic hepatitis B (CHB) will be asymptomatic and will only be diagnosed by finding elevated transaminases. With time, the ongoing inflammation, necrosis and scarring will lead to cirrhosis and liver failure.

Chronic hepatitis B
Patients with CHB should be evaluated to determine the stage of the viral infection and the severity of liver disease. HBeAg is present in the earlier stages of the disease and indicates a high level of viremia and a high likelihood of active hepatic inflammation. Conversely, the presence of anti-HBe indicates a later stage of disease, low levels of viremia and a low likelihood of inflammation. Only patients with elevated transaminases need be considered for specific treatment. Most patients with elevated transaminases will be HBeAg-positive, but a small proportion will be anti-HBe-positive. Indeed, in anti-HBe-positive patients with elevated transaminases, elevated liver enzymes are usually due to some other cause, and such patients should be investigated for other liver diseases. The most common conditions that might coexist with hepatitis B in these patients are chronic hepatitis C, fatty liver and alcoholic liver disease.

Therapy in CHB is most appropriate for HBeAg-positive patients with ALT > 2 x N for four to six months (Perrillo, Schiff et al., 1990). Anti-HBe-positive patients respond less well and are not suitable for interferon therapy. Many patients with elevated liver enzymes will remit spontaneously in four to six months. Treatment is then no longer required. Thus a four- to six-month waiting period is required to avoid treating such patients undergoing spontaneous remission. A liver biopsy is recommended but not mandatory.

Interferon therapy

Currently the only drug licensed for CHB is interferon-alfa. The dose is 27–35 million IU weekly for four months. A response is defined as normalization of the transaminases, seroconversion from HBeAg-positive to anti-HBe-positive, and, where measured, loss of hepatitis B virus DNA from serum. In the HBeAg-positive group the response rate is 40 to 50 per cent (Perrillo, Schiff et al., 1990). In anti-HBe-positive patients with elevated liver enzymes the long-term response rate is only about 10 per cent (Brunetto, Oliveri et al., 1995). Interferon-induced remissions are usually permanent, whereas spontaneous seroconversions may relapse in up to 15 per cent of patients.

Not all patients are suitable for interferon therapy. Patients with hepatic decompensation who are treated with interferon may develop life-threatening infections or may have an exacerbation of the hepatitis B, leading to hepatic failure (see below for other contraindications).

Patients with normal or near-normal transaminases should be followed at six-month intervals with transaminases and liver function tests. Active hepatitis may be intermittent in these patients and may flare in the future, at which stage the patients may become candidates for therapy.

MANAGING HEPATITIS C

As with hepatitis B, patients with elevated liver enzymes need further evaluation. The presence of liver disease should be assessed. If the transaminases are elevated, the patient needs to be assessed for therapy. The indication for therapy in chronic hepatitis C is ALT elevated more than 1.5 x N for six months. Again, a liver biopsy is advisable but not mandatory.

Interferon therapy

The treatment for chronic hepatitis C is interferon, 3 million IU three times/week for 12 months (Reichard, Foberg et al., 1994). On this regimen about 30 per cent of patients will remit (i.e., will have normal ALT more than six months after completion of therapy). The response rate is decreased by several factors,

333

including the concentration of hepatitis virus particles in serum, the genotype of the hepatitis C virus and the presence of cirrhosis. None of these factors alone is sufficient to allow withholding of therapy, but in combination they may predict treatment failure with sufficient probability as to make treatment not worth undertaking.

Some patients who will fail therapy can be identified early. Failure of the transaminases to normalize after two months of therapy predicts treatment failure. There is no point in treating these patients beyond two months. There does not appear to be any advantage to increasing the dose of interferon in such patients (Lin, Roach et al., 1995).

TABLE 3: Factors Predictive of a Sustained Beneficial Response to Interferon Alfa in Patients with Chronic Hepatitis[†]

Chronic Hepatitis B	Chronic Hepatitis C
Short duration of disease	Short duration of disease
High serum aminotransferase concentrations[††]	Young age
Active liver disease with fibrosis[††]	Absence of cirrhosis, or minimal amounts of hepatic fibrosis[††]
Low HBV DNA levels[††]	Low HCV RNA levels[††]
Wild-type (HBeAg-positive) virus	Genotype 2 or 3 or absence of a high degree of genetic heterogeneity (quasi-species)[††]
Absence of immunosuppression	Low hepatic iron stores

[†] Reprinted with permission from Hoofnagle & Di Bisceglie, 1997. Copyright 1997, *New England Journal of Medicine*.
[††] This factor is one most frequently associated with a high likelihood of response to therapy.

CONTRAINDICATIONS TO INTERFERON THERAPY

Patients who continue to drink or to use substances should not be treated. Interferon therapy is difficult and requires a high degree of compliance if it is to be successful. Patients who are actively abusing alcohol or drugs may not be able to comply adequately with treatment. In addition, IDUs run the risk of reinfection with hepatitis C while on therapy.

Interferon is contraindicated in the presence of autoimmune diseases as it is an immune stimulant. There are several reports of exacerbation of autoimmune diseases on interferon therapy, including psoriasis and ulcerative colitis. The sole exception may be autoimmune thyroiditis because long-term hypothyroidism may be an acceptable price to pay for some patients. Interferon also suppresses the bone marrow. Thus significant thrombocytopenia and granulocytopenia are also contraindications. Interferon can cause depression, and suicides have been recorded. Therefore interferon should not be used in patients with severe depression or psychoses. Hepatic decompensation is a contraindication to interferon use. In hepatitis B, an interferon-induced flare may be fatal. In hepatitis C, patients with decompensation are unlikely to have any long-term benefit even from successful treatment. They are also less likely to respond to treatment and should become candidates for liver transplantation rather than interferon.

TABLE 4: Side-Effects of Interferon Alfa†

SYSTEMIC EFFECTS	Fatigue, fever, headache, myalgia, arthralgia, backache, anorexia, weight loss, nausea, vomiting, diarrhea, abdominal cramps, hair loss and hypersensitivity reactions.
NEUROLOGICAL EFFECTS	Difficulty concentrating, lack of motivation, sleep disturbance, delirium, disorientation, coma, seizures, electroencephalographic changes, decrease in hearing, tinnitus, dizziness, vertigo, decrease in vision, retinal hemorrhages and cotton-wool spots.
PSYCHOLOGICAL EFFECTS	Anxiety, irritability, depression, social withdrawal, decreased libido, paranoid or suicidal ideation, and return of craving for alcohol or drugs.
HEMATOLOGICAL EFFECTS	Decrease in platelet count, white cell count and hematocrit.
IMMUNOLOGICAL EFFECTS	Increased susceptibility to bacterial infections, especially bronchitis, sinusitis, furuncles and urinary tract infections. In rare instances: pneumonia, lung abscess, brain abscess, septicemia and bacterial peritonitis.

Table 4 continued

AUTOIMMUNE EFFECTS	Development of autoantibodies and anti-interferon antibodies, hyperthyroidism, hypothyroidism, lichen planus, diabetes, hemolytic anemia, thrombocy-topenic purpura and lupus-like syndromes.
Other	In rare instances: pneumonia, proteinuria, interstitial nephritis, nephrotic syndrome, cardiac arrhythmia, congestive heart failure and acute exacerbation of liver disease.

† Reprinted with permission from Hoofnagle & Di Bisceglie, 1997. Copyright 1997, *New England Journal of Medicine*.

HEPATOCELLULAR CARCINOMA

Both hepatitis B and hepatitis C are associated with an increased risk of hepato-cellular carcinoma (HCC). In hepatitis B this can occur in the non-cirrhotic liver, whereas in hepatitis C this only occurs in patients with cirrhosis. The high frequency of HCC in these patients has led to the development of programs to screen such patients with alphafetoprotein and ultrasound at regular intervals. To date there is no evidence that screening is effective in reducing the mortality from the disease. Nonetheless, screening has become so widespread that it is difficult not to provide it. However, screening should be selective. In hepatitis B, screening should not start before age 30. Patients who are HBeAg-positive are less likely to get HCC since they are relatively early in the course of their disease and may therefore not be suitable for screening. Patients with decompensated liver disease should not be screened because, in Canada, liver transplantation is seldom an option for such patients.

In patients with hepatitis C the presence of cirrhosis is a necessary prerequisite for screening. Hepatic decompensation is not a factor because liver transplantation is available. However, most liver transplantation programs will not transplant patients who are not rehabilitated from their addiction. Such patients should probably also not be screened.

MANAGEMENT OF CONTACTS

Patients with hepatitis B may transmit disease to their sexual partners and family members. All such contacts should be screened for hepatitis B. In many jurisdictions, public health authorities are responsible for this contact tracing, hepatitis B testing and vaccination. However, this is not equally well carried out in all jurisdictions. Thus the physician should ensure that appropriate follow-up has been provided for contacts.

In hepatitis C, sexual transmission is less of a problem. Sexual transmission of hepatitis C may occur, albeit at very low efficiency (Setoguchi, Kajihara et al., 1994). Therefore the spouses of infected patients should be tested. Repeated testing of the spouse in monogamous relationships is probably not necessary. However, to the extent that it can be done, contact tracing among IDUs is important. All those who shared needles with the index case should be traced (if possible), and tested.

EDITOR'S NOTE[†]

From the time that this section was written, significant progress in the treatment of hepatitis C has been made. Until recently, the treatment for chronic HCV was monotherapy with interferon, 3 million IU three times/week for 12 months. Ribavirin is a synthetic guanosine analogue that eliminates the HCV when administered concomitantly with interferon alfa-2b. The combination of interferon alfa-2b and ribavirin in marketed in Canada as Rebetron®. Recent randomized clinical trials have demonstrated that Rebetron is more effective than interferon alone, either as an initial treatment or as a retreatment of patients who have failed initial interferon treatment (Davis, Esteban-Mur et al., 1998; Poynard, Marcellin et al., 1998; McHutchinson, Stuart et al., 1998).

[†] Peter Selby, Ed.

12.3

HIV AND SUBSTANCE ABUSE

David C. Marsh, MD

TRANSMISSION

The worldwide epidemic of human immunodeficiency virus (HIV) infection has significantly increased the problems associated with drug use on many levels. Injection drug use poses the direct risk of HIV transmission through contaminated needles or injection equipment. Non-injection drug use, including alcohol consumption, increases the likelihood of behaviors that put one at risk of infection such as unsafe sex or unsafe needle use (Second National Workshop on HIV, Alcohol and Other Drug Use, 1994). Moreover, in most developed countries HIV infection among drug users is linked to heterosexual transmission, often to non-drug-using partners, and vertical transmission from mother to child.

PREVALENCE

HIV seroprevalence in populations using injection drugs varies widely from location to location, and over relatively short periods of time. In Canada, HIV seroprevalence among injection drug users in Vancouver was four per cent in 1992–1993 and 23 per cent in 1996–1997. In Toronto, the rate was 4.5 per cent in 1991–1992 and 9.5 per cent in 1997. Montreal's rate of HIV seroprevalence among IDUs was five per cent in 1988 and 19.5 per cent in 1997 (Health Canada, 1998). It has been suggested that once levels of infection reach 10 per cent of an injecting population, spread of the virus can increase exponentially (Second National Workshop on HIV, Alcohol and Other Drug Use, 1994). In Brooklyn, New York, the seroprevalence is 50 per cent. In Edinburgh, Scotland, seroprevalence among injection drug users increased from five per cent in 1983 to 57 per cent in 1985. In Bangkok, Thailand, rates rose from one per cent in 1987 to 43 per cent in 1988. In both Edinburgh and Bangkok the explosive spread of HIV was associated with the limited availability of sterile injection equipment. With the potential for rapid spread of HIV within a given population it is important for HIV testing, with appropriate pre- and post-test counselling, to be incorporated into all drug treatment programs (see Table 5).

TABLE 5: Counselling Checklist for HIV Testing

PRE-TEST

☐ Clearly establish the history of risk and communicate reasons for test.

☐ Review basics of HIV transmission and methods of risk reduction, including using needle exchanges.

☐ Discuss sexual activity and preference and encourage safe sex practices.

☐ Fully explore the implications for the individual of a positive result, including establishing how the result will be communicated and the availability of social supports.

☐ Obtain informed consent.

☐ Ensure confidentiality.

☐ Plan a follow-up appointment.

POST-TEST

If seronegative
☐ Convey result with clear explanation of seroconversion and message that recent risks would require retesting in three to nine months.

☐ Strongly encourage safer sex practices and the use of sterile needles and needle exchange.

☐ Stress that a negative result is not a licence for high-risk behavior.

If seropositive
☐ Convey result with a clear explanation of the implications.

☐ Strongly encourage safe sex and safe injection practice for secondary prevention.

Table 5 continued

☐ Discuss notification of contacts and implications of local public health policies.

☐ Refer to appropriate local peer support programs.

☐ Arrange follow-up with HIV primary care physician and drug treatment services.

ALWAYS

☐ **Most importantly,** carefully assess psychological impact, bearing in mind the high risk for suicide at this time. Counter this by ensuring that social supports are available and offering hope for a future with appropriate management of HIV infection.

PREVENTION

A comprehensive harm-reduction approach to drug use is required to prevent the rapid spread of HIV infection. Elements of this approach include the ready availability of clean syringes, access to flexible and liberal methadone programs and an end to social marginalization and criminalization of drug users (Riley, 1993). Nowhere is the challenge of prevention as acute as within correctional institutions. For example, in Canadian prisons, hepatitis C seroprevalence, a marker for previous use of contaminated injection equipment and therefore high risk of acquiring HIV infection, is between 28 and 40 per cent of *all* inmates (Jurgens, 1994). Many individuals report sharing injection equipment for the first time while incarcerated, and needle exchanges or other preventive measures are rarely available to inmates.

Methadone maintenance

One key element in secondary prevention of HIV transmission is the provision of methadone maintenance to HIV-positive individuals with opioid dependence. These individuals should be fast-tracked for admission to methadone treatment programs. Methadone maintenance dramatically reduces the frequency of injection drug use. Given the rapid rate of relapse to daily needle use following cessation of methadone, a good argument can be made for all HIV-positive patients with opioid dependence to be maintained on methadone for life.

340

COMPLICATIONS

HIV infection in a drug user adds complications in terms of medical management. By far the most common cause of death associated with illicit drug use is suicide (Single, Robson et al., 1996). This must be borne in mind when HIV testing is offered and test results delivered to individuals with a history of substance abuse.

Several physical complications of drug use can resemble sequelae of HIV infection, which adds complexity to the diagnosis once infected individuals become ill. Cocaine-induced multi-infarct dementia can be indistinguishable clinically from AIDS cognitive-motor complex. Pneumonitis produced by crack cocaine inhalation has been misdiagnosed as *Pneumocystis carinii* pneumonia. Hepatitis B and C must be added to the list of infective agents, which can account for elevated liver function tests in HIV-positive injection drug users.

Many infections associated with injection drug use have a more malignant course in the presence of HIV infection. These include pulmonary and extra-pulmonary tuberculosis, human papilloma virus (and associated cancer of the cervix), genital and oral herpes simplex virus infection and primary and secondary syphilis. There are conflicting data concerning the course of chronic hepatitis B and C infection in those who are HIV-positive. However, acquisition of any viral hepatitis after the immune-suppressive effects of HIV are in place can precipitate an acute, fulminant hepatitis. The range of organisms that can cause infective endocarditis expands as the patient's CD4 cell count falls. Bacterial pneumonia is more common and more deadly in injection drug users. When combined with HIV infection, mortality approaches 15 per cent (Selwyn, Feingold et al., 1988).

HIV and active substance use

Finally, active drug use significantly complicates management of HIV infection. Compliance with antiretroviral and antituberculosis medication is often poor. For those on methadone maintenance therapy, compliance can be improved by daily dispensing of all medications at the time of methadone administration. Peripheral intravenous access is rarely available and placement of an indwelling central line often provides a site for self-administration of drugs. Non-specific complaints about sleep or generalized pain are common in advanced HIV infection. However, benzodiazepines, barbiturates and opioids should be used with caution in patients with a history of substance abuse. Some medications (such as rifampin and phenytoin) increase the metabolism of methadone, requiring dosage adjustments to prevent withdrawal. In other cases pharmacokinetic interactions are known but the clinical significance is not as clear (such as inter-

341

actions between methadone and zidovudine or fluconazole). Moreover, the potential interactions between antiretrovirals, antibiotics and illicit drugs are largely unexplored.

LOOKING TO THE FUTURE

In the face of the challenges of concurrent HIV infection and substance abuse, pessimism can come easily. Nevertheless, there are some grounds for hope. Some studies have found a high rate of long-term non-progressors among drug users. Methadone maintenance clearly leads to improvement in CD4 count, immune status and clinical course.

The increasing overlap between two epidemics facing modern society — HIV infection and substance abuse — will continue to require the development of innovative measures which limit the consequences of substance abuse for individuals and communities.

R E F E R E N C E S

Ball, J.C. & Ross, A. (1991). *The Effectiveness Of Methadone Maintenance Treatment: Patients, Programs, Services, and Outcome.* New York: Springer-Verlag.

Brunetto, M.R., Oliveri, F., Colombatto, P., Capalbo, M., Barbera, C. & Bonino, F. (1995). Treatment of chronic anti-HBe-positive hepatitis B with interferon-alpha. *Journal of Hepatology, 22(1 Suppl),* 42-44.

Coates, R.A., Rankin, J.G., Lamothe, F., Arshinoff, R., Raboud, J., Millson, M.E., Halliday, M.L., Bruneau, J., Soto, J., Vincelette, J., Brabant, M.& Fauvel, M. (1992). Needle sharing behaviour among injection drug users (IDUs) in treatment in Montreal and Toronto, 1988-1989. *Canadian Journal of Public Health, 83(1),* 38-41.

Davis, G.L., Balart, L.A., Schiff, E.R., Lindsay, K. & Bodenheimer, H.C., Jr. (1989). Treatment of chronic hepatitis C with recombinant interferon alpha; a multicenter randomized, controlled trial. *New England Journal of Medicine, 321(22),* 1501-1506.

Davis, G.L., Esteban-Mur, R., Rustig, V., Hoefs, J. Gordon, S.C., Trepo, C., Shiffman, M.L., Zeuzem, S., Craxi, A., Ling, M-H. & Albrecht, J. (1998). Interferon alfa-2b alone or in comparison with ribavirin for the treatment of relapse of chronic hepatitis C. *New England Journal of Medicine, 339(21),* 1493-1499.

Di Bisceglie, A.M., Martin, P., Kassianides, C., Lisker-Melman, M., Murray, L., Waggoner, J., Goodman, Z., Banks, S.M. & Hoofnagle, J.H. (1989). Recombinant interferon alpha therapy for chronic hepatitis C: A randomized, double-blind, placebo-controlled trial. *New England Journal of Medicine, 321(22)*, 1506-1510.

Garfein, R.S., Vlahov, D., Galai, N., Dohery, M.C. & Nelson, K.E., (1996). Viral infections in short-term injection drug users: The prevalence of the hepatitis C, hepatitis B, human immunodeficiency, and human T-lymphotrophic viruses. *American Journal of Public Health, 86(5)*, 655-661.

Health Canada. (1998). *HIV/AIDS Epi Update*. Ottawa: Health Canada.

Hoofnagle, J.H. & Di Bisceglie, A.M. (1997). The treatment of chronic viral hepatitis. *New England Journal of Medicine, 36(5)*, 347-356.

Jurgens, R. (1994). *HIV/AIDS in Prisons: Final Report of the Expert Committee on AIDS and Prisons*. Ottawa: Correctional Services Canada.

Lin, R., Roach, E., Zimmerman, M., Strasser, S. & Farrell, G.C. (1995). Interferon alfa-2b for chronic hepatitis C: Effects of dose increment and duration of treatment on response rates. Results of the first multicentre Australian trial. Australia Hepatitis C Study Group. *Journal of Hepatology, 23(5)*, 487-496.

McHutchinson, J.G., Gordon, S.C., Schiff, E.R. Shiffman, M.L., Lee, W.M., Rustig, V., Goodman, Z.D., Ling, M-H., Cort, S. & Albrecht, J. Interferon alfa-2b alone or in combination with ribavirin as initial treatment for chronic hepatitis C. *New England Journal of Medicine, 339(21)*, 1485-1492.

Metzger, D., Woody, G., De Philippis, D.D., McLellan, A.T., O'Brien, C.P. & Platt, J.J. (1991). Risk factors for needle sharing among methadone-treated patients. *American Journal of Psychiatry, 148(5)*, 636-640.

Osmond, D.H., Padian, N.S., Sheppard, H.W., Glass, S., Shiboski, S.C. & Reingold, A. (1993). Risk factors for hepatitis C virus seropositivity in heterosexual couples. *Journal of the American Medical Association, 269(3)*, 361-365.

Perrillo, R.P., Schiff, E.R., Davis, G.L., Bodenheimer, H.C., Jr., Lindsay, K., Payne, J., Dienstag, J.L., O'Brien, C., Tamburro, C., Jacobson, I.M. et al. (1990). A randomized, controlled trial of interferon alfa-2b alone and after prednisone withdrawal for the treatment of chronic hepatitis B. The Hepatitis Interventional Therapy Group. *New England Journal of Medicine, 323(5)*, 295-301.

Poynard, T., Marcellin, P., Lee, S.S., Niederau, C., Minuk, G.S., Ideo, G., Bain, V., Heathcote, J., Zeuzem, S., Trepo, C., Albrecht, J. (1998). Randomised trial of interferon alpha2b plus placebo for 48 weeks for treatment of chronic infection with hepatitis C virus, *Lancet, 352(9138),* 1426-1432.

Reichard, O., Foberg, U., Fryden, A., Mattsson, L., Norkrans, G., Sonnerborg, A., Wejstal, R., Yun, Z.B. & Weiland, O. (1994). High sustained response rate and clearance of viremia in chronic hepatitis C after treatment with interferon-alpha 2b for 60 weeks. *Hepatology, 19(2),* 280-285.

Remis, R.S., Millson, M., Major, C. (1997, July). *The HIV Epidemic Among Injection Drug Users in Ontario: The Situation in 1997* (Report prepared for the AIDS Bureau, Ontario Ministry of Health). Toronto: Ontario Ministry of Health.

Riley, D.M. (1993). *The Policy and Practice of Harm Reduction.* Ottawa: Centre on Substance Abuse.

Samet, J.H., Shevitz, A., Fowle, J. & Singer, D.E. (1990). Hospitalization decision in febrile intravenous drug users. *American Journal of Medicine, 89(1),* 53-57.

Second National Workshop on HIV, Alcohol and Other Drug Use. (1994). *Second National Workshop on HIV, Alcohol and Other Drug Use — Proceedings.* Ottawa: Canadian Centre on Substance Abuse.

Selwyn, P.A., Feingold, A.R., Hartel, D., Schoenbaum, E.E., Alderman, M.H., Klein, R.S. & Friedland, G.H. (1988). Increased risk of bacterial pneumonia in HIV-related intravenous drug users without AIDS. *AIDS, 2(4),* 267-272.

Setoguchi, Y., Kajihara, S., Hara, T., Motomura, M., Mizuta, T., Wada, I., Yamamoto, K. & Sakai, T. (1994). Analysis of nucleotide sequences of hepatitis C virus isolates from husband-wife pairs. *Journal of Gastroenterology & Hepatology, 9(5),* 468-471.

Shindo, M., Di Bisceglie, A.M., Cheung, L., Wai-Kuo Shih, J., Cristiano, K., Feinstone, S.M. & Hoofnagle, J.H. (1991). Decrease in serum hepatitis C viral RNA during alpha-interferon therapy for chronic hepatitis C. *Annals of Internal Medicine, 115(9),* 700-704.

Single, E., Robson, L., Xie, X. & Rehm, J. (1996). *The Costs of Substance Use in Canada.* Ottawa: Canadian Centre on Substance Abuse.

Tassopoulos, N.C., Papaevangelou, G.J., Sjogren, M.H., Roumeliotou-Karayannis, A., Gerin, J.L. & Purcell, R.H. (1987). Natural history of acute hepatitis B surface antigen-positive hepatitis in Greek adults. *Gastroenterology, 92(6),* 1844-1850.

U.S. Public Health Service Inter-Agency. (1991). U.S. Public Health Service inter-agency guidelines for screening donors of blood, plasma, organs, tissues, and semen for evidence of hepatitis B and hepatitis C. *Canada Diseases Weekly Report, 17(46),* 251-257.

van den Hoek, J.A., van Haastrecht, H.J., Goudsmit, J., de Wolf, F. & Coutinho, R.A. (1990). Prevalence, incidence, and risk factors of hepatitis C virus infection among drug users in Amsterdam. *Journal of Infectious Diseases, 162(4),* 823-826.

Vento, S., Garfano, T., Renzini, C., Cainelli, F., Casali, F., Ghironzi, G., Ferraro, T. & Concia, E. (1998). Fulminant hepatitis associated with hepatitis A virus superinfection in patients with chronic hepatitis C. *New England Journal of Medicine, 338(5),* 286-290.

Wolk, J., Wodak, A., Morlet, A., Guinan, J. J. & Gold, J. (1990). HIV-related risk-taking behaviour, knowledge and serostatus of intravenous drug users in Sydney. *Medical Journal of Australia, 152(9),* 453-458.

Wong, V., Wreghitt, T.G. & Alexander, G.J. (1996). Prospective study of hepatitis B vaccination in patients with chronic hepatitis C. *British Medical Journal, 312(7042),* 1336-1337.

Zeldis, J.B., Jain, S., Kuramoto, I.K., Richards, C., Sazama, K., Samuels, S., Holland, P.V. & Flynn, N. (1992). Seroepidemiology of viral infections among intravenous drug users in northern California. *Western Journal of Medicine, 156(1),* 30-35.

Older Adults and Substance Use

13 OLDER ADULTS AND SUBSTANCE USE

13

OLDER ADULTS AND SUBSTANCE USE

Luis Fornazzari MD

A GROWING AT-RISK POPULATION

The population of those aged 60 years and over will triple worldwide during the first quarter of the 21st century, growing from 600 million in 2000 to 1,135 million in 2025. This explosive growth in the number of older adults is obviously an important sociological event, posing significant, multifaceted challenges to medical practitioners.

An elderly population disproportionately experiences, among other pathologies, emotional and mental health disorders when compared with a younger cohort (Blazer, Crowell & George, 1987). Within the substance-abusing population of older adults there is a higher incidence of both primary and secondary mental health diagnoses. Moreover, in part due to biological changes associated with aging, the elderly have an increased sensitivity to the effects of alcohol and other psychoactive drugs (Linnoila, Erwin et al., 1980).

EPIDEMIOLOGY

Alcohol abuse and dependence

Studies of populations of older adults estimate the prevalence of alcohol abuse and dependence to be in the range of 0.6 per cent to 3.7 per cent. Studies using criteria based on the DSM-IV have reported rates of 1.2 per cent for men and 0.3 per cent for women (Grant, Harford, et al., 1994). Data on heavy drinking show that among older adults 31 per cent of men and 22 per cent of women reported consuming more than three drinks per day (Paganini-Hill, Ross & Henderson, 1986). In a study conducted in a hospital setting in England, it was found that of elderly patients admitted, 7.8 per cent abused alcohol. Of those who abused alcohol, 24 per cent of the admissions were alcohol-related (Mangion, Platt & Syam, 1992). In the United States, 1.1 per cent of all admissions of Medicare beneficiaries in 1989 were due to alcohol-related causes, a rate similar to that for admissions due to myocardial infarction (Adams, Yuan et al., 1993). In primary care settings and outpatient clinics the estimates of rates of alcohol dependence among older patients range from six per cent to 10 per cent (Magruder-Habib, Saltz & Barron, 1986). These statistics are even higher in emergency facilities where almost 15 per cent of elderly patients present with alcohol dependence (Tabisz, Badger et al., 1991).

Substance Use Disorders

The data on Substance Use Disorders in older adults are less well studied. Indirect data suggest a potentially serious problem. Older adults comprise no more than 12 per cent of the North American population, but they consume approximately one-third of all prescription medications (Arnett, Blank et al., 1990). We should also consider that geriatric patients commonly experience anxiety, insomnia and pain syndromes. So the potential for abusing anxiolytics, hypnotics and analgesics is quite high.

The point at which the use of a psychoactive drug becomes abuse, dependence or harmful use is not well defined (Graham, Saunders et al., 1995). But for both Alcohol Use Disorders and Substance Use Disorders, early and late onset abusers are well characterized. In all cases, it is quite difficult to know the role the clinician or the patient plays in the development of this disorder. In general, when the use of any prescription medication results in physical, functional or psychosocial impairment, it should be considered a Substance Use Disorder (Reid & Anderson, 1997).

MORBIDITY OF ALCOHOL USE DISORDERS AND SUBSTANCE USE DISORDERS

Once alcohol is in the bloodstream, it affects all tissues in the body. It has been shown that measurable physical damage is detectable in every human system. Reports indicate that over 90 per cent of actively drinking older alcoholics present with a major health problem (Schuckit, 1982; Smith, 1986).

The pharmacokinetics of alcohol (absorption, metabolism, and excretion) are not altered in the elderly. But changes in body components, such as a decrease in lean body mass and a diminution in alcohol dehydrogenase, the degrading enzyme of alcohol, leads to 20 per cent higher blood alcohol concentrations in the elderly when compared with younger adults (Vestal, McGuire et al., 1977).

Some of the more important medical complications of alcoholism in the elderly are:

• Hematological and immune system disorders, manifested as anemias and decreased ability to control infections (e.g., pneumonias) and malignancies (esophageal, prostrate and liver cancer). In drinkers who smoke, there is a tenfold increase in pharyngeal cancer.
• Hypertensive and cardiovascular disorders such as cardiac arrhythmias, myocardial infarction, and cardiomyopathy and an associated increased incidence of hemorrhagic stroke.
• Cirrhosis and other liver diseases.
• Chronic gastritis and gastric ulcers.
• Malnutrition.

Special considerations in this population include alcohol-related physical damage, cognitive impairment, loss of functional abilities and the interaction of alcohol with other prescribed medications.

Alcohol-related injuries and physical damage
Older adults are at greater risk for alcohol-related injuries. Alcohol-related injuries and physical damage are due in part to the effects of alcohol on balance, gait and cognition, in combination with the effects of aging on bones, muscles and the circulatory system. All these factors contribute to an increase in falls, fractures and convalescence-related complications of immobilization such as thromboembolism (Ziring & Adler, 1991).

Moreover, heavy alcohol intake can lead to a vascular compromise of bone structures, particularly to the head of the femur (avascular necrosis) requiring hip replacement without a particular history of trauma (Rosenkranz, 1983).

Cognitive impairment and alcoholic dementia
Specific functions such as psychomotor performance are more affected in older adults who use alcohol than among those who do not (Vogel-Sprott & Barrett, 1984). In young adults, chronic alcohol abuse and/or dependence leads to memory impairment and brain imaging changes that improve with abstinence (Carlen & Wilkinson, 1983). However, even though we understand that morphological changes to the brain and memory impairment occur, alcohol-related dementia remains poorly understood among elderly patients. This, in part, is due to the clinical characteristic of the disorder which is rather unspecific in the aging population. Older adults usually experience a decrease in cognitive functioning due to physiological reasons. Another factor is the lack of specific neuropathological markers, as in Alzheimer's disease and frontotemporal dementias, where clinicopathological correlations are possible. Also, the

351

quantity and the duration of alcohol consumption necessary to produce severe cognitive impairment compatible with the diagnosis of dementia remain uncertain. All these considerations do not apply to the well-known effect of alcohol in Wernicke's encephalopathy and the Korsakoff amnestic syndrome.

Interactions with other prescribed and over-the-counter medications

Aging is frequently associated with increased use of prescribed medications. Between 60 per cent and 78 per cent of older adults receive some form of prescribed medication. The percentage using over-the-counter or self-administered medications is not known (Chrischilles, Foley et al., 1992). The interaction of alcohol with medications is a very serious issue. Acute and/or chronic use of alcohol may either prolong or decrease the half-life of medications (Forster, Pollow & Stoller, 1993). One study reported that 27 per cent of older adults combine alcohol and ASA, while 11 per cent combine alcohol and sedative/hypnotics (Adams, 1995).

SUBSTANCE USE AND OLDER ADULTS

The deleterious effects of analgesic abuse in elderly populations are now being reported (Elseviers & De Broe, 1998). In developed countries, analgesics and non-steroidal anti-inflammatory substances (NSAIDs) are among the most frequently used pharmaceutical products, particularly among the elderly. Classic analgesics like paracetamol, salicylates and pyrazolone derivatives are frequently used for minor pain syndromes and fever, while NSAIDs are used for arthritis and musculoskeletal disorders. Classical analgesic nephropathy is a chronic renal disease caused by the excessive consumption of analgesic mixtures containing at least two antipyretic analgesics combined with caffeine or codeine.

As with ethanol, benzodiazepines are central nervous system depressants that produce drowsiness, confusion, ataxia, dizziness and impaired motor coordination (Wattis, 1981). There are suggestions in the literature that the elderly may experience more severe complications from benzodiazepines, including rage reactions, delirium, dementias and depression (Solomon, Manepalli et al., 1993). An increase in fall rates has been reported in older adults taking either long- or short-acting benzodiazepines. These falls have devastating effects on mobility and cause hip fractures (Sorock & Shimkin, 1988).

CONCURRENT DISORDERS AND SUICIDE IN THE ELDERLY

The leading psychiatric diagnosis of hospitalized older adults is Depression. Over one-third of these patients have a Substance Use Disorder. Three-quarters of the group with a dual diagnosis abuse alcohol, while 29 per cent abuse other substances. Older adults with concurrent disorders are more frequently admitted for attempted suicide compared with those with a mental disorder diagnosis alone. Important consideration should be given to these findings in order to prevent depression and suicide in the elderly (Blixen, McDougall & Suen, 1997; Sadavoy, Smith et al., 1990).

SCREENING AND EARLY DETECTION

Screening and identification of substance use problems are important for early intervention and treatment. Physicians commonly miss drinking problems among elderly patients, especially women. All older adult patients should routinely be asked about alcohol use. (Techniques used in taking an alcohol history are outlined in Section 1.1.) Older patients who are reluctant to discuss their drinking can be asked questions like, "Do you ever have a drink during the holidays or at New Year's?" or "Do you sometimes have a drink to help you sleep?" Patient trust can be developed by assuring the patient, when appropriate: "Many people have one or two drinks under those circumstances." This approach helps patients admit to drinking without feeling ashamed or guilty.

Physicians should be alert to common and early presentations of alcohol use in the elderly, including unexplained falls and injuries, fatigue, failure to thrive, weight loss, confusion, depression, anxiety and insomnia, dyspepsia and ulcers and hypertension and arrhythmias. Information from family members can be invaluable in identifying alcohol problems.

Screening tools and older adults

Early detection at the primary care level is essential for early and successful intervention because it helps to avoid complications and added pathologies. The CAGE questionnaire (see Section 1.1, Table 2) does not appear to be ideally sensitive in the elderly population. However, when combined with questions on the quantity and frequency of drinking, the CAGE questionnaire can be effective in detecting problem drinking in this population (Adams, Barry & Fleming, 1996). Laboratory measures such as GGT and MCV also lack sensitivity and should not be used as sole screening measures, but can be used to confirm clinical suspicion and to monitor progress in treatment.

TREATMENT

Treatment of older adults with Alcohol Use Disorders, Substance Use Disorders and concurrent disorders is complex and may require specialized treatment approaches and treatment settings. Many of these patients are also coping with poor general health and may be experiencing loss. Any successful treatment program should consider the patient's physical and psychological condition and must involve the family or spouse. It is important to note that elderly alcoholics are as successful as younger alcoholics in treatment programs, though those in age-specific group treatment programs tend to stay in treatment longer (Atkinson, Tolson & Turner, 1993; Kofoed, Tolson et al., 1987).

Alcohol withdrawal management

Studies suggest that the severity and duration of alcohol withdrawal symptoms increase with age. Older patients have significantly more withdrawal symptoms, and of longer duration, compared with younger adults (nine days versus six days, respectively) (Brower, Mudd et al., 1994).

Older patients may require hospitalization for withdrawal management. As an emergency medical condition, correction of fluids and electrolytes and protection of the airways is mandatory. Prevention of Wernicke's encephalopathy with thiamine, symptomatic treatment of withdrawal symptoms and prevention of usual complications such as seizures and delirium tremens should be considered. The use of benzodiazepines, of proven efficacy in alcohol withdrawal, should be carefully guided by the use of standardized withdrawal assessment indexes, such as the Clinical Institute Withdrawal Assessment for Alcohol Scale (CIWA) (see also Section 3.2). When liver disease is suspected, the use of short-acting benzodiazepines, such as lorazepam, is preferred over long-acting diazepam.

Withdrawal management, other drugs

Any geriatric patient with a clinical picture characterized by forgetfulness, confusion, depression, anxiety, falls, incontinence, poor hygiene and sleep disturbance, and who is using a psychoactive drug, is a candidate for a trial of withdrawal management and abstinence. The withdrawal management should be carried out in hospital.

Rehabilitation

Treatment for older adults who abuse alcohol or other drugs should involve rehabilitation programs designed for geriatric patients and staffed by clinicians who possess a good understanding of aging and the complex issues faced by this population.

R E F E R E N C E S

Adams, W.L. (1995). Potential for adverse drug-alcohol interactions among retirement community residents. *Journal of the American Geriatrics Society, 43*(9), 1021-1025.

Adams, W.L., Barry K.L. & Fleming, M.L. (1996). Screening for problem drinking in older primary care patients. *Journal of the American Medical Association, 276(24),* 1964-1967.

Adams, W.L., Yuan, Z., Barboriak, J.J., Rimm, A.A., Adams, W.L.,Yuan, Z., et al. (1993). Alcohol-related hospitalizations of elderly people. Prevalence and geographic variation in the United States. *Journal of the American Medical Association, 270(10),* 1222-1225.

Arnett, R.H., Blank, L.A. Brown, A.P., Cowan, C.A., Donham, C.S., Freeland, M.S., Lazenby, H.C., Letsch, S.W., Levit, K.R., Maple, B.T. et al. (1990). National health expenditures, 1988. Office of National Cost Estimates. *Health Care Financing Review, 11(4),* 1-41.

Atkinson, R.M., Tolson, R.L. & Turner, J.A. (1993). Factors affecting outpatient treatment compliance of older male problem drinkers. *Journal of Studies on Alcohol, 54(1),* 102-106.

Blazer, D., Crowell, B.A. Jr. & George, L.K. (1987). Alcohol abuse and dependence in the rural South. *Archives of General Psychiatry, 44(8),* 736-740.

Blixen, C.E., McDougall, G.J. & Suen, L.J. (1997). Dual diagnosis in elders discharged from a psychiatric hospital. *International Journal of Geriatric Psychiatry, 12(3),* 307-313.

Brower, K.J., Mudd, S., Blow, F.C., Young, J.P. & Hill, E.M. (1994). Severity and treatment of alcohol withdrawal in elderly versus younger patients. *Alcoholism, Clinical and Experimental Research, 18(1),* 196-201.

Carlen, P & Wilkinson, A. (1983). Assessment of neurological dysfunction and recovery in alcoholics: CT scanning and other techniques. *Substance and Alcohol Actions/Misuse, 4(2-3),* 191-197.

Chrischilles, E.A., Foley, D.J., Wallace, R.B., Lemke, J.H., Semla, T.P., Hanlon, J.T., Glynn, R.J., Ostfeld, A.M. & Guralnik, J.M. (1992). Use of medications by persons 65 and over: Data from the established populations for epidemiologic studies of the elderly. *Journal of Gerontology, 47(5),* M137-M144.

Elseviers, M.M. & De Broe, M.E. (1998). Analgesic abuse in the elderly. Renal sequelae and management. *Drugs and Aging, 12(5),* 391-400.

Forster, L.E., Pollow, R. & Stoller, E.P. (1993). Alcohol use and potential risk for alcohol-related adverse drug reactions among community-based elderly. *Journal of Community Health, 18(4),* 225-239.

Graham, K., Saunders, S.J., Flower, M.C., Birchmore Timney, C., White-Campbell, M. & Pietropaolo, A. (1995). *Addiction Treatment for Older Adults: Evaluation of an Innovative Client-Centered Approach.* Binghamton, NY: Haworth Press.

Grant, B.F., Harford, T.C., Dawson, D.A., Chou, P., Dufour, M. & Pickering, R. (1994). Prevalence of DSM-IV alcohol abuse and dependence; United States, 1992. *Alcohol Health and Research World, 18,* 243-248.

Kofoed, L.L., Tolson, R.L., Atkinson, R.M., Toth, R.L. & Turner, J.A. (1987). Treatment compliance of older alcoholics: An elder-specific approach is superior to "mainstreaming." *Journal of Studies on Alcohol, 48(1),* 47-51.

Linnoila, M., Erwin, C.W., Ramm, D. & Cleveland, W.P. (1980). Effects of age and alcohol on psychomotor performance of men. *Journal of Studies on Alcohol, 41(5),* 488-495.

Magruder-Habib, K., Saltz, C.C. & Barron, P.M. (1986). Age-related patterns of alcoholism among veterans in ambulatory care. *Hospital and Community Psychiatry, 37(12),* 1251-1255.

Mangion, D.M., Platt, J.S. & Syam, V. (1992). Alcohol and acute medical admission of elderly people. *Age and Ageing, 21(5),* 362-367.

Paganini-Hill, A., Ross, R.K. & Henderson, B.E. (1986). Prevalence of chronic disease and health practices in a retirement community. *Journal of Chronic Diseases, 39(9),* 699-707.

Reid, M.C. & Anderson, P.A. (1997). Geriatric substance use disorders. *Medical Clinics of North America, 81(4),* 999-1016.

Rosenkranz, L. (1983). Aseptic necrosis of bone and chronic alcoholism. *Journal of Family Practice, 17(2),* 323-326.

Sadavoy, J., Smith, I., Conn, D.K. & Richards, B. (1990). Depression in geriatric patients with chronic medical illness. *International Journal of Geriatric Psychiatry, 5,* 187-189.

Schukit, M.A. (1982). A clinical review of alcohol, alcoholism and the elderly patient. *Journal of Clinical Psychiatry, 43(10),* 369-399.

Smith, J.W. (1986). Alcohol and disorders of the heart and skeletal muscles. In N.J. Estes & M.E. Heinemann (Eds.), *Alcoholism: Development, Consequences, and Interventions* (3rd ed.). St. Louis: C.V. Mosby.

Solomon, K., Manepalli, J., Ireland, G.A. & Mahon, G.M. (1993). Alcoholism and prescription drug abuse in the elderly: St. Louis University grand rounds. *Journal of the American Geriatrics Society, 41(1),* 57-69.

Sorock, G.S. & Shimkin, E.E. (1988). Benzodiazepine sedatives and the risk of falling in a community-dwelling elderly cohort. *Archives of Internal Medicine, 148(11),* 2441-2444.

Tabisz, E., Badger, M., Meatherall, R., Jacyk, W.R., Fuchs, D. & Grymonpore, R. (1991). Identification of chemical abuse in the elderly admitted to emergency rooms. *Clinical Gerontologist, 11,* 27-39.

Vestal, R.E., McGuire, E.A., Tobin, J.D., Andres, R., Norris, A.H. & Mezey, E. (1977). Aging and ethanol metabolism. *Clinical Pharmacology and Therapeutics, 21(3),* 343-354.

Vogel-Sprott, M. & Barrett, P. (1984). Age, drinking habits and the effects of alcohol. *Journal of Studies on Alcohol, 45(6),* 517-521.

Wattis, J.P. (1981). Alcohol problems in the elderly. *Journal of the American Geriatrics Society, 29(3),* 131-134.

Ziring, D.J. & Adler, A.G. (1991). Alcoholism. Are you missing the diagnosis? *Postgraduate Medicine, 89(5),* 139-145.

Women and Substance Use

TABLES AND FIGURES

14

WOMEN AND SUBSTANCE USE

Peter Selby, MD, and Lynn Wilson, MD

OVERVIEW

Alcohol and drug problems are less likely to be recognized in women than men, especially among elderly women or those in high socioeconomic categories. The patterns of use, and reasons that women use drugs, differ significantly from those of men. Women are more likely to see their alcohol consumption as a response to a specific traumatic event or as a way of coping with stressful social situations. Biological, psychological, social and cultural factors account for differences between male and female patients in terms of the effects of substances of abuse and responses to treatment interventions.

Little is known about treatment effectiveness for women. More programs tailored to women are needed. A comprehensive approach to the female substance user is recommended, including the provision of adequate social support, medical and obstetric care, family involvement in therapy, child care, educational and vocational assistance, programs for survivors of sexual abuse and/or violence, treatment of concurrent disorders such as depression, women-only therapy groups, treatment for multiple drug abuse and parenting programs.

EPIDEMIOLOGY

Alcohol use

In Canada, 67 per cent of women report using alcohol. This represents only a slight increase in drinking rates since the 1960s, despite the dramatic changes in women's social roles. Men consume alcohol in greater quantity and frequency than women. One per cent of women consume 15 or more drinks per week (compared with 10 per cent of men), and 5 per cent of women consume eight to 14 drinks per week (Canadian Centre on Substance Abuse & Addiction Research Foundation, 1997).

Alcohol use during pregnancy

Drinking during pregnancy has declined dramatically in recent years, but 25 per cent of pregnant women still report having consumed alcohol in the previous month. In 1992–1993, there were 250 pregnant women treated for substance dependence in Canada (Canadian Centre on Substance Abuse & Addiction Research Foundation, 1997). This is most likely a gross under-representation of the true prevalence of substance misuse during pregnancy.

Stewart and Streiner (1994), using a General Health Questionnaire, surveyed 561 pregnant women over 20 weeks' gestation, drawn from both urban and rural, specialist and primary care practices in Ontario. Of the 466 respondents, 22.7 per cent reported regular weekly drinking of about 1.97 standard drinks, 8.2 per cent drank more than seven standard drinks and 3 per cent drank more than 14 standard drinks per week. Women who drank more than seven drinks per week were more likely to be socially disadvantaged, unmarried, unemployed and to use tobacco and other drugs. These women were also more likely to have been physically abused and have emotional problems or psychiatric conditions. Fried and co-investigators (1980) found that use of alcohol during pregnancy by heavy social drinkers declined during the last two trimesters.

Prescription drug use

Women have historically been more likely to use "socially acceptable" (i.e., prescription) drugs. For example, in a Canadian national survey, 5.3 per cent of women reported using tranquillizers in the past year, as compared with 3.4 per cent of men. Use of prescription opioids in the past year was reported by 14.1 per cent of women versus 12 per cent of men. And in the past year, 5.4 per cent of women (compared with 3.7 per cent of men) had used sleeping pills (Canadian Centre on Substance Abuse & Addiction Research Foundation, 1997). On the other hand, more men use illicit drugs, with the exception of stimulants. Of women attending Alcoholics Anonymous, 40 per cent are also addicted to another drug.

Factors contributing to substance use

Various studies have reported that 44 to 80 per cent of women treated for alcohol dependence are survivors of sexual abuse. Female victims of violence are twice as likely to use sleeping pills or tranquillizers. As with men, alcohol-dependent women have a higher familial incidence of alcohol dependence (Ferrence, Ross & Janecek, 1990). Women suffering from alcohol abuse and/or dependence are more likely than men to have a concurrent disorder, such as major depression. In the past, women were labelled as "sicker" and "less motivated" because the antecedents, consequences and treatment needs of male substance abuse were considered to be the norm.

Tobacco use

In Canada, more men than women are smokers — 28 per cent versus 26 per cent. A growing concern is the fact that more young women than young men are choosing to smoke. Of females between 10 and 19 years of age, 15.6 per cent are current smokers in contrast to 14.9 per cent of young men of the same age (Canadian Centre on Substance Abuse & Addiction Research Foundation, 1997).

Lung cancer has been the leading cause of death among women in the United States since 1986, and in Canada since 1993 (Peto, Lopez et al., 1994; National Cancer Institute of Canada, 1993). This is attributable to the increased prevalence of female smoking in the period following the Second World War.

SCREENING

All women should be screened from adolescence onwards for the use of drugs, including over-the-counter and herbal remedies. Women who are at high risk are described as young, involved with a substance-using peer group, having a heavy-drinking spouse, depressed, experiencing a life crisis and frequently using alcohol and/or other drugs to cope with daily problems.

Screening tests such as T-ACE and TWEAK (see Section 1) are more specific than the CAGE, especially in pregnant women. The TWEAK and T-ACE questionnaires have about 90 per cent sensitivity and 78 per cent specificity, while the CAGE has 49 per cent sensitivity with 93 per cent specificity to detect women who are hazardous drinkers.

It is imperative to assess substance use in women who present with psychiatric problems such as depression, anxiety and eating disorders, or those with histories of sexual abuse or who are victims of violence.

Clinical indicators

The physician should be aware of the ways in which female substance abusers may present. These indicators may be medical, psychosocial/behavioral or historical (see table below).

363

TABLE 1: Indicators Suggesting Alcohol or Other Drug Dependence in Women

MEDICAL	• gastritis, esophagitis, non-specific dyspepsia, anorexia • neuropathy • hypertension • liver disease • menstrual disorder • macrocytosis, thrombocytopenia • sexually transmitted disease • obstetric complications
PSYCHOSOCIAL/BEHAVIORAL	• interpersonal conflicts • domestic violence • employment problems • trauma • depression, anxiety, insomnia, suicidal ideation • missed medical appointments • alcohol on the breath at appointments
HISTORICAL	• alcohol- or drug-abusing partner • frequent primary care or emergency room visits • psychiatric treatment or hospital admissions • low birthweight infants or children with FAS/FAE • frequent use of psychoactive medication • family history of substance use disorder • family breakdown

BIOLOGICAL CONSIDERATIONS

Women tend to have greater body fat and less body water than men. Therefore, the pharmacokinetics and dynamics of alcohol and other drugs differ in men and women. In women of child-bearing age, the phase of the menstrual cycle has also been shown to alter drug effects and response to treatment (Jones & Jones, 1976).

Nicotine withdrawal

Symptoms tend to be recalled as more severe by women than by men. Nicotine polacrilex gum in the 2 mg dose is more effective in men than women, who might require the 4 mg dose. Also, women should be tapered more slowly. The effect of the menstrual cycle among women experiencing nicotine withdrawal is controversial. However, withdrawal symptoms, especially cravings for cigarettes, increase in women with premenstrual syndrome (PMS). Therefore, it is preferable to time the quit date to coincide with the first half of the cycle.

Alcohol metabolism

Because women have lower levels of gastric alcohol dehydrogenase and a lower percentage of body water, they achieve higher blood alcohol levels than do men for the same amount of alcohol consumed (Freeza, DiPadova et al., 1990). They are also more likely to develop cirrhosis at lower levels of alcohol consumed in a shorter period of time. Therefore low-risk drinking guidelines are lower for women (see Appendix 2).

Reproductive effects

Alcohol and illicit drugs such as heroin and cocaine tend to disrupt the hypo-thalamic-pituitary-ovarian axis, leading to anovulation and amenorrhea. Though fertility is reduced, these women can still get pregnant and should receive contraceptive counselling. Smoking and alcohol dependence are associated with an increased risk of first trimester abortions.

Pregnancy

Among drugs of abuse, alcohol is the only proven teratogen. Alcohol exposure during pregnancy has been associated with a spectrum of disorders including fetal alcohol syndrome (FAS), fetal alcohol effects (FAE), alcohol-related birth defects (ARBDs) and alcohol-related neurological defects (ARND) (see Table 2). The current estimate of the incidence of FAS in North America ranges from 0.5 to three cases per 1,000 live births (Abel, 1995).

Binge drinking is thought to be more harmful than chronic low-level drinking. However, the safe limit of alcohol consumption in pregnancy is unknown. Since there is no known benefit from consuming alcohol in pregnancy, and the risk of harm is possible, women should be advised to refrain from drinking while pregnant.

Substance use in pregnancy is associated with spontaneous abortion, premature labor, toxemia, low birthweight, placenta previa and abruptio placentae.

TABLE 2: Diagnostic Criteria for FAS and Alcohol-Related Effects†

1. FAS with confirmed maternal alcohol exposure

    1.1 Alcohol exposure in the mother is heavy and characterized by intoxication and withdrawal, including several consequences in various domains of her life.

    1.2 Characteristic facial anomalies in the infant (flat philtrum, short palpebral fissure).

    1.3 Growth retardation (prenatal/postnatal growth retardation with height/weight below the 10th percentile).

    1.4 CNS neurodevelopmental abnormalities (developmental delay, skull and brain malformations, intellectual impairment, behavioral problems, attention deficit, impulsivity).

2. FAS without confirmed alcohol exposure

Same as above except alcohol exposure is not confirmed.

3. Partial FAS with confirmed alcohol exposure. 1.1 plus 1.2 or 1.3 or 1.4

4. Alcohol-related effects with a history of maternal alcohol exposure

    4.1 Alcohol-related birth defects (ARBD). These birth defects can be cardiac, skeletal, renal, ocular and/or auditory.

    4.2 Alcohol-related neurodevelopmental disorder (ARND).

        4.2.1 CNS neurodevelopmental abnormalities.

        4.2.2 Complex behavioral or cognitive abnormalities.

† Reprinted with permission from *Fetal Alcohol Syndrome: Diagnosis, Epidemiology, Prevention and Treatment.* Copyright 1996, Institute of Medicine.

TREATMENT ISSUES

Numerous factors have been identified as barriers to engaging and/or retaining women in treatment (Table 3). Many of these barriers are related to women's social environment. When women do enter and continue in treatment, it is generally due to family support and to the availability of gender-sensitive treatment.

TABLE 3: Barriers to Treatment of Substance Use Disorders in Women

- low self-esteem
- lack of support from partner
- opposition to entering treatment from families and friends

Table 3 continued

- child-related and other familial responsibilities
- discomfort with identification of substance abuse as primary problem
- guilt, shame, embarrassment, fear of rejection
- lack of identification by physician
- fear of damaging the relationship with family physician
- fear of criminal prosecution
- fear of loss of child custody
- lack of women-oriented services
- gender stereotyping, racism, sexism and harassment within treatment programs
- underemployment and financial difficulties
- psychiatric disorders

Care of the pregnant substance-abusing woman

Pregnancies complicated by substance use should be regarded as high risk. Once identified, a pregnant substance abuser needs to be promptly assessed by a physician who specializes in this area. The woman must *not* be told to stop her drug(s) of abuse suddenly because of the risk of precipitating withdrawal with subsequent fetal loss. She should be offered admission to hospital where she can undergo withdrawal management (e.g., benzodiazepine loading for alcohol dependence) or stabilized on replacement therapy (e.g., methadone for heroin dependence). In addition to routine prenatal care, pregnant substance users should be screened for STDs, HIV, HCV and HBV in the first and third trimesters. Serial assessments of fetal growth and health should be performed. (See also "Pregnancy and Cocaine Use" in Section 6.1, and "Methadone Treatment during Pregnancy and Lactation" in Section 8.2.).

Prenatal care may need to be provided opportunistically since some women will not adhere to a regular appointment schedule. A non-judgmental and caring attitude can facilitate engagement in treatment and attendance at prenatal visits. Neonates of drug-exposed mothers require careful assessment and follow-up.

Neonatal care

Birth defects (i.e., FAS, ARBDs) should be identified. Neonatal abstinence syndrome can occur for a number of substances (e.g., alcohol, opioids [including methadone], benzodiazepines). A large proportion of neonates whose mothers are physically dependent on opioids will experience a neonatal abstinence syndrome characterized by features such as tremors, high-pitched cry, irritability and excessive sucking. As opposed to adult opioid withdrawal, neonates can experience seizures. These infants, therefore, should be observed closely in

367

hospital (for a minimum of five days) using the Finnegan Neonatal Abstinence Scoring System (Finnegan & Kandall, 1997) and should be treated with paregoric or oral morphine according to existing protocols. The onset of withdrawal is typically two to three days after birth, but late onset may occur within two weeks. Therefore, careful follow-up after discharge is imperative (see also Section 8.2).

R E F E R E N C E S

Abel, E.L. (1995). An update on the incidence of FAS: FAS is not an equal opportunity birth defect. *Neurotoxicology and Teratology, 17(4),* 437-443.

Canadian Centre on Substance Abuse & Addiction Research Foundation. (1997). *Canadian Profile: Alcohol Tobacco and Other Drugs.* Toronto: Canadian Centre on Substance Abuse and Addiction Research Foundation.

Ferrence, R., Ross, H.E. & Janecek, E. (1990). *Women and Substance Abuse: Literature Review.* Toronto: Addiction Research Foundation.

Finnegan, L.P. & Kandall, S.R. (1997). Maternal and neonatal effects of alcohol and drugs. In J.H. Lowinson, P. Ruiz, R.B. Millman & J.G. Langrod (Eds.), *Substance Abuse: A Comprehensive Text* (3rd ed.). Baltimore: Williams & Wilkins.

Freeza, M., DiPadova, C., Pozzato, G., Terpin, M., Baroona, E., Lieber, C.S. (1990). High blood alcohol levels in women: The role of decreased gastric alcohol dehydrogenase activity and first-pass metabolism. *New England Journal of Medicine, 322,* 95-99.

Fried, P.A., Watkinson, B., Grant, A. & Knights, R.M. (1980). Changing patterns of soft drug use prior to and during pregnancy: A prospective study. *Drug and Alcohol Dependence, 6(5),* 323-343.

Jones, B.M. & Jones, M.K. (1976). Women and alcohol: Intoxication, metabolism and the menstrual cycle. In M. Greenblatt & M.A. Schuckit (Eds.), *Alcohol Problems in Women and Children.* New York: Grune and Stratton.

National Cancer Institute of Canada. (1993). *Canadian Cancer Statistics.* Toronto: Canadian Cancer Society.

Peto, R., Lopez, A.D., Boreham, J., Thun, M. & Heath, C. Jr. (1994). *Mortality from Smoking in Developed Countries 1950–2000.* Oxford: Oxford University Press.

Stewart, D.E. & Streiner, D. (1994). Alcohol drinking in pregnancy. *General Hospital Psychiatry, 16(6),* 406-412.

Stratton, K.R., Howe, C.J. & Battaglia, F.C. (1996). *Fetal Alcohol Syndrome: Diagnosis, Epidemiology, Prevention and Treatment.* Washington, DC: Institute of Medicine.

S U G G E S T E D   R E A D I N G

Canale, M.D. (1996). *The Hidden Majority: A Guidebook on Alcohol and Other Drug Issues for Counsellors who Work with Women.* Toronto: Addiction Research Foundation.

Adolescent Substance Use and the Family

15 ADOLESCENT SUBSTANCE USE AND THE FAMILY

15

ADOLESCENT SUBSTANCE USE AND THE FAMILY

Patrick D. Smith, PhD, and Gloria Chaim, MSW

BACKGROUND

This section identifies some of the key issues physicians should be aware of when encountering adolescents and/or their families in their practices. It is not an exhaustive or in-depth discussion of the issues and does not, in particular, address issues specific to special populations within this group, such as native youths and street-involved youths. The purpose is to highlight the crucial role the physician can play in exploring substance-using behaviors along with other life problems with this population.

The prevalence of substance use in the adolescent population, and the complex issues that form the context for adolescents and their families, may present a forbidding picture to the health care provider. While adolescence can be viewed as a time of "crisis," it should be understood as a time of opportunity for growth (Schroeder, 1989), a hopeful stage when youths can anticipate many years of personal development. Although most, if not all, adolescents will experience a range of difficulties, such problems are commonly outgrown as young people mature into adulthood.

Alcohol and drug abuse among adolescents represents a significant problem in North America. While substance abuse among teens is not a new phenomenon, relatively little is understood about the etiology or consequences of problematic use among adolescents. Many of the difficulties faced in the attempt to accurately determine rates of problem substance use among teenagers result from a lack of agreement on appropriate definitions of problematic substance use. What are needed are definitions that account for the developmental process of adolescence.

Early identification

Early identification and setting appropriate goals are crucial. Because of their frequent contact with this population, physicians can be instrumental in facilitating the adolescent's growth during this period, either directly or indirectly, through referral or intervention with collaterals, particularly family members. It is important to keep in mind that although substance use is widespread, problematic use is rare. Even when problematic use occurs, the problems generally occur with a different set of circumstances than those of adult users. Physicians should attempt to understand, rather than label or classify, the adolescent, and facilitate the appropriate level and type of intervention (Best, 1996).

Context of use

As with any population, the identification of problematic substance use among adolescents must take into consideration the scope of the problem for the individual and its impact on his or her social environment. For the adolescent abuser it is crucial to identify familial factors that may contribute to problematic use, and to appreciate the impact that the use has on the family. The interaction between the adolescent's own developmental process and the developmental stage of his or her family tends to play a crucial role in the development of the substance use problem and, hence, in treating the problem effectively.

Screening and assessment

Screening for problematic substance use among adolescents and identifying those in need of treatment is difficult. Adolescents often hide substance use from parents and any other adults in positions of authority. Many teens also consider even heavy substance use as normal in the context of their peer groups and tend to minimize their use when reporting. Physicians and other health care professionals who are involved in screening for substance abuse and providing intervention or referring for treatment report feeling most frustrated and least effective when working with teenagers.

SCOPE OF THE PROBLEM

Since many adolescents underreport substance use to health care providers, the data available for problematic substance use in this population are not good diagnostic indicators. It is widely felt that survey data representing confidential self-reports of substance use yield the most accurate estimates of the scope of the problem. The longest ongoing study of adolescent drug use in Canada, the *Ontario Student Drug Use Survey,* has been tracking substance use among Ontario students in grades 7, 9, 11 and 13 for two decades (Adlaf, Ivis & Smart, 1997). The 1997 survey found that 59.6 per cent of students reported alcohol use in the past year, 27.6 per cent reported cigarette use and 24.9 per cent reported cannabis use. These three drugs are consistently reported as the most commonly used among adolescent populations in North America. Approximately one-third of the Ontario sample reported no drug use (including tobacco or alcohol) during the past year; about one-third reported only alcohol or tobacco use; and the remaining third reported use of some type of illicit drug during the past year.

Other drug use reported in the *Ontario Student Drug Use Survey* includes LSD (7.6 per cent), other hallucinogens such as mescaline and psilocybin (10.1 per cent), stimulants used for non-medical purposes (6.6 per cent), barbiturates used for medical purposes (6.0 per cent), stimulants used for medical purposes (3.7 per cent), methamphetamine (3.6 per cent), Ecstasy (MDMA) (3.1 per cent), cocaine (2.7 per cent), solvents (2.6 per cent), barbiturates used for non-medical purposes (2.5 per cent), crack cocaine (2.2 per cent), tranquillizers used for medical purposes (2.1 per cent), PCP (2.0 per cent), heroin (1.8 per cent), tranquillizers used for non-medical purposes (1.7 per cent) and glue (1.5 per cent). Males reported higher rates of heroin and methamphetamine use and females reported higher rates of non-medical stimulant use.

It is important to note that adolescent females in other studies have indicated use of stimulants for appetite and weight control (Smith, Gottleib et al., 1994) and this may account for their high rates of use relative to males.

While most drugs showed higher rates of use among older students, the use of inhalants was greater among the younger students. Limited access to other drugs at younger ages may contribute to the relatively higher use of inhalants for the younger adolescents. There was also some indication that first drug use was occurring at an earlier age than was the case in previous surveys.

While alcohol and tobacco are responsible for the greatest harm to the physical, social and psychological well-being of adolescents, it is important to not dismiss other drug use because of relatively lower prevalence rates. The *Ontario Student Drug Use Survey* indicates that even low rates of use actually represent a large number of students. For example, while only 2.2 per cent of the students reported having used crack cocaine in the Ontario survey, this represents 20,600 individuals. It is also important to appreciate that the problems a particular drug poses depend not only on the percentage using but also on the likelihood that current use will lead to dependence and other related negative consequences.

DEFINING PROBLEMATIC USE

How does a physician know when adolescent substance use constitutes a problem? Drugs such as alcohol have posed challenges to defining the problem.

Researchers and clinicians often disagree on what constitutes alcohol abuse or problem drinking in adult populations. It is not surprising, therefore, that there is even more confusion and disagreement about definitions for problem drinking among adolescents. Many of the traditional definitions of problem drinking have been based on older, male, inpatient populations and do not adequately address problem drinking among adolescents.

Inadequacy of quantity/frequency measures

One factor complicating agreement over definitions of problem drinking in adolescents is that quantity/frequency measures of drinking have often been used as the only, or the primary, source of information for understanding and evaluating problem drinking. Such measures cannot be accurately applied to adolescents, who often experience problems with lower quantities and frequencies of consumption, compared with adults, due to inexperience or underdeveloped tolerance. In addition, many traditional screening instruments overemphasize physical complications of alcohol use and withdrawal to determine problematic use. As a result, many adolescent problem drinkers do not receive treatment because their use typically does not yield the same medical complications and physiological dependence found in older, longer-term drinkers.

Use of appropriate screening questions

Traditional methods of measuring and defining problem drinking focus on the impairment of social roles. Often the social roles included for screening and assessment (e.g., marriage, career) are not applicable for adolescents, and difficulties in areas more salient to adolescents (e.g., impaired school performance, missed classes, regretted sexual experiences) are omitted (Hurlbut & Sher, 1992). When screening for problem substance use among adolescents, it is important to be aware of social roles that are appropriate to the adolescent being assessed.

Defining problematic use in females

Given that traditional definitions of problem drinking are based primarily on data from adult male problem drinkers, assessment tools have traditionally not been gender-sensitive. Pope and Smith and their colleagues (1994) addressed the complications associated with using these assessment tools to compare males and females relative to problems with alcohol. An individual is frequently classified as a problem drinker based on the quantity of alcohol consumed in one sitting or on reported multiple negative consequences resulting from drinking. Reliance on the measurement of the quantity of alcohol consumed ignores the fact that women's bodies, in general, have a higher percentage of fat and less water per pound than men's bodies. Because alcohol is distributed in total body water, an equivalent amount of alcohol per pound will result in a higher blood alcohol concentration for women than for men (Blume, 1990). Additionally, women experience more day-to-day variation in peak blood alcohol levels than men. This variation, which appears to be related to the menstrual cycle, makes it more difficult for women to predict the effects a given amount of alcohol will have on their bodies (Johnson, 1991). Given the increased irregularity of menstrual cycles among adolescent females, hormonal effects may be even more prevalent among adolescent girls than adult women.

Assessing problem drinking on the basis of associated negative consequences is also problematic. Again, most of the negative consequences included in traditional assessment instruments are based on reports of male drinkers. Many of the consequences addressed (e.g., legal problems, fighting because of drinking) are more common for males than for females. It has been reported that males have a tendency to be more aggressive, have more behavioral problems at school and in general exhibit more externalizing behaviors than females, regardless of drinking status (Prior, Smart et al., 1993). Conversely, females tend to report more internalizing consequences of drinking (e.g., anxiety, depression) than males, and have been found more often to drink to get drunk (Pope, Smith et al., 1994; Petersen, Sarigiani & Kennedy, 1991; Waite-O'Brien, 1992). Pope, Smith and their colleagues (1994) highlight the need for the assessment of drinking and problem drinking to include more internalizing consequences so female problem drinkers are not underidentified and differences in prevalence rates between males and females overestimated.

Adolescent norms and substance use

It is important to appreciate that norms for substance use vary considerably based on age. Patterns of frequent, heavy drinking are considered more normal among older teens than in an older adult population (Smith, Wells & Abdul-Salaam, 1997). For example, it is known that many college students with high quantity and frequency of alcohol consumption return to non-abusive patterns of drinking after graduation. While many young people will experiment with substance use, and even use regularly for a period of time, the majority will not develop serious problems or experience significant negative consequences related to use (Bailey, 1989). In the case of drinking, data demonstrate that most adolescents and young adults "mature out" of alcohol abuse (Kandel & Logan, 1984).

Some believe that since adolescents are not of the age of legal consumption, any use of what otherwise are considered legal drugs among teens is illegal and, therefore, constitutes problematic use. While this may be interesting as an intellectual debate, this premise is not helpful for the health care professional who is attempting to differentially determine cases where intervention is needed. It is, however, important to appreciate how underage use of even tobacco or alcohol can contribute to significant family problems.

377

PHYSICIAN'S ROLE IN SCREENING AND TREATMENT

Adolescents appear in physicians' offices for many reasons ranging from an annual physical to acute medical or psychological problems. (See Table 1 for a list of clinical indicators that may be associated with substance abuse.) The presenting problem may in fact not be the actual or only concern. As a result, the physician's task is complex. In order to diagnose and treat the problem the physician must also gather accurate and complete information from the patient, as well as, if possible, from collaterals.

The adolescent needs to be engaged in a process where he or she feels respected and able to trust the physician enough to participate in an open, honest exchange. The physician must clarify the boundaries of the confidential relationship and be able to provide the privacy usually necessary to begin an open dialogue. It is important for the physician to provide a rationale and convey a willingness, desire and expectation to discuss a variety of issues including substance use and sexual behavior/involvement — areas often felt to be taboo. Experimentation with high-risk behaviors and particularly with substances, usually more than one, is to be expected in adolescence and therefore should be dealt with in a matter-of-fact manner. The physician should be perceived as supportive, non-judgmental and empathic. By normalizing fears, concerns and ambivalence about disclosure as well as indicating that it is routine procedure to explore substance use experience, the physician sets the stage for gathering information that may contextualize the individual's presenting concerns and indicate the need for further exploration or treatment.

Assessment tools

The physician is in an excellent position to ask for and receive information that could lead to early identification of areas of concern, and prevent further problems. George and Skinner (1991) and Winters and Stinchfield (1995) review a number of screening and assessment instruments used in the investigation of adolescent substance use. The battery of assessment instruments developed by Winters and Henly (1988) is of particular interest. Their Minnesota Chemical Dependency Adolescent Assessment Package includes a brief 40-item screening instrument, the Personal Experience Screening Questionnaire; a structured interview format, the Adolescent Diagnostic Interview; and an in-depth self-complete questionnaire, the Personal Experience Inventory. The latter is available in a paper-and-pencil or computerized version. The computerized score report includes quite detailed narratives as well as statistical scores on each of the areas covered including substance use severity, psychosocial risk and mental health concerns including suicide risk. Generally, the physician's role would be to screen for substance use and related problems and refer to other specialized treatment resources for further assessment, diagnosis and treatment

378

planning, if indicated (see Section 2). In some cases, depending on the setting, mandate and availability of other resources, it may fall to the physician to do the complete assessment and treatment.

A screening consists of a brief self-report questionnaire as well as a brief structured interview of the adolescent. Areas of focus should include drug use frequency, onset and functions of use. It is often thought that laboratory tests should accompany screening, but such tests should be used with caution as there are significant limitations to what can be detected. Generally, for drugs other than cannabis and benzodiazepines, only recent use can be detected from analysis of urine or blood (see Section 1.3). Self-reporting is a valuable tool for generating information about recent substance use. However, whenever possible, brief interviews with collaterals are recommended. These can be very useful for information gathering as well as eliciting support for the adolescent. Although many youths are isolated, homeless, estranged from their families or refuse to have their families involved, they may identify a peer or other significant person as their "family." Collaterals often accompany youth to appointments and often welcome the opportunity to participate. It is recommended that the adolescent be interviewed privately but that the collateral be interviewed with the adolescent present (Winters & Stinchfield, 1995).

When discussing substance use, it is helpful to describe it in behavioral and quantitative terms, avoiding using labels like "alcoholic" or "drug addict." Because adolescence is a time of experimentation and change, applying labels implies a chronic, lifelong problem that is not only contraindicated but may become a self-fulfilling prophecy. Labelling can also have a profound impact on the patient's family and others around him or her, affecting how they relate to and treat that individual. Intervention must be undertaken with care since the goal of screening for, identifying and dealing with problematic substance use is to ameliorate problems as opposed to exacerbating them.

Early identification

Kaminer (1991) points out the importance of identifying abuse at its outset, or when the symptomatology is mild, and of dealing with it to prevent further development of the problem(s). Berg and Gallagher (1991) caution us to continually contextualize substance abuse in terms of the adolescent's developmental stage. Parents often report concern and would like to exert control over the adolescent's peer group, particularly if they suspect or have evidence of substance use, sexual experimentation or other behaviors within the group that they are concerned about. The child who is struggling to become an autonomous adult does not share the parents' concerns and frequently struggles harder to experiment and find a place in the social world without the parents' "interference." Adolescents may perceive experimentation with substances as "normal" and it may well be only a minimal part of experimenting with various roles and relationships. Therefore substance abuse should be prioritized along with other presenting problems, and may in fact not be the first or primary issue to be addressed. In many cases the physician will encounter substance use as an experiment with independence and autonomy rather than as a serious medical problem.

Although initially substance use may be assessed as experimental, it is crucial that ongoing screening and monitoring take place. It is possible, and often likely, that the use and any initial or isolated clinical indicators (Table 1) will diminish or disappear over time. However, it is important to be alert for changes with regard to frequency, variety or evidence of substance use or any of the clinical indicators. A failing grade on a test for a high-achieving student may be a warning sign or an anomaly. However, repeated failure, or failure coupled with illegal behavior and a change in peer group, should be cause for concern and lead to further exploration.

It is important to address any substance use and/or the associated behaviors because even limited involvement can have serious consequences. For example, an adolescent who drinks for the first time may be charged with driving while impaired. In this case, the charge is an indicator of an adolescent, first, who demonstrated poor judgment, possibly due to limited experience with substances, and second, whose judgment was impaired by use of a substance. Intervention strategies will vary depending on whether the problem is assessed as substance abuse, or poor judgment or acting out. Regardless, it is important that the adolescent is helped to take responsibility for his or her behavior and to develop suitable alternatives and strategies.

TABLE 1: Clinical Indicators of Alcohol and Other Drug Use by Adolescents

PSYCHOSOCIAL/BEHAVIORAL	• poor/changed school performance • involvement in illegal/delinquent activities • sexual acting out — e.g., promiscuity, prostitution • increased demand/need for money • change in peer group/involvement with substance-using peer group • driving under the influence of substances

Table 1 continued

MEDICAL	• frequent injuries • suicide attempts, gestures, ideation • unexplained/sudden weight loss or anorexia/bulimia • coughing, wheezing, "chronic" cold symptoms • gastrointestinal complaints including nausea and vomiting • insomnia • infections • chronic use of inhaled drugs • anxiety • depression • sexually transmitted diseases
Historical	• parental alcohol or drug use • estrangement from family • family relationships perceived to be poor • abuse or neglect • psychiatric disorders (particularly conduct disorder) • early experimentation with alcohol/drugs

Follow-up to screening

Once the screening is complete and contextualized, it is important for the physician to give adolescents objective, behavioral feedback and make recommendations. Motivating patients to commit to treatment recommendations, and following up to ensure that they have complied, are crucial steps for the physician to take. It would be helpful for the physician to have an understanding of the concepts and skills involved in the motivation and change process, particularly as they apply to adolescent substance abusers. In-depth discussion of this, however, is beyond the scope of this section.

It is important for physicians to be informed about drugs (both licit and illicit), and drug effects and interactions. Physicians can play an important role in counselling adolescent patients on the harms associated with high-risk behaviors. Harm-reduction strategies include adequate vaccination against hepatitis B, provision of condoms and needle exchange, to name a few. Having pamphlets about alcohol and drugs and high-risk behaviors available for patients is helpful as well. Similarly, the physician should have information about local treatment resources so that appropriate referral can be made should the screening indicate that such a step is warranted.

ROLE OF THE FAMILY

Many studies have examined complex family dynamics in an attempt to sort out the protective role of families, the risk factors associated with families and their impact on adolescents' approaches to substance use.

Family context and peer influence

Many studies have identified that adolescents in "intact" families (i.e., two-parent families) are less likely to use substances or to report associated problems than adolescents in other family structures. Adlaf and Ivis (1996) present evidence that family interactions and relationships are more influential than family structure alone on adolescent substance using and other problematic behavior. They found, as did Sokol-Katz and colleagues (1997), that familial factors mediated peer influence, known to be very powerful in adolescence. They found the amount of time adolescents spent with their family, regardless of its structure, to be the most influential factor. It appears that this and other family relational factors, such as the perception of getting along well with parent(s), confiding in them and having their activities monitored by them, have significant effects on peer association and consequent potential substance use.

Positive familial relations also mitigate the potential negative influence of family structures that have been disrupted by separation, divorce or death. Smith, Rivers and Stahl (1992) identified that the quality of family cohesion alone did not constitute a risk/protective factor but rather that the adolescent's perception and evaluation of the level of conflict/cohesion was the important factor. Therefore, when interviewing an adolescent, it is crucial to discuss his or her feelings and perceptions about the "reality" of the family context rather than gathering information that is more objective. This information will inform treatment and will suggest intervention with the family to effect change at that level. Whether or not adolescents currently live with their families, family intervention to either facilitate change in the system or to help the members come to terms with, accept and develop functional coping strategies is strongly recommended in lieu of or in conjunction with other treatment modalities focused solely on the substance abuse.

Parental substance use

Adolescent expectations are strongly influenced by parental attitudes towards substance use, and by parental substance use itself. Adolescents with an abusing parent expect more positive consequences of use than other adolescents. Their expectations are influenced by direct and vicarious experience. At the same time, they perceive their families as providing little preparation for social roles. Family cohesion and positive expression are perceived to be low in these families (Smith, Rivers & Stahl, 1992). O'Farrell (1995) notes that parents who

382

use substances in a problematic way, or who are recovering, may have particular difficulties in communicating with their adolescent children and managing the adolescents' behavior.

Prevalence of childhood trauma

A study carried out by the Connecticut Department of Children and Families in 1994 found that between 75 per cent and 80 per cent of children from substance-abuse-affected families experienced abandonment, emotional neglect, physical neglect and physical abuse (Connecticut KidsLink, 1997). As a large number of adolescents who present with substance abuse come from families where substances, primarily alcohol, are abused, it is important to screen for other trauma and, at a minimum, work towards providing the adolescent with coping and protective strategies. Some adolescents are parents themselves and the risks to their own children need to be assessed.

The physician and the family

Family members may attribute the adolescent's difficulties to substance use rather than other life concerns the adolescent may be struggling with. It is important for the physician to help both the adolescent and the family members to explore the context of use and to prioritize issues of concern, as opposed to immediately focusing on the need for treatment of substance use. When distraught parents present to the physician, with or without their child, their concern can be overwhelming to both the parents and the physician. Allow parents to tell their stories, and provide support and reassurance to validate their concerns. Be aware though that theirs is only one perspective on the "story" and that other perspectives, particularly that of the adolescent, are also important.

Reassure parents that experimentation is "normal" and that further exploration and assessment of the situation are necessary before conclusions can be reached. Referral to resources such as parent support groups, or addiction treatment facilities that provide education and/or treatment for family members of substance users, can be helpful both to parents who have a realistic assessment of the problems the adolescent presents and to those who are "overreacting." While both will benefit from the information and support, the former may have the opportunity to develop helpful strategies to cope with their child and the latter may be able to gain a more realistic perspective about the problems. Family therapy may be recommended as a forum for both parents and adolescents to negotiate this difficult stage, regardless of the assessed severity of the substance use.

The developmental context

How individuals and families cope with the challenges of adolescent development affects the way that substance use is viewed and managed. Erikson saw adolescence as a time of stress and strain between the self and society. To work through the tasks inherent in separation and individuation, the adolescent challenges roles, rules, values and norms, particularly those of the family. As a result, when a child enters this stage, the family is itself transformed and enters a new phase in its development. At the same time, parents may be struggling with some of the same individual concerns as the adolescent, such as forming new identities, re-evaluating hopes and dreams and possibly making major changes in their lives. For example, changes in career or marital relationships are common at this time (Preto & Travis, 1985). Viewing substance use in the developmental context helps to normalize experimentation and hold out the expectation for maturation as the adolescent moves into adulthood.

The physician needs to consider gender-related issues, including sexual orientation and/or confusion, which are prominent during adolescence. This context reinforces the importance of negotiating goals and expectations with adolescents and their families that allow room for experimentation and exploration. It also underlines the usefulness of a harm-reduction approach when dealing with substance use as opposed to abstinence-oriented approaches. This is a time when the adolescent needs some freedom to connect to peers in a positive way, to separate from parents, and yet have guidance and appropriate limits. Threats of change, and actual change, often produce anxiety (Schroeder, 1989). Depending on the level of substance use involvement, the role of the physician may be to provide information, guidance and reassurance to the family, rather than to intervene with the adolescent. Family education and/or therapy may be very helpful to families who need help managing during this transitional time.

R E F E R E N C E S

Adlaf, E.M. & Ivis, F.J. (1996). Structure and relations: The influence of familial factors on adolescent substance use and delinquency. *Journal of Child & Adolescent Substance Abuse,* 5(3), 1-19.

Adlaf, E.M., Ivis, F.J. & Smart, R.G. (1997). *Ontario Student Drug Use Survey: 1977-1997* (ARF Research Document Series No. 136). Toronto: Addiction Research Foundation.

Bailey, G. (1989). Current perspectives on substance abuse in youth. *Journal of the American Academy of Child and Adolescent Psychiatry,* 28(2), 152-162.

Berg, I.K. & Gallagher, D. (1991). Solution focused brief treatment with adolescent substance abusers. In T.C. Todd & M.D. Selekman (Eds.), *Family Therapy Approaches with Adolescent Substance Abusers.* Toronto: Allyn and Bacon.

Best, D. (1996). Put away adult things. *Addiction Research 4(4),* 393-394.

Blume, S. (1990). Chemical dependency in women: Important issues. *American Journal of Drug and Alcohol Abuse, 16,* 297-308.

Connecticut KidsLink. (1997). DCF inter-agency committee on substance abusing mothers and their children in Connecticut: A summary of problems and solutions (a report summary by Andy Dodge). New Haven, CT: Consortium for Substance Abusing Women and Their Children.

George, M.S. & Skinner, H.A. (1991). Assessment. In H.M. Annis & C.S. Davis (Eds.), *Drug Use by Adolescents: Identification, Assessment and Intervention.* Toronto: Addiction Research Foundation: Ottawa: Minister of Supply and Services, Canada.

Hurlbut, S. & Sher, K. (1992). Assessing alcohol problems in college students. *Journal of the American Medical Association, 41,* 49-58.

Johnson, S. (1991). Recent research: Alcohol and women's bodies. In P. Roth (Ed.), *Alcohol and Drugs Are Women's Issues.* Metuchen, NJ: Women's Action Alliance and Scarecrow Press.

Kaminer, Y. (1991). Adolescent substance abuse. In R.J. Frances & S.I. Miller (Eds.), *Clinical Textbook of Addictive Disorders.* New York: Guilford Press.

Kandel, D. & Logan, J. (1984). Patterns of drug use from adolescence to young adulthood: I. Periods of risk for initiation, continued use, and discontinuation. *American Journal of Public Health, 74,* 660-666.

O'Farrell, T.J. (1995). Marital and family therapy. In R. Hester & W.R. Miller (Eds.), *Handbook of Alcoholism Treatment Approaches* (2nd ed.). Boston: Allyn and Bacon.

Petersen, A., Sarigiani, P. & Kennedy, R. (1991). Why more girls? *Journal of Youth and Adolescence, 20,* 247-271.

Pope, S., Smith P., Wayne, J. & Kelleher, K. (1994). Gender difference in rural adolescent drinking patterns. *Journal of Adolescent Health, 15,* 359-365.

Preto, N.G. & Travis, N. (1985). The adolescent phase of the family life cycle. In M.P. Mirkin & S.L. Koman (Eds.), *Handbook of Adolescent and Family Therapy.* New York: Gardner Press.

Prior, M., Smart, D., Sanson, A. & Oberklaid, F. (1993). Sex differences in psychological adjustment from infancy to 8 years. *Journal of the American Academy of Child and Adolescent Psychiatry, 32,* 291-304.

Schroeder, E. (1989). Therapy for the chemically dependent family. In P.B. Henry (Ed.), *Practical Approaches in Treating Adolescent Chemical Dependency.* New York: Haworth Press.

Smith, P.D., Gottlieb, A., Cleveland, E., Flick, E. & Capps, J.P. (1994). Alcohol use and eating disorders: Their co-occurrence among adolescent female cheerleaders. Paper presented to Southern Society for Pediatric Research, New Orleans, LA.

Smith, P.D., Rivers, P.C. & Stahl, K.J. (1992). Family cohesion and conflict as predictors of drinking patterns: Beyond demographics and alcohol expectancies. *Family Dynamics of Addiction Quarterly, 2(2)*, 61-69.

Smith, P.D., Wells, D.B. & Abdul-Salaam, K. (1997). Assessing alcohol problems in student populations. In P.C. Rivers & E.R. Shore (Eds.), *Substance Abuse on Campus: A Handbook on Substance Abuse for College and University Personnel.* Westport, CT: Greenwood Press.

Sokol-Katz, J., Dunham, R., & Zimmerman, R. (1997). Family structure versus parental attachment in controlling adolescent deviant behavior: A social control model. *Adolescence, 32(125)*, 199-215.

Waite-O'Brien, N. (1992). Alcohol and drug abuse among female adolescents. In G.W. Lawson & A.W. Lawson (Eds.), *Adolescent Substance Abuse — Etiology, Treatment, and Prevention.* Gaithersburg, MD: Aspen.

Winters, K.C. & Henly, G.A. (1988). Assessing adolescents who abuse chemicals: The Chemical Dependency Adolescent Assessment Project. In *Adolescent Drug Abuse: Analyses of Treatment Research.* (NIDA Research Monograph No. 77). Rockville, MD: National Institute on Drug Abuse.

Winters, K.C. & Stinchfield, R.D. (1995). Current issues and future needs in the assessment of adolescent drug abuse. In E. Rahdert & D. Czechowicz (Eds.), *Adolescent Drug Abuse: Clinical Assessment and Therapeutic Interventions.* (NIDA Research Monograph No. 156). Rockville, MD: National Institute on Drug Abuse.

Concurrent Disorders

16 CONCURRENT DISORDERS

TABLES AND FIGURES

16

CONCURRENT DISORDERS

Blenos A.T. Pedersen, MD

SUBSTANCE USE PROBLEMS AND MENTAL HEALTH PROBLEMS

A 19-year-old man with hallucinations and paranoid ideas was picked up by police and brought to a hospital emergency department after he broke a store window. The police made the assumption that he was mentally ill. The young man was not known locally, so there was no way to gather information about his medical history. A diagnosis of Schizophrenia was made and he was referred to a community mental health program. After the patient changed doctors, the diagnosis of Schizophrenia was questioned. At the time of initial treatment he had been using cannabis and cocaine daily for several months. When he was picked up he had no money and was not taking care of his appearance. He looked to be chronically mentally ill at the time, but the alternate diagnosis of drug-induced psychosis needed to be considered.

Integrated mental health and addiction services

Physicians, psychiatrists and allied health workers frequently encounter the kind of interface between addictions and mental health that is illustrated above. As a result, there is a growing concern about how such cases are managed. The long-standing division between addiction and mental health services is being challenged by an interdependent model of service, education and research. This section aims to present basic issues around which the two parts of the health-care system can share concepts, clinical language and skills.

EPIDEMIOLOGY

A recent textbook reports the following data concerning the prevalence of concurrent disorders:

- of persons with mental disorders, 29 per cent have a Substance Use Disorder
- 47 per cent of individuals with Schizophrenia have substance use problems
- 25 per cent of persons with Anxiety Disorders have a substance use problem
- 47 per cent of substance abusers have mental health problems
- a mental disorder or alcohol problem is found in 72 per cent of abusers of other drugs
- in a psychiatric hospital, almost one-third of admissions have comorbid substance-related problems (Beeder & Millman, 1997).

Since addiction is a common concurrent reality in patients presenting for medical care, the combined mental and substance-related problems must be regarded as a part of everyday clinical practice.

Epidemiological surveys

There have been a number of large-scale general population surveys in North America in the past 20 years, including the Epidemiologic Catchment Area Survey and the National Comorbidity Survey in the U.S., and the Ontario Mental Health Supplement Survey in Canada, where the issue of concurrent disorders has been examined. Although findings vary, each study confirms the fact that there is a significant co-occurrence of psychiatric disorders and Substance Use Disorders among populations who present with either a psychiatric disorder or a Substance Use Disorder. The reader is directed to the following papers as sources on prevalence and/or use of services by individuals with concurrent disorders: Regier, Farmer et al., 1990; Narrow, Regier et al., 1993; Kessler, Nelson et al., 1996; Ross, 1995; Ross and Shirley, 1997. Regier, Farmer et al. is particularly valuable because it presents data on the prevalence of concurrent disorders in the community and in specialty addiction medicine settings and prison samples.

There are widely varying estimates of the prevalence of co-occurring substance use and mental disorders, depending in part on the samples studied, the interview instruments chosen (clinician-administered such as the SCID [Structured Clinical Interview for DSM-IV] or lay-administered such as the DIS [Diagnostic Interview Schedule] and the CIDI [Composite International Diagnostic Interview]) and diagnostic criteria (lifetime or current, DSM-III, DSM-IIIR, DSM-IV or ICD-10) employed, as well as the disorders studied. There are also problems with making diagnoses of "independent" psychiatric disorders in the presence of active substance abuse because symptoms of the latter may mimic or hide symptoms of the former. For example, "major depression" may turn out to be "substance-induced" and clear up within a relatively short time following cessation of drinking.

FUNDAMENTAL PRINCIPLES

Treatment planning
The effectiveness of treatment for Substance-Related Disorders is well established (see Section 2.1). As has been pointed out throughout this manual, the effectiveness of treatment is enhanced when the treatment plan is *matched* to the needs of the individual. A team approach to treatment should be employed wherever possible, involving the physician, addiction counsellors, psychiatrists and other services as needed, as well as family members. This approach is fundamental when concurrent disorders are encountered. A 1990 report to the United States Congress, *Broadening the Base of Treatment for Alcohol Problems,* argued in favor of a such a "broadly based" approach wherein biopsychosocial perspectives are carefully matched to individual patient needs (Institute of Medicine, 1990). Experience has shown that the application of this fundamental principle is essential for successful concurrent disorder treatment outcomes.

Mental signs and symptoms
Mental signs and symptoms are common when encountering Substance-Related Disorders. Such clinical observations should be expected in connection with the use of psychoactive drugs. However, it is important not to misinterpret mental signs and symptoms to mean that most individuals with substance-related problems have what is traditionally called a mental disorder. It merely indicates that the varied effects of alcohol and drugs on the central nervous system are common, significant and need to be understood clinically. This may begin by understanding the varied effects of the substance groups on the mental state of the user.

Altered mental status
While a mental status examination, or some part of it, is usually included in every medical assessment, the effects of substance use on mental status are not commonly taught or considered clinically. In each of the various routines and instruments available for mental status examinations, mental status can be altered in patients who present with concurrent disorders and non-concurrent addiction problems. A mental status examination makes observations of behaviors, speech, mood, thought, perceptions and cognition. Different substance groups can affect any or all of these components in a variety of ways. Further, the same substance group may effect mental status differently at various stages of use, such as intoxication, withdrawal or chronic use.

393

SUBSTANCE-RELATED DIAGNOSTIC CATEGORIES AND ALTERED MENTAL STATES

The *Diagnostic and Statistical Manual of Mental Disorders* (DSM-IV) is essential reading for all clinicians who are involved in the assessment and management of mental and substance-related problems. In the DSM-IV it is suggested that there are two categories available to classify substance use problems, Substance Use Disorders and Substance-Induced Disorders, and the possible combination of these two. The combination of the two categories with a mental disorder may be expressed as *concurrent disorder = mental disorder + use disorder ± induced disorder.* Each of these disorders affects the mental state of the user, and they interact to produce varying mental states.

Use Disorders
Use Disorders manifest as addictive behaviors in persons with abuse or dependence. The Use Disorders alter mental states by a variety of "addictive behaviors" which may mimic Personality Disorders (Vaillant, 1983).

Induced Disorders
Induced Disorders may result from use of any of the substance groups. These are associated with specific toxic effects on the brain leading to symptoms *(altered mental state)* that are characteristic of the substance group. (Some examples of induced symptoms are provided below.)

Concurrent Disorders
Concurrent disorders are the potential interactive combinations noted above. The combinations interact to produce effects on the mental state that are not simply additions to the two basic disorders. Understanding the varied effects of the combinations is essential clinical knowledge. Due to the combinations, there may be exaggeration of symptoms, or masking of symptoms usually expected from either of the combined disorders. This may be different from what is seen when the disorders are not combined. The interaction varies with the combinations, but also with the phase of the substance use. For example, symptoms vary with intoxication and withdrawal.

SUBSTANCE USE DISORDERS AND MENTAL HEALTH

Clinical criteria for Substance Use Disorders
Use Disorders present clinically as behavioral symptoms of abuse and dependence (see Table 1). These clinical manifestations, sometimes called "addictive behaviors," may be misinterpreted as Personality Disorders (Kaplan & Sadock, 1998; Nace, Davis & Gaspari, 1991; Brooner, Schmidt et al., 1992). This can easily

394

lead to misdiagnosis and inappropriate treatment if the substance-related possibility is not considered. Frequently, patients with mental symptoms do not tell their doctor about substance use and physicians often do not ask. When a substance-related history is taken, the criteria for dependence should be noted.

Substance use behaviors with or without Personality Disorder

In past nomenclatures, substance-dependent individuals were referred to as "sociopaths." However, in many cases altered behavior is limited to periods of substance use. That is, Substance Use Disorders are time limited, whereas personality characteristics are usually lifelong regardless of the circumstances.

Addictive behaviors associated with a Use Disorder can present in two ways. That is, addictive behaviors can occur in a user who does not have a Personality Disorder and in a user who has a pre-existing Personality Disorder. In the latter case, the Substance Use Disorder in combination with a Personality Disorder may exaggerate the manifestations of the personality problems. Antisocial Personality Disorder is the most common concurrent mental disorder with Substance-Related Disorders. In such cases, considering the effects of the substance use is vital.

TABLE 1: Abbreviated List of Criteria for Use Disorders: Abuse and Dependence†

Preoccupied with substance use
Increased use of substance beyond socially expected
Inability to *control* use of substance
Symptoms of *withdrawal*
Signs of *tolerance*
Restricted activities
Impaired functions
Hazardous use
Patients who meet two criteria suffer from Substance Abuse.
Patients with three or more criteria suffer from Substance Dependence.

† Abbreviated list is an aid to remembering key words. See DSM-IV for details.

SUBSTANCE-INDUCED DISORDERS AND MENTAL HEALTH

Mimicking mental disorders

Substance-Induced Disorders can alter mental status in ways that mimic virtually all common categories of mental disorders. Therefore, it is essential to know which symptoms are caused by which substance groups. It is also essential to know which "groups of symptoms" particular substances may cause. For example, cocaine use can lead to the manifestation of groups of symptoms that mimic a Major Depressive Episode. Other examples are given below. These are also tabulated and summarized in DSM-IV.

It is clear that clinicians who are not aware of the mimicking potential of Substance-Induced Disorders may make inappropriate mental disorder diagnoses. For example, chronic alcohol users who do not tell their physicians about their substance use may present with all the symptoms of depression or Dysthymia. Of course, treating the depression does not treat the alcohol dependence. If substance use is not assessed, the possibility of misdiagnosis is high and inappropriate treatment may be given.

Common examples of Substance-Induced Disorders mimicking mental disorders

Substance-Induced Disorders mimic primary mental disorders in a variety of ways. Not only do the various substance groups cause different symptoms, but the same substance may present differently, depending on the phase of substance use. The following examples illustrate the range of clinical presentations.

• Cocaine *Intoxication* may induce symptoms similar to mania.

• Cocaine *Withdrawal* may induce a depressive episode ("the crash").

• Alcohol-Induced Mood Disorder, *regular use.*

A 30-year-old mother of three children presents to a family practice office because her mood has been down for several months. She does not disclose that in order to relax she drinks two or three glasses of wine each evening. The differential diagnosis is between an Alcohol-Induced Mood Disorder and a primary Major Depressive Episode with concurrent alcohol use.

• Benzodiazepine-Induced Anxiety Disorder, *withdrawal.*

The same mother in the above example has for several years received benzodiazepines from her family doctor for insomnia. When her doctor finds out

396

about her wine consumption, he stops providing her with benzodiazepines. When the benzodiazepines run out, the mother begins to have anxiety symptoms and panic attacks for the first time. In fact, these symptoms also exaggerate her need for alcohol.

• Cannabis-Induced Psychotic Disorder, *chronic use.*

A 25-year-old university student has failed academically over the last two years. His friends take him to the school's health services because he has been experiencing hallucinations. He is a chronic daily marijuana smoker but on close questioning he discloses that his recent source of "grass" is from plants with a very high THC content. Still further questioning leads to the admission that for several months he has been paranoid. After six weeks with no cannabis use his symptoms disappeared.

• Cannabis-Induced Sexual Dysfunction, *chronic use.*

The same 25-year-old in the above example has had difficulty with erections for several years. This, too, resolves after he is abstinent for some time from cannabis.

• Caffeine-Induced Sleep Disorder, *regular use of increased amounts.*

Insomnia, a commonly presenting problem in general practice, must have among its differential diagnosis Substance-Induced Insomnia. Most of the substance groups can cause sleep disturbances. The diagnosis of Substance-Induced Insomnia is difficult to manage for the clinician given that the patient often seeks another substance to relieve the problem (see Section 5.2).

It would be a clinical error to mistakenly diagnose the above examples of Substance-Induced Disorders as primary mental disorders and to treat them as such. The appropriate assessment and treatment is the assessment and treatment of the addiction.

VARIATIONS WITH SITE OF PRACTICE

In community settings such as general practice, Substance-Induced Disorders alone are much more common than combined or concurrent disorders. (The differential diagnosis will be discussed below.) In contrast, in a psychiatric hospital, concurrent disorders are much more common than addictions alone.

ASSESSMENT PRINCIPLES

Decision trees are used to reach psychiatric diagnoses. Many of these are illustrated in the DSM-IV. The decision tree method first considers if altered mental status is caused by a physical illness or is a Substance-Related Disorder. Because either a physical illness or a Substance-Related Disorder can cause or mimic mental disorders, they must both be demonstrated or excluded before a primary psychiatric diagnosis is made. The main purpose for using decision trees is to exclude such possibilities before making a psychiatric diagnosis. However, the incidence of a concurrent disorder must be considered. Such assessment considerations are presented in Figure A. This decision process considers not only diagnoses but factors necessary to treatment. It involves detailing biopsychosocial problem lists. (See Figure A for a discussion of developing problem lists that are organized in terms of the different elements of assessment: addiction assessment, physical assessment, mental assessment, social assessment and spiritual assessment.)

Induced Disorders — time interval considerations

By definition, a Substance-Induced Disorder should disappear after a period of abstinence from the involved substance(s). The type of substance, dose and chronicity of use all influence the period of abstinence required. At this time, there is no consensus about the period of abstinence required. A reliable average period of abstinence is three to four weeks. It must be remembered though that some symptoms, such as mood or personality problems (addictive behaviors), might take longer to ameliorate. Symptoms of anxiety or psychosis usually disappear within two to three weeks.

Severe symptoms often call for the immediate use of medication. If this is the case, then several months into treatment it is appropriate to conduct a trial without medication in order to confirm the diagnosis. This is based on the assumption that the substance-induced symptoms will not return but the primary disorder symptoms, if existent, will. This delayed trial without medication can save a patient from a long-term misdiagnosis and unnecessary treatment.

FIGURE A: Assessment of Concurrent Substance and Mental Disorders

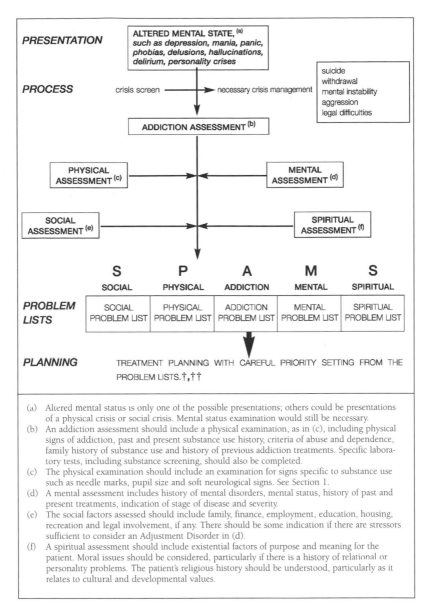

(a) Altered mental status is only one of the possible presentations; others could be presentations
     of a physical crisis or social crisis. Mental status examination would still be necessary.
(b) An addiction assessment should include a physical examination, as in (c), including physical
     signs of addiction, past and present substance use history, criteria of abuse and dependence,
     family history of substance use and history of previous addiction treatments. Specific labora-
     tory tests, including substance screening, should also be completed.
(c) The physical examination should include an examination for signs specific to substance use
     such as needle marks, pupil size and soft neurological signs. See Section 1.
(d) A mental assessment includes history of mental disorders, mental status, history of past and
     present treatments, indication of stage of disease and severity.
(e) The social factors assessed should include family, finance, employment, education, housing,
     recreation and legal involvement, if any. There should be some indication if there are stressors
     sufficient to consider an Adjustment Disorder in (d).
(f) A spiritual assessment should include existential factors of purpose and meaning for the
     patient. Moral issues should be considered, particularly if there is a history of relational or
     personality problems. The patient's religious history should be understood, particularly as it
     relates to cultural and developmental values.

† See below, axial summary and examples.
†† See below, five-block format for treatment of concurrent disorders.

CONCURRENT DISORDERS

Possible combinations

Concurrent disorders may involve any mental disorder plus any Substance-Related Disorder. The latter includes any Substance-Related Disorder from any of the substance groups. In theory, a concurrent disorder is the combination of any of the substance-related categories in DSM-IV with any of the non-substance categories of mental disorders.

That is, concurrent disorders in this section are one or more mental disorders plus a Substance Use Disorder (usually Dependence) involving one or more substances with or without one or more Substance-Induced Disorders from those substances.

Concurrent disorders	= mental disorder(s) + Use Disorder ±	Substance-Induced Disorder(s)

In most medical practices, the variety and epidemiology of such combinations is limited. The most common examples in practice are Antisocial Personality Disorder, Mood Disorders, Anxiety Disorders and Schizophrenia with varied combinations of Substance-Related Disorders. Less common are Eating Disorder, Sleep Disorder and Sexual Dysfunction.

Although not expressed in the equation above, a concurrent disorder diagnosis *must always consider the social context and include any physical disorders that may also be concurrent.* Both of these may also lead to mental symptoms (altered mental status). In DSM-IV nomenclature these are called Adjustment Disorders and Mental Disorders due to a General Medical Condition (Kaplan & Sadock, 1998).

Heterogeneity

Grouping all of the possible combinations of Mental Disorders, Substance Use Disorders and Substance-Induced Disorders under the one heading of "concurrent disorders" should not imply that there is homogeneity in concurrent disorders. *Clinically, it is important to understand that just the opposite is true — concurrent disorders are fundamentally heterogeneous.* For example, Schizophrenia in a 19-year-old man combined with the use of alcohol, nicotine and cannabis is very different in assessment and treatment from Major Depressive Disorder in a 30-year-old woman who abuses benzodiazepines. They are both concurrent disorders, but the resemblance stops there.

Because of the heterogeneity of combined substance and mental disorders, clinical practitioners need to give the required attention to the specific diagnoses in the combinations. Therefore, it is important for clinicians to have an awareness of the most common combinations presenting at their site of practice. This will help clinicians to be consistent and specific in their management of such cases. It will also discourage physicians from regarding all Substance-Related Disorders in the same manner. With concurrent disorders, improved treatment outcomes are reliant on matching combinations with specific therapies.

RECORDING CONCURRENT DISORDERS

A common language used by all health disciplines would facilitate an understanding of the heterogeneous combinations of diagnoses and factors relevant to treating concurrent disorders. In the North American context, DSM-IV provides mental health and addiction services providers with such a language. The table below shows the five-axial format that includes both mental disorder diagnoses and biopsychosocial factors. Table 2 is an example of an axial report of a typical concurrent disorders case.

TABLE 2: Recording Multidimensional Aspects of Concurrent Disorders: DSM-IV Axial Summary of Potential Categories†

Axis I	Mental Disorder(s) Substance Use Disorder(s) Substance-Induced Disorder(s)
Axis II	Personality Disorder
Axis III	Physical Diagnoses
Axis IV	Social Issues (Psychosocial and environmental problems)
Axis V	Severity in the last year (Psychological and occupational functioning)††

† See DSM-IV for details.
†† The accepted approach for reporting of overall functioning in Axis V is the use of GAF scores (Global Assessment of Functioning). See DSM-IV for further details.

Axial records and the SPAMS problem list method

The axial record is useful because it includes a method of summarizing the concurrence of disorders. The axial reporting system is biopsychosocial in content, which helps to focus treatment planning in concurrent disorders since there may be problems specifically associated with each diagnosis on the list. These problems can be listed using the SPAMS (social, physical, addiction, mental and spiritual) problem list method outlined in Figure A. The use of axes and problem lists gives the treatment team a common focus for each concurrent disorders patient. The lists are revised as the patient moves through the treatment phases.

RECORDING CONCURRENT DISORDERS: EXAMPLES USING AXIAL RECORDS

Example one — chronic relapsing disorders

Below is an axial record of a concurrent disorders case encountered in a mental health centre.

Axis I	Schizophrenia
	Alcohol Dependence
	Nicotine Dependence
	Cannabis Abuse
	Alcohol-Induced Dysthymia
Axis II	Deferred*
Axis III	Bronchitis
Axis IV	Legal problems, with aggression
	Financial problems
	Housing problems
Axis V	GAF 50

* Addictive behaviors may mimic Personality Disorders and sometimes this is mistakenly recorded on this axis as a Personality Disorder.

The content of the axial report provided is typical in mental health centres treating chronic patients. Such patients are often repeatedly admitted with relapses of mental disorders, social crises or legal problems. In such cases it is important to address the substance use issues, which can reduce both recidivism and hospital costs.

Clinicians must not be discouraged by relapses. Persistence by those involved in treatment is essential for successful outcomes. A team approach, phased management, the use of problem lists, establishing priorities and well-matched, broadly based consideration continued into rehabilitation can lead to success demonstrated by improvements in the functional measure used in Axis V (Kent, Fogarty & Yellowlees, 1995a; 1995b).

402

Example two — Social Phobia and Substance-Related Disorders

Axis I   Social Phobia
             Alcohol Dependence
             Benzodiazepine Dependence
             Substance-Induced Panic Disorder

Axis II   No Personality Disorder, but the combination in Axis I might
             mimic Avoidant Personality Disorder, particularly if the problem
             is chronic, and dependence exaggerates social isolation behaviors

Axis III   No health problems

Axis IV   Unemployment and on long-term social support (medical welfare)

Axis V   GAF 50

The occurrence of Social Phobia in a concurrent disorders patient usually precedes the Substance-Related Disorders. Substance use often begins as self-medication for the phobia. A family history of Social Phobia or other Anxiety Disorder is common in these cases. A patient history of avoidance often dates to childhood. Typically in their late teens, these patients discover alcohol and begin to self-medicate. Unfortunately, addiction commonly follows. The use and abuse of benzodiazepines may follow a similar pattern.

In cases where there is a relationship between the mental and the substance disorders, treating the mental disorder successfully helps to treat the addiction. However, as previously stated, the addiction does have a life of its own and requires specific addiction treatment.

Example three — Antisocial Personality Disorder and Substance-Related Disorders

Axis I   Alcohol Abuse
             Cocaine Dependence
             Cocaine-Induced Depressive Disorder

Axis II   Antisocial Personality Disorder

Axis III   A past history of seizures

Axis IV   Many social issues including financial and legal

Axis V   GAF 60

403

The transference issues that are common with persons who have such an Axis II diagnosis make it difficult to focus on substance use problems. These patients frequently present other issues and are annoyed by a focus on addiction issues. They often stop coming for treatment. At times the only factor that keeps them coming for treatment is a legal order, such as a probation order. When they persist, it may be rewarding to patiently work with them and help them to associate many of their problems with addictive behaviors. If they see the connection, they may be motivated to modify their substance use and profit from addiction treatment.

Cocaine-induced depression is a typical reason such patients seek help. The patients often insist that their difficulties have nothing to do with cocaine but with a dysfunctional childhood. While a dysfunctional childhood may be at the root of many of their problems, helping them stop or reduce cocaine use will help them to address the deeper issues.

Summary of the three examples — heterogeneity of concurrent mental health and Substance-Related Disorders

The three examples demonstrate the heterogeneity of concurrent mental health and Substance-Related Disorders. Taken together, they highlight the need for varied and well-matched strategies for treatment. However, in all such cases an organizing system, such as the five-block format described below, will be useful. Within that format it is important to retain a biopsychosocial perspective. No one part of a biopsychosocial perspective is more important than the other. The social, physical, addiction, mental and spiritual perspectives all may play an essential role in the desired treatment outcome.

FIVE-BLOCK CLINICAL ASSESSMENT AND TREATMENT FORMAT FOR CONCURRENT DISORDERS

Field research conducted by the National Institute of Mental Health on the treatment of concurrent disorders has been organized and reported as "clinical tasks" (Drake & Noordsy, 1997). To assist systematic application in daily clinical practice, the tasks can be organized in a five-block format (see Figure B). The format includes the three treatment phases commonly seen in traditional addiction interventions. Staff education and case management blocks support the three phases.

FIGURE B: Five-Block Format for Treatment of Concurrent Disorders

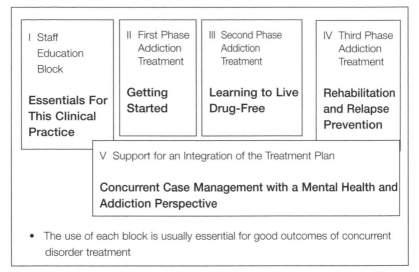

I Staff Education Block **Essentials For This Clinical Practice**	II First Phase Addiction Treatment **Getting Started**	III Second Phase Addiction Treatment **Learning to Live Drug-Free**	IV Third Phase Addiction Treatment **Rehabilitation and Relapse Prevention**

V Support for an Integration of the Treatment Plan

Concurrent Case Management with a Mental Health and Addiction Perspective

- The use of each block is usually essential for good outcomes of concurrent disorder treatment

BLOCK ONE: STAFF EDUCATION

Although a staff education block is not specifically about treatment, this block is essential in a concurrent disorders treatment plan. In most constituencies in North America, addiction and mental health services have been separated politically, financially and subsequently educationally. In most disciplines related to mental health, such as medicine, psychiatry, psychology, social work and nursing, there has been very little if any training curricula related to addictions and usually nothing about concurrent disorders. Efforts are now being made to change this lack of training, but it will take time to impact the system. Because this is only beginning to change, essential, basic and practical staff education about concurrent disorders is almost always required if effective treatment of these disorders is to be provided. This staff education is equally required in the addiction field where mental health education has seldom been provided. Some topics of a curriculum are introduced in this section. The education should also provide some skills training. The DSM-IV is a valued reference to both addiction and mental health categories and especially valuable as a reference of symptomatology.

Basic curriculum for staff education

Some basic topics for concurrent disorders training are listed in the table below. These topics are basic knowledge for any health professional working with this population and can be adapted for training psychiatrists, physicians, nurses, therapists or other clinicians.

405

TABLE 3: Some Recommended Essentials for Psychiatric Residency Training about Mental and Substance-Related Problems †

---

1. Significant epidemiology of concurrent disorders: "common things are common."
2. The case for an integrated assessment and treatment strategy.
3. A basic foundation: substances and their effect on the mental state.
4. Substance categories and their relation to mental symptoms.
5. Substance use, dependence and addictive behaviors as symptoms.
6. Substance-Induced Disorders, "mimicked mental disorders."
7. Combined disorders are not just concurrent: consequences of combinations.
8. Five-block format for treatment planning, including three phases of treatment, staff education and case management.
9. Common substance-related concurrent disorders and:

   Psychosis and substance
   Mood Disorders and substance
   Personality Disorders and substance
   Anxiety Disorders and substance
   Other Mental Disorders and substance

   The heterogeneity of concurrent disorders (varied combinations in practice) and the danger of generalizing are taught by considering specific concurrent disorders. Knowledge of which combinations usually present in the particular treatment centre in which one practises also helps to avoid these traps.
10. Awareness of more specialized topics such as pharmacology, substance and suicide, substance and violence.

---

† If a training program is developed, 1 to 8 can be phase one, the topics of number 9, phase two, and number 10 can be presented as a third phase as the discipline requires.

BLOCK TWO: FIRST PHASE OF TREATMENT

This is the first of three treatment phases. It includes an initial assessment of the addiction and mental disorders, screening for crisis needs and the provision of treatment and a more extended biopsychosocial assessment as a basis for matched treatment recommendations. Crisis management may include a need for management of substance withdrawal and/or the stabilization of the mental disorder. Motivational and engagement strategies are an important part of this phase because the patient is often at the precontemplation or contemplation stage related to his or her substance use. Each of these tasks is necessary to prepare the patient for phase two treatment.

Identification

Concurrent disorders sometimes confound diagnosis because Substance-Use Disorders and Mental Disorders can *mask* symptoms or *exaggerate* presenting symptoms. Careful assessment, and reassessment after periods of abstinence, may help to clarify the diagnosis. The clinician should take an addiction history and include questions about each substance group, family history of addiction and past addiction treatments (Minkoff & Drake, 1991). This is not a well-developed skill for many physicians or mental health workers and should be acquired. (For screening for clinically significant substance use consult Section 1.)

Withdrawal management

Withdrawal from a substance takes on extra significance in the context of a concurrent mental disorder. The physician must be alert to the clinical difficulty of sorting out symptoms because withdrawal may mask or exaggerate the symptoms of the mental disorder. Further, the multiple symptoms may present as a Substance-Induced Disorder and confuse the diagnosis. The physician must also be aware of the fact that symptoms of withdrawal, especially anxiety, agitation and aggression may mistakenly be accepted as part of a psychiatric problem. A withdrawal management plan is important for the comfort of both the patient and the staff. In an inpatient setting where patients with Schizophrenia are treated, appropriate withdrawal management should reduce aggression and thereby lessen the need for restraints and isolation. (See pharmacological management below.)

Stabilization

Another essential part of initiating treatment of concurrent disorders is the stabilization of the mental disorder. Patients with concurrent disorders frequently have stopped taking their medication while using substances. This is often the reason for the relapse of the mental disorder. Re-establishing appropriate medication is an important part of this phase of management. The appropriate medication is one that is best matched to the concurrent mental disorder. This medication is usually prescribed by a psychiatrist or physician experienced in mental health disorder treatments.

A frequent part of stabilization is the management of sleep problems, which are common after withdrawal. Unless a sleep problem is severe, it should be managed without the use of sedative/hypnotics because of their dependence liability. Zopiclone or trazadone hydrochloride are effective short-term medications. If a diazepam taper is used in detoxification, additional sleeping medication should not be required. The use and abuse of benzodiazepines in patients with concurrent disorders is a significant problem that must always be considered and monitored very carefully in concurrent cases. There are indications for the use of benzodiazepines, even in a substance-dependent person, but only in exceptional cases when there is no other option.

Physical assessment

Persons with concurrent disorders often have increased problems with their physical health. Some of these physical illnesses may also be a source of mental symptoms. For example, chronic debilitation and poor nutrition may be associated with depression. Medication used concurrently for physical illness may confound mental symptomatology. For these reasons, a careful and comprehensive medical history, examination and investigation are an essential part of this phase. In some centres where there is an emphasis on non-biological psychosocial modalities, physical assessments may be minimized. This lack of complete physical assessment can lead to misdiagnosis and inappropriate treatment.

Social assessment

Both research and clinical experience show that persons with concurrent disorders often have multiple and complicated social problems. The problems may relate to family, finance, employment, education, housing or legal issues. These problems may need priority attention in order to stabilize situations so that other treatment can be maintained. The relevance of the social context reinforces the need for concurrent case management discussed below. Excluding these considerations in the treatment plan will often defeat even the best efforts in other aspects of treatment.

Due to complications caused by the combination of the above biopsychosocial needs, the need for longer-term inpatient care is often necessary. Given the current emphasis on "shorter stays," this may require advocacy by the treatment team. Advocacy also needs to extend into the community in order to secure drug- and alcohol-free community housing options. Such planning is vital for successful treatment, especially in this early phase. If overlooked, the potential for relapse increases. Long-term assertive case management is necessary especially in patients with chronic or severe concurrent problems.

Engagement and motivation

The engagement of the patient and his or her motivation towards treatment is fundamental at this phase. Given the heterogeneity of concurrent disorders, the skills and strategies vary with the combinations of disorders. Consider the different implications of such diagnoses as Schizophrenia, Antisocial Personality Disorder, Bipolar Disorder or Social Phobia. Each involves specific strategies related to the diagnostic category. This also will vary with the substances that are part of the combinations. Motivation strategies need to be adapted to the patient's point in the cycle of change (Drake & Noordsy, 1997).

Appropriate treatment referral

Assuming the success of the above approaches to treatment, the aim is to help the concurrent disorders patient continue in an appropriate addiction treatment

408

program. The patient may use a program that is integrated into the admitting program (e.g., an addiction service within a mental health program) or a parallel program that is external to the admitting program. In either case, careful plans must be made to help the services complement each other. The patient must not "fall between the cracks." Advocacy to admit persons with concurrent disorders to an appropriate addiction program is essential.

At this time integrated services are not common and more integrated services are needed in the future. Because of the number of concurrent disorders presenting to physicians and health services, particularly in psychiatric centres, some clinical responsibility for integrating treatment in these centres is the only realistic solution. There are simply not enough addiction services to parallel all the mental health services.

Advocacy in a parallel addiction service, such as a self-help organization, may require special attention to the need for medication. Alcoholics Anonymous publishes a pamphlet about this issue which is very helpful. Patients must be advised that some well-meaning persons in self-help groups might encourage them to "stop their meds." They should be warned that discontinuing their medication often causes a relapse of the mental disorder.

BLOCK THREE: LEARNING TO LIVE DRUG-FREE

This is the second phase of the addiction treatment. Having moved beyond the contemplation stage of phase one, the patient is now assisted to understand the need to overcome his or her substance use problems and learn strategies to do so. With concurrent disorders this invariably means abstinence. This may not always be possible, particularly in persons with both chronic and severe disorders. However, experience to date shows that abstinence usually leads to better functional recovery and an improved basis for continued management of the mental health issues.

Matched treatment approaches

As in phase one of treatment, the treatment strategies must be carefully matched to the specific mental disorders that are combined with the addiction. That is, the strategies are matched to variations like Psychotic Disorders or Mood Disorders, Anxiety Disorders or Personality Disorders. In each variation, the matching strategies would usually follow recommended protocols for the mental disorder, but consider the presence of the combined addiction. The improvements from addiction treatment develop over a time period. Most of the improvement is in the first eight to 16 weeks, but some neuropsychological improvements, as in chronic Alcohol Dependence, continue for periods of up to

409

24 months. These improvements provide a better physical and psychological foundation for the concurrent disorder. Through the successful treatment of a substance use problem, there are possible benefits for the outcomes of most mental disorders. It is an approach that is definitely worth the effort.

What must be re-emphasized though, is that the *treatment of the mental disorder is not the treatment of an addiction*. They are independent conditions that require separate but well-integrated treatments. The treatment of one disorder is not the treatment for the other, even though the treatments impact positively on one another. Integration means planning for both aspects of treatment and making them both work in a timely way.

The components of this phase are parallel to other addiction programs and include:
• Counselling
• Self-help
• Group work and support
• Addiction education
• Concurrent disorder education
• Introduction to relapse prevention strategies
• Concurrent case management (see Block 5).

Details of these strategies for addiction treatment are considered elsewhere in this manual. In contrast to treating an addiction alone, when treating concurrent disorders clinicians must be systematically aware of the nature and effects of the mental disorder. For example, if the concurrent disorder is Schizophrenia, the clinician must consider problems such as thought disorder and low motivation. If the concurrence is with a Personality Disorder, consideration must be given to issues of self-perception and relational difficulties. In most of the mental disorders, particularly chronic disorders, one must consider pharmacotherapy and issues of compliance. These considerations are just a few examples of issues and challenges to the successful integration of treatment that are not part of the usual non-concurrent addiction management.

BLOCK FOUR: REHABILITATION AND RELAPSE PREVENTION

Rehabilitation and relapse prevention is a third phase in addiction treatment. In the case of those with chronic concurrent disorders, a traditional mental rehabilitation program needs to be supplemented by a structured relapse prevention component (Annis, Herie & Watkin-Merek, 1997). Substance use relapse prevention significantly aids the successful management of the mental disorder and its social issues (Minkoff & Drake, 1991). (See also Section 2.1.)

The duration and intensity of rehabilitation may need to be increased in light of the chronicity and severity of individual conditions, especially with regard to the mental disorder (e.g., Schizophrenia). Experience shows that sufficient rehabilitation time is rewarded with better outcomes. The need for greater staff input during a lengthy period of rehabilitation is often not adequately funded, but reaps great cost benefits.

In chronic patients, relapse prevention is aided by random urine drug screen monitoring. Seeking agreement from the patient for this strategy not only helps to monitor progress but is helpful to many patients to reinforce abstinence. Self-help groups provide structure for community rehabilitation. An additional advantage is the availability of self-help groups in every community. An informed sponsor is helpful to the mental health patient when adjusting to the program. In larger communities there are some self-help groups especially for concurrent disorders (e.g., "double trouble groups"). Some community mental health groups may be able to provide long-term support. Part of a long-term strategy is placing the patient in supportive community housing that is also committed to providing a drug-free environment.

BLOCK FIVE: CASE MANAGEMENT

Case management is an approach that is continuous through all the treatment blocks described. It is the main strategy for integrating timely, matched and comprehensive modalities through what can be a complicated treatment format. The case manager should keep the focus on the necessary broadly based bio-psychosocial commitment of the program (Drake & Noordsy, 1997).

A biopsychosocial perspective, as pointed out at the beginning of this section, is almost always necessary in concurrent disorders. Just as a car cannot run on three tires, no matter how good the tires are, or how carefully they have been installed, effective case management should be committed to using all modalities and matching each to the patient's needs. This perspective usually requires

411

a team of disciplines working carefully together in order to have the necessary care in each area. The case manager should have basic skills in both mental health and addictions. The case manager should also be comfortable working in both the addiction and mental health systems in order to be able to advocate for patients who frequently need to straddle both systems (Minkoff & Drake, 1991).

SUICIDE: A SPECIAL CONSIDERATION

Depression is the most common mental problem associated with suicide. Substance-Related Disorders, especially Alcohol Dependence, are second in the list of causes of suicide. In concurrent disorders, the combination of these factors is common and makes those with concurrent disorders a high-risk population.

PHARMACOTHERAPY OF CONCURRENT DISORDERS

General principles
Pharmacotherapy for concurrent disorders requires consideration of the medication used to treat the addiction problems, the medication used to treat the mental disorder, the pharmacotherapeutic action of the substances the individual may be using, medication for medical problems and the interaction between any of these. A comprehensive list of all of these should be made available and should be monitored by members of the treatment team, especially the responsible physicians. Unless a list is kept, it is easy to miss medications prescribed by a family doctor or an over-the-counter or herbal medication used by the patient.

Pharmacotherapeutic principles
Some of the usual pharmacotherapeutic principles are especially critical in cases of concurrence.
- When pharmacotherapy is used in concurrent disorders, it must *always* be in the context of a biopsychosocial strategy.
- Specific reasons for the use of individual medications with selected target symptoms are recommended. These reasons may be psychiatric, addiction-related or medical.
- The ever-present problem of drug interaction must be carefully considered and include the potential interactions of the varied medications and the substances being used. An example is the ability of some substances to exaggerate anticholinergic effects.
- Medications used to treat concurrent disorders should not include medications that have an abuse or dependence liability. When exceptional circumstances warrant the use of such medications, they must be chosen very carefully.

412

Pharmacotherapy — specific concurrent disorders considerations

All of the above points are accepted pharmacotherapeutic principles. However, they have heightened importance in the combinations used with concurrent disorders. Below are some specific considerations:

• Substance users are often non-compliant with their prescribed medication, leading to relapse of the mental disorder. This is often based on the patient's fear of using a substance and taking medication at the same time.

• Some abused substances are pharmacokinetically competitive with drugs used in mental health contexts. For example, nicotine interacts with many antipsychotic medications increasing the incidence of side-effects, including tardive dyskinesia. Caffeine also affects the bioavailability of some antipsychotics (Lucas, Pickar et al., 1990).

• Some substances with low abuse potential are more likely to be abused by individuals with mental disorders. For example, benztropine mesylate (Cogentin®), used to treat side-effects of antipsychotics, is sometimes abused by patients with Schizophrenia for its anticholinergic effects. Some patients with chronic psychiatric disorders also use dimenhydrinate (Gravol®). In large doses, dimenhydrinate can lead to drug-induced delirium and psychosis. When abused by patients with Schizophrenia this can present a very confusing clinical picture.

TABLE 4: Interactions between Drugs of Abuse and Common Therapeutic Agents[†]

Drug of Abuse	Therapeutic Agent	Interaction and Mechanism (if known)
Ethanol	• Disulfiram	Acetaldehyde dehydrogenase inhibition produces flushing, hypotension, nausea, tachycardia. Fatal reactions possible.
	• MAO inhibitors	Impaired hepatic metabolism of tyramine in some beverages produces a dangerous, possibly fatal pressor response.
	• Tricyclic antidepressants	Acute ethanol may inhibit first-pass TCA metabolism, yielding additive CNS impairment. Chronic ethanol use induces hepatic TCA metabolism up to three fold.

413

Table 4 continued

Drug of Abuse	Therapeutic Agent	Interaction and Mechanism (if known)
Ethanol (cont'd)	• Neuroleptics	Cumulative CNS impairment of psychomotor skills, judgment and behavior. Possible increased risk of akathisia and dystonia.
	• Anticonvulsants	Chronic ethanol use produces prolonged hepatic microsomal enzyme induction, reducing phenytoin levels. Possible seizure risk.
Barbiturates	• Tricyclic antidepressants	Increased TCA metabolism may reduce efficacy. Acutely, combination may potentiate respiratory depression.
	• MAO inhibitors	May also inhibit barbiturate metabolism, prolonging intoxication.
	• Neuroleptics	Induced hepatic microsomal enzymes may reduce chlorpromazine levels.
	• Anticonvulsants	Valproic acid increases phenobarbital levels and toxicity. Induced hepatic microsomal enzymes may lower carbamazepine levels. Combined induction and competitive inhibition yield unpredictable phenytoin levels.
Benzodiazepines	• Disulfiram	Inhibited hepatic oxidation may enhance benzodiazepine effects. Oxazepam and lorazepam (inactivated by glucuronidation) are not thus affected.
	• MAO inhibitors	Two reports describe edema with chlordiazepoxide.

414

Table 4 continued

Drug of Abuse	Therapeutic Agent	Interaction and Mechanism (if known)
Opiates	• MAO inhibitors	Meperidine has produced severe excitation, diaphoresis, rigidity, hypertension or hypotension, coma and death.
	• Neuroleptics	Chlorpromazine and meperidine may produce hypotension and excessive CNS depression.
	• Anticonvulsants	Propoxyphene inhibits oxidation of carbamazepine, yielding toxic levels. Methadone metabolism may be increased by carbamazepine or pheny-toin via hepatic enzyme induction, causing withdrawal.
Stimulants	• MAO inhibitors	MAO inhibitors increase neuronal catecholamine storage; amphetamines and cocaine provoke abrupt release, hyperpyrexia, severe hyper-tension, and death.
	• Neuroleptics	Amphetamines and cocaine exacerbate positive symptoms of chronic psychosis. Conversely, neuroleptics may effectively treat stimulant-induced psychosis.

† Reproduced with permission. Copyright 1997 W.B. Saunders.

Selection of medication

The important principle of specificity of medication selection was emphasized above. To aid in these selections, Table 5 below includes potential considerations for medication that may occur in concurrent disorders. Each of these potentials must be clinically clarified within the appropriate phase of treatment.

UNDERSTANDING CONCURRENT DISORDERS

An understanding of the identification and treatment of concurrent disorders is imperative for physicians treating patients with substance use problems and for those treating patients with mental health problems. Although there is increasing recognition of the high prevalence of concurrent disorders, there still exists an urgent need for additional clinical research in this area.

TABLE 5: Selected List of Pharmacotherapies for Concurrent Disorders

Some pharmacotherapy is available for some or some combinations of the following:

Use Disorders: (substance specific)
  treatment of dependence
  treatment of severe intoxication
  treatment of withdrawal

Induced Disorders: (substance specific)
  treatment of induced psychoses
  treatment of induced Mood Disorders
  treatment of induced Anxiety Disorders
  treatment of induced Sleep Disorders
  treatment of induced Sexual Disorders

Any of the above may also be treated in combinations such as the following:

Primary Psychotic Disorders with
  treatment of dependence
  treatment of intoxication
  treatment of withdrawal
  treatment of one or more of the induced disorders

Primary Mood Disorders with
  the same list as psychoses above

Primary Anxiety Disorders with
  the same list as psychoses above

Primary Personality Disorders with
  the same list as psychoses above

Other primary Mental Disorders with
  the same list as psychoses above

416

R E F E R E N C E S

American Psychiatric Association. (1994). *Diagnostic and Statistical Manual of Mental Disorders: DSM-IV* (4th ed.). Washington, DC: American Psychiatric Association.

Annis, H.M., Herie, M.A. & Watkin-Merek, L. (1997). Structured relapse prevention. In S. Harrison & V. Carver (Eds.), *Alcohol and Drug Problems: A Practical Guide for Counsellors* (2nd ed.). Toronto: Addiction Research Foundation.

Beeder, A.B. & Millman, R.B. (1997). Patients with psychopathology. In J.H. Lowinson, P. Ruiz, R.B. Millman & J.G. Langrod (Eds.), *Substance Abuse: A Comprehensive Textbook* (3rd ed.). Baltimore: Williams and Wilkins.

Brooner, R.K., Schmidt, C.W., Felch, L.J. & Bigelow, G.E. (1992). Antisocial behavior and intravenous drug abusers: Implications for diagnosis of antisocial personality disorder. *American Journal of Psychiatry, 149(4),* 482-487.

Drake, R.E. & Noordsy, D.L. (1997). Treatment of comorbid disorders with a case manager approach. In N.S. Miller (Ed.), *The Principles and Practice of Addictions in Psychiatry.* Toronto: W.B. Saunders.

Institute of Medicine. (1990). *Broadening the Base of Treatment for Alcohol Problems.* Washington: National Academy Press.

Kaplan, H.I. & Sadock, B.J. (1998). *Synopsis of Psychiatry* (8th ed.). Baltimore: Williams and Wilkins.

Kent, S., Fogarty, M. & Yellowlees, P. (1995a). A review of studies of heavy users of psychiatry services. *Psychiatric Services, 46(12),* 1247-1253.

Kent, S., Fogarty, M. & Yellowlees, P. (1995b). Heavy utilization of inpatient and outpatient services in a public mental health service. *Psychiatric Services, 46(12),* 1254-1257.

Kessler, R.C., Nelson, C.B., McGonagle, K.A., Edlund, M.J., Frank, R.G. & Leaf, P.J. (1996). The epidemiology of co-occurring addictive and mental disorders: Implications for prevention and service utilization. *American Journal of Orthopsychiatry, 66(1),* 17-31.

Lucas, P. B., Pickar, D., Kelsoe, J., Rapaport, M., Pato, C. & Hommer, D. (1990). Effects of the acute administration of caffeine in patients with Schizophrenia. *Biological Psychiatry, 28(1),* 35-40.

Mathew, R.J. & Wilson, W.H. (1990). Behavioral and cerebrovascular effects of caffeine in patients with anxiety disorders. *Acta Psychiatrica Scandinavica, 82(1),* 17-22.

417

Minkoff, K. & Drake, R. (1991). *Dual Diagnosis of Major Mental Illness and Substance Disorder.* New York: Jossey-Bass.

Nace, E.P., Davis C.W. & Gaspari J.P. (1991). Axis II comorbidity in substance abusers. *American Journal of Psychiatry, 148(1),* 118-120.

Narrow, W.E., Regier, D.A., Rae, D.S., Manderscheid, R.W. & Locke, B.Z. (1993). Use of services by persons with mental and addictive disorders. Findings from the National Institute of Mental Health Epidemiologic Catchment Area Program. *Archives of General Psychiatry, 50(2),* 95-107.

Regier, D.A., Farmer, M.E., Rae, D.S., Locke, B.Z., Keith, S.J., Judd, L.L. & Goodwin, F.K. (1990). Comorbidity of mental disorders with alcohol and other drug abuse. Results from the Epidemiologic Catchment Area (ECA) Study. *Journal of the American Medical Association, 264(19),* 2511-2518.

Ross, H.E. (1995). DSM-III-R alcohol abuse and dependence and psychiatric comorbidity in Ontario: Results from the Mental Health Supplement to the Ontario Health Survey. *Drug and Alcohol Dependence, 39(2),* 111-128.

Ross, H. & Shirley, M. (1997). Life-time problem drinking and psychiatric co-morbidity among Ontario women. *Addiction, 92(2),* 183-196.

Vaillant, G. (1983). *The Natural History of Alcoholism.* Cambridge: Harvard University Press.

Drug-Seeking Behavior in Patients

17 DRUG-SEEKING BEHAVIOR IN PATIENTS

TABLES AND FIGURES

17

DRUG-SEEKING BEHAVIOR IN PATIENTS

Meldon Kahan, MD

DRUG SEEKING

Drug seeking may be defined as the attempt to obtain prescriptions for psychoactive drugs by making false or deliberately exaggerated claims of pain or distress. Drug seeking is a common and serious problem. The inability to identify and manage drug-seeking patients can make a physician's practice unpleasant and frustrating.

Drug seekers tend to gravitate towards clinical services with a high volume of new patients, such as recently opened medical practices, walk-in clinics and emergency departments. They also seek out physicians who are known to prescribe opioids. Most drug seekers attempt to obtain prescription opioids such as oxycodone preparations (Percocet®, Tylox®), hydromorphone (Dilaudid®), meperidine (Demerol®) or anileridine (Leritine®). Others attempt to obtain benzodiazepines such as lorazepam (Ativan®) or alprazolam (Xanax®), barbiturate preparations such as Fiorinal®, or stimulants such as methylphenidate (Ritalin®).

Some drug seekers are dependent on the drug that they are seeking. Others are dependent on illicit opioids such as heroin, and use prescription opioids to relieve symptoms of withdrawal. Still others are addicted to drugs such as cocaine, and obtain prescription opioids to support their habit through trafficking. Others are not dependent on drugs at all but are professional drug dealers. Percocet®, for example, sells for $5 on the street; a 10-minute office visit, therefore, may generate profits of $500 or more. A subset of drug seekers have true chronic pain and have developed a secondary opioid addiction (see Section 8.3). Finally, a very small number of individuals who appear to be drug seekers have undertreated true chronic pain; this phenomenon is known as "pseudoaddiction."

CLINICAL FEATURES

Drug seekers often have the following clinical features:

- They ask for their drug of choice by name (although they would prefer that the physician name it first: "It starts with an F; it is a dark blue capsule...").
- They refuse all other therapeutic options, claiming that they cause adverse effects or that they do not work.
- They make it difficult to confirm their story regarding drug use. For example, they may come to the office late Friday afternoon knowing their regular physician will be difficult to reach.
- Their presenting medical condition lacks objective signs (e.g., migraine headache), making a definitive diagnosis impossible. Common ailments claimed by drug seekers include acute low back pain, migraine headache, toothache and renal colic.
- If the physician shows reluctance to prescribe the desired medication, drug seekers will pressure the physician through pleading, bargaining, anger or dogged persistence. They will attempt to create a sense of urgency — they are in desperate pain and need the medication right away. When refused, they may become angry.

MANAGEMENT OF DRUG SEEKING

Drug seeking can be minimized by adopting the following protocol:

USE GENERAL POLICY STATEMENTS
Definite and categorical statements leave little room for argument, thus avoiding prolonged negotiations with the drug seeker. Say to the patient, "I never prescribe Fiorinal," or "This clinic does not allow physicians to prescribe narcotics to new patients."

ONLY GIVE OPIOIDS IF YOU HONESTLY BELIEVE THAT THE PATIENT IS "ON THE LEVEL"
Giving patients a prescription to get them out of the office is a mistake. These patients will return to the physician again in a short time requesting more medication, and if they are refused, the confrontation will likely be angrier and more time-consuming than if the physician had said no in the first place. These patients might also refer friends to your practice.

DON'T MAKE DECISIONS BASED ON STEREOTYPES

While drug seekers are often young, it is a mistake to rely on age, appearance, or social class in deciding whether someone is a drug seeker.

BE SKEPTICAL OF THE PATIENTS' STORIES OF WHY THEY RAN OUT OF MEDICATIONS

For example, if the medication is so important to the patients that they cannot live for one more day without it, then ask why they allowed the medication to run out.

MAKE YOUR SYSTEM FOR DISPENSING PRESCRIPTIONS "TAMPER-PROOF" (SEE TABLE BELOW)

Some patients are content to leave the office without a script for opioids because they have stolen one or more blank scripts.

TABLE 1: Tips for "Tamper-Proof" Prescribing

Although care is required whenever a prescription is written, extra care must be taken when writing prescriptions for psychoactive medications, especially those with a high dependence liability. Below are some simple tips to avoid the diversion or misuse of licit medications. • Record the amount to be dispensed in both words and numbers on the prescription. • Put several lines through unused space on the prescription. • Use an opioid flow sheet that records dates and amounts prescribed (see Addendum 5 to Section 8). • Do not allow phone repeats. • Keep your prescription pad in a secure location. • If possible, use numbered or non-reproducible prescription pads.

ASK PATIENTS WHETHER THEY HAVE RECEIVED AN OPIOID PRESCRIPTION FROM ANOTHER PHYSICIAN WITHIN THE PAST 30 DAYS

In Canada, patients are required by law to inform the physician writing a narcotic prescription if they have received narcotics from another source within the past 30 days, even if the physician did not ask them. Commonly prescribed opioids such as Tylenol® #3, Fiorinal® C1/2, Percodan® and Percocet® are considered narcotics under this act.

DO NOT LEAVE YOUR PRESCRIPTION PAD LYING ABOUT
Each blank script fetches up to $5 on the street. Treat the prescription pad as if it were your own personal cheque-book.

ASK PATIENTS WHETHER THEY HAVE A PROBLEM WITH THE DRUG THEY ARE REQUESTING
A non-confrontational approach to the patient is necessary. The physician may simply say to the patient, "This drug is potentially addicting, and some patients who take this drug regularly develop problems with it. Do you think you have a problem like this?" Occasionally patients will acknowledge their drug problem if approached in this manner.

DO NOT ATTEMPT AN OUTPATIENT OPIOID TAPER
Even if the patient acknowledges his or her dependence, opioid tapering should only be attempted when (a) the patient's diagnostic work-up establishes a probable organic basis to his or her pain of sufficient severity to warrant opioid treatment; and (b) the physician has a long-standing relationship with the patient and is fairly certain that the risk of double-doctoring is minimal. The majority of drug seekers will not meet these two conditions. Remember that although opioid withdrawal is uncomfortable, it is not dangerous, and the physician is not obligated to provide an opioid prescription to a dependent patient. (See Sections 8.1 and 8.3 on opioid withdrawal and chronic non-malignant pain for further discussion on opioid tapering.)

DO NOT USE OPIOID DRUGS OTHER THAN METHADONE IN THE TREATMENT OF OPIOID DEPENDENCE
In other words, it is not acceptable for a physician to maintain an opioid-dependent patient on opioids until he or she gets into treatment.

PRESCRIBING OPIOIDS WHEN DRUG SEEKING IS SUSPECTED

Some physicians suspect that a patient is a drug seeker but feel obligated to prescribe opioids because the patient might in fact have legitimate pain. The following protocol includes some of the key points in the assessment and management of this difficult clinical situation. For a more detailed discussion, refer to Section 8.3, particularly the sections on the assessment and management of opioid dependence in patients with chronic pain.

424

TAKE AN ALCOHOL AND DRUG HISTORY

Patients with a current or past history of dependence on other drugs are at greater risk for opioid dependence.

ALWAYS ORDER AT LEAST ONE URINE DRUG SCREEN

If the physician is prescribing oxycodone for the first time, the presence of hydromorphone in the urine before the patient fills this prescription suggests that the patient is double-doctoring; the absence of oxycodone after the prescription has been filled suggests that the patient is diverting it to other sources.

LOOK FOR CLUES TO INJECTION DRUG USE

Be alert to such objective signs as track marks and elevations in hepatic transaminases.

GET CORROBORATING INFORMATION FROM PREVIOUS PHYSICIANS AND FAMILY MEMBERS

It can take many months to confirm or rule out a diagnosis of opioid dependence; information from previous physicians and others can shorten this time considerably.

HAVE THE PATIENT SIGN A TREATMENT CONTRACT THAT SPELLS OUT CONSEQUENCES FOR BREAKING THE CONTRACT

The contract should specify that opioids will be prescribed by only one physician and scripts will not be renewed early. (See Addendum 4 to Section 8 for a sample treatment contract.)

AVOID SHORT-ACTING OPIOIDS WITH A HIGH DEPENDENCE LIABILITY

These include Percocet®, Dilaudid®, Demerol®, Leritine® and Fiorinal® C1/4 or C1/2.

PRESCRIBE SMALL AMOUNTS FOR SHORT PERIODS OF TIME

Frequently reassess the patient.

REFER THE PATIENT FOR CONSULTATION

However, be aware that physicians who continue to prescribe opioids in the hope that the specialist's appointment two months hence will resolve matters are often disappointed. The consultant should be informed of any concerns about drug seeking and asked about the role of opioids in the patient's treatment. The referring physician should ask the consultant specific questions such as, "In your experience, do patients with this condition require opioids in this amount and for this duration?"

BE ALERT TO BEHAVIORAL PATTERNS THAT SUGGEST SUBSTANCE DEPENDENCE

Look for signs such as:

- double-doctoring
- prescription forgery
- acquiring opioids from the street
- unauthorized opioids in the urine drug screen
- signs of opioid intoxication (drowsiness, nodding off, pinpoint pupils, etc.)
- repeatedly running out of medication early
- taking opioids in doses far in excess of what is normally required for patients with the presenting condition
- repeatedly refusing to try non-opioid treatments.

STOP PRESCRIBING OPIOIDS IF SUBSTANCE DEPENDENCE IS DIAGNOSED

Once a diagnosis of substance dependence is made, the physician should cease prescribing opioids, treat with clonidine and refer the patient to a drug treatment program.

The Impaired Physician

18 THE IMPAIRED PHYSICIAN

18

THE IMPAIRED PHYSICIAN

Graeme Cunningham, MD

PREVALENCE

The prevalence of alcohol and drug problems among physicians is no different from that found in the general public (Adler & Potts, 1985).

In 1992, Hughes and colleagues described a survey of 5,426 physicians who completed an anonymous questionnaire on their use of 13 substances during their lifetime, in the previous year and in the past month. This study described six per cent of physicians as heavy drinkers, while finding that physicians were five times more likely than non-physicians to self-medicate with benzo-diazepines and opioids (Hughes, Brandenburg et al., 1992). Also in 1992, Brewster sent a questionnaire to 3,000 physicians and found that six per cent of physicians who responded to the questionnaire were heavy drinkers.

Both surveys found that although substance use disorder did occur in the medical profession, it was no more prevalent than in the general public. Nonetheless, physicians who are abusing substances and still practising are a cause of concern among hospital administrators, chiefs of staff and chiefs of departments.

Brewster has suggested that physicians who are training in emergency medicine or psychiatry are more likely to use mood-altering substances than their colleagues, but no particular medical specialty has a markedly high risk for substance abuse. Anesthetists seem to be overrepresented in treatment programs, which is believed to be a function of their easy access to powerful opioids (Brewster, 1992).

429

Factors Contributing to Substance Abuse in Physicians

The calm, professional façade of some physicians can hide emotional turmoil. Medical training is demanding and intense, while respect for physicians is viewed by many as diminishing. The result is that physicians often experience dissatisfaction with the conditions and considerable stresses of practice. Some physicians may then resort to unhelpful defence mechanisms. In addition, physicians' training and their focus on the well-being of their patients may not adequately equip them to deal with the myriad of emotions they experience in the course of their daily rounds. In such a context, many drift into an overwork syndrome that is characterized by ritualized behavior, irritability, and neglect of self and family. Those who have not learned to examine their feelings about death, disease and the tragedies they encounter daily may turn to suppression and denial to cope. Although clearly unhealthy, self-medication soon becomes an important part of this cycle. While often not evident to the physician or those around him or her, use of alcohol and prescription drugs may increase in an attempt to maintain control in an otherwise chaotic life. For most, relationships and personal health suffer long before there is any obvious professional impairment.

Bloom and Wallinger (1989) provide an insight into the psychological profile of the substance-abusing professional. Typically, the substance-abusing professional was raised in a dysfunctional family, lacking strong support structures. He or she may have low self-esteem and be filled with self-doubt and feelings of inadequacy. Emotionally immature, the addicted person may have difficulty organizing and expressing feelings, be unduly sensitive and combine a low tolerance for frustration with an unrealistic need for perfection. These people are goal-directed and often at the top of the class academically. In a profession that demands perfection of its practitioners, the rewards of this work ethic are often all too few. Behavior that would be expected to lead to ill health in their patients can become an easy way to escape for physicians at risk. Not unexpectedly, there is often a family history of substance use disorders.

Intellectualization, denial, guilt, shame and secrecy become factors that serve to perpetuate the professional's abuse. The silence of colleagues and loved ones often completes the picture. Fear of "ruining a career" and the "risk of being wrong" become excuses for overlooking the obvious.

Recognizing the Substance-Abusing Physician

There are no specific behaviors that can conclusively identify a substance-abusing physician. Some non-specific clues, outlined in the table below, may be helpful when substance abuse is suspected.

430

TABLE 1: Indicators of Substance Abuse

Substance abuse by a physician may be accompanied by the following behaviors:

- isolation, professionally and socially, which may be a forerunner of impairment, but almost always accompanies it
- inappropriate prescribing of large doses of opioids to patients
- change of personality
- loss of efficiency and reliability
- increase in number of sick days
- development of indecision
- heavy "wastage" of drugs
- unpredictable work habits
- sloppy charts and writing
- mood swings
- changes in routine
- desire to work alone
- wearing of long sleeves
- presence of a disabling anxiety
- frequent trips to the bathroom
- frequent presence in department when off-duty
- increase in number of complaints from patients about the physician's attitude and behavior, especially regarding a change in demeanor
- physical changes
- memory loss
- suicide intent

Even if he or she is not clinically addicted, a physician who uses drugs or alcohol while practising must be confronted.

Mood swings and slurred speech over the telephone are often noted by colleagues, and ultimately office conduct is affected by substance use. By the time the inappropriate substance use manifests itself in a hospital setting the doctor is usually very ill.

DIAGNOSIS AND INTERVENTION

Early recognition of a physician's problematic substance use is often inhibited by the failure of colleagues and other medical staff to observe the signs, the sequential impact and the progression of the addiction and their own denial of the situation. Ultimately, a lack of adequate training prevents colleagues' early recognition of the impaired physician's problematic substance use.

431

The early diagnosis of a physician's substance use disorder is critical to increasing both the chances for successful recovery and the ability to retain professional standing and reputation. The hallmark of addiction is denial — waiting for spontaneous insights from the impaired physician is futile and dangerous. While anger is a typical reaction to intervention or confrontation about substance use, most physicians ultimately express gratitude to those involved, even if only after successful treatment.

According to Benzer (1991), the basic principles of a successful intervention are as follows:

- It should be carried out by more than one colleague, particularly those in positions of authority, such as chairpersons of departments or chiefs of staff.
- It should occur when the physician is sober and soon after an incident precipitated by the problem.
- The location should be quiet and non-threatening.
- Documentation of specific incidents of impaired behavior should be used if available.
- Colleagues should have a non-judgmental attitude. They should anticipate possible reactions such as denial, anger and threats, including legal threats.
- The goal is for the physician to agree to an assessment by an independent specialist rather than to accept a stigmatizing diagnosis and mandatory treatment.

The possibility of substance use disorder should be approached like any other serious medical condition. The physician should be referred to an appropriate specialist for assessment with the agreement that the assessment will be shared with the referring physician and, if necessary, their business associates and hospital officers. Based on this assessment, a decision for further treatment or return to work can be made.

TREATMENT

Like anyone else with a drug or alcohol problem, an addicted physician requires treatment. The initial goal when treating a physician is abstinence following detoxification, which may require medical supervision. In the longer term, the goal is for the physician to control his or her substance use.

Residential treatment
The requirement for residential treatment for physicians is a controversial subject. It is indicated for physicians who have failed to remain abstinent after

intervention or community-based treatment, for those who have concurrent medical or psychiatric problems and for those who have experienced serious consequences, such as licence loss, legal repercussions or loss of social supports. Residential treatment ranges from one to three months.

Physician-only treatment centres are not necessarily indicated if the physician can easily accept the patient role. Thus, a conveniently located treatment centre may be sought to allow for follow-up.

Duration

What is significant for treating substance-abusing physicians is that the duration of treatment, specifically follow-up, should be at least two years. The most important aspect of treatment for an addicted physician seems to be peer group therapy over a prolonged period (Gallegos, Talbott et al., 1992). Studies have shown that physicians who attend 12-step-based support groups are more likely to recover than those who do not (Galanter, Talbott et al., 1990).

Treatment programs

There are positive, sympathetic approaches to the occurrence of substance abuse among physicians. In Ontario, for example, the Ontario Medical Association sponsors the Physician Health Program. An outline of the program is included as an addendum to this section as an example of how the treatment of substance-abusing physicians can be carried out.

While the Ontario program advocates the unbiased treatment of physicians and highlights the need for confidentiality as an impetus for entering treatment, it also clearly outlines the circumstances under which a physician's impairment would be reported to the professional regulating body.

WOMEN PHYSICIANS

Physicians should be aware that alcohol and drug addiction is as much a problem for women physicians as it is for their male colleagues. Yet, of the 250 physicians who participated in a Canadian program for addicted physicians over a four-year period, only 12 were women (Cunningham, 1994). Clearly women are underrepresented in this group, as they are in other populations who seek addiction treatment (Reed, 1985).

Physicians should also be aware that the stigma of addiction in women can be very significant. Further, the demands of family and profession can delay entry into treatment and interfere with follow-up and continuing care.

PROGNOSIS

A number of studies have demonstrated an excellent prognosis for physicians who receive treatment for substance abuse problems and who participate in a long-term monitoring program (Reading, 1992). The monitoring program may simply be attendance at mutual help group meetings and/or a health professional support group, or it may be more intense, involving random urine drug screens as well as continuing care contracts.

Monitoring

Close monitoring may account in part for the excellent prognosis for physicians: Shore (1987) found a 96 per cent "improved" rate in monitored physicians versus 64 per cent in unmonitored physicians. The physicians in this study were rated as "improved" if they were engaged in professional activities and had stable interpersonal relationships. Shore concluded that there is increasing evidence that a two- to four-year follow-up period is positively correlated with a favorable treatment outcome.

R E F E R E N C E S

Adler, G.R. & Potts, F.E. (1985). Narcotics control in anesthesia training. *Journal of the American Medical Association, 253(21),* 3133-3136.

Benzer, D.G. (1991). Healing the healer: A primer on physician impairment. *Wisconsin Medical Journal, 90(2),* 70-79.

Bloom, M.A. & Wallinger, C.L. (1989). Lawyers and alcoholism, is it time for a new approach? *Pennsylvania Bar Association Quarterly, 60* 187-200.

Brewster, J.M. (1992). *Drug Use among Canadian Professionals.* Ottawa: Health and Welfare Canada.

Cunningham, G.M. (1994). A treatment program for physicians impaired by alcohol and other drugs. *Annals of the Royal College of Physicians and Surgeons of Canada, 27,* 219-221.

Galanter, M, Talbott, D., Gallegos, K. & Rubenstone, E. (1990). Combined Alcoholics Anonymous and professional care for addicted physicians. *American Journal of Psychiatry, 147(1),* 64-68.

Gallegos, K.V., Lubin, B.H., Bowers, C., Blevins, J.W., Talbott, G.D. & Wilson, P.O. (1992). Relapse and recovery: Five and ten year follow-up study of chemically dependent physicians. The Georgia experience. *Maryland Medical Journal, 41(4),* 315-39.

Hughes, P.H., Brandenburg, N., Baldwin, D.C. Jr., Storr, C.L., Williams, K.M., Anthony, J.C. & Sheehan, D.V. (1992). Prevalence of substance abuse amongst US physicians. *Journal of the American Medical Association, 267(17)*, 2333-2338.

Reading, E.G. (1992). Nine years experience with chemically dependent physicians: The New Jersey experience. *Maryland Medical Journal, 41(4)*, 325-329.

Reed, B.G. (1985). Drug misuse and dependency in women: The meaning and implications of being considered a special population or minority group. *International Journal of the Addictions, 20(1)*, 13-62.

Shore, J. (1987). The Oregon experience with impaired physicians on probation: An eight-year follow-up. *Journal of the American Medical Association, 257(21)*, 2931-2934.

ADDENDUM

THE PHYSICIAN HEALTH PROGRAM OF THE ONTARIO MEDICAL ASSOCIATION*

A CONFIDENTIAL PROGRAM

1. The Physician Health Program (PHP) of the OMA is a program designed by physicians, for physicians. We provide prompt advice and support to physicians who feel at risk or think they have a problem, their families and concerned colleagues. Intervention co-ordination, referral for assessment and treatment, recovery monitoring and advocacy are components of our comprehensive service.

    We respect a physician's privacy and maintain confidentiality to the greatest possible degree. Names of referral sources are also held in confidence.

2. The PHP will receive calls from any physician, family member or concerned individual.

    If necessary we will evaluate the problem and organize and help conduct an intervention with discretion and compassion.

    Excellent treatment resources are available, and once primary treatment is completed, the PHP will conduct long-term monitoring to enhance the quality of the recovery process.

    We proudly advocate for physicians in our program and help them cope with any issues that arise during recovery.

---

* Reprinted with permission of the Ontario Medical Association, copyright 1999.

3. *Confidentiality*

   The PHP is a program of the Ontario Medical Association. We respect the confidentiality of those who contact us and physicians who use our program. We DO NOT automatically report their names to the College of Physicians and Surgeons of Ontario.

4. Our confidential number is 1-800-851-6066, and can be called anytime. In Toronto call 340-2972. Our ad appears every month in the *Ontario Medical Review*, and we are also featured on-line at the OMA Weblink Internet site at www.oma.org. We welcome calls from anywhere in Ontario, from physicians and their families of any background.

APPENDICES

Overview of Epidemiology of Substance Use in Canada and the United States

STATISTICS ON SUBSTANCE USE — CANADA

STATISTICS ON SUBSTANCE USE — UNITED STATES

APPENDIX 1

OVERVIEW OF EPIDEMIOLOGY OF SUBSTANCE USE IN CANADA AND THE UNITED STATES

Peter Selby, MBBS

STATISTICS ON SUBSTANCE USE — CANADA

Statistics can be useful to physicians in clinical encounters because they provide independent, objective information that may help motivate patients to change their behavior (see Section 2.5).

Costs of substance abuse

Single and his colleagues (1996) have estimated that substance use cost Canadians $18.45 billion (or 2.7 per cent of the GDP) in 1992 (Table 1). Included in this conservative estimate are the health, social and economic costs to society.

TABLE 1: Cost of Substance Use in Canada in 1992[†]

Substance	Cost in billions of $	% of total cost
Tobacco	9.56	51.8
Alcohol	7.52	40.8
Illicit drugs	1.37	7.4
Total	18.45	100.0

† Adapted from Single, Robson, et al., 1996.

TOBACCO

Prevalence of use

In 1995, there were about 6.1 million smokers in Canada aged 15 or older. The prevalence of smoking has declined from 49.5 per cent in 1965 to 27.4 per cent in 1995. However, there has been little change since 1990 (Canadian Centre on Substance Abuse & Addiction Research Foundation, 1997). According to *Canada's Alcohol and Other Drugs Survey 1994,* 27 per cent of Canadians were current smokers, 26 per cent former smokers and 46 per cent non-smokers. Men aged 18 to 19, people of lower socioeconomic status and people with lower levels of education were more likely to be current smokers. Among the provinces, Quebec had the highest prevalence of smokers at 33.6 per cent, while Ontario had the lowest, at 22.4 per cent. Across Canada, francophones were more likely to be smokers than non-francophones. Daily smokers averaged 15 cigarettes per day while non-daily smokers averaged two cigarettes per day (Health Canada, 1997).

In 1994, of 3.9 million youths aged 10 to 19, the prevalence of smoking rose from 2.5 per cent among 10- to 12-year-olds, to 29 per cent among 18- to 19-year-olds. Young females were more likely to be current smokers, especially between the ages of 13 and 17 (Health Canada, 1997).

Mortality

In 1992, there were approximately 33,498 deaths attributed to tobacco in Canada, or an average of 91 deaths per day. This accounted for 17 per cent of total mortality. Males accounted for 69 per cent of these deaths. Of deaths attributed to tobacco, 35 per cent were due to lung cancer, 20 per cent to ischemic heart disease and 17 per cent to chronic obstructive pulmonary disease (COPD). Tobacco accounted for 495,640 potential years of life lost (PYLL) (Single, Robson, et al., 1996).

Morbidity

In 1992, tobacco-related causes accounted for 208,095 hospital separations. Of the over three million hospital days attributable to tobacco-related illness, the majority were due to COPD, followed by stroke, ischemic heart disease and lung cancer (Canadian Centre on Substance Abuse & Addiction Research Foundation, 1997).

FIGURE A: Smoking Status of Canadians†

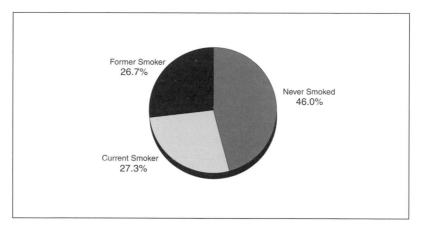

Former Smoker
26.7%

Never Smoked
46.0%

Current Smoker
27.3%

† Adapted from Health Canada, 1997.

ALCOHOL

Prevalence of use, problems and dependence

The number of Canadians who drank declined from 84 per cent in 1979 to 72 per cent in 1994. Beer was the most commonly consumed beverage, followed by wine and hard liquor. According to the 1997 *Canadian Profile,* one in 10 drinkers (9.2 per cent) reported at least one problem (including social, health, happiness, home life, work/school and finances) due to alcohol consumption. Health problems were experienced by 5.1 per cent of drinkers, while 4.7 per cent of drinkers had financial problems. Heavy drinkers (at least one episode of consuming five or more drinks in the week prior to the survey) tended to be young males with high incomes. Men were almost twice as likely to have drinking problems, especially between the ages of 15 and 24 or if they were single or divorced. People with low incomes and those in the Atlantic Provinces also reported more problems with alcohol. In 1991, the prevalence of dependence was 1,700 per 100,000 population, down from a peak of 2,600 per 100,000 population, which was last reported in 1978 (Canadian Centre on Substance Abuse & Addiction Research Foundation, 1997).

Mortality

In 1992, 6,701 Canadians, or three per cent of total mortality, died due to alcohol-related problems. The majority of deaths were due to motor vehicle accidents (1,477), followed by cirrhosis (960) and suicides (918). Alcohol accounted for 186,257 PYLL (i.e., 27.8 years lost per alcohol-related death) (Canadian Centre on Substance Abuse & Addiction Research Foundation, 1997).

445

Morbidity

In 1992, two per cent of all hospitalizations were due to alcohol-related problems, while a total of 86,076 hospital separations were attributed to alcohol. The majority were accounted for by accidental falls (16,901), followed by alcohol dependence syndrome (14,316) and motor vehicle accidents (11,154) (Canadian Centre on Substance Abuse & Addiction Research Foundation, 1997).

Drinking and driving

In 1993, 46 per cent of fatally injured drivers had some measure of alcohol in their blood. Of those drivers, 39 per cent were over the Canadian legal limit of 80 mg% and 30 per cent over 150 mg%. In 1993, one in eight adults reported driving in the preceding year after consuming two or more drinks. Typically, males between age 18 and 45 with high incomes were more likely to be impaired drivers (Canadian Centre on Substance Abuse & Addiction Research Foundation, 1997).

Beneficial effects of alcohol

In 1992, Single and colleagues (1996) found that alcohol prevented more total deaths than it caused, mainly by preventing ischemic heart disease. However, this benefit is only seen among older adults and therefore the PYLL due to alcohol is almost double the potential years of life saved by alcohol. Also, the number of hospitalizations due to alcohol consumption were greater than those prevented by low levels of drinking.

FIGURE B: Drinking Patterns in Canada†

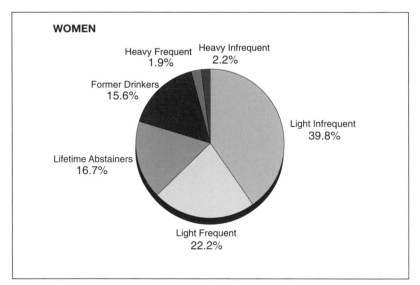

Figure B continued

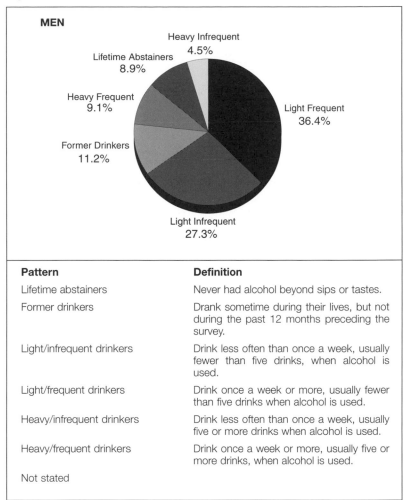

MEN

Pattern	Definition
Lifetime abstainers	Never had alcohol beyond sips or tastes.
Former drinkers	Drank sometime during their lives, but not during the past 12 months preceding the survey.
Light/infrequent drinkers	Drink less often than once a week, usually fewer than five drinks, when alcohol is used.
Light/frequent drinkers	Drink once a week or more, usually fewer than five drinks when alcohol is used.
Heavy/infrequent drinkers	Drink less often than once a week, usually five or more drinks when alcohol is used.
Heavy/frequent drinkers	Drink once a week or more, usually five or more drinks, when alcohol is used.
Not stated	

† Adapted from Health Canada, 1997.

PRESCRIPTION DRUG USE

Prevalence of use

According to *Canada's Alcohol and Other Drug Survey 1994*, approximately eight per cent of adults over the age of 15 used sleeping pills in the prior year. Greater consumption was reported among the elderly and among women. Of those surveyed 13.1 per cent used opioid narcotic pain relievers (codeine, meperidine, morphine). Consumption was highest among younger people, women, or individuals who were divorced, separated or had lower incomes (Health Canada, 1997).

Drug diversion

In 1994, there were 1,115 thefts and other losses of narcotic and controlled substances reported. The two leading sources of thefts and losses were pharmacies, with 486 reports of theft or loss, and hospitals, with 394 reports of theft or loss (Canadian Centre on Substance Abuse & Addiction Research Foundation, 1997).

Prescription forgeries

Of the 1,072 prescription forgeries detected in 1994, most occurred in Ontario. The overwhelming majority, 1,052, were for narcotics, mainly codeine and oxycodone. Fifty were for other controlled substances such as methylphenidate and barbiturates (Canadian Centre on Substance Abuse & Addiction Research Foundation, 1997).

ILLICIT DRUG USE

Prevalence of use

The true prevalence of illicit drug use is unknown due to the difficulty of collecting such data. However, in 1994, 28.2 per cent of Canadian adults reported using cannabis sometime in their past, 3.8 per cent crack, 5.2 per cent LSD, 1 per cent amphetamines and 0.5 per cent heroin (Health Canada, 1997).

FIGURE C: Lifetime Use of Drugs by Canadians†

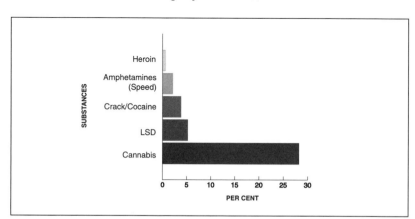

† Adapted from Health Canada, 1997.

448

Mortality

Illicit drug use led to 0.4 per cent of total mortality in Canada. The majority of those deaths, 87 per cent, were of men. Of the total deaths, 42 per cent were due to suicide, 14 per cent were due to opioid poisoning, nine per cent were due to cocaine poisoning and eight per cent were due to AIDS acquired through the use of illicit drugs. In 1992, illicit drug use accounted for 31,147 potential years of life lost, an average of 42.6 years per death (Canadian Centre on Substance Abuse & Addiction Research Foundation, 1997).

Morbidity

Of all hospitalizations, .02 per cent were attributable to illicit drug use. Drug psychosis, assault and cocaine abuse precipitated 50 per cent of those admissions (Canadian Centre on Substance Abuse & Addiction Research Foundation, 1997).

HIV AND SUBSTANCE USE

Prevalence

The most recent figures published by Health Canada show that the prevalence of HIV in Canadian injection drug users in Toronto increased from 4.5 per cent in 1991–1992 to 9.5 per cent in 1997. In Vancouver, the prevalence rose from four per cent in 1992–1993 to 23 per cent in 1996–1997. In Montreal, the prevalence increased from five per cent in 1988 to 19.5 per cent in 1997 (Health Canada, 1998).

It is believed that if the prevalence rate crosses 10 per cent, the spread of HIV will become very difficult to control. On the basis of this argument, a national harm-reduction strategy needs to be implemented to keep the prevalence of HIV low in Canada (see Section 12.3).

Magnitude of the problem

Although the quoted statistics reflect the best estimates of the nature of HIV prevalence, it is important to emphasize that they are only estimates. The true magnitude of the problem is not known. The social stigma surrounding substance misuse and the likelihood of surveys missing people with more severe problems may lead to this bias. For more detailed analysis of the data, the reader is referred to *Canadian Profile: Alcohol, Tobacco and Other Drugs* (Canadian Centre for Substance Abuse & Addiction Research Foundation, 1997).

STATISTICS ON SUBSTANCE USE — UNITED STATES

TOBACCO

Prevalence of use
An estimated 64 million Americans (30 per cent of the population aged 12 or older) were current smokers in 1997 (Substance Abuse and Mental Health Services Administration, 1998).

Approximately 4.5 million youths aged 12–17 were current smokers in 1997. The rate of smoking among youths aged 12–17 was 20 per cent. Current smokers aged 12–17 were about nine times as likely to use illicit drugs and 16 times as likely to drink heavily as their non-smoking peers (Substance Abuse and Mental Health Services Administration, 1997).

Among adults, men had somewhat higher rates of smoking than women, but rates of smoking were similar for males and females aged 12–17. The rate of current smokeless tobacco use was significantly higher for men than for women in 1997 (6.0 per cent vs. 0.5 per cent). Over 90 per cent of smokeless tobacco users were men (Substance Abuse and Mental Health Services Administration, 1998).

The prevalence of smoking declined from 42.3 per cent in 1965 to 30 per cent in 1997 (Substance Abuse and Mental Health Services Administration, 1998).

Tobacco and other drug use
According to the *1996 National Household Survey on Drug Abuse,* current smokers were more likely to be heavy drinkers and illicit drug users. Among smokers, the rate of heavy alcohol use (five or more drinks on five or more days in the past month) was 12.8 per cent and the rate of current illicit drug use was 14.7 per cent. Among non-smokers, only 2.5 per cent were heavy drinkers and 2.6 per cent were illicit drug users. An estimated 6.8 million Americans (3.2 per cent of the population) were current users of smokeless tobacco (Substance Abuse and Mental Health Services Administration, 1997).

ALCOHOL

Prevalence of use, problems and dependence
According to the *National Household Survey on Drug Abuse: Population Estimates 1997,* approximately 111 million Americans age 12 and older, or 51 per cent of

450

the population, had used alcohol in the past month (Substance Abuse and Mental Health Services Administration, 1998).

Drinking patterns
In 1996 it was found that about 32 million persons (15.5 per cent) engaged in binge drinking (five or more drinks on at least one occasion in the past month) and about 11 million were heavy drinkers (drinking five or more drinks per occasion on five or more days in the past month) (Substance Abuse and Mental Health Services Administration, 1997).

About 9.5 million current drinkers were aged 12–20. Of these, 4.4 million were binge drinkers, including 1.9 million heavy drinkers. Among youths aged 12–17, the rate of current alcohol use was 49.8 per cent in 1979, 32.5 per cent in 1990, 21.1 per cent in 1995 and 18.8 per cent in 1996 (Substance Abuse and Mental Health Services Administration, 1997).

Fifty-nine per cent of men were past-month alcohol users, compared with 44 per cent of women. Men were much more likely than women to be binge drinkers (22.8 per cent and 8.7 per cent, respectively) and heavy drinkers (9.3 per cent and 1.9 per cent, respectively) (Substance Abuse and Mental Health Services Administration, 1997).

In contrast to the pattern for illicit drugs, the higher the level of educational attainment, the more likely was the current use of alcohol. In 1996, 66 per cent of adults with college degrees were current drinkers, compared with only 39 per cent of those having less than a high-school education. Binge alcohol use rates did not vary across different levels of education. However, the rate of heavy alcohol use was 3.7 per cent among adults who had completed college and 6.8 per cent among adults who had not completed high school (Substance Abuse and Mental Health Services Administration, 1997).

Drinking and driving
The U.S. Department of Transportation's Fatality Analysis Reporting System routinely collects blood alcohol concentration (BAC) data on fatally injured drivers. Twenty states consistently report BAC data for over 80 per cent of fatally injured drivers. Based on those 20 states, in 1997, 30 per cent of fatally injured passenger vehicle drivers had a BAC above 100 mg% (Insurance Institute for Highway Safety, 1998).

451

ILLICIT DRUG USE

Prevalence of use

According to the 1997 *National Household Survey on Drug Abuse,* an estimated 13.9 million Americans were current illicit drug users, meaning they had used an illicit drug in the month prior to the interview. The number of current illicit drug users was at its highest level in 1979, when there were 25 million (Substance Abuse and Mental Health Services Administration, 1998).

Following a significant increase from 1992 to 1995, between 1995 and 1996 there was a decrease in the rate of past-month illicit drug use among youths aged 12–17. The rate was 5.3 per cent in 1992, 10.9 per cent in 1995, and 9.0 per cent in 1996. The decrease between 1995 and 1996 occurred in the younger part of this age group — i.e., those aged 12–15 (Substance Abuse and Mental Health Services Administration, 1997).

For those aged 18–25, the rate of past-month illicit drug use increased from 13.3 per cent in 1994 to 15.6 per cent in 1996. The rate of past-month cocaine use also increased in this age group during this period, from 1.2 per cent to 2.0 per cent (Substance Abuse and Mental Health Services Administration, 1997).

An estimated 2.4 million people started using marijuana in 1995. This was about the same number as in 1994. The annual number of marijuana initiates rose between 1991 and 1994 (Substance Abuse and Mental Health Services Administration, 1997).

The overall number of current cocaine users did not change significantly between 1995 and 1996 (1.45 million in 1995 and 1.75 million in 1996). This was down from a peak of 5.7 million in 1985. Nevertheless, there were still an estimated 652,000 Americans who used cocaine for the first time in 1995 (Substance Abuse and Mental Health Services Administration, 1997).

There were an estimated 141,000 new heroin users in 1995, and there has been an increasing trend in new heroin use since 1992. A large proportion of these recent new users were smoking, snorting, or sniffing heroin, and most were under age 26. The estimated number of past-month heroin users increased from 68,000 in 1993 to 216,000 in 1996 (Substance Abuse and Mental Health Services Administration, 1997).

PERCEIVED RISK OF HARM FROM DRUG USE

The percentage of the population reporting that they perceived great risk of harm in using marijuana once a month increased from 40 per cent in 1994 to 44 per cent in 1996. However, the percentage reporting great risk in using marijuana more frequently (once or twice a week) did not change. Among youths aged 12–17, there was no change in perceived risk of marijuana use between 1994 and 1996. Among youths, the perceived risk of harm increased from 1985 to 1990, then decreased from 1990 to 1994. This trend in perceived risk mirrors the trend in the use of marijuana among youths. As the perceived risk increased, use decreased, and vice versa (Substance Abuse and Mental Health Services Administration, 1997).

Among youths aged 12–17, there was a significant decrease in the perceived risk of occasional (once a month) use of cocaine from 1994 to 1996. Since 1990, the percentage of youths reporting great perceived risk in using cocaine once a month decreased from 72 per cent to 54 per cent. This measure of perceived risk had previously increased significantly, from 58 per cent in 1985 to 70 per cent in 1988 (Substance Abuse and Mental Health Services Administration, 1997).

Among youths aged 12–17, the percentage reporting great perceived risk in smoking one or more packs of cigarettes per day has steadily increased, from 45 per cent in 1985 to 54 per cent in 1996 (Substance Abuse and Mental Health Services Administration, 1997).

A significant shift in perceived risk of alcohol use occurred between 1993 and 1996. In 1993, 70 per cent of the population aged 12 and older reported great perceived risk in having four or five drinks nearly every day, and 60 per cent reported great risk in having five or more drinks once or twice a week. By 1996, daily use of alcohol (four or five drinks) was associated with great risk by 77 per cent of the population, an increase in perceived risk. However, the perceived risk of having five or more drinks once or twice a week decreased to 53 per cent. This diverging trend was evident not only for the total population but for youths aged 12-17 as well. Among youths, the percentage reporting great perceived risk in having five or more drinks once or twice a week decreased from 58 per cent in 1992 to 45 per cent in 1996, while during that same period the percentage reporting great perceived risk in having four or five drinks nearly every day increased from 61 per cent to 67 per cent (Substance Abuse and Mental Health Services Administration, 1997).

453

R E F E R E N C E S

Canadian Centre for Substance Abuse & Addiction Research Foundation. (1997). *Canadian Profile: Alcohol, Tobacco and Other Drugs.* Toronto: Canadian Centre for Substance Abuse and Addiction Research Foundation.

Health Canada. (1998). *HIV/AIDS Epi Update.* Ottawa: Health Canada.

Health Canada. (1997). *Canada's Alcohol and Other Drugs Survey 1994: A Discussion of the Findings.* Ottawa: Health Canada.

Insurance Institute for Highway Safety. (1998). *Fatality Facts: Alcohol* (On-Line). Available at: http://www.highwaysafety.org/safety_facts/fatality_facts/alcohol.htm.

Single, E., Robson, L., Xie, X. & Rehm, J. (1996). *The Costs of Substance Abuse in Canada.* Ottawa: Canadian Centre on Substance Abuse.

Substance Abuse and Mental Health Services Administration. (1997). *Preliminary Results from the 1996 National Household Survey on Drug Abuse.* Washington, DC: US Department of Health and Human Services.

Substance Abuse and Mental Health Services Administration. (1998). *National Household Survey on Drug Abuse: Population Estimates 1997.* Washington, DC: US Department of Health and Human Services.

Guidelines on Low-Risk Drinking[*]

[*]These guidelines are produced as public information and are reproduced here as a resource for physicians who wish to provide their patients with information about responsible alcohol consumption. *Feel free to make individual copies of the guidelines whenever the need arises in your practice or a request for information is made.*

GUIDELINES ON LOW-RISK DRINKING

Healthy people who choose to drink and who are of legal drinking age can minimize the risk of alcohol-related problems, such as health and social problems, injuries and alcohol dependence, by observing the following low-risk drinking guidelines: There are some people who should not use alcohol, or should limit their use to less than the maximum amounts set out in the guidelines. Please read "When the Guidelines Don't Apply" to see if you belong to one of these groups.

LOW-RISK DRINKING GUIDELINES

- Drink no more than two standard drinks on any day (see below for the definition of a standard drink).

- Limit your weekly intake to 14 or fewer standard drinks for men and nine or fewer standard drinks for women.

- Drink slowly to avoid intoxication, waiting at least one hour between drinks and taking alcohol with food and non-alcoholic beverages.

- If you abstain, don't start drinking alcohol for its protective effect against heart disease. There are less risky alternatives such as exercise, better nutrition and quitting smoking.

- If you choose to drink, the protective effect of alcohol can be achieved with as little as one drink every other day.

- If you are seeking help for a drinking problem, follow the advice of your counsellor or health professional.

If you exceed the daily or weekly limits on a regular basis, there is an increased risk of problems. If you exceed the daily limit, you should take precautions to avoid injuries and other problems.

WHEN THE GUIDELINES DON'T APPLY

There are some people who should not use alcohol at all, or who should limit their use to less than the maximum amounts specified in the guidelines. This is the case for:

- people with certain health problems, such as liver disease or certain psychiatric illnesses

- people taking certain medications, such as sedatives, sleeping pills and pain-killers

- people with a personal or family history of serious drinking problems

- women who are pregnant, trying to conceive, or breast-feeding

- people who are operating vehicles such as automobiles, motorcycles, boats, snowmobiles, all-terrain vehicles or bicycles

- people who need to be alert — for example, while working with machinery or dangerous equipment, while engaging in challenging physical activities or when responsible for the safety of others or public order

- people who are under any legal or other restriction on drinking — personally or because of the environment they're in.

A STANDARD DRINK

One standard drink contains 13.6 grams of alcohol. That is the amount of alcohol in one 12 oz. regular-strength beer (5% alcohol), one drink containing 1.5 oz. spirits (40% alcohol) or one 5 oz. glass of wine (12% alcohol).

ENDORSEMENTS FOR THE LOW-RISK DRINKING GUIDELINES

These guidelines are based on research analysis conducted by medical doctors and social scientists affiliated with the ARF Division of the Centre for Addiction and Mental Health, and the University of Toronto.

These guidelines have been endorsed by the College of Family Physicians of Canada and the Canadian Centre on Substance Abuse.

Facts for Patients Series: Drug Information Sheets

APPENDIX 3

FACTS FOR PATIENTS SERIES:
DRUG INFORMATION SHEETS

This series of information sheets is intended to be a resource for physicians who wish to provide their patients with basic information about a number of types or classes of drugs in a non-confrontational manner. *Feel free to make individual copies of the information sheets whenever the need in your practice arises or a request for information is made.*

These sheets are ideal for patients who are concerned about their substance use, or for family members who are concerned about the substance use of someone in their family. While some technical or medical information is included in the series, they are meant to present factual information, using everyday language.

This series of information sheets is based on the "Do You Know..." series published by the Addiction Research Foundation, now the Centre for Addiction and Mental Health. The "Do You Know..." series, and other products for professionals and the public, can be ordered from the Centre for Addiction and Mental Health. See the back cover of this book for details.

ALCOHOL...
FACTS FOR PATIENTS

Street names
Booze, brew, hooch, grog.

Alcohol is a drug
Alcohol is called a depressant drug because it *slows down* your brain's ability to think and to make good decisions. Whether the alcohol comes in beer, wine or liquor doesn't matter. It's the *amount of alcohol* in your drink, not the *type* of drink, that affects you.

Problem drinking
If drinking interferes with your life or your health, you have a drinking problem.

If drinking, to you, means getting drunk, not remembering what you did, passing out, or feeling embarrassed about the night before, these are signs of a problem. Other signs are:

- getting into fights when you drink
- having sex with someone you don't particularly like when you drink
- being frequently hung over or late for work or school
- being charged with impaired driving.

And if drinking is your major way of coping with stress, or if you cannot control how much you drink at one time, you are experiencing problem drinking.

Sensible drinking
Sensible drinking does not interfere with:

- your health
- your job or studies
- your relationships
- your safety
- the safety of others.

A pattern of sensible drinking means days of not drinking mixed with days of light drinking.

Drinking can hurt you physically
Drinking a lot of alcohol over a long time can do serious damage to your body.

- Brain damage, ulcers, liver disease, malnutrition, heart disease, and various cancers are more common among heavy drinkers.
- People who drink heavily are likely to die younger than people who drink lightly or not at all.
- Pregnant women who drink risk having babies with birth defects, sometimes very serious ones. It is known that the more a pregnant woman drinks, the higher the risk; but it is not known whether just one or two drinks are really "safe."

Mixing alcohol with other drugs can be dangerous

- Taking a few drinks with other depressant (or "downer") drugs, such as tranquillizers and sleeping pills is especially dangerous. The alcohol and the other drug boost the effect of each other, and a person unexpectedly may seem very drunk, pass out, go into a coma, or even die. Even common non-prescription drugs such as antihistamines (for colds and allergies) can make you dopey and clumsy when you take alcohol at the same time.
- Taking stimulant drugs such as caffeine, cocaine, or amphetamines after drinking a lot of alcohol isn't a good idea either. These drugs can trick you into thinking you are sober, but you're really not — you are just wider awake and more hyper.
- Researchers now believe that alcohol makes the body absorb the cancer-causing chemicals in tobacco and cannabis more quickly. If you drink and smoke, you may be more likely to get cancer of the mouth, neck or throat.
- Some medicines can't do their job as well if they are mixed with alcohol. Other medicines can interact violently with alcohol, causing side-effects such as cramps, vomiting and headaches.

When it comes to alcohol and other drugs, the best advice is: don't mix.

ALCOHOL, OTHER DRUGS AND DRIVING... FACTS FOR PATIENTS

Driving under the influence and the law
Most people know that driving while impaired by alcohol is against the law. Not so many realize that driving while impaired by any drug is a crime.

Alcohol is the most widely used drug, and the one most often linked to motor vehicle accidents. But other drugs can affect the way you drive. This is especially when they are combined with alcohol. It makes sense. Driving requires attention, judgment, perception, decision making, physical reaction, and the ability to co-ordinate these skills. It is dangerous to drive or operate machinery under the influence of any drug that alters behavior or mood.

Other drugs, besides alcohol, that drivers take
A 1992 study by the Addiction Research Foundation discovered that, after alcohol, the drugs most commonly found in accident victims were: cannabis (e.g., marijuana and hashish), benzodiazepines (i.e., tranquillizers), and cocaine. Other drugs found were: morphine, barbiturates, codeine, meperidine (e.g., Demerol®), diphenhydramine (e.g., Benadryl®), and pheniramine, an ingredient in many cold preparations.

Prescription drugs can be dangerous
Some drugs prescribed for medical reasons have little or no effect on driving if they are taken by themselves and in the recommended doses. Many others, however, can affect how you drive, even when they are taken in recommended doses. Some carry a warning to be careful if you are going to be operating complex machinery. Ask your doctor or pharmacist about whether or not your prescription drugs can affect how you drive.

How depressant drugs affect you
Depressant drugs, such as tranquillizers, sedatives, or sleeping pills, slow down your central nervous system. They can make you drowsy, slow your reaction time, and hinder your ability to pay attention or concentrate.

The same is true for drugs with depressant side-effects. These include drugs such as cold remedies, cough medicines, antihistamines to control allergy symptoms, and drugs to prevent nausea or motion sickness. The sedative effect of some antidepressant drugs can also affect your driving ability.

Mixing any depressant drug with alcohol, which is also a depressant, can be extremely dangerous. The combined effects of the two drugs are sometimes much greater than the effect of either one alone.

465

Stimulants and other drugs that make you more alert

You might think that because depressant drugs add to the depressant effect of alcohol, stimulants would counteract this effect. This is not the case. Only time can lessen impairment by lowering the concentration of alcohol in your blood, or lowering the level of any other drug in your system.

Stimulants such as the caffeine in coffee, tea, cola drinks, or "stay awake pills" may make you more alert, but they still leave you impaired. Also, their effects may wear off quickly, leaving someone who is very tired asleep at the wheel. Although basic driving skills do not seem to be affected by medical doses of amphetamines, these stimulant drugs make some people overconfident, which may lead to dangerous driving. High doses of amphetamines make some people hostile and aggressive, which may also lead to risky driving.

Illegal drugs like cannabis and cocaine

Some believe it is safer to drive under the influence of cannabis than of alcohol. However, like alcohol, marijuana and hashish impair the skills important for driving, mostly those necessary for perceiving and responding to potentially hazardous situations. And their effects can last for hours, long after the high is gone.

Many cocaine users say the drug actually improves their driving ability. This is not surprising. Cocaine is a drug that makes many people feel they have greater mental and physical abilities than they actually do. Cocaine also dramatically affects vision, and some users have complained of sound or smell hallucinations. For example, they hear bells ringing or smell smoke or gasoline. These hallucinations have caused them to drive dangerously.

What you should know before taking any drug and driving

Best advice for alcohol is NEVER drink before driving. Even small amounts of alcohol can impair your ability to drive safely.

Best advice for anyone using illicit drugs or legal drugs in a non-medical way is... DON'T, and certainly not if you intend to drive. Illicit drug users usually can't be sure what drug or drugs they are taking or of the dose they are getting.

Best advice for anyone taking any prescribed or over-the-counter medication, is...ASK a pharmacist or doctor about how the drug might affect you and your driving. You should also ask whether even a small amount of alcohol will increase the drug's effects on your driving ability. Be aware, too, that the same drug can affect you differently at different times. The most dangerous time may be when you first start treatment, because you may not be used to the effects.

466

AMPHETAMINES (SPEED)...
FACTS FOR PATIENTS

Street names
Speed, ice, glass, crystal, crystal meth, crank, poor man's cocaine, pep pills, bennies, uppers.

How amphetamines work
Amphetamines and related drugs "speed up" the body's central nervous system, which is why one slang name for them is "speed." They mimic adrenaline, a hormone that is one of your body's natural stimulants. At the same time, they affect your heart, lungs, and many other organs.

Some of these drugs are available by prescription from a medical doctor. Some of them are now made in illegal laboratories.

Uses of amphetamines
Amphetamines were developed first as a medicine for sinus congestion. Later, doctors prescribed them for depression and for weight loss ("diet pills") but stopped because people became dependent on them very quickly. Today they are prescribed for only a few conditions — such as hyperactivity in children, and a rare sleep disorder called narcolepsy. But they are still around — and dangerous — on the street.

What "street" amphetamines look like and how they are used
On the street, amphetamines can come in crystals or powders that are off-white to yellow in colour. They have been swallowed, injected, sniffed or smoked.

"Crystal" or "crystal meth" is a powder form of methamphetamine that is injected, inhaled or taken by mouth. "Ice" and "glass" are smokable forms of methamphetamine and, like "crack" cocaine, their effect is strong and fast — but it lasts much longer.

Other amphetamine-like stimulants include methylphenidate (Ritalin®), diethylpropion (Tenuate®) and fenfluramine (Ionamin®). These medications come as tablets or capsules and are swallowed.

Look-alike stimulants are often misrepresented as "speed" and made to look like amphetamines. They contain various amounts, or combinations, of stimulants called ephedrine, phenylpropanolamine or caffeine.

How stimulants affect you
People use illegal stimulants because they make them feel alert, confident and full of energy. Basically, they "turn off" appetite and "turn up" the mind. A small

467

dose will probably give you a surge of energy and make you feel alert, talkative and restless. Your heart beats faster, your blood pressure rises, and the pupils of your eyes get bigger.

Larger doses and longer use of stimulants can make people behave very strangely. They feel they are bigger and better than others, and can become hostile, violent and paranoid (seeing "enemies" everywhere). Large doses also cause fevers, sweating, headaches, irregular heartbeats, blurred vision, tremors, seizures, heart attacks and strokes.

Injecting, snorting or smoking amphetamine-like drugs makes all these effects happen faster because the drug gets to the brain faster.

Stimulants are dangerous
Here are some reasons why:

- Stimulants, especially in large doses, can cause serious changes in heartbeat, increased blood pressure, stroke, heart attack or high fever, sometimes resulting in death.

- Some people who smoke or inject amphetamines "chase" the high by raising their dose, sometimes smoking or shooting repeatedly for days, eating little and sleeping less. This pattern can lead to delusions, paranoia and psychosis sometimes leading to violence and accidental death.

- People who inject also run the risk of infections from dirty needles or impurities in the drug. They risk getting hepatitis or HIV if they share needles with others. Some injectors have developed serious lung disease due to deposits of the drug or tablet fillers.

Amphetamine-like stimulants are addictive
You can rapidly become both psychologically and physically dependent on these drugs, especially if you inject, snort or smoke them.

Your body quickly becomes tolerant to the effects on mood — that is, you need a larger dose to get as high as you did at first. You reach a point, however, where even more of the drug won't work.

If you've used stimulants regularly and you suddenly stop taking them, you will experience withdrawal symptoms — feeling extremely tired, hungry, irritable and depressed. As a way of coping with these unpleasant symptoms, users often turn to such other drugs as barbiturates, alcohol and opioids, running the risk of becoming addicted to them as well.

468

BARBITURATES (DOWNERS)...
FACTS FOR PATIENTS

What barbiturates are

Barbiturates are powerful depressant drugs — which means they slow down your central nervous system. That's why the slang word for them is "downers."

Barbiturates are occasionally prescribed for their sedating effects and to treat migraine headaches. They are also available, with a doctor's prescription, under such trade names as Seconal®, Amytal®, Nembutal®, Tuinal® and Fiorinal®. Currently, doctors don't prescribe them very often for anxiety or sleep disorders because there are safer drugs now available. When they are sold illegally on the street they are often named for the colors of their capsules. For example, Amytal is called "blue heaven" and Nembutal "yellow jackets."

How barbiturates are used

Doctors sometimes prescribe barbiturates (e.g. phenobarbital) for people who have a seizure disorder called epilepsy. Rarely, they also prescribe them for people who can't sleep or are anxious or tense (but these days, they will more likely prescribe medications called benzodiazepines, which are less dangerous).

But some people take barbiturates for what they think is the "fun" of it. Others are trying to calm down from the effects of some other drug that speeds up their bodies — amphetamines or cocaine, for example.

How barbiturates will make you feel

A small amount (e.g., a prescribed dose) will make you feel calm, relaxed, and mildly happy. Your breathing and reflexes slow down and you may become sleepy. (However, some people also feel dizzy, nauseated and mentally foggy.)

A higher dose often has the effect of a few alcoholic drinks. You may become cheerful and talkative, or depressed and edgy. Your speech may slur, your vision may blur and your movements may be clumsy.

If you use high doses of barbiturates often and for a long time, you can start behaving in strange and unpredictable ways because your memory and judgment break down. You may also feel depressed, very tired, irritable and paranoid (seeing "enemies" everywhere). You may even have thoughts of suicide.

Barbiturates are dangerous

Barbiturates are among the most dangerous of the drugs used illegally. Here's why:

- Your body quickly becomes tolerant to the drug's pleasant effects — meaning that you need a bigger dose to get the "high." But the body does not become tolerant to the effect the drug has on breathing — meaning that the more you take, the weaker your breathing becomes. At some point you may become unconscious, go into a coma, or even die.

- Mixing barbiturates with other "downers" such as alcohol, tranquillizers or heroin, or even with some antihistamines, is very dangerous because they also slow your heart and breathing rates.

- If you regularly take a lot of barbiturates and suddenly stop, you can suffer withdrawal symptoms, including seizure and heart irregularities, severe enough to cause death.

- If you inject barbiturates you run even more risks, such as tetanus or other infections from dirty needles — or hepatitis or HIV from needles shared with others.

- Pregnant women should not take barbiturates except under a doctor's supervision. Prolonged use may cause babies to suffer withdrawal symptoms due to their mother's drug use.

You can become addicted to barbiturates

Barbiturates used for pleasure — or even prescribed pills taken too long and too often — can cause a strong physical and psychological dependence. Withdrawal can be unpleasant, dangerous, and even deadly. If you are addicted to these drugs, make sure you get medical help to quit.

BENZODIAZEPINES...
FACTS FOR PATIENTS

What benzodiazepines are

Most medications prescribed today to treat anxiety and insomnia belong to a group of drugs called benzodiazepines. Benzodiazepines work by calming your central nervous system.

Frequently prescribed benzodiazepines include lorazepam (e.g., Ativan®), alprazolam (e.g., Xanax®), diazepam (e.g., Valium®), temazepam (e.g., Restoril®) and triazolam (e.g., Halcion®). Often, their chemical names end in the letters "pam" or "am."

Used correctly, under the direction of your doctor, these medications are effective and safe. For anxiety and sleep problems, benzodiazepines are usually prescribed only for short periods — a few weeks or months. However, some people may need to take benzodiazepines for a longer period of time.

How benzodiazepines will affect you

The way these medications, or any other drug, affect you depends on many factors, including:

- the amount you take
- how long you take a drug
- whether you're also taking other medications or drugs
- your age.

Benzodiazepines can help relieve sleep problems and symptoms of anxiety. They have also been used in the treatment of panic disorders, seizures and muscle spasms.

Generally speaking, a small dose tends to make you feel relaxed and calm. A larger dose may make you feel drowsy and clumsy. These medications should be taken as directed by your physician. You should never take more than your doctor prescribes. Otherwise, you may become too sedated.

If you take benzodiazepines regularly (e.g., every day) for a long time, they may become habit-forming.

The safety of benzodiazepines

These medications are generally considered safe when taken as directed by your doctor. In current medical practice, they are usually prescribed in low dosages for short periods (i.e., a few weeks or months).

When you start taking benzodiazepines, you may experience side-effects such as drowsiness, dizziness and light-headedness. You may be unsteady on your feet and less alert. Often these symptoms pass as your body adjusts. Until you are sure of your reaction to this drug, avoid driving and always use caution in tasks demanding alertness.

Side-effects concern everyone, especially seniors, who are more sensitive to the effects and side-effects of drugs. Some people may feel "hung over" on the day after taking the medication and may be more prone to falls and injuries. These issues may be of particular concern with long-acting benzodiazepines like flurazepam. It has also been suggested that benzodiazepines can impair the ability to learn and remember new information.

Benzodiazepines may be prescribed to relieve sleeplessness. But some people who have trouble sleeping may have a hidden reason for their insomnia (such as depression or another illness). A physician may prescribe benzodiazepines until the underlying reason for the insomnia is discovered. Then, a more appropriate treatment may be suggested. This is one reason that benzodiazepines tend not to be prescribed for long periods of time to treat insomnia. Another is that, over time, these medications become less effective in promoting, and may even impair, restful sleep.

Your doctor or pharmacist can warn you about medications to avoid while taking benzodiazepines. Benzodiazepines can increase the effects of alcohol and other drugs (e.g., cold, allergy and pain preparations, and other sleep medications).

Remember, avoid driving when you have taken a benzodiazepine and have also had some alcohol. Mixing benzodiazepines with other drugs may cause excessive drowsiness and potentially dangerous sedation.

An overdose of benzodiazepines can cause unconsciousness or even death. Warning signs that you've take too much include:

• severe drowsiness
• slurred speech
• weakness and staggering.

If you notice any of these signs after taking the medication, contact your doctor.

A few people have experienced mental and behavioral changes while taking benzodiazepines. If you experience any changes in your behavior or mental state (such as confusion, bizarre behavior, aggression, etc.), consult your doctor immediately.

472

If you're taking benzodiazepines and are pregnant or thinking about becoming pregnant, talk to your doctor because they may affect your baby. For example, using benzodiazepines while you're pregnant can lead to withdrawal symptoms in your baby after it is born. Benzodiazepines are also passed on through breast milk. You shouldn't stop the medication on your own; check with your doctor first.

As with all medications, keep benzodiazepines out of the reach of children — they're more sensitive than adults to the effect of benzodiazepines.

Benzodiazepines can be addictive

They may cause physical and psychological dependence. It depends on how much of the medication you take and how long you take it. If you have been dependent on any other drug, you may be at a greater risk.

If this medication is used regularly for more than a few weeks, your body may become used to the presence of benzodiazepines and you may feel that you need them.

To avoid becoming dependent on benzodiazepines, don't take more of the medication than your doctor prescribes, and don't take it more often or for longer than directed.

Do not stop taking benzodiazepines without first consulting your doctor. Stopping suddenly may bring symptoms that are similar to conditions for which the medications were originally prescribed. Withdrawal symptoms can be mild (e.g., trouble sleeping, feeling unwell) or severe (e.g., anxiety, trembling, cramps), and, in rare cases after high doses are stopped quickly, psychosis and convulsions can occur.

Usually, physicians taper you off the medication slowly, over time. Even then, there is a chance that you may experience some temporary discomfort. Any withdrawal symptoms will subside with time, as the body readjusts.

Regularly discuss your need for the medication with your doctor. In most cases, benzodiazepines do not need to be used regularly for longer than four to six weeks.

Alternatives to the use of benzodiazepines

Although some people with specific conditions might have to take benzodiazepines for a long period of time, others may benefit from alternatives to relieve anxiety and sleeplessness.

473

To relieve stress, it may be useful to try relaxation exercises and tapes, take long walks, find new interests and hobbies and talk about your troubles with a friend.

People who take benzodiazepines to help them sleep may find that the medication is less effective after a few weeks. For a more permanent solution, and as an alternative to drug therapy, consider the following tips:

- Exercise regularly and get some fresh air during the day, but avoid strenuous activity before bed.
- Avoid naps during the day.
- Have a warm glass of milk or a light snack before bed.
- Take a warm bath before bed.
- Try not to dwell on your problems at night.
- Share your worries with close friends.
- Make your sleeping area a comfortable, soothing place.
- Keep alcohol and caffeinated drinks to a minimum, especially in the evening.
- Go to bed when you are tired and not before.
- Get up at the same time each morning.
- If you can't fall asleep, get up and do something relaxing until you are drowsy.

Also, remember that sleep patterns change as you get older. Seniors, for example, may not need as much sleep as they once did.

If you have any concerns about your benzodiazepine use, consult your doctor or pharmacist.

CAFFEINE...
FACTS FOR PATIENTS

What caffeine is

Caffeine is a stimulant that speeds up your central nervous system. Found in coffee, tea, cola drinks, cocoa and chocolate, as well as in stay-awake pills and some headache medicines, it is the world's most popular drug. In purified form it is a white, bitter-tasting powder.

Amounts of caffeine in common products

The following are approximate amounts of caffeine in products you may use regularly. (A cup refers to an average serving — about 200 mL.)

- cup of brewed/percolated coffee: 100 mg
- cup of instant coffee: 65–100 mg
- cup of decaffeinated coffee: 2–6 mg
- cup of tea: 50 mg
- soft drink containing caffeine (280 mL): 50 mg
- chocolate bar (50 g): 3–35 mg
- cup of hot cocoa: 50 mg
- stay-awake pills: 100 mg

The amount of caffeine in headache and cold medicines varies from product to product. It is shown on the label of over-the-counter medications but not on prescription drugs.

Why caffeine is so popular

About nine out of 10 Canadian adults consume caffeine, mainly in coffee and tea. For most of us, drinking these beverages is something we do at certain times of the day and around certain activities — when we need a pick-me-up or want to relax and socialize, for example. It is caffeine's stimulating effect — the "lift" — that we are after.

Some people think the caffeine in coffee sobers you up when you've had too much alcohol. It's not true. The caffeine may make you more alert, but you're still drunk — just wider awake and more hyper. Your co-ordination and concentration will still be impaired.

And some people take caffeine without even knowing it — in the form of headache medicines (e.g., Anacin®, Instantine®, Tylenol #1®, Exedrin®, 222s®, Atasol-8®).

475

How to know when you've had too much caffeine
Too much caffeine can give you a headache, upset your stomach, make you nervous and jittery and leave you unable to sleep. Some people feel these effects even with a small amount.

Too much caffeine can be dangerous
Moderate amounts of caffeine — up to about 300 mg a day (e.g., three average cups of coffee) — will rarely harm an otherwise healthy adult.

But if you regularly drink six to eight cups of coffee — or your daily dose of caffeine from a combination of products containing caffeine is higher than 600 mg — you may have trouble sleeping, feel anxious, restless, and depressed and develop stomach ulcers. Higher amounts can make you extremely agitated and give you tremors and a very rapid and irregular heartbeat.

Since small amounts of caffeine have a greater effect on children because of their smaller body size, it is wise to be aware of how much caffeine your children consume in chocolate products, soft drinks and medications.

At doses of 1,000 mg or higher, caffeine may produce vomiting, seizures, abnormal heart beat and rapid respiration. Although caffeine has not been proven to cause birth defects in humans, pregnant women are advised to take as little of it as possible to reduce possible risks to their own and their baby's health.

What happens when you stop having caffeine
Regular use of more than about 350 mg of caffeine a day (e.g., three to four cups of coffee or nine or 10 cola drinks) makes you physically dependent on caffeine. That means that if you abruptly stop using caffeine-containing products, you may feel edgy and tired and have to take caffeine again. The symptoms go away when you take caffeine again. They also gradually disappear after several days if you stop using caffeine. The more caffeine you consumed, the greater the withdrawal symptoms will be.

CANNABIS...
FACTS FOR PATIENTS

What cannabis is

Marijuana, hashish and hash oil all come from *Cannabis sativa*, a plant that grows in many parts of the world. Cannabis contains THC, a chemical that changes the way you think, feel and act. Cannabis is much more powerful today than it was 20 years ago because growers have developed strains that contain much more THC than before.

Cannabis is the most commonly used illegal mood-altering drug in North America. In 1994, 7.4 per cent of Canadians over 15 reported using it at least once during the past year.

How cannabis will affect you

Cannabis affects different people in different ways, depending on the mood they are in, how they expect they are going to feel, the amount they take, how strong it is and whether they eat it or smoke it.

Soon after smoking cannabis, most people feel "high" — more relaxed and talkative and less concerned about what they say or do. However, cannabis makes some people nervous, dizzy and upset.

Later on, you may become reflective and sleepy. Physically, you will probably notice that your eyes redden, your heart beats faster and your appetite is enormous (often called "the munchies"). Cannabis can affect your balance, judgment, memory, reactions and perceptions, especially if it is used together with alcohol. In fact, very large amounts can cause hallucinations — seeing and hearing things that don't really exist.

Cannabis can be dangerous

There is scientific evidence that cannabis carries these health risks:

Regular use of cannabis can impair your short-term memory in particular, and your ability to learn new things. You will be less able to speak, read, compute or reason. It also slows down your reaction time, making it dangerous to perform complex tasks such as driving a car. The combined use of alcohol and cannabis will increase these effects.

When cannabis is used by women during pregnancy, babies may be born prematurely, with low birthweights or with other abnormalities.

Cannabis smoke contains up to 50 per cent more tar and cancer-causing chemicals than tobacco cigarettes, and can cause bronchitis and increase the smoker's risk of developing such major lung diseases as emphysema and cancer. If you also smoke tobacco, cannabis adds to the harmful effects on the lungs. It may also harm the immune system, which helps you fight off infections and diseases in the body.

If you have high blood pressure or heart problems, smoking cannabis may be risky because it can increase your heart rate. Your heart has to work harder and your blood pressure can go up.

For people with a history of emotional problems or mental illness, regular cannabis use can bring on their symptoms or make them worse.

You can become dependent on cannabis
With regular use, people can become *psychologically dependent* on cannabis. They crave the "high," and become edgy and anxious if they cannot get the drug.

People who use large doses on a daily basis can become physically dependent and experience *withdrawal symptoms* when they stop using the drug. For less than a week or so they may have trouble sleeping, feel anxious and irritable, and lose their appetite.

478

COCAINE...
FACTS FOR PATIENTS

Street names
Coke, crack, rock, freebase, C, blow, dust, flake, snow, star dust.

What cocaine is
Cocaine comes from the leaves of the tropical coca plant. It has two major effects — it is a powerful stimulant that speeds up your central nervous system and it is an anesthetic that numbs whatever mucous membranes it touches, such as the inside of your mouth and nose.

Cocaine is usually sold as a white or pink crystalline powder that is inhaled or sniffed ("snorted"). It can also be injected and, in some forms, smoked.

Injecting the drug produces a fast, powerful response that peaks in minutes.

Crack and freebase are both smokable forms of cocaine and carry a kick similar to injecting the drug. Crack is the street name for cocaine in the form of rock-like chunks of impure freebase. Both crack and freebase give an intense high that quickly fades into a craving for more of the drug.

What cocaine does to your body
Basically, cocaine overworks your body and brain. It sends the body into overdrive — boosting your heart rate, blood pressure and body temperature.

Its action in the brain can initially make the user feel alert, energetic, more sociable, confident and in control. This feeling can be so powerful and pleasurable that many users immediately want more of the drug. For others, it isn't like that at all; they feel withdrawn, restless, anxious or even panic-stricken.

Tolerance develops to cocaine's high. Many users use larger amounts to try to experience the original high. Eventually, if you use cocaine often and long enough, the "high" gives way to negative effects. These include paranoia (suspecting "enemies" everywhere), hallucinations (seeing and hearing "things"), and an unwell feeling because you can't sleep and don't feel like eating.

Cocaine is dangerous
It is difficult to predict which individuals will have an adverse or toxic effect from cocaine. For some occasional users, and for those who use it frequently — especially if they inject or smoke it — cocaine use can be a serious health problem. Here's why:

479

- Damage to heart tissue and rapid heartbeat can cause heart failure and sudden death, even though you are otherwise healthy.
- A cocaine-triggered rise in blood pressure can explode weakened blood vessels in the brain, causing a stroke.
- It's possible to overdose on crack, freebase, or injected cocaine — even on small amounts of the drug. You can die from seizures, strokes or heart failure.
- Those who inject cocaine run the risk of infections from dirty needles and impurities in the drug. They risk getting hepatitis or HIV if they share needles with others.
- Those who smoke cocaine risk damaging their entire breathing system.
- Finally, as with other stimulant drugs, heavy or long-term use can simply cause the body to burn itself out. Insomnia, weight loss, paranoia and malnutrition are among the first signs of a serious problem.

You can become addicted to cocaine

It is true that fewer than one in 10 people who have ever tried cocaine continue to use it once a week or more. However, some regular users, chasing a longer and stronger high, keep increasing their dose. For those who do get hooked, cocaine seems to be one of the hardest drug habits to shake.

Regular, heavy users find that when the high fades, it is followed by a low as the central nervous system rebounds and works more slowly than normal. It's called the "crash" — a nagging depression that sends many users back for more of the drug.

ECSTASY...
FACTS FOR PATIENTS

What "ecstasy" is

Ecstasy, or MDMA, is a drug with properties related to both amphetamines and hallucinogens. Among the other names ecstasy goes by are E, XTC, Adam, euphoria, X and MDM.

Ecstasy is sometimes referred to as a "designer drug." It is usually produced in underground laboratories and has no approved medical use. Ecstasy is usually sold in tablets or gelatin capsules and taken orally. It may also be sold as a powder. Sometimes the tablets are crushed and then snorted. The drug comes in different shapes, sizes, and colours depending on who is making it. Ecstasy produces effects that usually begin within one hour, and may last for four to six hours.

As with other street drugs, what is sold as ecstasy may actually contain other drugs, such as amphetamines, caffeine, LSD or other drugs.

MDMA was first produced in 1914 by pharmaceutical researchers as an appetite suppressant. In the 1970s, a small number of psychotherapists in the United States began to use MDMA as a component of therapy. In the 1980s, MDMA, soon to be known as ecstasy, gained popularity as a recreational drug. Ecstasy is a restricted drug in Canada.

Ecstasy's use has been associated with young adults who go to concerts, clubs, or attend "rave" parties.

The effects of ecstasy

Ecstasy can produce a mild intoxication, a sense of pleasure, and feelings of euphoria. There is often an increased sense of sociability or closeness with others. Users may also feel a sense of heightened perception. Like all stimulant drugs, ecstasy may make users feel full of energy and confidence. However, some people find ecstasy's effects disturbing. Users may experience an increase in sweating, increased blood pressure and heart rate, nausea, grinding of the teeth and jaw pain, anxiety or panic attacks, blurred vision and vomiting.

Even small doses can cause strong negative effects, which may last for days or weeks. These include confusion, panic, insomnia or even convulsions. Ecstasy may distort perception, thinking or memory. It also can produce psychosis, paranoia, hallucinations and long-lasting bouts of anxiety or depression in susceptible users. There is evidence from animal research that recreational doses of ecstasy can cause permanent neurological damage. There is concern that this may occur in humans and studies into this are being conducted.

Regular users, and some occasional users, have reported weight loss, confusion, irritability, depression, paranoia and exhaustion. Reactions may be severe and unpredictable. Long-term use of ecstasy has not been thoroughly studied, but jaundice and liver damage were reported after repeated use.

There have been several fatal incidents associated with ecstasy use at raves. In England, deaths have occurred from kidney or cardiovascular failure induced by a very high body temperature and dehydration. Ecstasy can cause an increase in body heat, a reaction which is enhanced by higher temperatures at parties. Young people attending all night raves sometimes overexert themselves while dancing. Combine this with the heat, heavier sweating, and failure to drink enough fluids, and the risk is even greater.

People who use ecstasy at raves should wear loose, thin clothing, take breaks from dancing, and drink plenty of water or other non-alcohol beverages.

"Herbal ecstacy"

Herbal ecstacy — the name is deliberately misspelled — has gained popularity recently among ravers as a "safer" alternative to ecstasy.

Some proponents of herbal ecstacy claim that the product is all natural and contains no chemicals. However, herbal ecstacy often contains caffeine and the herb known as Ma Huang, which contains ephedrine. The combination of caffeine and this herb in certain weight-loss products has caused heart attacks and a number of deaths.

Ephedrine is a stimulant that some athletes use to enhance their performance. Ephedrine can cause headache, dizziness, insomnia, irritability, hypertension and stroke.

HALLUCINOGENS...
FACTS FOR PATIENTS

Street names
Acid, blotter, microdot, windowpane (for LSD); angel dust, killer weed, green, super pot (for PCP); love drug (for MDA); magic mushroom (for psilocybin).

What hallucinogens are
Hallucinogens are drugs that can distort your perceptions so that you see and hear things that don't really exist. They can make you experience hallucinations.

There are many drugs in this category. Some come from plants and others are made in illegal laboratories.

Although such drugs as amphetamines and alcohol are usually not called hallucinogens, large doses of them can sometimes cause hallucinations.

How hallucinogens make you feel
Hallucinogens are unpredictable. Their effects are fast changing and unexpected. How they affect you depends a lot on your "mind-set" — your expectations, experience, and mood — and on the setting. (You're likely to have a different "trip" at a rock concert than listening to soft music at home.)

Here is what some different hallucinogens look like and a few of their effects.

LSD
The most powerful of the hallucinogens, LSD has no colour, odor or taste. It is so strong that a dose (30 micrograms) is too small to see. It is packaged in miniature powder pellets ("microdots"), gelatin chips ("windowpane") or squares of LSD-soaked paper ("blotter"). LSD is usually swallowed but may also be "snorted" or injected. It has some effects on the body, causing weakness, clumsiness, nausea, chills, enlarged pupils and rapid heartbeat. But it mainly distorts the way you think, feel and act.

Psilocybin
Psilocybin is found in very specific types of mushrooms. The mushrooms can be dried and sold as is, or as a powder in capsules. Purified psilocybin forms white crystals. The drug is usually swallowed but can be injected. It may make you feel relaxed or tired, and you may have mystical or "religious" experiences.

483

PCP

Often sold in white or colored chunks or crystals, PCP can also come in the form of a powder or tablet. Mixed with tobacco, marijuana, or dried parsley, it is usually smoked, but it can be swallowed or injected. Effects can last as long as two weeks. Although it makes users "high," it also often makes them violent towards themselves and others. An overdose can be deadly, and PCP's effect on the mind has caused many deaths by accident, suicide and homicide.

Mescaline

The "buttons" of the peyote cactus containing the drug are dried, then chopped or ground and sold in capsules. It is usually swallowed, but it can be smoked or injected. Physical effects include enlarged pupils, high temperature, muscle weakness and vomiting. Mental effects include rapid mood changes, a sense of separation from your body and a belief that you are experiencing greater awareness or "truth."

Other hallucinogens

The active ingredient in morning glory seeds is related to LSD, but is weaker. The seeds are often treated with insecticides and other chemicals that can be poisonous.

Nutmeg powder, which is sometimes eaten or sniffed, is chemically related to mescaline. Both getting, and recovering from, a nutmeg high can be unpleasant.

Besides giving you hallucinations, the leaves and berries of jimson weed make your skin hot and dry, your eyes blurry and your mouth dry. Jimson weed has also caused a number of deaths.

Hallucinogens can be dangerous
Here's why:

- Users may display unpredictable, bizarre, dangerous behavior while under the influence, possibly resulting in harm to themselves or others.

- Sometimes, for no obvious reason, hallucinogen users have a "bad trip," experiencing confusion, disorientation or fearfulness. They suddenly feel paranoid (seeing "enemies" everywhere) and intensely anxious about losing control. These feelings can lead to bizarre and even violent behavior, especially with PCP and sometimes with LSD. Because these drugs are powerful and unpredictable, using them in a situation in which you don't feel safe and at ease is asking for trouble.

484

- Dealers often substitute another drug, sometimes a stronger drug, for the one you think you are getting (e.g., LSD or PCP for mescaline or psilocybin). You don't know what you're taking or how it will affect you.

- Days, weeks or months after you stop taking these drugs you can suddenly have a "flashback," a vivid rerun of a previous drug trip, usually a bad one. Flashbacks usually last only a few seconds or minutes but seem much longer. They can happen over and over again, unpredictably.

- If you inject hallucinogens, you run such risks as infections from dirty or shared needles — including hepatitis or HIV.

- Although little is known about the effects of other hallucinogens on pregnancy, women who use LSD during pregnancy have more risk of problem pregnancies and birth defects in babies.

- The toxic effects of hallucinogens include: restlessness, nausea, loss of co-ordination, hallucinations and later on, confusion, anxiety and depression. There is also the risk of the drugs precipitating psychosis or heart problems such as arrhythmia which might lead to the need for hospitalization.

Hallucinogens and addiction

Taking such hallucinogens as LSD, mescaline, or psilocybin for a few days will make you tolerant to their effects; even with higher doses you won't feel the hoped-for high. If you regularly use hallucinogens you can become psychologically dependent on them, feeling that you have to have them. As the drug wears off, users sometimes suffer a "crash" period that can last for a few days.

OPIATES...
FACTS FOR PATIENTS

What opiates are
Opiates are very strong painkillers (much stronger than the pills that people take for minor pain). The name "opiates" comes from opium, a gummy substance collected from the seed pod of the opium poppy.

Morphine and codeine are drugs made from opium. Heroin is made by adding a chemical to morphine.

Today, many drugs in the opiate category don't actually come from opium at all. Instead, they are made synthetically from chemicals. Some examples are oxycodone (in Percodan®/Percocet®), meperidine (Demerol®), hydrocodone (in Novahistex DH®), hydromorphone (Dilaudid®) and methadone.

What opiates look like
Heroin on the street is usually a white or brownish powder. It is usually dissolved in water and injected under the skin or into a vein or muscle, but it can also be sniffed into the nostrils or smoked ("chasing the dragon").

Opium comes in dark brown chunks or powder, and is usually eaten or smoked.

Other opiates come in a variety of forms: tablets, capsules, syrups, solutions and suppositories.

Uses of opiates
Doctors and dentists prescribe opiates for patients who are in moderate to severe pain. Because these painkillers are addictive, they shouldn't be taken steadily for a long time. But they are safe in the short term — for example, if you have had surgery or have an abscessed tooth. When someone is dying from a painful disease, the risk of addiction is not important, and opiates are given for as long as needed to keep the person in comfort.

Certain kinds of prescribed opiates can help people who are addicted to illegal opiates such as heroin. People addicted to opiates are given a safer, legal drug (usually methadone) so that they can live a more normal life off the "street" and, in many cases, finally become drug-free.

Other medical uses of opiates are to control bad coughs or diarrhea. Some non-prescription products contain a small amount of codeine.

People who use opiates illegally are looking for a different effect — a "high" and a mellow, relaxed feeling. Although heroin is the most well-known opiate, many users take illegally obtained prescription drugs.

486

Some of the most commonly used and abused opiates are codeine-containing preparations such as Tylenol #1, 2 and 3®, 292s®, Atasol 8, 15 and 30®, and Exdol 8, 15, and 30®.

Opiates can be dangerous

Opiates can be dangerous if they are used without medical supervision. Here are some of the reasons why:

• These drugs (especially heroin) can kill you if you seek the "high" by taking larger doses than your body is used to. With street heroin, it is easy to overdose accidentally because the purity of the drug varies so much — anywhere from zero per cent on the low end to almost pure on the high end. The purer the heroin, the more likely an overdose.

• Many people inject opiates because the effect (called the "rush") is faster and stronger. But they run extra risks: skin infections, heart infections and HIV or hepatitis from needles and paraphernalia shared with others.

• Many heroin users also abuse other drugs, such as benzodiazepines, alcohol, cocaine and amphetamines, with the risk of becoming hooked on these drugs as well.

• Pregnant women who take these drugs risk problems during pregnancy and childbirth. Their babies suffer from withdrawal symptoms and can die if not treated.

Opiates are addictive

You can quickly become physically and psychologically dependent on opiates. If you use them steadily, you become tolerant to the desired effect. That is, you must take more and more of the drug to get a "high" or even to control pain. If it's the high you're after, however, at a certain point no amount of the drug will work unless you stop taking it for a few weeks. If you stop taking heroin for a few weeks and then inject the same amount you were using prior to stopping, you risk overdosing. This is because your body has lost its tolerance to the drug.

Once you become physically dependent on opiates, stopping use abruptly will make you sick. Although people rarely die from withdrawal, it can be miserable (much like a bad case of flu). People often also feel very depressed and anxious, are unable to sleep or eat, and desperately want more of the drug (psychological dependence). This craving is especially great for heroin, and heroin is therefore one of the hardest drugs for an addicted person to quit.

SOLVENTS AND AEROSOLS...
FACTS FOR PATIENTS

Street names
Glue, gas, sniff.

Solvents and aerosols are drugs
Solvents and aerosols are drugs that were never meant to be drugs. Solvents are made by the chemical industry and are used in many products: gasoline, shoe polish, paint removers, model airplane glue, nail polish remover, spray deodorants, hairsprays and insecticides. These are only a few of the hundreds of products that contain them.

But people, especially young people, found that a whiff of these chemicals can give them a "buzz." And so solvents and aerosols also became "drugs." Because they are breathed in (inhaled) — like some other drugs, such as ether, amyl nitrate, and nitrous oxide — scientists call them "inhalants."

How solvents and aerosols affect you
In seconds after sniffing, you will feel the effects. That's because the drug floods directly from your lungs into your bloodstream. From there it quickly goes into the brain and liver, which are the organs with the largest blood supply.

The result for many users is an immediate "high." They become giddy, outgoing and full of confidence. They hear and see "things," objects around them take on strange sizes, shapes and colors. Time and space seem to shrink and expand.

Physically, the effects of sniffing are no fun at all. Sneezing, coughing, vomiting and diarrhea are common. Users also have slurred speech, double vision, drowsiness, muscle pain — and a hangover after the effects wear off.

Solvent and aerosol abuse is dangerous
Sniffing solvents and aerosols can kill you or leave you permanently damaged. Here's why:

- In one common way of sniffing inhalants, users put a solvent-soaked cloth in a plastic bag that they hold tightly around their nose and mouth. Some users have suffocated when they fell asleep or passed out.

- Some users suffer heart failure if stress or strenuous exercise follows several deep inhalations ("sudden sniffing death").

- Some users have overdosed.

488   Copyright © 1999 Centre for Addiction and Mental Health

- The feeling of being all-powerful can make users reckless and violent, and they can purposely or accidentally hurt or kill themselves or others.

- Some users don't get high, they just get depressed. Some have attempted suicide.

- People who use solvents regularly for a long time can damage their liver, kidney, lungs, heart, brain and blood. Sometimes this damage heals when drug use is stopped; sometimes the damage is permanent.

- Some users have suffered severe brain damage. Their brains have actually shrunk, and their ability to think and to control their movement has been seriously affected.

You can become addicted to aerosols and solvents

If they use them often, young people are especially vulnerable to becoming psychologically dependent on these chemicals. Solvent use becomes a more and more important part of daily life and is very hard to stop. Users also become tolerant to the chemical and need to keep taking more and more to get high. They can become physically dependent, and may develop withdrawal symptoms. Withdrawal symptoms are more likely to occur after stopping heavy use. Symptoms may include irritability, depression, tremors and loss of appetite.

STEROIDS...
FACTS FOR PATIENTS

Street names
The juice, the white stuff, roids.

Anabolic steroids
Steroids include a wide variety of chemicals found in both plants and animals. For example, cholesterol and sex hormones are both steroids. Here we are concerned about only one member of the steroid family, anabolic steroids, which are a manufactured version of the male sex hormone, testosterone.

These drugs are used by some athletes who are trying to build up their bodies for sports and by people who think they will look better with bigger muscles.

Medical uses for anabolic steroids
Anabolic steroids are only used medically to treat very specific conditions. When steroids are used to improve sports performance, or to add muscle mass, they are a serious concern. Some doctors used to prescribe anabolic steroids to athletes to help them improve their performance. However, the medical profession and most sports organizations now forbid the use of steroids for this purpose.

Why some people take anabolic steroids
Athletes taking steroids *believe* that they help them perform better by increasing their size and strength, and by allowing them to train for long periods of time with less pain and fatigue. They also *say* steroids make them feel more competitive, confident and enthusiastic. Some users take them to look muscular while others feel that steroids increase their sex drive. However, there is controversy among scientists regarding the effects of these drugs on athletic performance.

How steroids affect you
Steroids can make you feel aggressive (it's sometimes called "roid rage" or "killer instinct"), very edgy, impatient and paranoid (seeing "enemies" everywhere). Mood swings are quite common — you may feel happy one moment and depressed the next.

Steroids can give you headaches, nosebleeds, stomach aches and acne. They can increase blood pressure in both men and women. Some people complain that their body becomes less flexible — their tissues retain fluids and their muscles tighten up. As well, they have more injuries while on steroids because of tendon problems.

Females who use steroids for a long time become more masculine looking. Their voices deepen and they grow more body and facial hair (although, not on their heads — they may actually suffer from male pattern baldness). Steroids have left some women unable to bear children.

There is also bad news for males if they use steroids for a long time. Their breasts develop, their testicles become smaller, their sperm count drops, and they may sometimes become impotent.

Steroids are dangerous
Here's why:

• Steroids can stop a young person from ever growing to his or her full height. It's a serious consequence and there's no second chance.

• Heavy use of steroids over a long period of time can cause irreversible liver damage and hardening of the arteries that may end in a heart attack or stroke.

• Personalities can change for the worse. Long-term users can become extremely paranoid, even violent. Often they don't realize what is happening to them and they end up losing friends and family.

• Those who inject steroids run the risk of infections from dirty needles, and of hepatitis or HIV if they share needles with others. Recent evidence suggests that steroids may affect the immune system making a person more susceptible to infections.

• Prolonged use of steroids can cause physical dependence resulting in withdrawal symptoms after use of the drug is stopped suddenly.

TOBACCO...
FACTS FOR PATIENTS

Why tobacco can harm you
Tobacco smoke is made up of many components. The main ones are nicotine, tar and carbon monoxide.

Nicotine is a highly addictive drug, partly because it produces its effects so quickly. It reaches the brain seconds after you puff on a cigarette. Many people find cigarettes just as hard to give up as heroin or cocaine.

Tar is made up of hundreds of chemicals; many of these cause cancer.

Carbon monoxide is a gas formed when tobacco is burned. The same gas is found in your car exhaust. Carbon monoxide lowers the amount of oxygen carried in your blood, and therefore the amount your body gets.

Risks related to smoking
There are still about 6,000,000 Canadians who smoke cigarettes. Of a total of 190,000 deaths in Canada each year, at least 40,000 are due to smoking.

Smoking:

- is the main cause of lung cancer
- increases the risk of cancers of the colon, mouth, throat, pancreas, bladder and cervix
- causes most cases of chronic bronchitis and emphysema
- is a major cause of heart disease and stroke
- greatly increases the risk of stroke for a woman who takes birth control pills
- increases a pregnant woman's risk that her baby will be underweight or will die in infancy.

The more you smoke and the longer you smoke, the greater the chance of serious trouble.

Pipes and smokeless tobacco
All forms of tobacco increase your risk of disease and early death.

Benefits of quitting
Yes, if you quit. Research shows the health benefits are almost immediate. And the longer you've quit, the better your health gets:

Within 24 hours:

- your blood pressure and pulse rate start to return to normal
- the carbon monoxide level in your blood decreases
- your chance of having a heart attack goes down.

Within a year your risk of a heart attack is cut in half. Over 10 years, your risk of developing lung cancer drops significantly until it is only slightly greater than that of people who never smoked.

What you should know about quitting

If at first you don't succeed, keep trying. Most smokers quit more than once before they finally give up cigarettes for good. Most try several times. In fact, only one in five makes it on the first try.

Here are a few things to be aware of when you try to quit:

- Withdrawal symptoms are normal. You might feel nervous, irritable and hungry. You might also have headaches, and trouble concentrating or sleeping. These symptoms usually disappear within a few days to a few weeks. It probably will take longer for you to get over wanting a cigarette, but that will get easier as time goes on.

- Cutting down instead of quitting is not a good idea. Many people just change the way they smoke — by taking more puffs or longer puffs — to get the same effect from fewer cigarettes.

- Many people worry they will gain weight when they quit. Only about one-third of people who quit gain weight, and that gain is usually only a small amount (one or two kilograms). Cutting down on snack food and exercising more can bring your weight back to where you want it.

- Everyone trying to quit has to find a personal reason for giving up smoking. Anyone who really wants to quit can do it.

- Most quitters stop smoking on their own — sometimes with the help of pamphlets, books, guides or videos. If you think that you need help, ask your doctor or talk to your local health agency. It's important to remember that no single method works for everyone. You may try several different approaches before finding the one that works for you.

Resources for Professionals

APPENDIX 4

RESOURCES FOR PROFESSIONALS

Prepared by Reference Services, Centre for Addiction and Mental Health Library

HOTLINES

ONTARIO

Addiction Clinical Consultation Service (ACCS)
1-888-720-2227, (416) 595-6968
Call for information, advice and professional support in treating patients' alcohol and drug-related problems.
Professionals only.
A service of the Centre for Addiction and Mental Health.

Drug and Alcohol Registry of Treatment (DART)
1-800-565-8603
The Drug and Alcohol Treatment Line offers an Ontario-wide treatment referral service.
Professionals and public.

Centre for Addiction and Mental Health Information Line (formerly INFO-ARF)
1-800-463-6273, (416) 595-6111
Call for information, taped messages on alcohol and other drugs, public information materials and referrals. A good information source for patients.
Professionals and public.
A service of the Centre for Addiction and Mental Health.

Drug Information and Research Centre
1-800-268-8058, (416) 385-3472
Provides drug information and consultant services.
Professionals only.
Subscription required.
A service of the Ontario Pharmacists' Association.

Ontario College of Physician and Surgeons
(416) 961-1711
Professionals and public.
A source for information about methadone treatment in Ontario. Ask for the Methadone Inquiries Line.

Ontario Problem Gambling Helpline
1-888-230-3505
An Ontario-wide information and referral service.
Professionals and public.
A service of the Ontario Ministry of Health.

CANADA

Motherisk Alcohol and Substance Abuse Helpline
1-877- FAS-INFO (327-4636)
Call with questions about alcohol and other drug use during pregnancy and breast-feeding.
Professionals and public.
A service of the Motherisk Program, The Hospital for Sick Children, Toronto, Ontario.

Canadian Centre for Ethics in Sport
1-800-672-7775, (613) 748-5755
Call for information about anabolic steroids and other performance-enhancing substances.

Depression Information Resource and Education Centre (DIRECT)
Physician Information Line on Depression
1-888-557-5050 code 800
DIRECT offers up-to-date information and general guidance about mood and anxiety disorders.
Access taped messages or consult with an information officer.
The service also has a line for the general public: 1-888-557-5051 code 8000

Provided by Psychiatry and Neurobehavioural Sciences, McMaster University, Hamilton, Ontario.

INTERNET RESOURCES

Web accessible databases indexing/abstracting peer reviewed clinical and research literature:

ETOH: Alcohol and Alcohol Problems Science Database
etoh.niaaa.nih.gov
Comprehensive research database covering alcohol abuse and alcoholism literature.
Producer: National Institute on Alcohol Abuse and Alcoholism (NIAAA).

Information about Drugs and Alcohol (IDA)
http://sadatabase.health.org/ida/
Covers scientific literature relating to alcohol and substance abuse prevention, as well as sociological literature.
Producer: National Clearinghouse for Alcohol and Drug Information (NCADI).

MEDLINE Databases
www.nlm.nih.gov/databases/freemedl.html
Provides access to both PubMed and Internet Grateful Med.
Producer: National Library of Medicine (NLM).

ORGANIZATIONS

ONTARIO

Centre for Addiction and Mental Health (CAMH)
www.camh.net
Many useful resources, including the CAMH Product Catalogue, clinical training opportunities, news in the field, and information about CAMH programs and services. This site links to the Substance Abuse Network of Ontario (SANO) currently at www.arf.org.

Drug and Alcohol Registry of Treatment (DART)
www.dart.on.ca
Provides a searchable database of treatment programs in Ontario.

Motherisk Program (The Hospital for Sick Children)
www.motherisk.org
The program provides information and guidance concerning drug use during pregnancy and breast-feeding.

CANADA

Alcohol Risk Assessment and Intervention (ARAI) Project
www.cfpc.ca/serv02.htm
The College of Family Physicians of Canada runs the ARAI training program to assist physicians in the assessment and intervention of alcohol-related problems.

Canadian Centre on Substance Abuse (CCSA)
www.ccsa.ca
As well as being a key policy organization, the CCSA manages an information clearinghouse for Canadian resources dealing with gambling and substance abuse issues. The site has a host of useful directories, databases and full text documents.

Canadian Society of Addiction Medicine (CSAM)
www.csam.org
CSAM is a national organization of medical professionals and other scientists interested in substance use disorders and addictive behavior.

Health Canada Online
www.hc-sc.gc.ca
Although broad in spectrum, consult this site for health alerts and news as issues arise. The site also includes some on-line publications for health professionals.

National Clearinghouse on Tobacco and Health (NCTH)
www.cctc.ca/ncth
The information service of the Canadian Council for Tobacco Control, NCTH offers resources on the health-related effects of tobacco.

UNITED STATES

American Society of Addiction Medicine (ASAM)
www.asam.org
ASAM is dedicated to educating physicians and medical students about addictions, and improving access to and the quality of treatment for addictions.

500

ASAM offers certification in addiction medicine and publishes the well-known reference book *Principles of Addiction Medicine.*

American Psychiatric Association
www.psych.org
Access ordering information for DSM-IV products and full text Practice Guidelines.

National Clearinghouse for Alcohol and Drug Information (NCADI)
www.health.org
NCADI is the information service for the major U.S. health institutions dealing with alcohol and other drugs. See the NCADI catalogue to access useful protocols and research summaries. This site includes publications from both NIAAA (**www.niaaa.nih.gov**) and the National Institute on Drug Abuse, NIDA (**www.nida.nih.gov**).

I N D E X

12-Step program, 47, 51, 53, 207, 265, 433. *See also* Alcoholics Anonymous.

2-Ethylidene-1,5-dimethyl-3,3-diphenylpyrrolidine. *See* EDDP.

6-Monoacetylmorphine. *See* MAM.

A

Aboriginal (Native) populations, 294

Abstinence, 3, 41, 47, 92, 106, 117, 178, 303, 351, 354, 407, 409, 411; and alcohol tolerance, 74; and "alcoholic heart disease," 100; and alcoholic liver disease, 91; and cerebral atrophy, 96; and clonidine, 140; and cocaine, 177, 182, 183; and health risks, 103; and hypertension, 100; and intensive treatment, 50; long-term (or prolonged), 41, 54, 76, 230; nicotine, 136, 139, 140; and pseudo-Cushing syndrome, 99; and pseudo-Parkinsonism, 96; syndrome, 234; and thrombocytopenia, 99; as treatment goal, 110, 112; versus cutting down, 135; and withdrawal, 110

Abuse, 175, 381; and alcohol, 6; and amphetamines, 6; and anxiolytics, 6; and binges, 54; and cannabis, 6; and cocaine, 6; and hallucinogens, 6; and inhalants, 6; and opioids, 6; and PCP, 6; and sedative/hypnotics, 6. *See also* Violence.

Acamprosate (biacetylhomotaurinate), 119

Acetaldehyde dehydrogenase, 118, 413

Acetaminophen, 90, 92, 147, 231, 232, 250, 251, 253, 255, 277, 310-311; overdose, 312

Acetylcholine, 215

Acetylsalicylic acid. *See* ASA.

Acquired immune deficiency syndrome (AIDS). *See* HIV/AIDS.

Action phase, 59, 60, 134, 143-144. *See also* Stages of change.

Acupuncture, and smoking cessation, 137

Addiction, 260, 279, 280; assessment, 398, 399; biological basis for, 55; counsellors, 42, 48, 393; definition of, 3, 127; education, 410; history, 264, 407; pharmacological hallmarks of, 127; service providers, 401

Addiction treatment, 296; agencies, 105; medicine, 244, 392; services, 58; specialist, 165, 193, 261, 262

ADH. *See* Alcohol dehydrogenase.

ADH blocker, 4-methylpyrazole (4-mp), 316

Adolescent diagnostic interview, 378

Adolescents, 194, 207, 286, 287, 288, 289, 292, 296, 373, 376, 378, 379, 382, 383, 384; males, 285; and smoking, 133; substance abuse by, 378

Aerosols, 292

Affect: disorders, 25, 182, 245; flat, 23; instability, 182. *See also* Lability.

Age and aging, 111, 349, 351, 352, 354, 377; patients, 157. *See also* Elderly patients; Older adults.

Aggression, 190, 286, 293, 399, 407

Agitation, 79, 86, 191, 193, 206, 213, 293, 407; and benzodiazepine withdrawal, 160, 161; and cocaine, 177, 179, 181; as indication for hospital admission, 84; severe, 81

Agonists-antagonists, mixed, 5, 244, 277

AIDS. *See* HIV/AIDS.

Amino acids, 119, 294; supplements, 93

Ammonia derivatives, toxic, 94

Amnesia, 6, 214, 290; and alcohol, 6; and anxiolytics, 6; and sedative/hypnotics, 6. *See also* Blackouts.

Amobarbibtal, equivalence to phenobarbital, 153

Amotivational syndrome, 211; and heavy use of cannabis, 206. *See also* Chronic intoxication state.

Amphetamines, 6, 29, 55, 180, 188ff, 192, 415; abuse, identification of, 191; adulterants, 191; and anxiety, 6; and cross-reactivity, 29; diagnoses associated with, 6; dosage, 189, 191; duration of detectability of, 33; effects, 176, 190; immunoassay testing for, 29; indications, 188; intoxication, 191; lethality, 191; neuropharmacology, 189; psychosis, 193; routes of administration, 189; screening for, 28; sources and form, 189; tolerance, 191; treatment, 191

Anabolic steroids, 285; cardiovascular effects, 285; endocrine effects, 286; hepatic effects, 286; psychiatric effects, 285

Analgesia, 116, 117, 225, 253, 257, 278

Analgesic, 225, 244, 250-252, 253, 254, 255, 258, 276, 316, 350-352; abuse, 352; antipyretic, 352; effect, 214; equivalences, 262; medication, 248; WHO ladder, 250, 251, 253, 255, 277

Anemia, 90, 99, 332, 336, 351; aplastic, 295; sideroblastic, 98

Anesthetic, 117; agent, 213; dissociative, 215; gases, 291; general, 85, 181, 213; properties, 175, 184; topical, 175

ANEXIA, 254. *See also* Hydrocodone.

Anileridine, 254, 277, 421. *See also* LERITINE.

Anorexia nervosa, 88, 141, 160, 188, 189, 195, 203, 289, 296, 335, 364, 381

ANTABUSE. *See* Disulfiram.

Antacids, 97, 251

Anti-craving medications, 54. *See also* Naltrexone.

Anti-epileptics, 191, 251

Anti-inflammatories, 249, 316

Anticholinergic: drug interactions, 412; effects of TCAs, 320

Anticoagulants, 105, 113

Anticonvulsants, 84, 151, 181, 235, 250-252, 414, 415

Antidepressants, 31, 105, 113, 140, 155, 186, 249, 413, 414. *See also* Tricyclic antidepressants.

Antifreeze, 314

Antihistamines, 31; and insomnia, 155

Antipsychotics, 31, 159, 193. *See also* Neuroleptics.

Antiretrovirals, 342

Antisocial personality disorder, 395, 400, 403

Antitussives, 225

Anxiety, 6, 20, 21, 23, 24, 25, 27, 80, 158, 190, 191, 204, 206, 210, 229, 245, 246, 249, 260, 261, 285, 335, 350, 353, 354, 363, 364, 377, 381, 384, 392, 397, 400, 403, 406, 407, 409, 416, 431; and alcohol, 6, 79, 105; and amphetamines, 6; and anxiolytics, 6; and barbiturates, 149, 150, 152; and benzodiazepines, 154, 160, 161,

B

C

Detection, of alcohol problems, 13, 15, 20ff; of drugs, 22, 32ff; laboratory markers for alcohol, 20; times, 33; in urine, 33

Detoxification, 42, 45, 48-52, 230, 232, 296, 311, 407, 432; and benzodiazepines, 49, 84; centre, 46, 83-84; clonidine, 230; home, 45; medically supervised, 46; methadone, 231, 232; and thiamine, 95, 181. *See also* Withdrawal management.

Developmental: delay, 366; effects, 240

Dexamphetamine, 6

Dextroamphetamine, 6; 192; dosage, 189

Diabetes, 20, 42, 99, 105, 113, 227, 336

Diabetic neuropathy, 250

Diagnosis, 43, 44, 149, 156, 178, 248, 273, 277, 378, 398, 422, 432; associated with class of substances, 6; dual, 353. *See also the individual drugs.*

Diagnostic and Statistical Manual of Mental Disorders, 4th ed. *See* DSM-IV.

Diagnostic interview schedule, 392

Diaphoresis, 81, 415; and barbiturate withdrawal, 149, 150; and benzodiazepines, 161

Diarrhea, 24, 25, 88, 215, 226, 228, 229, 289, 335; chronic, 98; recurrent, 21

Diazepam, 33, 157, 165, 181, 231, 245, 305, 306, 354; absorption, 163; and alcohol, 74; and anxiety, 155; equivalent drugs and dosages, 163, 164, 165, 166; half-life of, 81, 163; intolerance of, 82; intramuscular injection of, 82; intravenous, 180; need for, 81; oral, 82; take-home prescriptions, 81, 82; treatment (of withdrawal), 54, 84, 163; and seniors, 158; tapering, 164, 168-169, 407. *See also* Benzodiazepines.

Diazepam loading, 76, 81, 84, 118; alternatives to, 83; dosage, 81, 82, 84, 85, 86; precautions for, 82-83; protocol, 82, 83. *See also* Alcohol withdrawal treatment.

Diet, 86, 92, 93, 104, 276; deficient, 98; low-protein, 94; supplements, 88

Digitalis, 105

DILAUDID, 254, 263, 421, 425; -HP, 254. *See also* Hydromorphone.

Dimenhydrinate (GRAVOL, DRAMAMINE), 2, 230, 231, 288; fatal doses of, 290

Diphenhydramine (BENADRYL), 288, 289, 290, 313, 319

Discontinuation, abrupt, 178

Disinhibition, 205, 216, 293, 318, 319; and alcohol, 74

Disorientation, 81, 183, 205, 335

Distortions, 210; cognitive, 249

Disulfiram (ANTABUSE), 54, 117, 118, 186, 413-414; as alternative to naltrexone, 116; contraindications for, 118; mechanism of action, 118; risks, 118

Disulfiram-like reactions, and alcohol, 74

Diuretics, 243; overuse of, 94

Divorce, 110, 382

Dizziness, 79, 190, 288, 335, 352; and methylphenidate, 193; and naltrexone, 116; and nicotine, 130, 132

Done nomogram for salicylate toxicity, 318

Dopamine, 54, 55, 176, 186, 187, 189, 215, 320; agonists, 186; blocking, 141; receptors, 209

Dopaminergic: neurons, 54; systems, 195

Double-doctoring, 31, 157, 165, 166, 230, 232, 245, 256, 260, 262, 424, 425

E

F

Functional: abilities, 351; impairment, 350; improvement, 276; status, 253, 257, 259, 261, 273

G

GABA. *See* Gamma-amino butyric acid.

Gabapentin (NEURONTIN), 250, 251.

GAF scores (Global Assessment of Functioning), 401, 402, 403

Gait, 351; ataxic, 96, 148

Gamma-amino butyric acid (GABA), 54, 318

Gamma glutamyl transferase (GGT), 20, 90, 114, 286, 353; screening for alcohol abuse, 90

Gas chromatography-mass spectroscopy (GC-MS), 28, 31

Gasoline, 5, 291, 292, 294, 295

Gastric: lavage, 132, 186

Gastric alcohol dehydrogenase. *See* Alcohol dehydrogenase, gastric.

Gastritis, 21, 98, 105, 113, 351, 364; alcoholic, 97

Gastrointestinal (GI): bleeding, 88, 94, 110; complaints, 381; decontamination, 317; signs, 21, 23; symptoms, 20, 293; tract, 206, 229, 234, 310; upset and naltrexone, 116

Gastrointestinal complications related to alcohol, 97ff. *See* Diarrhea; Esophagitis; Gastritis; Liver disease; Mallory-Weiss tear; Pancreatitis.

GEN-XENE. *See* Clorazepate.

Gender: -related issues, 384; -sensitive treatment, 366; stereotyping, 367

General Health Questionnaire, 362

Genetic factors, 215; and alcohol, 75

Genetic pleomorphism, and liver disease, 87

Genetics, 128, 334

Genital herpes simplex virus, 341

Geriatric patients, 350, 354. *See also* Elderly patients; Older adults.

GGT. *See* Gamma-glutamyl transferase.

Glaucoma, 203

Gluconeogenesis,,99

Glucuronidation, 311, 414

Glucose, 84, 90, 310; intolerance, 99; and thiamine, 82, 86. *See also* Blood sugar.

Glue, 375

Glutamate, 54, 119

Glutamic acid, 215

Glutathione (GSH), 311

Glycine, 318

Goals: realistic, 144; setting of, 51; of treatment, 110, 112, 248

Gonorrhea, 26, 328

Goose bumps, 229

GRAVOL *See* Dimenhydrinate.

Growth, 287; retardation of, 366

Guide Your Patients to a Smoke-Free Future, 136, 143-144

Guilt, feelings of, 15, 17, 18, 44, 47, 61, 141, 353, 367, 430

Gynecomastia, 89, 97, 286

H

H_2 receptor blockers, 97, 251

HABITROL, 139. *See also* Nicotine.

Hair loss, 335

HALCION. *See* Triazolam.

Halfway house, 47, 52

Hallucination, 27, 80, 188, 191, 193, 206, 210, 211, 213, 289, 293, 319, 320, 391, 397, 399; and alcohol withdrawal, 76, 77, 78, 79, 148; auditory, 81, 182, 214; and barbiturate withdrawal, 148, 150; and benzodiazepine withdrawal, 160, 161; cocaine and, 182; as indication for hospital admission, 84; and MDMA, 195; visual, 81; during withdrawal, 86

Hallucinogen persisting perception disorder (HPPD), 210

Hallucinogens, 4, 22, 183, 209, 288, 375; abuse of 211; and anxiety, 6; diagnoses associated with, 6; list of, 6; and psychosis, 23

Hallucinosis, 80, 81, 82

Halogenated compounds, 5, 291

Haloperidol (HALDOL), 82, 86, 186, 216, 310

HALT states (hungry, angry, lonely, tired), 47

Hashish, 203, 204, *See also* Cannabis.

Hazardous alcohol consumption, 114, 363; incidence of, 108

HBV. *See* Hepatitis B virus.

HCC. *See* Hepatocellular carcinoma.

HCV. *See* Hepatitis C virus.

HDL/LDL ratio, 285

Head: fullness in, 79; injury, 96, 227

Headache, 79, 96, 118, 190, 193, 248, 250-252, 276, 287, 335; medication-induced, 225, 250; migraine, 147, 225, 250-251, 422; and nicotine, 130, 132; rebound, 252; sudden onset, 184, 185

Health: education, 46; effects of alcohol, 112; profile, 108

Health care: professionals, 58, 175; resources, 57, 62

Health care costs, 41; and alcohol, 71; and tobacco, 71

Heart, 100, 329; and alcohol, 102; failure, unexplained, 100; rate, 130, 177, 190, 204, 206, 211

Heart disease, 42; alcoholic, 100; benefits of alcohol against, 4, 103, 104, 107; medications, 105. *See also* Cardiovascular complications; Cardiovascular disease; Ischemic heart disease.

520

I

521

M

O

534

S

U

V

544

W